TWO LIVES IN ONE

IN MEMORY OF MY HUSBAND
W. S. WOYTINSKY

PRESENTED BY
E. S. WOYTINSKY

TWO LIVES IN ONE.

EMMA S. WOYTINSKY —

FREDERICK A. PRAEGER, *Publishers*

New York • Washington

BOOKS THAT MATTER

Published in the United States of America in 1965
by Frederick A. Praeger, Inc., Publishers
111 Fourth Avenue, New York 3, N.Y.

© 1965 by Emma S. Woytinsky

Library of Congress Catalog Card Number: 65–13124

Printed in the United States of America

Your dear image, unforgettable,
Is before me, always, everywhere . . .

—F. TYUTCHEV

Contents

TWO LIVES IN ONE

1. *Our Love*

MY LIFE BEGAN on March 14, 1916—the night when, for the second time, I met Wolik, for whom I had been waiting all my youth. Strangely enough, neither of us had recognized our destiny at our first meeting, in Irkutsk, the capital of Eastern Siberia, on the preceding December 16. A mutual friend, Apollon Kruglikov, had invited both of us to his box in the theater. That night, I felt so low, so depressed, that I wanted to be left alone. In the dark box, I could hardly see Wolik. But in the brightly illuminated foyer, I saw his burning-red hair and several times caught his intense look, as if he wanted to penetrate my thoughts. This increased my uneasiness, and I tried to look aside.

From the Fortress of Peter and Paul in Petrograd (now Leningrad), where he was imprisoned by the Communists after he had been defeated in the resistance against their *coup d'état* in 1917, Wolik wrote me:

> It was amusing to recall that night. You hardly turned your head when I entered the box and were so cold that I said to myself, "Well, well," or something of the sort. All evening I cast sidelong glances at you but met frowning brows and could hardly see your eyes. Yet I did see that you were heavenly lovely, and I tried to figure out with whom you were so cross and whether you were always in such an angry mood. After long hesitation and inner struggle, I asked you to go to the foyer with me during the intermission. After another struggle, I offered you my arm in the crowd. While trying to entertain you, I studied your face . . . In the mirror I saw all of you—tall, slender, proud, with infinitely sad eyes! . . . Back in the box, you turned away from the stage, moved to the rear.
>
> . . . But somehow I felt sympathy with you, and this feeling of sympathy and compassion eased the impression that you were proud and unfriendly. You see, I did not understand you then. There remained an impression of something infinitely beautiful and inaccessible. I was afraid to acknowledge to myself how much that unapproachable, proud beauty of yours attracted and lured me. Next morning I went to Apollon to find out in a roundabout way who that girl in the box was. But he screwed up his left eye and asked,

"Why? Did she hook you? A beauty, eh?" I answered with dignity, "Nothing of the sort, just so-so . . ." and wanted to hear more, but he would not say a word. And I, my dearest love, thought for three months of that girl in the theater with such sad eyes, until I met her again . . .

FIRST MEETINGS

On that decisive winter night of March 14, 1916, I had rushed to a theater within walking distance of my home with my childhood friend Manya, who had come to teach, along with me, in a public school and was staying with us that year. Behind us was an uneventful day, and in an upsurge of gaiety I said to Manya at the entrance, "Let us spend the whole evening with the first acquaintance we meet tonight." She nodded yes. We were a few minutes late and got to our seats noiselessly. When the curtain went up and lights appeared, I saw Wladimir Savelievich Woytinsky at my right. All I had heard of him since our last meeting was that he was an outstanding writer and speaker among the political exiles and that he was absorbed in his work. Because of his heroic past, his name was pronounced almost with awe.

Manya and I exchanged the meaningful looks of two plotters. He, too, seemed to be pleased, stayed with us through the intermissions and took us home. Not expecting that he would care to come in, I said good-bye at our door, and he left.

Manya reproached me, "That was not nice. You should have asked him in!"

"Oh, he wouldn't care to come, but if you feel I was not courteous, I'll apologize right away." Through the stillness of the night, I called him back and said, "I am terribly sorry. Manya scolded me for being rude —she thinks I should have invited you to come to see us. If you have an evening free, please, do come!"

To Manya, I said, "He will never come!"

Next morning, before we left for school, Wolik* telephoned to ask whether he could visit us that night. All day long I smiled deep inside myself so as not to betray my unaccountably high spirits. That night, I felt close to him, as much at home with him as with myself. My reserve melted, and I laughed and teased him. On leaving, he forgot, or so I thought, his brief case. Early the next morning he called up to ask whether he might pick it up. This was a pretense, of course, but nobody could have been more unsuspecting than I was. And I am sure that none of his friends would have believed that their serious colleague was artful at such tricks.

In another letter from the Fortress, Wolik wrote:

* Diminutive names are a part of the Russian folklore. The usual diminutive for Wladimir is Volodya, but I preferred Wolik.

I was so miserable those days, lonely, needed by nobody, so forlorn. To forget myself, to think of nothing, I went to the theater. And suddenly—I saw next to me the beautiful girl from that theater night. I was so confused that I did not know what to say, how to greet you. Remember, you came to my help. I was so grateful. . . . Then I took you home and worried all the way whether you would ask me to come to see you. Frankly, I even hoped that you might ask me in right then for an after-theater snack. A foolish dream! I was so sad, I could almost have cried and started home calling myself an ass. Then I heard your voice calling me back. When I reached you, you invited me. You were so beautiful, with flushing cheeks and innocent eyes! To hide my excitement I replied awkwardly that though you invited me out of politeness, I should nevertheless be glad to come. You laughed, and I went home, carrying with me the sound of your laughter, the brilliancy of your eyes, and your sweet image.

. . . The next evening I sat on the chair at the window, opposite the couch where you and Manya were. I was charmed by you, stirred by your beauty, your eyes, but I tried not to show my feelings, talked, laughed, joked and told stories. I cannot remember a word of what I said but I recall vividly how you sat, bent slightly forward, and how you once took Manya's hands into your own. I envied her even then: I wanted to be close to you, only to sit next to you and look at you.

From then on Wolik came to see us almost every night. At home and in school, I thought only of him, but I did not understand that this was love. I worried that I was so unworthy of him. I feared that he liked me for my appearance, and so his feeling for me could be only superficial. Wolik, for his part, thought that I was used to adulation and wanted to add him to my conquests:

I invented all sorts of pretexts to visit you, looked for excuses to justify my frequent visits, as if the love surging in my heart was not justification enough. . . . I could not believe that you, so radiantly beautiful, could have chosen me from among all the others and were beginning to love me. I thought you were as friendly with everybody as with me . . . that you were playing with me, that it was your whim, your fun to subject and torment me. Such a fool I was to think of you so! You said: "You do not know me," said it quietly, sadly. I did not believe you. I was moving toward the highest, fullest happiness in the world, but I thought I was going toward torture. Yet even if my love for you had brought me the cruelest tortures, I would have taken that road and given my life and soul for your love . . .

I remember how I came to take you for the first time for a walk along the Angara River. You came out in a black suit and a hat with a broad brim. It was a sunny spring day. You looked so adorable and you must have felt the power of your beauty for a moment or have read the ecstasy in my eyes. You blushed, looked shyly at me and became lovelier than ever. . . . My friends asked me who the girl was with whom they had seen me. I felt my face redden but would not tell your name . . . I could not understand . . . why you permitted me to come so often. I looked at you as one looks from the ground to the sun, looked at you as a queen whom I would never dare approach as an equal.

I, too, was deeply troubled. In a family of superbly handsome people, I had considered myself, from childhood, an ugly duckling. Hundreds of times I had caught admiring looks and heard myself complimented, but I had always been sure that this came from friendship, from love, which blinded the eyes. Being plain, as I thought I was, had never bothered me. I was a bookworm and had my plans for an interesting, useful life. Now, the more I saw admiration in Wolik's eyes, the more I feared that he would never love me for what I really was, that he was attracted by something of little importance.

The love I desperately wanted was an all-absorbing passion, a complete unity and happiness that had no bounds, that would nearly choke me. Nothing less would satisfy me—in that rejection of anything else was my delight and my torture. I asked myself again and again, Was that what Wolik would bring me and what he, too, wanted? But troubled as I was, I became gay and carefree when Wolik appeared in the evening. We understood each other from the first word, though he often teased me: "You are too quick for me!"

Somehow, I never gave much thought to Wolik's appearance. He was just himself to me, all of him, including the twinkle in his eyes, his young laughter, his red hair, freckled face, and artist's hands. One night, shortly after I had first met Wolik, an outstanding "political" nicknamed Florianych was taking me home from a masked ball, and when the conversation happened to concern Wolik, who then meant nothing to me, he had said, with unexpected emphasis, "I have often noticed that women are not good judges of a man's looks. Wladimir Savelievich has a fine, distinguished face, but I have not noticed that women would think the way I do." Subsequently, this remark and Wolik's attitude toward my appearance led me to ask myself several times if it would matter if Wolik looked different. My conclusion was always the same—no! There was something very attractive, even touching, in his appearance, but this appeal was not physical. It came from a kind of shyness though not awkwardness, a simplicity combined with inborn dignity.

Despite the bitter cold, Wolik always wore only one glove, on his left hand. I was intrigued, but felt I could not ask him about it. I found out later that his coat pockets were full of left gloves because in taking off the right glove to greet people, he so often had lost it. Wolik wore gloves on the train as protection from dust. Cold was a less important matter to

him. Later, in cold weather, when I reminded him that he was not wearing his gloves, he would assure me that the essential thing was having
the gloves, and that in this context they were as effective in his pockets
as on his hands.

I had several friends in Irkutsk who, for one reason or another,
tried to throw cold water on my feelings, though I never said a word
about Wolik to anyone but Manya. Even she was not entirely sure that
Wolik would satisfy my hopes. My mother said nothing, but I knew that
she, like my late father, had always expected me to marry some outstanding scholar—and here was Wolik, a man deprived of all civil
rights, just out of the penitentiary. Even a little pupil of mine, the daughter of the next-door neighbor, came to implore me not to marry
Wolik: "He has such red hair, and freckles, too. You think nothing of
it, but I assure you, they cause a lot of trouble. I know, I have red hair
and freckles, and everybody makes fun of me!"

Wolik's friends, almost exclusively political exiles, were surprised and
displeased at his choice. They did not see how a man with such a past
and such a reputation could get excited about a sixteen-year-old girl. (I
was actually twenty-three but looked much younger; Wolik was thirty-
one.) Moreover, I came from a middle-class, bourgeois family and had
shown no particular interest in politics. Would I try to keep him away
from his friends and political activities? One of his closest friends, Irakli
Tseretelli, insisted on meeting me, and Wolik gave in, for two reasons, as
he later explained to me: He wanted to show me off, and also, perhaps
unconsciously, he wanted to expose me to his very handsome friend, who
had a name glorified throughout Russia and who had a magnetic charm
for the ladies.

Manya, Wolik, and I took the train for the hour ride to Usolye, some
30 miles away, where Tseretelli lived. The first surprise came when
Tseretelli, tall and slim, did a handstand and walked toward us on his
hands. The whole day was full of pranks, fun, and jokes, with Tseretelli
teasing Wolik and me throughout. When we passed a shack, Tseretelli
suddenly slipped in, sweeping me in, too, to scare Wolik and see how
he would react to my disappearance. Wolik and Manya went back and
forth looking for us, until we jumped out of our hiding place. Tseretelli
insisted that it was Wolik who had run away from us. Poor Wolik, confused and worried, defended himself, but to ensure that he wouldn't
leave us again, I tied him to me with Tseretelli's handkerchief.

Wolik described his feelings that day:

> At the table I laughed, made jokes, talked nonsense, but I was wor-
> ried and watched you. Then when you disappeared, I was upset for
> a moment. I was almost ready to go to my room, pack, and go back
> to Irkutsk. I did not do it because I was afraid of causing you
> grief and offending you. What would you have thought, my sweet-
> heart, if I had suddenly left Usolye? Would you have understood that
> love was so close to us? Then you returned and tethered me with a

handkerchief and kept me close to you until evening. All that time I not only saw you, not only heard your voice, but felt the warmth of your body and was intoxicated by your beauty, your closeness, almost to the point of losing consciousness. In those hours you found your Wolik and I found my darling.

Next morning, Wolik and Manya left—he to take care of some of his publications, and she to return to teaching school. Wolik begged me to stay in Usolye one more day and promised to return that night. It was a long day, and both Tseretelli and I were thoroughly bored with each other. He tried to entertain me and several times offered to tell me of Wolik's life, but I refused to learn anything from anybody but Wolik himself. Finally, we went to the station to meet Wolik, and at the sight of him I felt such an upsurge of happiness and relief that I had to make an effort not to give my feelings away. We took Tseretelli home and then Wolik took me to my hotel in a carriage. I felt so close to him that I let him put his arm around me. Wolik said, "I did not know whether to come back here or not. If you knew why I hesitated, you would forgive me. I am afraid I cannot control my feelings any more." My heart shook, but I said softly, "I would have never forgiven you."

The next day we spent together on the bank of the Angara, and Wolik told me later how he wanted to kiss my hand but that he would have dared to swim across that wide river before he would have dared to touch me. When on our return to Irkutsk, he kissed me for the first time, he was immediately jealous of himself. How could I have permitted this? Permitted just him, or others, too? As he wrote in one of the Fortress letters, "I had a foreboding that you would torment me, and at the same time was jealous of myself."

I was so inexperienced and innocent that I understood his kiss to mean an engagement and love forever. Next day, on my return from the school, I found a gorgeous basket of white roses in my room. But when I asked in the evening, "Forever?" Wolik hesitated: "I do not know." As he recalled in the next letter:

> . . . your exclamation full of horror and reproach, "You kissed me not loving me? How could you?" I wanted to redress the wrong I did, to ask for forgiveness, but stronger than this desire was the feeling that everything would be lost if I should say one insincere word in that critical moment. And so with some difficulty I squeezed out of myself, "Oh no, I did kiss you lovingly." This was not what you expected. . . . You got up and said coldly, "Please, take me home . . ." When I met you a day later at a mutual friend's house, you asked me to take a walk with you and said, "Don't ever come again." I was heartbroken and said sadly, "Yes, I am not worthy of your love." You had pity on me and said softly, "I cannot accept what you offer me. It is too little. . . . I cannot see you any more." Yes, this is too little for you, I know. I offer myself, all of myself, but it is too little. It looked as if you were not listening to me. But you lis-

tened to the sounds in your heart, and there love was alive already
. . . and love forgave me for the torment that my kiss had caused
you.

In my diary, I wrote:

> When I think how little happiness has been in his life, I am so sad
> and I wish to intoxicate him with joy . . . Yet I cannot say the
> words he so ardently wants me to say: "I love you." They are not
> yet born in my heart, and I cannot violate it.

And three days later:

> The great, irrepressible joy . . . Happiness that floods my whole
> being. Everything that was before, everything that troubled me is
> so small, so insignificant. I know only my love, my Wolik . . . Of
> him I have thought those endless nights, for him I have waited so
> many years grieving that he did not come . . . He is mine, he has
> lived for me. The war did not take him, he did not perish in the
> prison, no other woman has entered his life, he was destined to be
> mine. This is why I never could have loved anyone else, he is mine
> forever.
>
> I am ashamed that I did not tell him "I love you." I do want him
> to know that he is all my life . . . Why did I torture myself, why did
> I reproach myself for his first kiss, for my weakness? He is mine, and
> the days interlace in one radiant chain.
>
> There are no words so powerful, so rich and strong that they can
> express what I feel . . . My heart undividedly belongs to Wolik,
> and it is full of songs, proud and passionate . . . My heart is full
> of dazzling, brilliant light, and I close my eyes when I look into it.

OUR "WEDDING"

The marriage ceremony was a formality neither of us cared about. But
my mother cared, and we did not want to cause her sorrow. We could
not be married officially. My family was Jewish. Wolik's father had belonged to the group of Jewish intellectuals who believed in assimilation
with the Russian people. At the peak of his career, as dean of a technical institute, a professor of mathematics, and holder of two Government medals, he had converted himself and his family to Christianity.
Wolik had been baptized as a child, but neither he nor his brothers and
sister had remained in the new religion. Each, in his own time, returned to Judaism, not because of religious feelings, but in protest
against the persecutions of the Jews by the Tsarist Government. All this
I learned later. We never talked about marriage or the future. We were
together, we were in love, and that was all we needed to know.

Like many people in the city, Mother knew that political exiles represented a special group within its population, that there were many
outstanding personalities among them. But our family never had any

social contacts with them, and I doubt if Mother had heard anything about Wolik, his family, or his unusual position in Russia's intellectual circles. As a matter of fact, I met political exiles for the first time that very year—at a community group organized to help the refugees streaming into Siberia from the western provinces ravaged by the Government's "scorched earth" policy against the advancing German troops. Indeed, I had met Kruglikov, who introduced me to Wolik, only once, at an evening party a few nights before.

One day Wolik said: "Darling, to marry you, I shall ask to be reconverted to Judaism. This is now possible, but it may take some time." I did not care, but what could we do about Mother's concern? Wolik consulted the Rabbi, who explained: "I cannot perform an official wedding, but tell your fiancée's mother to come to me. I shall tell her that our religion considers a marriage fulfilled when the man puts the ring on his fiancée's finger and says the sacramental words, which I shall inscribe for you in Russian characters so that you can say them, in the presence of two witnesses." My mother went to him and returned reassured. In half an hour, we were "married," in June, 1916. The marriage was not official. But that did not bother us.

What mattered was that we were free to live our own way. Wolik suggested that we spend a few weeks in Arshan, about a hundred miles away, where he had hiked the summer before our meeting.

ARSHAN

Arshan, on the Mongolian border, was a tiny resort, or rather a faint foreshadowing of what a resort would be. There were a few toylike cabins, a few houses, a store or two, but no pharmacy or other medical sources. We found a primitive cabin with the barest of furnishings and chinks in the walls and ceiling. Yet we could not have been happier if it had been a palace. The finest resort could not have been more beautifully located—among imposing, snow-capped mountains cut by canyons with magnificent waterfalls and mountain streams.

We went hiking, climbing the rocks, crossing mountain streams to penetrate into the virgin forest, here on the right bank, there on the left. We were in an enchanted world, and everything—the lacelike clouds, the fresh, luscious green of the trees and grasses, the proud inaccessible peaks, the roar of the rapids, the din of the waterfalls—merged into one jubilant feeling of ecstasy and love.

We watched the waterfalls rushing out of dark, narrow canyons. Some twisted like a serpent before they spread themselves fanwise over a rocky projection that seemingly hung in the air; others ran with reckless madness down, down into a deep, huge bowl of blue, pink, and white marble. The water danced and shone in all colors through the mist of silver spray.

We looked up and up from that playful water to the line of slowly rising mountains crowned by glittering ice. Many had never been trod by human foot. We walked in the quiet virgin forest, where the dim air breathed a profound peace.

Between us, the feeling of closeness grew with every day. We never talked about our future, made no plans for the life ahead of us, did not work out a "design of life," unlike Beatrice and Sidney Webb, with whom we were often compared in later years. We were almost like children—everything was fun and filled us with wonder; we lived the life around us and were supremely happy.

In the evening, we read by flickering candlelight and looked at the stars shimmering through the holes in the ceiling. Once, Wolik caught a cold that lasted two terrifying days. Coming from a healthy family, and with no recollection of illness, I was totally ignorant of what to do. I asked advice from the owner of the cabin, and he suggested rubbing Wolik with kerosene. I reported this to Wolik, but he laughed and said, "Why not use wood, a local resource? It will be just as effective!" I almost cried from worry, but two days later he was up, saying that his own prescription—having me read him the poetry of Rabindranath Tagore—had cured him.

I had an occasional pang when I realized how unlike Wolik's image of me I was. I tried several times to persuade him that it was his love that made me appear so wonderful and so beautiful to him, that I was afraid of his disillusionment when he would see me as I really was, but he laughed and said: "Yes, you think I am just a fool and you are so smart to warn me! No, my love, you have no idea how cunning I am, and so you are mine!" Later, Wolik wrote from the Fortress:

> Don't worry that I think so much of your "appearance." Your beauty which I so admire is not "appearance," or anyhow not merely appearance . . . Your eyes are a part of your soul, a part of your love. No matter how radiant your beauty, your eyes would not be so marvelously adorable if your soul were not free of all vanity and your love were not pure and hot as the sun.

From Arshan we went to Lake Baykal, in the south of Siberia, and decided to travel down the Angara River.

ON THE ANGARA

We bought a large boat with two pairs of oars, loaded it with our luggage, and started off. The Angara is extremely wide and deep, and 1,100 miles long. Its water is crystal clear and, because the subsoil is frozen, is icy even under a burning sun. In many parts of the Angara, there are long, rocky islands, and on both sides of it, the *tayga*, the primeval forest, stretches for hundreds of miles. Villages were few and far between, some thirty or thirty-five miles apart, with no sign of human life between.

Every morning we started early and spent the day in the boat. In the middle of it, Wolik had fashioned a kind of a hearth over a thick layer of sod. We were completely alone. The sun roasted us mercilessly, the rain drenched us to the bones and put out our fire, the wind chilled us, but we were floating in heaven.

The news of Wolik's presence spread like wild fire among the political exiles scattered along the Angara, and we were greeted in many villages by people who knew of him and of whom he had heard. They were eager to talk with him and to hear what was happening in the world.

Usually we stopped late in the evening when we reached a village, tied up our boat, and knocked at the nearest peasant house and asked for hospitality. If we arrived very late, we groped our way through the darkness, our arms outstretched so as to touch a house, and I would ask if they would take us in; a woman's voice was reassuring, and we never had any difficulty. Once we were in, the samovar appeared on the table, along with bread, butter, cottage cheese, eggs, and milk, and occasionally some fish. The Siberian peasants lived more like American farmers than like peasants of European Russia; they had not known slavery, and they had land and well-built houses to withstand the cold winters. More often than not, we could detect, on entering a house, how many daughters were in the family. The clue was the number of Singer sewing machines, the typical dowry at that time, that were lined up along the wall.

We slept in the *gornitsa,* a kind of living room and, except for two nights that we lay on the floor on bags filled with hay, we had clean and fairly comfortable beds. There was never any fear of polluted water or milk, and we ate and drank everything offered to us. Next day we lived on food given us by the night's hosts. Sometimes they caught fish early in the morning, and we were treated not only to fresh buns but even to a fish pie. On leaving, we gave a silver ruble (roughly equivalent to the American half-dollar) to our hosts, and they, impressed by city people's generosity, thanked us again and again.

One morning our hosts warned us not to stop at the next village, which had the uninviting name Razboynikovo (Robbers' Den), but to try to reach the second village before dark. Our efforts to heed their advice failed because of a sudden storm that drove our boat here and there until, totally exhausted, we landed in Razboynikovo. The houses did not face the river; their windows turned away from it toward the road or the forest. With the warning in mind, we asked for the alderman's house so as to make known our overnight stay in the village. When we entered his house, he threw one look at Wolik's Swedish black leather jacket lined with red wool and bowed respectfully. Evidently the red lining, similar to that usually seen on generals' outfits, had persuaded him that Wolik was a high official. To cap the confusion and perhaps increase our danger, the alderman informed us: "We have the gendarme and two policemen in the village today. They brought the payments to soldiers' widows. The gendarme got the best room, and is sleeping now. But I shall send the boy to waken him and vacate the room for you." Meeting the police was the last thing we wanted: Wolik, whose status in

Siberia was that of exile, had not reported his trip to the Governor General's office.

The still sleepy gendarme arrived and though he, too, was impressed by the red lining, he inquired, "What is your business, sir?" Wolik had arranged before the trip to send a series of articles on his impressions to the largest newspaper in Petrograd and had received payment in advance by telegraph. He was working on an article about the villages that Catherine the Great had ordered established in the area and that, accordingly, were shown on all Siberian maps although they never had been built. To impress the gendarme, he said, "I am here from the Geodetic Survey. This is the map of your region, and I am to check it and eliminate all non-existent villages. Look here—have you ever seen this village? Or this?" The gendarme buried himself in the map, fascinated by the villages that ought to be in his area yet did not exist. The map and the impressive "Geodetic Survey," of which he had never heard, convinced him. He saluted, and the alderman sent a boy to take us to the designated house. We shut ourselves in and never showed our faces in the village. Around 5 A.M., we heard a knock at the door. Anticipating trouble, I went to open it. A policeman greeted me and said they were leaving, and the gendarme wanted to know if we would like to be escorted because travelers in that area were occasionally bothered. I asked him to convey our thanks to the gendarme for his thoughtfulness but said that we were too tired for so early a start. Two hours after the police left, we went to our boat.

Days passed. We were alone on the Angara, talking, telling of our life before, of our families, resting, making tea. For days at a time, we never saw another boat, never heard another human sound. Then one day came the roar of impassable rapids some twenty miles away. We knew we had to make our last stop before reaching them, at Bratsky Ostrog, where a large colony of political exiles lived.

There we were met with great friendliness by several exiles, and Wolik had to promise them he would speak to the colony that night about the war and the situation in the country. This was my first underground meeting, and I watched intently the arrangements made against intrusion by the police. I had never participated in any political activity, but like all other students at that time I had progressive leanings. Everything connected with underground work had great fascination. To hear Wolik for the first time talk to a crowd in the half-darkness, often turning his eyes toward me, to see their respect for him and their eagerness to know his opinions—all this was enormously exciting, and I felt a part of an important world.

We gave our boat to an older member of the colony and returned to Irkutsk by relay. The road was very bad and it was raining, but we were immune to such small discomforts. One coachman told us that he had shot a mother bear with her two cubs a few days before, and he offered to sell us the hides. We bought them sight unseen, paid the hunter, and gave him our address in Irkutsk. A week or so later, the hides arrived, smelling so terrible that the horse drawing the coach was terrified and dogs ran alongside barking wildly. We took the hides home and found a tanner who made beautiful rugs out of them, especially the large one. We put it in the living room, before the fireplace. It had deep, thick fur and was big enough for the two of us to lie on. Wolik considered it my rug and frowned when anyone stepped on it.

OUR PARENTS' ATTITUDE

Manya and I had so monopolized Wolik's visits that my mother had not got to know him well before our marriage. "Do you consider it proper to go out with him every night?" she had asked. And I had answered, "I would go with him to the end of the world." Mother had looked rather surprised and said sadly, "The end of his world is right here. I hope you will be happy within this little world." (If only she had known!) After that, she never asked or said anything, accepting the inevitable.

She had only a vague idea about our journey when we had left. When we returned, excited, and told her of our adventures, she was upset and said to Wolik, "Only a man like you could think up something like that!" We laughed, took her in our arms, and turned her round and round, until she, too, started laughing and said, "You two are quite a pair!"

For an entirely different reason, Wolik's mother was similarly cautious in accepting her new daughter-in-law. Wolik loved my black velvet outfit with the wide-brimmed hat, and asked me to have my picture taken in it. He sent the photograph to his mother. Her reaction was to worry whether I wasn't "too glamorous a girl" for her bookish son. She feared that this might be a passing whim for that girl, but a real heartbreak for her son. Fortunately, at the same time we had another photograph taken—of us together—and it reassured her.

Soon we heard that Wolik's father would come to see us. Wolik was very glad, and I was, too, although I was somewhat apprehensive of what his reaction to me would be. On the night he was to arrive, we waited at the station until 1 A.M. for the train from Petrograd, only to be told that it would not get there before six o'clock. We went home but were wakened by the maid when Wolik's father arrived unexpectedly. I waited for Wolik to go out of the bedroom first, then went to greet his father. He looked at me, and tears filled his eyes. "She is so natural," he said. Sensing disapproval, I was shocked at his hasty judgment and felt I had not had a fair chance.

But his reaction was the opposite of what I thought. At that time, modernistic currents in art and literature were in vogue in Russia, particularly in Petrograd. As in all new trends in any field of art, exaggerations, aggressiveness, and intentionally sharpened declarations of the new "faith" were the order of the day. Wolik's sister, Nadya, who still lived with her parents, was a highly educated, very attractive and artistic person, and eagerly took part in those sophisticated activities, which, to her father, seemed artificial and senseless. He was tired of Nadya's friends, their mannerisms and pretentious discussions behind which he, a mathematician and profound scholar, saw only a deficiency of knowledge and a disregard for realities. In contrast, my plainly combed hair, lack of make-up, and generally unaffected appearance so touched him that tears came to his eyes. . . . Of course, futurism, cubism, and other modern currents in art and literature had reached Siberia, but they had not deeply penetrated the circles of the political exiles. Moreover, neither of us was under the spell of that movement.

Wolik's father spent several weeks with us, during which he and I became great friends. During the daytime, he did some sightseeing, and in the evening, we had long discussions, reminiscences, talks about other members of Wolik's family. He arranged to have butter and other foodstuffs shipped home, where they were in short supply by the end of World War I, while Siberia, despite huge procurements for the armed forces on the Western front, was swimming in surpluses. When Father left, he took with him our promise that I would go to Petrograd to meet Wolik's mother, for whom such a long trip—five days, even by express train—was much too strenuous.

LIFE IN IRKUTSK*

Our few months in Irkutsk between the return from our honeymoon late in the fall of 1916 and the outbreak of the Revolution in March, 1917, were crammed with emotion and work. Love was in and around us; every word, every look, was suffused with it. Indeed, it was difficult to understand how life around us could continue to be as ordinary as before. Strangely, nobody sensed the dazzling miracle that had transformed our lives, and even friends regarded our marriage matter-of-factly.

Work brought us back to earth. The morning after we settled down in two furnished rented rooms, Wolik asked me, "Would you like to work with me on my new project, 'The Labor Market in Siberia During the War'?" Thus began our teamwork, which was to last forty-four years. I entered on this path hesitantly, fully realizing the superiority of Wolik's mind, erudition, and talents. But unexpectedly for me, and to my greatest joy and satisfaction, it turned out that we worked together efficiently and that Wolik enjoyed introducing me to the broad intellectual world in which his mind operated.

The survey of the Siberian labor market was to cover the normal situation, the labor shortage resulting from military recruitment, the special labor demands created by large procurements for the front, the increase

* Irkutsk had been founded in the middle of the seventeenth century, on the right bank of the Angara River; the station of the Trans-Siberian Railroad is on the left bank. The economy of Irkutsk was based on the trade with China, trade in Siberian furs, and connection with the Lena gold fields. In our time, Irkutsk had broad, paved streets and many fine buildings. There were several high schools, a well-stuffed regional museum, a permanent theater, and two daily newspapers.

in unskilled labor with the influx of refugees from western provinces ravaged by the government's scorched-earth policy before the invading Germans, war wages, the role of women, and so on. Documentation was sketchy, but there were some possibilities of expanding it and using sampling methods. Publication of the survey was assured.

Wolik worked steadily, with full concentration, knowing no fatigue while at his desk. I adopted his work habits and gradually, over the years, acquired a capacity for disciplined, concentrated work, though I could never match Wolik's. Needless to say, despite my major in economics, I could assist him only in collecting material, preparing tables, and so on, not in planning the study of the labor market. However, Wolik was marvelous about sharing his ideas and his knowledge with me and initiating me into fact-finding work. I have never counted how many similar studies we later completed together or how many more we envisaged and discussed, only to give them up for one reason or another and to shift to another, more urgent or more appealing project.

Of course, the labor survey was not the only work to occupy us in those few months we lived in Irkutsk. Wolik wrote about our trips to Arshan and on the Angara. He sent the long essay "Arshan" to the well-known magazine *Vestnik Evropy* (*The Herald of Europe*). Although we did not see it in print, we were told that it did appear before that magazine went out of existence, as did all other independent publications after the Communist *coup d'état* in 1917. The articles about the Angara trip were published in the Petrograd daily, *Rech'* (September–October, 1916).

Wolik not only introduced me to research work but also strongly supported me in my special interest in educational matters, to which I had devoted much effort and time before our meeting. Shortly after our return from the boat trip on the Angara, the Municipal Council of Irkutsk organized a series of evening courses on educational matters for parents. The Council asked me to give a course of ten lectures on the psychology of children's reading. Feeling inadequately prepared and not wishing to fail in Wolik's presence, I was inclined to say no, but he urged me to accept. I gave in, outlined the course, and scared as a rabbit, mounted the lecturer's platform. I had just time enough to note that every seat was occupied when a tall gray-haired man in the first row got up, pushed back his chair, said loudly, "I did not come here to be enlightened by a kid," and left. Only the thought of Wolik gave me courage, and I started the lecture, though my voice trembled. Gradually, as the course developed, I gained the confidence of the listeners, who came to consult me after the lectures. Later, I repeated that course in the Fröbel Institute in Tiflis.

One of my points, which I illustrated with samples from the so-called children's books, was that it was preferable to introduce children to classical literature at the earliest possible age, depending on their individual abilities, than to feed them shallow little stories written especially for them. I felt strongly that what adults could enjoy, children could also, even if they did not understand every word or the full meaning of a story or fable. It was possible to select fairy tales, short stories, and descriptions in Russian and world classical literature whose beauty of images and language would captivate children. Exposing them to the best in literary writing at an early age would not only enrich their vocabulary but would also develop in them a more discriminating taste in literary style, better judgment about the quality of writing.

I also thought that once fine taste had been conveyed to the young readers, they would later return to the great books of classical literature that they had not fully understood earlier—perhaps return more than once to derive, with every successive reading, more pleasure and understanding. In contrast, who ever returns to children's stories? Interestingly, what I was discussing a half century ago in a remote Siberian city is still stirring the minds of educators today.

Although most of our time was given to work, my strongest interest was in reading everything Wolik had already published. I was shaken by his description of the prison years, but while my heart bled, I was overcome by another feeling, even more powerful than my love: I worshiped Wolik as a hero, a knight without fear and reproach, whom no ordinary mortal could even approach. How to be worthy of him and his love, how not to disappoint his expectations of me!

The pressure of work may have helped the merging of our personalities, so similar in many respects and so different in many others. The adjustment took time, of course, but it was achieved in an atmosphere of loving harmony and profound mutual respect. It is beside the point that Wolik was on an incomparably higher level than I—by his adoration and respect, he was raising me to his level!

FRIENDS IN IRKUTSK

Both of us were content to live quietly and work on Wolik's book, but he was too prominent a member of the political colony and the intellectual circle in the city not to be missed. Invitations were frequent, and so I met many outstanding people. Wolik was loved and respected, but it took some time before I was accepted wholeheartedly and suspicion vanished that I would tear him away from his political friends and interests.

The Irkutsk colony of political exiles—or "politicals," as they were usually called—was rather large. Among them were lawyers, doctors, teachers, political journalists, writers, and other professional people, on the one hand, and workers, peasants, soldiers exiled for participation in strikes and rioting, on the other. The dream of every exile was to be assigned to Irkutsk, the cultural center of eastern Siberia. Traditionally a progressive city, it both welcomed and needed the exiles who enriched its life. At our time, the colony was especially outstanding. The common characteristics of political exiles then were idealism, bravery, dramatic experiences in the past, and great hopes for the future of Russia, combined with a keen interest in political life at home and abroad. Within this broad spectrum were great individual differences and personal relationships.

Tseretelli, whom I mentioned earlier, was in a class of his own. An exceptionally gifted orator, a fearless defender of the people's aspirations for freedom, he absorbed many of the best features of the Russian intelligentsia while preserving the flair of the Orient in his behavior with people and in his manners. He was a lone wolf, and never married. He loved to tease his friends, and one had to be alert not to fall into his traps. I saw many who were bewildered by him and could not distinguish when he was joking and when he was serious.

Abram Gotz, a heroic figure among the exiled Socialist Revolutionaries, was one of Wolik's closest friends. He captured my heart at first sight—there was something so engaging in his broad smile, his affectionate looks at Wolik, his strong and friendly handshake, that I immediately felt at ease with him. He had broad philosophical interests; in his home, conversation covered a wide range of topics—literature, music, the theater, and, naturally, politics. In the evening, somebody would start to play the piano or the mandolin, others would sing, and there was much laughter and friendly joking. Abram's wife, a very warm and intelligent person, was a medical doctor and of a more quiet nature than he. There was something motherly in her hospitality toward me.

Apollon Kruglikov and his wife, Barbara, were other close friends who were very fond of Wolik. Wolik had brought about their marriage. When Apollon had been sentenced to ten years in prison and exile in Siberia thereafter, he had not wanted to bind his sweetheart, who lived in a provincial Russian town, to so terrible a future. He had written her that he no longer loved her and that she was free to arrange her life as she wished. Wolik, who knew the truth, wrote Barbara of Apollon's real motives. She gave up her work, came to Irkutsk, and married Apollon while he was in the penitentiary. By the time I met them, Apollon had completed his term and they were living together happily. It was Apollon's idea to repay his debt of happiness to Wolik by introducing him to me at the theater. Who knows? Perhaps I would not have met Wolik otherwise!

Another close friend was Eugene Timofeev, a man of exceptional strength and integrity whom nothing could induce to betray an iota of his convictions. With a five-year prison sentence, he was the leader and the soul of the political prisoners in the Alexandrovsk penitentiary, where he continued to write illegally, and smuggled out of the prison articles on the situation at the front during World War I. These articles, signed by initials only, were so informative and displayed such a technical grasp of what was happening on all parts of the front that the general public ascribed them to some military expert at Army Headquarters who wanted to preserve his anonymity. On the eve of his release from prison, Timofeev was accused of heading the activities of the Socialist Revolutionary Party in Irkutsk while serving his term, and a new penalty—ten more years of imprisonment—was imposed on him. A lesser man would have broken under such a cruel blow to all his hopes and plans, but not Eugene. He did not betray his emotions but remained composed and cold during pronouncement of the new sentence. A year later the Revolution of 1917 liberated him, but the new rulers of Russia considered him no less dangerous than did the Tsar. He was arrested for defending the Constituent Assembly and sentenced to death; the verdict was suspended, but he then was kept in prison for several years as a hostage, exiled to Siberia, arrested, released, rearrested, and finally was shot or died in one of Stalin's torture chambers. A few of his letters addressed to me under my maiden name slipped through the Communist censorship, but after the 1930's we had no communication from him or his wife.

There were the Arkhangelskys and Boris Rabinovitch, brother-in-law of Gotz, the Ermolaevs—Konstantine and his sister Vera—the young poet Prussak, and many others. To me this was a new world of which I had known only from books. The heroic figures of whom I had read now and then behind the teacher's back now came out of the shadow of my imagination. In sheer fascination I watched them and was forcefully drawn to them—Wolik's friends and therefore my friends.

To become a part of this tightly knit, mature group, in which everybody knew everything about everybody else and had lived through many common or similar experiences, was not easy for a young girl from an entirely different background. Besides, there was not enough time: Five months after our return from the boat trip, I left for Petrograd to meet Wolik's mother and other members of his family, and on the way there was surprised by the Revolution of 1917, which changed the course of our lives and theirs. I entered that circle shyly and could not help feeling that I was regarded with a certain curiosity and skepticism and that Wolik's close friends were weighing whether or not I was fit to be his wife. Yet they were so warm and natural that my self-consciousness rapidly disappeared, and though I did not contribute anything of substance to those friendly people, I felt closer and closer to them and sensed that they, too, had accepted me.

Not until thirty years later did I learn from Tseretelli, when he came to the United States, one reason for the cautiousness, even distrust, with which the Irkutsk politicals had regarded me: They had been sure that our marriage must have been celebrated with great pomp and that because of my attitude toward Wolik's friends, none of them had been invited. They could scarcely have been further from the truth.

Of my own friends, I had only Manya, who was to leave for Petrograd when school closed. We had grown up together, and she was closer to me than any of my sisters. Her sweetheart, Isaac, a young writer, was killed at the beginning of World War I during the first German attack, and she virtually died with him. She talked and taught, traveled and met people, but inside she was finished. I was her only tie with life, and though she picked out for me another of the politicals in Irkutsk, it gave her a great deal of satisfaction to see how the love I found in Wolik was born and grew. When we embraced at the railway station at her departure, neither of us realized that we would never see each other again!

2. *What Lay Behind Us*

BEFORE I TURN to the cataclysmic events of 1917, which completely changed our world, let me tell briefly of Wolik's life and mine before our two lives became one.

WOLIK'S CHILDHOOD AND YOUTH

Wolik was born into a rather sophisticated family. His father was a brilliant teacher of mathematics and dean of a polytechnic college; his mother came from an intellectual family, had graduated from a high school—a rare accomplishment for a woman some hundred years ago —and spoke German and French fluently. Her brother was an editor of a well-known magazine, *Rassvet* (*The Dawn*). Wolik had two brothers, Joseph and Nikolai, and a sister, Nadya. A German nurse lived permanently in the household, while French and English governesses alternated from year to year. The children were tutored at home; even the dancing teachers came to their house. Only for the last two or three grades were the children sent to school, at a private high school.

In his adult years, Wolik disapproved of this sort of education. If he had gone to a public school, or even a private school, from the first grade, he told me, he would have learned to work and play with other children, instead of withdrawing into himself. He learned a great deal from home tutoring, much more than even the best school could have given him, but at the price of loneliness, which he felt very keenly at times in both childhood and later years. He loved his family, but he needed broader horizons. The quiet, regular, and to some extent conventional pace of home life was not for this passionate rebel, yearning to give himself to great causes.

He felt closest to his father, and an intellectual affinity existed between the two. A witty man who told funny stories, had absolute pitch, and could sing operatic arias after only one hearing, his father showed an unconcern for small, practical matters, an attitude that appealed to Wolik. Wolik and his father shared a love of travel, ancient books and manuscripts—particularly old parchments with mathematical essays—and all kinds of collections. Wolik's father visited Europe every summer, and antiquarians in several countries held things that they believed he would buy on his arrival. Often he took Wolik with him on such trips— to Germany, Italy, Sweden. In the winter months, he studied the maps and guidebooks and discussed his next trip with Wolik, the only other member of the family who showed an interest in them. Wolik's mother, dismayed by this pastime, would point out that he had just returned from a trip but that his thoughts were already back in Europe and he would answer good-naturedly: "I get a double pleasure at no extra cost —first by reading about a trip and then by taking it." Wolik, too, loved such map explorations and brought home library books about countries he expected to visit.

Occasionally his father's carefree attitude and passion for collecting got him in trouble. At the outbreak of World War I, finding himself in Brussels, he decided to bring home some of the colorful posters put out by the Belgian Government with appeals to the population to remain calm or with instructions to the recruits. He had taken several of them from walls and put them in his brief case when the police stopped him. The matter looked serious until the chief of the police, a stamp collector, recognized a kindred soul and, after a grave warning, let him take the train to Petrograd.

A common love of mathematics strengthened the bond between father and son. Wolik wrote in his memoirs, *Stormy Passage:* "When I was twelve, my father introduced me into the mysteries of calculus. Although I preferred various branches of geometry, at fourteen I was also fairly familiar with advanced algebra." * Around that time, Wolik established his own system of disciplining his use of time. Each day he registered in a special ledger the hours he spent "usefully," on reading, writing notes, studying, and those he "wasted," on chatting and playing. His mother told me that she once had interrupted his reading to consult him on some family matter and noticed that although he obligingly put aside his book, he entered a mark in his ledger. As she got up to leave his room, she saw him glance at his wrist watch and again make a mark in his ledger. Curious, she asked him what it was all about, and the boy showed her his notebook where he had entered the time spent with her in the "wasted" column. Surprised and hurt, with tears in her eyes, she stayed fifteen or twenty minutes longer to discuss his behavior. Next day, in reply to her direct question, he confessed that he had entered the time spent in comforting her in the "wasted" column.

Each night, before going to bed, he totaled the number of "useful" and "wasted" hours and made notes on each book he had read. This self-imposed discipline, practiced from early years, accounts in part for Wolik's exceptional literary productivity. His mind was never idle or concerned merely with trivial matters, but operated on a much higher level. His response to complex theoretical problems was immediate. No matter what topic was raised, his reaction always gave the impression that he had just finished studying it and was prepared to discuss it.

* New York: Vanguard Press, 1961.

When he had a little free time, Wolik liked to spend it with the old carpenter, a simple but intelligent man, who lived on his father's property in Finland. The carpenter was deaf and dumb, but he could express himself by signs and knew the sign-language alphabet used by deaf mutes. Wolik soon learned to talk to him and later enjoyed telling his own family complicated stories by using signs and pantomime. I recall several gatherings at our home when Wolik let his imagination play and told, without saying a word, the story of the origin of religion, of the world's creation, of the different social classes and their relationships. His eyes twinkled, as new ideas came to his mind, and his mimicry was so expressive that nearly everybody understood him.

In his youth, Wolik was very fond of one close friend who shared his interest in economics, Boris Raitz. Wolik found Boris an exceptionally brilliant and attractive boy—lovable, warm, always cheerful—and felt that his own ideas were sharpened by his efforts to convince Boris of them. Nadya, Wolik's sister, also was captured by Boris' charm. Both were deeply grieved by the tragic end of Boris' life: Vacationing in the Swiss Alps, he went mountain-climbing and, as he wrote to Wolik, liked to take short cuts, that is, to descend the rocky slopes instead of following the serpentine paths. On one such direct descent, he tried to pick some edelweiss but lost his balance and was killed instantly in the fall. For a long time, Wolik could not reconcile himself to his death, and Nadya's life was also affected by this loss of the first and probably the strongest love of her life. Wolik dedicated his first book on economics, *Market and Prices,** to the memory of Boris and in several footnotes pointed out that certain ideas had been suggested to him by Boris.

Neither in high school nor in his father's preparatory courses did Wolik establish any permanent friendships, perhaps because of shyness fostered by home tutoring and the lack of contacts with youngsters that he would easily have found in a school. Later he found another friend to whom he was strongly drawn—Andrea Caffi—but their different pursuits separated them for so many years that this friendship never developed as fully as it might have.

STUDENT AND REVOLUTIONIST

Wolik's father conducted summer courses on his estate in Terioki, Finland, to prepare high-school graduates for the competitive entrance examinations for specialized colleges, other than the one of which he was dean. While still in high school, Wolik lectured at his father's courses. He wrote: "I looked older than I was, had inherited some of my father's speaking ability, and was rather successful in this role." † He taught mathematics and physics, and the students preferred him to several older teachers. The high school he entered had been the alma mater of the famous mathematician, A. A. Markov, and Wolik was soon called

* *Rynok i Jseny* (St. Petersburg: 1906).
† *Stormy Passage.*

"the second Markov." The school and his father expected him to concentrate on and excel in mathematics. At about fifteen, however, he became engrossed in economics, its theory and history: "I devoured the British classics, books of the German historical and Austrian psychological schools, Marxian literature, works of French Socialists and Syndicalists . . ." * Then with youthful boldness he undertook to write a book on the general theory of value. He worked on it during his last year in the high school, to the great regret of his father, who clung to the hope that his son would become a mathematician. Wolik sent his manuscript, about a thousand pages in longhand, to the famous professor M. I. Tugan-Baranovsky, who, ousted by the Tsar from St. Petersburg University, now lived on his estate in the south of Russia. Believing that this was the work of a young unknown professor, Tugan-Baranovsky commented warmly on it and recommended it for publication in a slightly condensed form. He started his letter to Wolik with "Dear Colleague," wanted to see his previous published works, and asked several personal questions. Wolik's father was surprised and very pleased at this, and thereupon became reconciled to the prospect that Wolik would excel, if not in mathematics, in another branch of science.

Informed that *Market and Prices* had been written by a high-school boy, Tugan-Baranovsky recommended the manuscript to his own publisher and wrote the foreword for it. By the time the book appeared, in April, 1906, Wolik's heart and soul were in the revolutionary movement, remote from scholarly work.

Interestingly, this book by a precocious youth expressed ideas and attitudes that remained characteristic of Wolik's mature work in economics. Tugan-Baranovsky stressed its most important feature in his foreword, in which he wrote that the author "strives to build his decisions on an empirical foundation, as close to life as possible: his abstractions do not hang in the air, they are grounded in historical soil." †

At St. Petersburg University, one man in particular exercised a profound influence on Wolik's thinking, Professor of Law L. Petrazhitsky (in Russia, economics was taught by the law faculty), and Wolik returned again and again to his ideas and thinking. Petrazhitsky's interpretations of the basic concepts of law, the state, and the moral pattern of human progress were close to Wolik's attitude toward life and his scale of values. Though he felt rather an outsider in Petrazhitsky's seminar because his

---

* *Ibid.*

† Or, as Wolik expressed it: "The economic science must never, even for a moment, break its contact with people and life." His characterization of a consumer in a capitalist society, written in 1904, is valid for today, describing "his insatiability, his persistent striving for new and newer goods and new and ever newer enjoyment, changeability of his tastes, his endeavor to imitate new and ever newer patterns, his contempt for tradition. On these features of the consumer depend such characteristic phenomena of the capitalist market as fashion, instability in demand, rapid changes in goods offered in the market, development of advertising and so on." *Market and Prices: Theory of Consumption, Market and Market Prices*, trans. Emma S. Woytinsky (New York: Augustus M. Kelley, 1964).

absorbing interest was in economics, he participated actively in the discussions and presented several papers of his own. One of these involves a monkey and was taken as a joke by the students, until the professor took Wolik's side, saying that the subject merited scholarly attention.

Wolik's topic was the sense of contractual rights among monkeys, and his own experiments were the basis of his paper. He had spent some time in Berlin and had visited the monkey section of the zoo every day. There he established contact with a large monkey, showing her a pear which he took out of his pocket and then put back in. The monkey watched him closely, and when he made a gesture asking her to jump, she obeyed. Wolik cut a slice from the pear and rewarded her with it. He repeated the gesture several times, and each time the monkey obliged with a jump and was rewarded. But when, after one jump, Wolik cut a much smaller slice from the pear, the monkey apparently felt cheated and refused to accept the slice. Wolik re-established good relations, and then demanded two jumps instead of one; the monkey jumped twice, received two standard slices of the pear, and was satisfied. Wolik varied his requests, now asking for one jump, now for two, and rewarded the monkey accordingly. All was well. Then he asked the monkey to jump twice, and as she did so, he calmly put the pear back into his pocket, as if he were about to leave. The monkey went wild, shook the bars violently, and bared her teeth. Wolik brought the pear out and cut one slice from it. The monkey took it, but waited for the second. Instead, Wolik signaled her to jump again; she did not budge, but waited for what she had rightfully earned. Variations of this economic exchange went on and on, and formed the basis for Wolik's conclusion that monkeys have a clear-cut sense of contractual obligations and rights.

In the seminar on economics, Wolik, a freshman, astonished the older members of the group with his knowledge of the writings of Karl Marx, then a proof of one's intellectual maturity. He could quote whole paragraphs, even pages, by heart. Because of his critical attitude toward Marx, unusual in those days, he was called a "Marx-eater." Soon he stood out in the crowd of students—at the age of twenty, a mathematician, author of a book on economic theory, well versed in several modern European languages, as well as in Latin and Greek, well read in history and literature, able to hold an audience with both the content and the humor of his speeches. Without trying to do so, he gained popularity among the students and respect from the professors for his love of study and gentlemanly behavior. The students nicknamed him the "Scythian" because of his red hair, his impetuous movements, his swift reactions, and, in general, for his unusualness, as if he had been thrown among them by some elemental force. Apparently, they were not alone in being impressed by his combination of forcefulness and refined culture; after we were married, I found among Wolik's possessions a wooden statue made in Siberia by Vera Ermolaeva which depicted him as an aristocratic gentleman with a fine, intelligent face; he was wearing a tuxedo but from beneath the back of the jacket there emerged a little tail.

We lost this original creature, along with all our other possessions, when the Communists occupied Georgia.

Almost immediately after Wolik entered the university, he was elected to the Student Council. On his return from a Christmas vacation in Italy and Germany, after Bloody Sunday, January 5, 1905, he joined the Social Democratic Party, and in no time was recognized by both students and workers as one of its most effective speakers. Resourceful, daring, ready to risk his life again and again in the fight against the Tsarist Government, capable of kindling the imagination of people and inspiring them to action, he became, without trying to assume the role, the rallying point of the large St. Petersburg student body. He was also very popular in the factory districts of the capital.

From 1905 through 1907, Wolik was arrested several times and spent some months in prison because of his political activities. On a speaking tour of the villages, he experienced a terrible ordeal at the hands of peasants enraged by his statement that Russia had no use for the Tsar. Only the arrival of troops at the station where he and several of his colleagues had been attacked prevented him from having his eyes gouged out; a scar over his left brow remained for many years. For weeks after Wolik told me this story, I had nightmares and could not help thinking of the impact on his parents when they read the terrifying news in the newspapers without being able to do anything for him.

After the revolution of 1905 was put down, thousands of industrial workers in St. Petersburg were thrown out of work and left to starve in the streets: 74 industrial plants and steel mills with 110,000 workers were closed. Singlehandedly and against his party's policy, Wolik organized these desperate men into the Council of the Unemployed, which could defend their interests before the reactionary Municipal Council. Almost incredibly, scores of thousands of angry, hopeless men on the brink of violence submitted themselves to the leadership of a twenty-two-year-old youth. He kept them within legal limits and exercised great authority by an amazing combination of moral strength, leadership, youthful revolutionary spirit, and the ability to use words for their cause. He actually got for them bread, work, and hope! The Municipal Council of St. Petersburg opened stations that provided 40,000 meals a day, advanced money to pay rent and interest on pawned items, and, most important, organized public works with decent working conditions.

The unemployed workers' devotion to him was extraordinary. No less extraordinary was the fact that he not only was capable of handling the unruly crowd of the unemployed but had enough political acumen and maneuverability in his actions and speeches to deal with the reactionary Municipal Council. By keeping open the communication channels with the Municipal Council, he could protect "his" unemployed by preventing police intervention.

Later in the year when many leaders of the defeated revolution fled abroad, Lenin urged Wolik to leave Russia and offered him the editorship of one of the party's magazines, with full independence in his work.

Wolik refused, saying that thousands of those who had followed the call of revolutionary leaders, his call among others, had paid for it with their lives or their freedom, and he wanted to share their fate. He remained in Russia, but, being too well known to the police for underground work in the capital, went to Ekaterinoslav in southern Russia. There he was soon arrested, court-martialed, and sentenced to four years in the penitentiary, to be followed by permanent exile in Siberia—for belonging to the Social Democratic Party.

PRISON YEARS

The prison in Ekaterinoslav was horrible. Hunger, filth, lice, freezing temperatures in the wards, constant beatings—all these he experienced, yet he maintained not only sanity but dignity. Worse than all these was having to witness the sadistic tortures inflicted on other prisoners in the corridor outside his cell. To watch, to hear the screams, to shake with hatred and indignation and be unable to do anything! In his book *Vne Zhizni (Shut Away from Life)*,* he wrote:

> Such scenes cannot be forgotten. I still smart with shame and anger when I recall that horrible "search in cell 9." And then . . . then I stood at the "eye" in my cell's door and could not tear myself away from it. Bit my lips so that blood appeared, in order to keep myself from screaming, looked and listened. Blood hammered in my temples, and my body shook with choking rage. I wanted to shout, to do something, so as to distract the butchers if only for a moment, to interrupt their "entertainment." But I stood without moving, clinging to the "eye," sticking to the crossbeams of the door so as not to fall. Watched and listened . . . I wanted to run away, to throw myself on the cot, to bury my head in the pillow, not to hear and not to see what was going on in the hall. But I had a vague feeling that I must not do this. A voice inside me insisted: "Stand here . . . See, listen . . . !"
>
> One who has not experienced this, who has not been in a prison when inmates are mistreated, will not understand what a torment it is to hear a few steps from you, behind your wall, that they are torturing somebody, perhaps your comrade, your close friend; to hear the sounds of blows, the screams of the victim, to hear how they pull his unconscious body along the floor, how his body strikes against the stairs, to hear all this and feel that you cannot do a thing, that you cannot even protest . . . You must sit and listen . . . One who has never lived through this, will never understand this torture.

When his turn came, he underwent the physical pain, the repeated attacks of dizziness, the sense of complete exhaustion. But morally he felt better:

* St. Petersburg: Jasny, 1914.

There was no longer that depressing, ugly feeling of humiliation which has never left me since the day I saw how they tortured Boris, and I was silent . . . Yes, I have carefully analyzed all my feelings during recent days and have been surprised by an unexpected discovery. When they beat my comrades before my eyes and I looked on and said nothing, the humiliation was a thousand times deeper and more poignant than a few hours ago when my head dangled helplessly under the blows and kickings of the butchers. Then, by my silence, I was a kind of involuntary participant in incredible infamy. Now I have been beaten up as if a beast had overtaken me during a hunt, as if I had crashed against rocks in falling from a mountain. Then I had the feeling of deep humiliation, now I do not feel it.

But even in such conditions, Wolik continued his scientific activity, writing a book on the theory of wages, on the basis of two bulletins of the Prussian Statistical Office admitted by the guards because of the big crowned eagles on the cover. Keeping his mind busy helped him to avoid self-pity and humiliation. He pretended that he had accepted a newspaper assignment to share prison life and to report on the conditions there. He took this assignment seriously and prepared a detailed report on the sadistic mistreatment of prisoners, hiding his papers in the cracks of the walls, the habitat of the bugs. When his report was completed—including names, dates, and precise details of beatings, some of them fatal—he had it smuggled out of the penitentiary in the seams of dirty shirts and underwear sent out to the laundry.

The article appeared simultaneously in several European capitals and in Russia. The effect was that of a bombshell. The reactionary Tsarist Government, more sensitive to public opinion than the Soviet Government, sent an investigating commission to Ekaterinoslav. On confirmation of the report, measures were taken to put an end to the sadistic infamy.

Wolik put himself at the disposal of the prisoners for any help he could give them; many turned to him for advice or to ask him to write legal papers for them or letters home. Because he helped not only political prisoners but also common criminals, the latter respected and trusted him, though ordinarily they were hostile to the politicals.

Although Wolik had spent most of his childhood summers in Terioki, close to the shore of the Baltic Sea, he had been so preoccupied with reading, writing, and teaching—in brief, with books and people—that nature had been unobserved by him. Confinement in prison brought about a complete reversal in his attitude. A passionate love of nature took hold of him, never to leave him. He described it in *Shut Away from Life:*

> Once, during the walk in the prison yard in the early spring I saw a few blades of grass. Behind the back of the guard, I picked them, hid them carefully under my shirt and took them to my cell. The

grass did not suffer from pulling. We looked tenderly at the soft green blades; those weak seedlings, which we would have crushed under our feet without mercy and coldbloodedly if we had been walking in freedom, appeared touchingly beautiful here. Each of us dreamt of a fragrant clearing, covered with flowers and shaded by the large branches of big trees. To stretch oneself on the grass, amid the flowers, listening to the murmur of the leaves, admiring the clouds passing overhead! What a joy it would be to live just one hour that way! . . .

I remember one spring evening when we watched a storm. The day was exceptionally stifling, and the stuffy air in the tower with its eternal musty smell of rot was particularly trying. We were exhausted and waited impatiently for the evening's coolness. The sky suddenly darkened, there was silence in the air. Then fast, heavy drops of rain started to drum playfully upon the iron sheets of the roof. Lightning cut through the darkness; deafening thunder rolled over the prison . . . The downpour became stronger and stronger, lightning sparkled brighter and faster . . . We opened the window, without thinking that the night check was over and that we could easily get a bullet from the guard for being at the window. The rain fell slantingly, and in one second water covered the window sill and ran over the floor. Soon a real pool was on the floor but this was not enough for us. We clung to the bars crossing the window, exposed our heads, our necks, our naked breasts to the cold spray of the rain. We tried to stretch out our arms beyond the bars so as to reach a stream of water running from some projection above the window and laughed loud while pushing one another from the narrow window. How cheerful we were that evening! It was fortunate that the guard did not hear our laughter amid the thunderstorm and did not notice us clinging to the bars when lightning flashed around us. Otherwise we would have paid dearly for that momentary gaiety. Anyhow, our cheerfulness was gone very quickly. Each of us must have thought with sadness how good it would be then in free air, somewhere in a field or a forest. At this thought confinement became so depressing, such a torture, that it seemed as if all the stones of the thick surrounding walls were pressing on one's breast. How wonderful the storm is, how wonderful life in freedom! How beautiful is everything of what the prison had deprived us! We did not talk about this that evening, perhaps because such thoughts would point to weakness of spirit or sentimentality, but these were the emotions which agitated us. By God, either my nervous system had given in or I lived before with closed eyes, without noticing how wonderful life was. This was what I thought turning sleeplessly from side to side that spring night.

I reacted even more sharply to the sight of the town when after a year's confinement, I had to go to the court to get the accusatory documents. I had walked those same streets many times as a free man and believed then that it would be difficult to create a duller, more vulgar, more repulsive town intentionally. But how different that town appeared to me now! I looked with a kind of rapture at the houses, the stores, the people in the streets, the trolley and the droshkas passing by. Everything charmed me. How bright, how rich, how animated and gay the streets seemed after our prison halls! How well-dressed the street crowd appeared after my eyes had become used to the filthy prison jackets, the rags of the transient prisoners and greasy uniforms of the guards! And the faces of all the people seemed healthy, cheerful, attractive . . .

Several times Wolik's parents bribed the wardens, even the Military Commander of the South, in an unsuccessful attempt to lighten his stay in the penitentiary, but their efforts only irritated him. He refused to accept any favor from the hated officials, wanting to share fully the sufferings of his comrades and friends. Several university professors tried to influence the military court in his behalf by stressing his exceptional scientific and literary talents. The result was the same: Wolik rejected any favoritism. Perhaps he carried this unbending attitude too far, but nothing could move him to agree to the slightest easing in his conditions as compared with others.

A typhus epidemic swept the prison, causing untold deaths and spreading from one ward to another. When no disinfection of the affected wards was undertaken, the prisoners organized a noisy demonstration. They appeared in relays at the open windows shouting the demand that the court attorney investigate the situation. After five hours of clamor, the attorney did come, and ordered the wards to be disinfected and the typhus-stricken prisoners transferred to the municipal barracks. But the epidemic continued.

Wolik, learning that there were few guards at the barracks and that there were no bars on the windows, concocted an escape plan. He would simulate typhus, get transferred to the barracks, and escape from there to freedom. That there was a much greater chance of catching typhus and dying from it was never even considered by the rebellious youth, eager to be out of jail. Indeed, he nearly did die. First, a drug smuggled in to him to create the appearance of illness left his body temporarily paralyzed; he felt as though he had plunged into icy waters. Then he nearly died from the starvation diet fed the dying patients in the barracks. Finally, he made his attempt to escape, was captured and taken back to the castle. He was proud, though, that he had not caught typhus.

In his third year in the Ekaterinoslav prison, Wolik noted enviously during his half-hour walk that some prisoners were working as carpenters. He applied for such work and was assigned to a group making market stands. The foreman of the group was a peasant serving a ten-year sentence for his role in a village riot. He was very proud to have such an educated man under him and tried to give Wolik the easiest work, yet had the tact to assure him: "This work may seem light, but it needs an educated man. The work is just right for you!"

In retrospect, Wolik considered those spring months as a carpenter, when he worked to the point of complete physical exhaustion each day, as his best period in that prison. When Nadya wrote him that he was to be transferred to a Siberian penitentiary, many inmates envied him. The foreman of his carpentry gang told him: "You will see, a year and then another will pass, and then you will be out of prison, and free to live in Siberia. You can marry there, any peasant girl will be glad to marry you. You are such a quiet man, and do not drink. But watch out: don't pick out some bad girl. You can get a good one! Just look around and get the best girl in the whole village!" (In later years, Wolik used to say that he had followed the foreman's advice to a T by picking out the best girl in the whole world.)

Wolik made the trip from the Ekaterinoslav to the Alexandrovsk penitentiary in Siberia with a convoy, the last part on foot. He had been put in chains, although the court had ruled that he should not be fettered. The warden overlooked this instruction, and Wolik would not remind him.

The Russian penal system was not monolithic but full of contradictions. It included the tortures of Ekaterinoslav Castle and the relaxed treatment of political prisoners in some other penal institutions. The penitentiary in Alexandrovsk was in the latter group, and the two years Wolik spent there belonged to the brighter side of his prison life. The politicals included many outstanding intellectuals of high moral standing, with whom he established lifelong friendships. The regime was much more humane, the head of the penitentiary had much respect for the politicals and most importantly, Knyasev, the Governor General of Eastern Siberia, a former judge, was a man of integrity under whom prison excesses were not permitted. In the last year of Wolik's term, he moved into his own log cabin within the prison compound: The penal code permitted prisoners who had served more than half of their term to build their own huts on prison grounds. Nadya, Wolik's sister, asked the Governor General to apply this law in Wolik's case. When Knyasev's counsel informed him that the law had never been repealed and made no distinction between common criminals and politicals, the Governor General agreed to Nadya's request. Wolik's log cabin was bought for about sixty dollars in the village, taken apart, brought to the prison, and then reassembled on the prison grounds. It consisted of two rooms with a stove and a covered porch.

In Alexandrovsk, Wolik wrote some of his most stirring articles about prison conditions. Several of them touch on problems that agitate legal and governmental minds to these days, such as capital punishment and its impact on the spread of crime in general, on the condemned, and on those outside prison walls but in trouble with the law, as well as on the "romance of the fist," as Wolik called the worship of sheer physical strength and the desperate gambling to which many prisoners succumbed. Yet there were no "purges" or "confessions" like those introduced later by the Kremlin. One weak attempt to inspire "confessions" in a case involving more than a hundred persons was defeated by a legal paper prepared by Wolik.

OUT OF PRISON

Wolik's release from the penitentiary came in December, 1912. Here are excerpts describing his feelings as a free man in his article "Prizraki" ("The Ghosts"), published in *Russkoe Bogatstvo* in 1913:

> Captivity lies behind me. There, in that realm of pain and torture, are my brothers in spirit. My thoughts return involuntarily to those somber walls. Again the familiar sorrowful ghosts surround me, those shadows of the years gone by. I do not drive away those shadows. No! They must remain with me forever. If I sank into the slough of sufferings and came up to the bright day with unbroken, undestroyed forces, I must keep, as my sacred duty, the memory of what I experienced there, in that hell . . .
>
> But why does not my thought of the past darken the brightness of freedom for me? Why have I not brought from prison either despair or disappointment or contempt for people? Instead, I have brought cheerfulness and joy which I had not known before imprisonment. . . .
>
> I entered prison, fatigued and gloomy, without much faith in life. The prison years passed by. Around me people perished. Comrades condemned to death were herded past me. Dead bodies were carried past me and dragged on the floor. As in a nightmarish ring, merged faces of the condemned distorted by fear of death, immobile masks of the dead, sallow faces of the inmates . . . Death in its ugliest form, humiliations, sadist tortures . . . And along with this —the moral destruction of the weak, the cowardly break with the past, forgetfulness of cherished ideals, attempts to save life at the price of betrayal and falsehood . . .
>
> I have experienced everything that imprisonment brings: the pain of loneliness during sickness, parting with friends taken to the gallows, hunger, cold, humiliations, beating, the horror of being caught at trying to escape, the dull despair of one who does not hope to return to freedom. The only pain I did not experience was fear of death, because I had not known the love of life while I was free. . . .
>
> Why then, after all this torture, have I brought out of prison only warm feelings for people, exhilarating joy in life and a fiery faith in myself, in my force, in life, in love, in beauty?

Then Wolik recalled a visit to the assistant warden when a sergeant was reporting the number of prisoners and the number who had died or been transferred to the death cells or the hospital, and so on. The warden used an abacus to keep count.

The assistant warden clicked the abacus adroitly. Like someone's teeth, the balls chattered sharply, gloomily. Suddenly an ugly thought gripped me: These were dead bones, the bones of those who had perished here, tortured to death. . . . The room swam before my eyes. The green light of the lamp appeared ominous, deadly . . .

The warden finished his calculations, cleared the abacus ringingly . . . It seemed that he was pouring our bones into a bottomless sack. My hands and feet were beginning to freeze. I rubbed my eyes to drive away the awful nightmare but could not banish the picture. I returned to my cell, with the ominous clank of human bones still in my ears. The importunate thought still drilled my brain that we, within those walls, were dead bones. The walls were like a huge bag into which we had been thrown for a time, to be poured into other bags, other boxes and covered with dust . . .

Then Wolik described another "insignificant, everyday scene." With other inmates, he was waiting his turn to be chained. The smith was a lifer who had betrayed other inmates and now was responsible for shackling the prisoners.

The smith sullenly rummaged in the heap of irons, measuring the crampon against my leg, trying one after another . . .

I sat on the ground, with my leg on the anvil. Over my body slid the repulsive rusty iron and the even more repulsive, hardened fingers of the traitor. Finally, he found the right crampon. "All right . . . Go ahead!" The hammer struck on the head of the clincher, flattening the iron. The fetters rubbed and struck my legs. There were no underfetters yet, and we did not know how to pull the chain and move cautiously . . . Blood began to run from under the iron crampons, and red drops flowed slowly down. But I did not feel the pain, only a boundless offense . . .

I remember walks in the prison. Like animals in a cage, we walked in the narrow, barred enclosure along the prison wall. We, the short-termers, walked the western wall while at the same time the lifers walked the eastern wall.

One could not look across to their side without feeling emotion and pain . . . Pale, greyish faces, expressionless eyes, hesitant steps, downcast heads, hanging arms, stooped shoulders and backs . . . As if the dead had come out of their tombs and were walking in the prison yard, walking to review the scene of their suffering and perform some mysterious ceremony to curse it . . . Those shadows of living dead haunted me like a nightmare, day and night. Now, as in a daydream, I see them before me—just as grey, somber, cursing silently, without words, as I saw them three years ago.

In those years when the ghosts of death hovered constantly before my eyes; when the moans, the shouts, the clanking of iron—in chains, in padlocks, in bars—hit my ears incessantly; in those first years of imprisonment I felt that the last shred of the will to live had disappeared from my heart. I did not think of freedom, and when occasionally a thought came to me of life after prison, it seemed to me that even in freedom smiles and joy would be forever impossible, inaccessible to me.

Why then do not all those recollections fill my soul with a deadly cold, why do they not paralyze my energy and love of life? Perhaps, in facing the joy of living, I am belying the ghosts that surround me? Perhaps, in my cheerfulness I am wronging friends tortured in the prison, comrades who are still suffering in chains, all those with whom I have shared sufferings and who now cannot share my joy with me? No! I stand before them in the right. I was gloomy and exhausted when I entered prison, and there, in that realm of sorrow, I found everything by which I am living now . . .

Other pictures of death, sorrow and pain are before me—that death, that sorrow, that pain which gave me faith in man and the beauty of life in those sad years. Out of the many comrades and friends who perished on the gallows, I remember one—the closest to me, whom I loved most, and whose death shook me more strongly, more deeply than anything else—because I did not understand the meaning of that death then.

I met Paul in prison, and his face struck me at once—he looked so different from all the others. A pale, sad face with a warm smile, a soft beard, big brown eyes, brave yet mellow eyes like those of a child; long, curling hair running down on both sides of his white forehead . . . His voice was soft, quiet, with a touch of melancholy. People in prison do not speak with such a voice. But as I learned more of him, I felt he could not have another voice—so much softness and love for people was in each word of his.

At the same time he was a man of iron will and incredible courage, a true knight without fear and reproach in all his dealings with friends and enemies alike. Hatred of enemies and oppressors usual in a revolutionary was absent from that sweet, infinitely kind man. Instead of hatred, he felt only love, sorrowful love for all who suffered and were oppressed. Only love had forced him to fight . . . And he went where love called him, trembling with horror and pain that he had to encounter bloodshed . . . "Freedom is dearer than life, and honor dearer than freedom"—that was Paul's stand. When I met him, the gallows awaited him, and he went toward it without fear . . .

By chance I met his father at the prison gate. He looked pitiful—bent by years and sorrow, gray-bearded, with dull, sunken eyes and tears running down his wrinkled face . . . Our eyes met for a moment, and to my great surprise I read in his look, behind the veil of tears, the expression of a quiet pride. I understood his pride and bowed deeply before him.

I saw Paul for the last time before his execution, at the window of the cell where the condemned awaited death. He came up to the bars, smiled at me, and shouted, "I am at peace. I have no fear." His truthful, lucid eyes told better than words that he was not pretending to be brave, was not suppressing fear, but, indeed, felt peace with all his soul, all his being . . .

I could not think of anything except Paul . . . It seemed to me that in his execution lay all the impotence, all the fruitlessness of purity and beauty of the human soul. Brute force won . . . For days I thought of Paul. Then suddenly I noticed that the thought of his death ceased to arouse feelings of despair and gloom. The gallows began to be supplanted, before my eyes, by Paul's face—his peaceful, sweet face with a sad smile and the eyes full of love and self-sacrifice . . . It was not brute force which had won; love was victorious. Therefore Paul was quiet and composed, therefore sparks of pride shone through the tears in his father's eyes . . .

Paul's words before his execution ring in my ears, and I cannot help thinking: No matter how many gallows people will erect, the beauty of life will not die! Life is beautiful if its children can so live and die. Death and brutality will never be the victors, because the oppressors have no power over life. Their power is only to repeat again, and again, for the thousandth time, Golgotha . . . Golgotha! This is not simply the symbol of death and pain. It is an image that calls to battle, to life, to joy. This is the symbol of the weakness of the evil and of the all-victorious power of love. With this image of love I shall never be under the spell of sadness and gloom. If I had brought out of prison only this single symbol, I would bless the years of suffering that gave that symbol to me, and in it, the basis for faith in life and man!

Wolik described further several instances of human weakness, scenes in the cells when some who had been heroic yesterday appeared petty today, when he lost faith in some of them. But as he looked closer, he began to feel that behind the silence, behind the masks the prisoners wore, were agonizing dramas more poignant than all the humiliations and even death—suffering for those beyond the prison walls, partaking of their sorrow and sadness.

Everyone lived his drama silently, without sharing it with others. Therefore they were so reserved, so suspicious, so easily irritated. They lived for the short moments of meetings with their loved ones. But each meeting added a new drop of venom. Everyone waited in torment and agitation for a line from the beloved, awaited mailday as a holiday. But afterwards the faces became more somber, more severe, and the inmates walked back and forth in their cells with expressions of greater pain . . . as if the soul longed to reach through the bars to loved ones, to get a glimpse of their life. But a glimpse of it brought only new pain . . . And again, in anxiety, there was the trembling wish to be closer even in pain to those whom they had left outside.

I remember one time when I watched the assistant warden sort letters for the prisoners. Envelopes, white and colored, big and small, covered by minute handwriting and almost illegible scribbles, flashed in his hands. Suddenly it began to seem that through his hands were streaming the tears of mothers, sisters, wives who suffered beyond the prison walls . . . helpless tears in response to unexpressed complaints, suppressed tears hidden in the prison walls. . . .

I began to feel pity for people, and in that pity contempt for their weakness drowned and disappeared. They were neither as they seemed to be in moments of enthusiasm, nor as they appeared to-day. They were just people, people suffering with the pain of broken links with life . . .

A comrade condemned to death asked me to give him some poison I had kept for myself. I hesitated, then broke a piece of glass from the window and made a cut in my flesh next to a vein. The glass entered the flesh as easily as steel would, and I saw that even without a knife I could open my veins, and that even without the poison I still had the power over my life. Then I gave him the poison . . .

When I entered prison and in my first years there I believed that my strength, my happiness lay in cold determination, in readiness to die, in proud loneliness, internal freedom. I could not be forced to suffer, to stand humiliation, because I could always choose death rather than take suffering and humiliation. I was ready then to despise those who suffered, who tormented themselves, had no hopes, expected nothing, and yet clung to life and tried to prolong their miserable existence . . .

But wordless dramas passed before my eyes. Against the moral disintegration, against the gloom, shone the brilliant threads which bind people together and save life through pain and suffering.

Without my noticing it, my attitude toward people and life was changing. My faith in people was becoming stronger, and my heart admitted love with all its burdens, all its pain. I grieved that I was so lonely and so free. I was willing to give up my proud strength and accept all the pains which love brings . . .

I remember an old woman who came from the Ukraine to see her son, a lifer. She lived near the prison for about a month, went to see him at permitted hours, took parcels prepared with touching motherly care. When I went with her to the prison, she talked constantly about her boy, recalled his childhood, laughed in telling of his pranks. She always entered the prison animated and gay. She looked the same way at her last visit, before she was to leave for the Ukraine. I liked her cheerfulness and thought: What an old lady!

So gay . . . But when she came out, her legs would not hold her. As soon as she was out of sight of the prison, she fell to the ground, with her face in the dirty snow, and sobbed and sobbed. She could not get up, could not walk. Her son's friends lifted her up and led her away. She kept repeating: "For good . . . for good . . . I have come to say goodbye . . . for good!"

How much her gaiety and high spirits had cost the poor mother before the meetings with the son whom the soulless prison had taken away from her . . .

The pale ghosts of despair and death may crowd around me. I was with you, shared your sad fate and will share it again when I am called upon to do so. But now nothing will silence those songs of the blue sky and snow-decked trees, the wild stream of the powerful Siberian river. Out of the penitentiary I have brought images of beauty and love, images bright as the sun. They call me to happiness and joy; they have kindled around me glittering stars which were absent from my life. They have filled the world with sounds my heart has not known before. As never before, I want to live. As never before, my heart is full of faith and happiness!

EXILE IN SIBERIA

When his prison term was completed, Wolik was first assigned to the village of Jilkino, on the high bank of the Angara River, across from the city of Irkutsk, the capital of Eastern Siberia. After he nearly lost his life crossing the Angara before it was completely frozen, his friends insisted that he should ask for permission to live in Irkutsk. He obtained it, made the move to Irkutsk, and immediately plunged into literary and political activities. He had lived through many challenging experiences, had witnessed acts of heroism and of human weaknesses, had seen horrible abuses of power by petty tyrants, and now he felt the urge to tell it all. He was already known in Russian literary and political circles, and the leading periodicals in St. Petersburg and Moscow were eager to print his articles, even at the risk of being fined or suspended. In the light of today's absence of free press in the Communist countries, one is surprised that it was possible for so fierce an opponent of the Government as Wolik to write, in the penitentiary and later in exile, vehement accusations against the regime and to have his writings printed for circulation throughout the country.

In the same period Wolik wrote for the local press as far as censorship permitted, organized several publications on burning political issues, published the book *Vne Zhizni (Shut Away from Life)*, prepared a historical survey of the Jewish population in Siberia as a project offered by the Irkutsk Jewish community, and was an active member of the Social Democratic group in exile.

When World War I started, Wolik spoke and wrote against the flag-waving, with caution, naturally, but clearly enough to be understood.

His views, however, did not keep him from being chosen chief statistician of the procurement mission of General Kozlov, who was charged with providing the Russian Army on the Western Front with cheap high-quality meat and dairy products from Siberia. The General knew of Wolik's past but he needed him; Kozlov's superiors in the capital liked Wolik's clear, informative reports and well-organized statistical data. When inspectors from St. Petersburg were expected, the General used to say to Wolik: "There is nothing to do in the office right now. You'd better work on your report at home."

To indulge his passionate love of the outdoors, Wolik wanted to spend some time exploring Siberia. He had no trouble in getting permission to leave Irkutsk, even to journey a thousand miles across that vast area. The first summer he went on short trips. Then he selected for his travels the almost uninhabited region reaching to the easternmost end of the mainland and facing Japan. He and his friend, Mikhail Vedenyapin, also a political exile, penetrated so deep in the *tayga* that they found themselves lost in a part of the Siberian wilderness that apparently had not been touched by human foot for a very long time. When they were about to reconcile themselves to death in the primeval forest, Wolik recognized on the horizon the shape of mountain peaks he had sketched at the beginning of their adventure. Their sense of direction regained, they crossed the *tayga* with the aid of a compass and reached human settlements and safety. Wolik described that trip in his book *V Tayge* (*In the Tayga*),* and wrote about other short trips in various articles.

Even in this period of comparative freedom in his personal life and political activities, Wolik had some trouble with the police, who never gave up hope of settling their score with him. He was arrested, released, and then re-arrested when the police decided to take the law in their own hands. But Wolik knew the law far better than those petty provincial officials. He appealed directly to Governor General Knyasev, gaining his release from the police sentence.

This was his last brush with the police before we met. They made one more try, while I was on the train to Petrograd to meet Wolik's mother and the other members of his family. Wolik, who had influenza at the time, was visited on March 13, 1917, by a police officer, who brought him an order to leave Irkutsk at once. Wolik promised to do so as soon as he recovered. Next morning, Irkutsk learned of the overthrow of the Tsarist Government, and on March 16 Wolik supervised the release of political prisoners from the local jail.

Thus his fight against the Tsarist regime ended in complete victory.

Wolik talked occasionally of his prison experiences; various incidents from that period of his life would come back to his mind in one connection or another. Characteristically, he never, in the forty-four years of our life together, said one word of complaint about the lost years, deprivation, mistreatment. There was not a trace of personal bitterness or self-pity in him, nor did he show any pride in his heroic past. Instead,

* Petrograd: Kniga, 1916.

he would relate a humorous episode or a warmly remembered story about a friend, or reflect on what he had learned in prison from contacts with all kinds of people and situations.

MY FAMILY

We lived in Polotsk, one of the oldest cities in Russia, located at the confluence of the Polota and West Dvina. The chronicler Nestor mentioned the principality of Polotsk as early as 862. In the following centuries, its capital, Polotsk, had a population of 100,000 and was an important trade center. In 1320, the principality fell to Lithuania, was subjected five times to a siege by Russia in the sixteenth century, and in 1563 was taken by Ivan the Terrible. The Catholic monks were killed, the Protestant churches destroyed, and the Jews forcibly converted to Christianity —or killed if they resisted conversion—by the Orthodox Russians with the help of Moslem Tatar soldiers in the troops of the Tsar. Soon thereafter the principality was taken by Poland, and at the end of the eighteenth century, it was reconquered by Russia. In 1812, when Napoleon invaded Russia, there was a fierce battle of Polotsk. Not much was left of the old architecture. Many wooden buildings were burned down, sharing the fate of other architecturally fine structures in Russia. There remained some old buildings, and one of these served as the compound for a military school.

At the dinner table we were fourteen: Father, Mother, seven boys, and five girls. The four older boys were my half brothers; my father's first wife had died at the birth of the last one. Mother had been very brave to marry a widower with four little boys.

Father was the hero of the family. Powerfully built, tall and strong as an athlete, with penetrating gray eyes and a fine voice, he looked very impressive. In the winter, when he went out in his fur-lined coat with a broad beaver collar, people called him the "Prince." There really was something princely about him, his simple dignity. He had had no formal schooling. Twice he had run away from home to go to a high school, but each time he had been caught and returned home. He had learned whatever he could, was well read, and had worked out his own attitude toward life and people. He combined common sense and an instinct for fairness with a sparkling personality. He never had to raise his voice—we felt his justice in all situations. He told us: "We are a kind of republic; every one of us has rights and obligations, and so there is peace. But we cannot live in anarchy!" He advised us: "Nobody forces you to give a present, but when you do want to give one, select, as you would do for yourself, something that you would want to have or to receive from a friend; don't act as if you were trying to get rid of some obligation." He showed great respect for Mother in all situations, and imposed a pattern of good manners and courtesy in our family life.

Father was a building contractor. Besides a large block of houses he had erected on his own account, he built churches, army barracks, railway sections. When he entered a bid for a project, he himself had drawn up the blueprints, and more often than not, he won the contract. The workers knew that he could outdo any one of them and understood every detail of the work, and they were generally on good terms with him. But once when a dissatisfied worker said a disrespectful word to my mother, Father grabbed the man's collar and threw him out the door.

Mother was strong and healthy, as were all the rest of us. She had lovely eyes and was very attractive, but with the years she began to gain weight.

Our parents' chief goal was to give us a good education. All my mother's children went to college, except one sister, Anne, who did not go beyond high school. Two brothers became lawyers; three sisters and one brother became doctors in different fields of medicine, and I studied economics and history. Father offered to send us abroad, as was not unusual in Russia, but all of us chose to study in Russia.

Father owned a block of houses built around a large court, and the one-story house in which we lived was inside at the end of the block. There were stables for horses, with a loft for hay and straw, a laundry house, a bathhouse for the tenants in two bungalows, and an icehouse.

Life at home was simple but cheerful and full of activities. Almost everything was prepared at home—barrels of pickles and sauerkraut, large jars of various preserves, gallons of cider and vinegar. Bread and cakes were baked, and wheat and rye flour were bought in 220-pound sacks. Chickens were raised in the back yard, and we had fresh eggs. Clothes were repaired and altered, and much of our clothing was made by Mother and Fruza, who stayed with us for eighteen years and was the only household help I ever knew.

Now it seems to me incredible that Mother and Fruza could manage such a large household in which so many things were done at home and without the gadgets and appliances deemed essential today—not even an electric light. Help from the children was unwanted in the kitchen, the rule being, "Do your homework, or read a book, practice on the piano, but leave us alone!"

Indeed, a bunch of youngsters in the kitchen would have been more nuisance than help, but what about all the dishes to wash, all the clothes to wash and iron? Looking back, I marvel at how smoothly and efficiently everything was run and how neat the house always looked. I cannot remember that Mother or Fruza even complained of the burden of housekeeping, though Mother occasionally said, "The annoying thing is that there is little change in housework: the same dishes have to be washed again and again, the same table set again and again."

Fruza came to work for us when she was fourteen and stayed until she married. She helped raise most of us from the day we were born, was our confidante and knew our little secrets. I cannot think of my childhood without remembering her cheerful face, her loyalty and pride in us, and all she did for us. Her wedding was a big day for the whole family, and after she left with her husband, a tall, good-natured sergeant, we felt a strange emptiness in the house.

Mother's life was made easier because we were exceptionally healthy. Except for measles and one case of scarlet fever, there was never any sickness in our home. I cannot remember any visits by or to a doctor.

Of all the children, Mother was most attached to Mark, her firstborn —not that she showed it in many ways, but we felt it, at least I did. She was proud of him, and with reason—he was brilliant, good-looking, extremely popular. Faina, my eldest sister, was next in her heart because she was not so strong as the rest of us. Very attractive, she liked music, dancing, had a small but pleasant voice, liked to dress and go places.

I was closest to Mark. He confided his innermost feelings to me and sought my advice on all important decisions. Of all the women he knew (and there were many), I was "the only one who had masculine strength of character while remaining fully feminine." He wrote this on the back of a photograph of himself that I still possess.

Of the younger children, both brothers were handsome, and the next two sisters were attractive, each in her own way. Finally, my youngest sister was a lovely girl.

I have not seen any of our relatives for nearly half a century, but I know that many of them have passed away.

A FORCED CONFESSION

As a young girl, I may have lied as small children innocently do, when the real world is sometimes hard to distinguish from dreams and fantasies. A child may easily confuse what has actually happened with what might have happened, and what he wanted to do with what he might have done. Such "lies" are forgotten as soon as they are uttered.

But I have never forgotten or forgiven the first lie extorted from me by a schoolteacher. I was eight years old. By the time I was five, I read fluently, having learned this skill while under the table listening to lessons given to my older sister and brother. After the tutor left, I would practice with them. Arithmetic fascinated me. So when I went to school I was often bored when other pupils struggled to read or add and subtract.

One day, during the arithmetic lesson, I listened to the monotonous counting of two plus three makes five, six plus four makes ten, and so on. To occupy myself, I began to pencil the answers along the long columns of exercises in the schoolbook. Suddenly the teacher looked at my book and said angrily, "Ah, this is why you always know the answers. You write them up at home. Who helps you?"

I blushed and said, "Nobody helps me. I wrote the answers just now in class."

"You little liar! It is not enough that you have cheated, you lie when you are caught!"

I insisted, "I am not lying. I wrote the answers here."

The teacher almost lost control of herself. "I shall teach you to stop lying. Stay here after the end of the lessons, and I shall have a talk with you."

The rest of the day I was miserable. It seemed to me that I was the most despised pupil in the room. I could not speak to anybody and kept trying desperately to think how I could convince the teacher that I had told her the truth. When all the pupils had gone, she came and demanded: "Will you tell the truth now?"

But my truth was a lie to her. She said angrily: "I have never seen such a stubborn liar," and left the room. After an hour that seemed an eternity to me, she returned and again tried to wring a confession from me. I did not yield. Then she dismissed me, threatening that if I did not repent by the next day, she would call my mother to the school and tell her of my unthinkable behavior.

At home, I could find no peace. Should I tell my mother? But she would be hurt, I thought, and would she believe me or the teacher? My elder sister sensed something and suggested: "Let us tell each other everything." How could I? "If you want to, we can start tomorrow," I said.

I was alone with myself. After a sleepless night in which I wanted to run away, then imagined myself dead and relished the picture of the teacher crying over my body, I still could not bring myself to tell Mother of my predicament. In school, when the teacher pressed me again and again, I finally squeezed out an "admission": "I did write at home." To her, this was a satisfying conclusion of a trivial story, and a few days later she undoubtedly forgot it. To me, she was no longer the same person.

That year she was my only teacher. All year I answered her questions, read and counted, never looking her straight in the face. As I was at the head of the class, she often complimented me, but that did not change my attitude toward her. When I moved on to the next grade, I discovered that she had become the class's counselor. In Russian high schools, a counselor was attached to each class to take care of the administrative details and assist the teachers in checking attendance, dealing with the parents, collecting and sometimes correcting compositions, consulting with pupils, and so on. More often than not, such a counselor continued with the same class from year to year. It happened that this teacher stayed with mine through all seven grades. I was the best pupil in the class and graduated with a gold medal. Naturally, she praised me to my parents and before other pupils and, in general, was very friendly. But I remained unsmiling and cold when I had to talk to her. On a holiday, when she invited the entire class to her house, I always refused to go on one pretext or another.

Then I left for the Women's College in St. Petersburg University. On my return home for the summer vacation, I met her in the street. She was all smiles and wanted me to visit her and tell of my experiences.

I looked at her and relived that day in class, heard her angry voice accusing me of a lie, saw her finger pointed at me, the "stubborn little liar," and said hurriedly: "Sorry. I must go. Mother is waiting."

ASPIRATIONS OF A BOOKWORM

If Wolik was born with paper and pencil in his hands, I must have been born with a book. Time and again, my parents and relatives told me that they always saw me bent over a book in some corner. My father's study had long shelves filled with the Russian classics, many thick bound volumes of an illustrated magazine, *Niva (Meadow)*, and various other books. The high-school library was also substantial, as was the library of the town in which we lived. I read everything that I could lay my hands on, indiscriminately. Much I did not understand, yet reading touched some sensitive cord and inspired my imagination.

At ten, I passionately wanted to do something big—to become an outstanding orator exhorting others to do great things, or a great writer, or an ideal teacher adored by children, a singer charming the audience. Sometimes I saw myself on the stage, captivating the audience, or living among the poor and bringing light into their lives. Somehow the books took me away from myself; I never thought about things little girls usually think about—my appearance, my dresses, and so on. My dreams and desires moved on another plane.

From the age of twelve or thirteen, my interests began to concentrate on teaching. I started reading periodicals on education, going back to what had been published years earlier in that field. My future profession appeared to me in a glowing light: I wanted to create a new type of school, a "school of life" where children would grow in contact with nature and real life, in a school located in the country, in the open air where they would learn to do things for themselves. Today, such a school would be called "progressive," but as early as the beginning of this century, Russian educational literature was permeated with such ideas.

Other emotions and inspirations sometimes swept me off my feet. I borrowed banned books from my classmates, books on the lives of outstanding Russian revolutionaries, their heroism and readiness to sacrifice their lives for the freedom of Russia. Such books were hard to get and in great demand, so that they were lent for only a night or two. I remember reading voraciously through *Underground Russia* by Stepnyak-Kravchinsky, a book of some 300 pages or more, in bed one night, by the light of a shielded candle so that nobody in the house would notice it. In comparison with his heroes, I felt very insignificant, and I burned to do something, if not heroic, at least helpful. At the very least, I could live among the poor people, work as they did, teach them to read. Yes, I would go straight to "the people."

Because my decision to run away from home was not impulsive or the consequence of a family quarrel or unhappiness, but to help in a great cause, time was needed for serious preparation. I told my friend, Ada Den, of my decision.

Ada was three years older than I, a tall, good-natured, rather heavily built girl with a round face, blue eyes, and a low-pitched voice. She was an orphan and knew little happiness except from our friendship. We were in the same class; she did not learn easily, and I often helped her with homework. My decision excited her, and soon she was under my spell. We would leave together and go—where? Somewhere, to work in a factory and live with the workers. Neither of us had any idea where that factory was, how to reach it, or whether a factory would hire us. But these were details; the important thing was to make the decision and prepare ourselves.

Ada lived not far from my home in a parson's house. She had a basement room, with windows reaching to the sidewalk. When I knocked lightly on the window, she would let me in, always cautioning me to make as little noise as possible. I would slide down the wall straight into her bed, and there we sat and whispered like two dangerous plotters.

I began to neglect my class work—it seemed senseless to exert myself when I soon would drop school altogether; fortunately, I was ahead in school and so maintained my marks. The Christmas vacation intervened, and Ada went to her sister's home in Riga. She wrote every day in our special code: We reversed the alphabet, using the last letter as the first, etc. In the beginning, it was quite a job to write in that code and to decode our letters, but after a few days I could write and read Ada's letters as effortlessly as ordinary mail.

Ada's absence seemed endless. I was lonely, yet could not divulge what was on my mind. Looking sadly at my mother and the rest of the family, I thought: "They know nothing. Will they miss me?"

The last two letters from Ada were confused as if she was too embarrassed to reveal something. She would tell me everything, she wrote; she hoped I would understand. Well, she did come and did tell me: At her sister's she had met a boy, and though she was not certain about his feelings, she liked him very much and would not have the heart to run away now . . .

I felt betrayed and at my age I could not understand what some strange boy had to do with our heroic plan. Yet he did kill our plan. Ada did not return after the summer vacation, and in the meantime I also changed my mind.

SCHOOL YEARS

There is so much and yet so little to tell about the formative years of my childhood. I matured gradually. So little of importance happened in the small real world in which I moved, so much went on inside me. Not that I was preoccupied with myself, but there was always some reason why I felt different from others. There was always something special on my mind.

First, it was religion that set me apart. Religion was seldom talked about in our family, it just was with us, like the air around us. We took it in as we breathed the air. I might have been eight or nine years old when, without my parents' knowing of it, I entered into a personal relationship with God. During the day, I did not think much about Him, but as soon as I was alone at night in my room and turned off the light, He came in. I could not see Him in the darkness, but I felt His presence. I talked to Him, gave an account of how I spent the day, repented if I had been inconsiderate or had told a lie or wanted more for myself than was right. With a burning desire to reach perfection, I promised to watch myself and try to satisfy Him. This was a deal for that night, and closing my eyes, I peacefully fell asleep.

Yet it was difficult to achieve the ideal, and I often asked God to give me another chance. This went on for a couple of years. What it amounted to was a kind of self-analysis, a check-up on myself. Nobody else knew of this; it was my secret. Whether any of my brothers or sisters had the same secret, I did not know. I never confided my feelings to other members of the family, and did not expect to be taken into their confidence, either. These nightly conversations ended as suddenly as they had begun. I do not recall when I stopped going over every detail of my day and reporting it to God. When I stopped, religion again became like the "air around me."

What remained was a habit of self-criticism, of remembering every wrong word I had said, every act of impatience. Sometimes thoughtless words or actions would come to me suddenly a year or so later, causing a sleepless night and a lot of discomfort.

However, when I was among other people, I forgot myself and became animated, gay, and ready for any prank. Several families with children lived in the apartments of the houses belonging to us, which formed a square around a large inner court. I played with the boys, climbed the roofs, slept in hay in the loft over the horse stalls. There was nothing the boys did that I could not match. Father pretended to be astonished, saying, "Look at this bookworm! She is a real tomboy!"

At another period, I insisted on being absolutely truthful—on saying what I meant or felt at home, in school, and to strangers. If the truth was offensive, I could keep silent but could not and would not be conventionally pleasant. This was not easy. I recall, for example, that a bunch of us were walking along a street, laughing loudly and cutting up. Suddenly, out of nowhere, appeared the head of the school. Everyone else stopped laughing and looked serious but not me. Not that I was disrespectful, but it was untruthful to pretend that we had been walking quietly before he appeared.

In another phase, I strove for absolute sincerity in my relations with schoolmates and teachers. A young woman, straight from graduation at

St. Petersburg Women's College, had come to teach us history. This was a time when a rebellious spirit was sweeping over Russia, stirring even us, teenagers, and she brought with her a breath of fresh air. Soon the teacher picked out a few of the brighter girls, asked us to her home, and organized a kind of seminar to study the history of civilization. We met once a week, realizing without her telling us that we must not talk about this "clandestine" activity, and became her friends. I thought the world of her, and she showed a fondness for me. As a token of my feelings for her, I gave her my picture. As time went on, I thought that more and more she was sinking into the school routine, and I was disappointed. I went to her, told her of my disillusionment, and asked her to give back my picture. She was offended and blushed, but returned the picture without a word. Guests who came to see my parents fell under my intent scrutiny. On looking at the little girl who said nothing but watched them closely, they must have felt occasionally that I read their thoughts, because I sensed their embarrassment when they turned their eyes away from me.

I relate these things not because they are important in themselves but because they seem to illustrate some subconscious emotions that agitated me. I felt that others would not understand them or would ridicule them if they knew about them.

I approached school work in my own way. Never satisfied with the dosage of science provided in class, I turned to books from which I could learn more. We were taught elementary physics, but I used the textbooks of my older brother Mark. In school, we had a dull, mediocre textbook on the history of Russia, but I read the works of the best historians —Platonov and Klyuchevsky; for the course on psychology in the last grade, I read the books suggested for university students; in the field of literature, I was thoroughly familiar with the Russian classics and with most important foreign works—not only classics but even the writings of such lesser authors as James Fenimore Cooper, Bret Harte, Jack London, and Alphonse Daudet.

This gave me an advantage over my classmates, which was a source of disappointment at examination time. I never knew the excitement, the sense of urgency in cramming for tests, nor did I know the elation others experienced at having passed. Calm and almost indifferent before and after an examination, I again felt apart from my classmates.

Certain fads that swept the school from lower to higher grades left me cool. For example, there was a sudden enthusiasm for American detective stories—with Nat Pinkerton, Nick Carter, and others. They were printed as serials, were sold for a few kopeks, and read everywhere. My brothers, though of different ages, swallowed each edition as soon as they got hold of it. Schoolgirls, too, were carried away by this passion. During classes, these booklets were read under the eyes of the teachers, smuggled from one row to another. The director of the military academy in our town ordered a search for the booklets in all the academy's classrooms and dormitories, then confiscated them and let them be stored in the attic. His daughter was my classmate, and so my school was abundantly provided with the forbidden stuff.

POGROM

In 1905, as a twelve-year-old girl, I did not know that the Tsarist police had whipped up the dregs of our town against its Jewish population—the "traitors" who had sold Russia to Japan. How otherwise, the inciting flyers demanded, could the gallant Russian Army and Navy have been defeated by those despicable, monkeylike Japanese? Death to the traitors!

That ominous day, a great roar filled the air of our courtyard, and I climbed to the roof of the stables to look. From there, I saw the large square in front of the military academy overflowing with a crowd, who were wildly waving arms and trampling feet. There was something almost bestial in that crowd, and I ran down to tell my parents. They needed no telling, they *knew*. My father and my half brothers quickly locked the heavy iron gate to our block. It reached from the ground to the second floor of the three-story house on the left side of our block. All the Jewish tenants came out into the yard and looked to Father for protection. He was calm and determined to fight. The apartment of the first floor in the house on the left was occupied by three bachelors—gentile engineers who always looked to us as if they had stepped out of the pages of Nikolai Garin's well-known book *The Engineers*. They were always friendly, always smiling or laughing, intelligent, wonderful with children, often riding us on their trotters which were constant prize winners in races. They begged Father to let us stay with them, but he refused: "We shall face danger together. Besides, the court is full of other children. God will strike me if I save my children and let others perish. I cannot do that." In any case, we would not have left him and Mother, even though we were very fond of the engineers.

There were frequent knocks at the gate by desperate men, women, children, imploring to be let in. Father opened the gate again and again. Then the roar came closer and closer . . . It seemed as if the earth was trembling under the feet of an endless crowd . . . People could not stop: those behind were pushing and pressing. In their rush, some tried to break down the gate. It withstood the test, and the mob was too excited and impatient to delay . . . Lots of booty was in sight, so what was the sense in expending oneself on a single obstacle? Onward! The waves rolled on, while the people inside the courtyard prayed and waited in silent anguish. Night descended, but there was no peace in town. Fires broke out at many places, and from the roof we could see shadows moving in the darkness; shots and screams rent the air.

It seemed strange to me, as to other children in the courtyard, that people we had never seen would want to kill us. But nobody had the time or desire to explain this to us. We whispered to each other, not daring to break the silence of the grownups. We got cold sandwiches to eat; the adults did not care about food. Everything was terribly unusual, ominous. Would a bright, gay, "normal" tomorrow ever come?

Some of the people in the courtyard talked with Father, and it was decided to wire Count Witte, then Minister of the Interior, to ask him to order the police to stop the pogrom. But how to get to the telegraph office, right in the center of the town where the rioting was at its peak? One of my half brothers donned a mujik's sheepskin coat and high boots, shoved an ax through his belt, and went forth. He kissed us all before leaving, but then laughed and said, "Don't worry! I shall be back!" It did not occur to him or to anyone in the courtyard that the clerks in the telegraph office might betray him or refuse to send the telegram. Fear was not as overpowering in Russia as it is today, and decency was expected and possible.

Time moved like a tortoise—now he must be at the square, now at Main Street, only a few blocks more. . . . He must be through by now, on his way back. Why does it take him so long? We counted and recounted the minutes and clung to the gate in the darkness—to let him in without delay. Just when we had began to despair, we heard quiet steps and his soft voice: "It's me!"

Scores of people were killed that day, many more beaten and tortured, hundreds of houses were destroyed. At dawn, when the lust and madness of the crowd were nearly exhausted, the town lay ravaged in dead silence. It was one of many towns that lived through a pogrom that day, while the Tsar and his Government were shaken by the assault of the workers and the progressives. The Tsar knew no way to quell the people's revolt except to direct the mob against some scapegoat—the Jews, the universities, the intellectuals.

Two days later, the Tsar had to capitulate with the Manifesto of October 17. Solemn funerals were arranged for the victims of the pogrom. The entire town participated, moving slowly behind the coffins, draped with black. Because two students and several Socialists had been killed along with the Jews, revolutionary songs were sung and a few red flags were carried.

Normal conditions were gradually restored in the city, but tension persisted in human relations. The gentiles felt guilty, and many of them took every opportunity to disassociate themselves from the Government-inspired pogrom. In the Jewish quarters there were, understandably, insecurity and distrust.

The "freedom" announced by the Tsar's Manifesto lasted only a few days. Mark, who attended a high school in the neighboring city of Witebsk, had come home with a friend of his. We were awakened at night by the police. They came with a search warrant, looked into Mark's room only, picked out some papers written in longhand by his friend, Sasha, and arrested Sasha. We were terribly disturbed, and next morning sent Fruza to talk to the police, and find out where they had put Sasha. She brought back word that he was being kept in the city's fire tower, and a policeman she knew had promised to pass on food packages to him. We spent much time in front of the tower, shouting to Sasha who, after a week of "investigation," was released and given back his papers. The title of one was "More Schools for the People," and of the other, even more radical, "Must Children Obey Their Parents?"

This was not an isolated example of police stupidity. A new mathematics teacher came to our school, a young extrovert with an easy smile who was accessible to our queries and occasionally to a discussion. He was at once popular with us, but he did not enjoy the confidence of the authorities. He taught for one year and was replaced the next fall by another teacher. Then we got word that he would pass through the town on his way to a new post. Wanting to say goodbye to him during the twenty-minute train stopover, about a hundred girls went to the station, only to find it ringed by police. A few girls got through and brought us his greetings. I was surprised and proud that out of all the students he singled me out to send a personal message, and I carried this excitement with me for several days.

COLLEGE YEARS

Though we were not wealthy, it was taken for granted that all of us —boys and girls alike—must have a college education, not too common a practice in the early 1900's. Mark studied at St. Petersburg University, my elder sister at Kharkov. I was next in line. Two years before graduation from high school, I decided to be financially independent. I am vague now as to why. Father was not very pleased, suspecting my desire to loosen my ties with the family. I was his favorite, and occasionally, caressing my black hair, he would say jokingly, "Black is never out of fashion."

To earn money, I started tutoring backward pupils in the evenings during the school months, and nearly every hour on the hour during summer vacation. The pay, it now seems to me, was rather high—two rubles (one dollar) an hour for a fifteen- or sixteen-year-old teacher. College tuition was not very expensive, and I managed modestly but without any deprivation to be on my own through my college years in St. Petersburg.

Studying and reading were the main occupations in college, but there were many extracurricular activities, too. One winter I volunteered to teach elementary grammar and arithmetic three evenings a week to workers. Another of my volunteer jobs was to prepare brief digests of books selected for a recommended popular reading set. We did this for a well-known public library headed by an outstanding woman.

I used my free hours to attend courses at the Institute for Teachers and various public lectures on education. I became interested in the work of Dr. Vladimirsky, who worked with so-called "difficult" children. I had opportunities to visit some outstanding schools, and I recall that some of those visits were exciting experiences, particularly for a budding educator. In one school, for example, I sat in on the lesson on zoology and was fascinated to see that, in order to learn the structure of an animal's eye, each pupil was provided with a bull's eye and was required to separate one layer after another with a lancet. Some pupils exhibited almost the skill of a surgeon in performing this operation, and all were completely absorbed. I could not help remembering how dull and uninspiring the zoology lessons in my high school had been.

Mark, my older brother, attended St. Petersburg University while I was in the Women's College there. We lived apart, but saw each other rather frequently. He tried to introduce me into his world, and one night took me to a boxing match. I disliked it greatly, and I never went to see another. Once he brought with him the student he was tutoring in law, a son of a Persian prince, with glowing black eyes and a broad grin that revealed two impeccable rows of glittering white teeth. He was unpretentious, thought the world of Mark and was clearly happy about that contact. Then, never having lived abroad, neither Mark nor I was conscious of how a foreigner felt in a strange environment; now I would have sensed his uneasiness immediately and could have made him feel more at home. Though there was something direct and attractive about the young man, many of his reactions were primitive. His ignorance about Russia and the world at large, though amusing at times, was irksome in the long run, and I lost interest in seeing him. He passed his exams and returned to Persia.

Mark also wanted me to meet his girl friends, and I was interested by the range of his affections. I remember in particular Genya, a proud, typically Russian beauty with blue eyes that looked straight into one's own and drew one to her; Olga, who must have attracted him by her special intelligence and intuitive understanding rather than her appearance (to my surprise, her hold over him was the strongest and longest); and Natasha, a petite, dazzling girl with a lively temperament, ready for any adventure that Mark suggested. There were others, too. My impression was that there was more fun and youthful merriment than real attachment, but I was too ignorant in that area to be perceptive.

The theater, the great love of the Russian people, was important in college life. We thought nothing of denying ourselves meals for several days in order to hear Chaliapin as Mephisto or Boris Godunov.

The entire student colony in St. Petersburg was stirred by the annual announcement, soon after New Year, of the forthcoming arrival of the Moscow Art Theater. Students carefully worked out plans on which plays to attend and on which dates; groups formed to alternate in the queues that extended for blocks three or four days before the ticket office opened. Two tickets per play per person was the rule, and it permitted all kinds of arrangements.

Guest performances of the Art Theater were usually scheduled for April or May, when it was still chilly in the capital, particularly at night. The first person to arrive at the ticket office started a waiting list, which became longer and longer as more people joined the line and added their names to the list. At first, a roll call every three hours was considered sufficient, then every two hours; on the last day and night, absence during a roll call at an unannounced time meant losing one's place in the line. There was no favoritism and no mercy: the matter was too important! To attend or not to attend the performances was almost as important as to be or not to be!

Of course, expensive seats were easily available, but by the end of the semester who had money enough for all the performances at front-row prices? And who wanted to be separated from his friends? Peddlers with hot buns and tea swarmed along the line; sandwiches were sold, and nuts and apples. The crowd was good natured, and there was much banter and laughter. But there was also much discussion. All the plays and all the actors were well known, preferences were solidly established, and there were heated debates about details of scenery or performance that were of no real consequence. The turmoil continued even after we had the tickets; dates were exchanged, combinations arranged for sitting together or meeting before, and so on.

Like everybody else, I was liberal-minded, though I was not in contact with any political party or group. I had my room walls decorated with portraits of Tolstoy, Chekhov, Block, Gorki, and some revolutionary leaders. I am sure that many students felt, as I did, a close relationship with various writers, a kind of personal involvement with their lives. When Tolstoy left his home and fell ill en route, all of us waited impatiently for bulletins on his condition from the house of the station master of Astapovo, where he had been taken. Nobody talked about anything else; the life of Tolstoy hung by a thin thread, and we were all concerned. I recall the evening when the bulletin came with the news of his death. Everybody rushed out into the street so as not to be alone, to share their feeling of sadness with others, known or unknown. All the theaters and even many stores closed their doors. A kind of numbness, bewilderment, was in the air—would life go on as before now that he was gone?

Next morning, the students from every institution marched to Isaakovsky Square to honor Tolstoy's memory. Because of his philosophy of "no resistance to evil," it was decided not to give the demonstration a revolutionary character and not to carry red banners, though its tenor was unmistakenly anti-Government.

AT FATHER'S WORKS

Father was engaged in building soldiers' barracks for the army in 1911. His brickworks were then in Nizhneudinsk, a small town on the Trans-Siberian railroad. He asked me to spend my summer vacation there, helping him with bookkeeping and other work. With him, he had 400 Chinese workers and two interpreters. The brickworks were several miles from the town and so included a commissary stocking essential foodstuffs and other necessities for the workers.

At first, all the workers seemed to me to have one face. I could not point out one to whom I had talked just a few minutes before, nor even distinguish who was young and who was old. Gradually I began to recognize individual faces and pick up a few Chinese words, which pleased the workers very much. When they saw me getting into the coach to go to town, they often asked me to buy something for them—a shirt, socks, a cup and saucer, and the like. Little by little, we got used to each other, and I gained their confidence. On hot days, they occasionally preferred to work in the evening by the light of lamps and lanterns on high poles. But on other evenings they would perform a Chinese play or wrestle or talk to me about their families. I liked such evenings very much, and felt myself one of a friendly crowd.

Finally, vacation was over, and I had to return to my college in St. Petersburg. I told the workers that I would be leaving in two days. Next morning, a delegation consisting of two men—the oldest and the youngest—came to beg me to take all 400 of them with me to my new job; they would rather work for me than for my father. I explained over and over again that I was not going to some works but to a school and would be living alone. A few hours later, the same men returned with another suggestion from the entire group: If I did not want to take all of them with me, they wanted me to accept those two; the older man would take care of me, and the younger would cook for me, and the two of them would maintain contact with the entire group. All of this seemed very foolish to my father, and he ordered the coach to take me to the train. But the workers unharnessed the horses and declared that they would take me to the station in a palanquin.

While I tried to persuade them that I could not possibly take the two men with me to St. Petersburg and that a parade to the railroad station of a palanquin escorted by 400 Chinese workers was out of the question, it became too late for the train anyhow. That evening when I went to my "room"—actually a part of the office partitioned off by a thin screen—I found a young pine tree erected in one corner and loads of fruit on the table. Our commissary carried no fruit; obviously some worker had been sent to town to buy this. The long negotiations and the sincere expression of friendliness toward me were fantastic and very touching indeed.

THE SCHOOL EXCURSIONS

School excursions were a common feature in Russia. They never started at the tender age at which Japanese kindergarten children, chaperoned by teachers, travel across the country to see Tokyo, Kyoto, Nara, and other famous cities, but Russian school authorities often organized highschool excursions to the Crimea or the Caucasus or boat trips along the Volga River.

Most popular were college excursions of different types. Some were like those in Europe or the United States, but there was one special type that I took twice. During my second year in college, my family moved from Polotsk to Irkutsk, Siberia, where Father had secured several substantial building contracts. I could go home only once a year, for the summer vacation; the trip in a coach took about eight days each way.

When forty students (boys and girls from the university and other institutions of higher learning) signed up for the home trip to Siberia, regardless of the particular city where they wanted to get off, a special coach was assigned to them and the key to it was entrusted to the leader they chose at a meeting before departure. Nobody except the railroad personnel could enter that coach. The fare for the students was one-fourth of the regular cost. In my case, the trip from St. Petersburg to Irkutsk cost 8 rubles ($4) instead of the regular 32. The cheap fare entailed an obligation: on returning to college, each participant had to present a paper in a seminar in the field of his or her studies on some feature of the region he had stayed in during the summer. I reported one year on the system of land ownership in Siberia; another year, on the history of settlements in that region.

The trip was great fun, though we traveled third-class with hard lower and upper bunks. Forty youngsters, few of whom knew one another, had eight days to spend together. As soon as the train left the capital, a mail box for internal correspondence was fastened at each end of the coach. Introductions were not needed; we were one crowd. Amidst laughter, singing, music (there was always somebody with a guitar, or a mandolin, or a balalaika), visits from one section to another, friendships and romances began, sometimes as short-lived as a butterfly, sometimes more lasting.

In addition to luggage, each of us carried our bedding and a teapot and other paraphernalia for tea. These were absolute essentials. Boiling water was available at every stop, free of charge; at lunch and supper time the train stopped for an hour or longer at a station with a restaurant. Peasant women swarmed around such stations, offering hard-boiled eggs, fried chickens, homemade cheese, bread, sweet buns, fruit, and so on. In the evenings, we made visits about the railroad coach, stopping here for a cup of tea, there for a treat of candy or ice cream. On the way from university to home town, economy was the rule; but from home to university, veritable feasts were held throughout the coach! Baskets of food prepared by mothers vied with one another in delighting young palates.

Though there were jokes and compliments, my recollection is that, on the whole, the atmosphere was almost Victorian. The boys carried the luggage, ran to fill the teapots or drop a letter into the regular mail box. Only one exception to this occurred in my own experience. Once when I was standing at the window looking at the scenery, a student pressed himself against my shoulder. Surprised, I looked at him disapprovingly, and he apologized.

Of course, there was the other side of the story—seeing unkempt, unwashed faces in the morning, having to appear in such a state, the waiting line before the washrooms, half undressing in the darkness on the hard bunk. All this was not too exalting. I may have shown that I felt some discomfort because I find in my diary that some student nailed down this feeling by saying to me: "You must travel first class, these surroundings are not meant for you!" I felt this remark as a blow but only said, "You don't want to hurt me, do you? I am enjoying this trip very much."

AMONG THE TATARS

More often than not, the college students were short of money, and it was not unusual for them to take tutoring jobs in summer vacations, or even during the school year, for the room, board, and pay offered by families living somewhere in the country. This was possible because the attendance system practiced in the United States was not used in Russian universities and colleges. Notices of tutoring positions were placed on a special board. During my third year in college, I saw an invitation from a Tatar family in Bakhchisaray, Crimea, to tutor two boys in French and German. The name of the city, celebrated in the famous poem of Pushkin, "The Bakhchisaraisky Fountain," echoed in my mind like an enchanting fairy tale, and I was excited at the prospect of life in a Tatar family. I wrote immediately and got a formal invitation in the return mail.

The Gasprinsky family consisted of the father, a widower with a sharply drawn face, an eagle's nose, and an appearance of energy and strength; the older daughter, with her Turkish husband and two small children; the younger daughter, Nina, very attractive but with the mind of a bird; and two sons, well-built teen-agers with little interest in and little promise for studies.

The only educated and interesting person in the family was Mr. Gasprinsky himself, editor of a Russian-language newspaper that supported assimilation of the Tatars with the Russians and their language and culture. At home, Russian was spoken along with Tatar. Despite the progressive attitude shown by Mr. Gasprinsky in many situations, family life was the same as it had been generations earlier. The women rarely left the house, which was surrounded by a tall brick wall and inaccessible to curious passers-by; when they did go, they wore a veil covering them from head to foot, with two narrow slits for their eyes. Naturally, I wanted this experience, and so I occasionally went out in a veil like theirs.

Bakhchisaray (which means "palace garden") was once the residence of the Tatar khans of Crimea. In 1519, they built the Khan-Saray, a beautiful palace, which was burned down in the first half of the eighteenth century and later restored, though not very successfully. This was a city of springs and fountains and of mosques—there were some 32 springs, nearly 120 fountains, and 35 mosques. The city was one wonderful garden, with beautiful cypress trees, vineyards on the slopes, and flowers, flowers everywhere.

There was much to see. Close to Bakhchisaray, on the mountain cliffs, was spread the old city of the Karaim Jews, Chufut-Kaleh, carved into the rocks and almost inaccessible. Once fully populated, it now had only a few families. In the synagogue of Chufut-Kaleh had been found one of the oldest scrolls, which was bought by the National Public Library of Russia. An old monastery hung on a forbidding cliff, between the Tatar and Jewish cities, and there were various Tatar ruins in the vicinity.

The most exciting event in Nina's life occurred when her father took her to a dentist in Simferopol, a neighboring, much larger city. He secured a separate room in the first-class coach and never left her alone except to go to the rest room. At such a moment, the mayor of Bakhchisaray, who happened to be traveling in the same coach and was not on speaking terms with Nina's father, seized the opportunity to insult his enemy. He rushed into the compartment, kissed Nina on both cheeks, and disappeared before her father returned. Had the latter known what happened in his absence, he would been beside himself and I don't know what he would have done to avenge his humiliator.

Nina, however, was too thrilled to care or even to understand the insult to her father's pride. Her greatest problem was with whom to share her enormous secret. It was impossible to tell her father, her sister, even the old nurse! And yet, how to keep such a wondrous thing to herself? The solution was at hand—as soon as they returned, Nina dashed into my room and breathlessly told me her little story. What amused me was that here was a girl not much younger than I, kept inside the tall walls of the house, always chaperoned, protected from the stranger's eyes like the greatest family treasure, and the result? She could be swayed by the first rascal!

The husband of the older daughter thought that I could not always be so reserved and quiet as I was in their family. Several times he said to me, "I would like to see you when you are drunk." As a matter of fact, I was not used to wine and most probably would have fallen asleep after the first glass. Apparently, he expected that I would become very animated, perhaps even lose control of myself. Of course, I never obliged the curiosity of that sensual Turk.

One of the Gasprinsky's maids married, and I watched the event with great interest. The maid had never seen her future husband and when, after a feast that lasted well into the night, she went to his home on a couch carrying her dowry and all the presents bestowed on her, she was still veiled. I was told that occasionally one daughter would be shown to the marriage broker and another, older or less appealing, sent with the dowry. The ceremony was monotonous and substantially the same at all income levels, except for the difference in the degree of luxury in food, clothing, music, and so on.

Soon after my arrival, Mr. Gasprinsky left for Turkey. After he returned some three months later, two old Tatar women paid me a visit. As custom required, I ordered coffee, and we chatted about this and that. Then one of them began to praise Mr. Gasprinsky—so clever, so respected, so good and kind to everybody. I agreed wholeheartedly. Would I be interested in marrying him? He would provide me with every comfort. I could hardly believe my ears; he could have been my grandfather. But Oriental custom did not permit me to show surprise or brush aside the suggestion or even answer lightly. The few months spent in the Tatar family had prepared me for correct behavior. I thanked them politely, said I was very flattered but that such an offer had to be considered seriously and I wanted to consult my parents. I also tried to find out whether the suggestion was of their own manufacture or was inspired by Mr. Gasprinsky himself, but the ladies skillfully evaded a straight answer.

A month later I got a wire from Irkutsk that my father had died. Next morning, I left Bakhchisaray to join Mother and the rest of the family. Mother needed me, and I skipped a year in college to remain with her, and then returned to St. Petersburg for the final year and graduation.

This was my first winter in Siberia. It was bitter cold, and the sharp, crisp air took my breath. Yet the sun was strong, the sky cloudless and blue, and young people skated in shirt sleeves on the rink in the open air. We lived in a cottage next to an icehouse. Mother bought half a carcass of an ox, and the butcher cut it into small pieces. The meat was kept in the icehouse and seemed to last forever.

I went to the farmers' market with Mother and heard her ask a woman if she had milk to sell. She did and, in turn, she asked my mother, "Whole or half? A big piece or a small?" I did not understand what she was talking about, but Mother showed no surprise and answered: "Half of a large." The farmer's wife turned to her husband and asked him to bring the sack with milk and the ax. Out of the sack she pulled a big round chunk of frozen milk and split it in half with the ax. I learned that on the eve of the market day, the farmers poured milk into bowls of two standard sizes, put a piece of wood into the bowl and let the milk freeze outside the house. In the morning, they pulled out the frozen milk with the aid of the wedge and filled the sacks with these chunks.

Without Father, we had to adjust ourselves to a more modest way of living, but my older brother and sister and I worked and two of our half brothers pitched in. The younger children continued to go to high school. On the whole, we managed rather well.

THE BEGINNING OF WORLD WAR I

After I graduated from college in the spring of 1914, I stayed with friends in Terioki, Finland, and tutored their daughter Sonya, an intelligent but capricious girl who was fond of me and therefore not too difficult to deal with. I spent my leisure hours with a book at the beach, watching the sea and its changing moods and colors.

Troublesome news began to break into the peaceful atmosphere of our life—the assassination of the Austrian prince, mobilization in Germany, in Russia, negotiations among the great powers. Rumors, now hopeful, now bad, filled the air. And then war!

Many Russian families who spent the summer in Finland started leaving for St. Petersburg. The change in attitude of the native population, the Finns, was unmistakable. They became silent and withdrew into themselves, while wild patriotism broke out among the Russians. The Balabanoff family, with whom I was staying, decided to return to the capital. There it looked as if the nation was united and accepted the war unreservedly. A son of my friends, a young officer, was called to arms, and we went to the station to say goodbye to him. Many women were presenting red roses as a last gift to the officers among their relatives and friends. Alas! A few days later the first troops to reach the front were mowed down by German artillery.

I got word that I had been appointed a schoolteacher at the elementary school in Stavropol, North Caucasus, and was asked to be there two days before the school opening on August 15. I made all the necessary preparations, but when I went to the station to buy a ticket, I could not get one; all the trains were requisitioned for the movement of troops. Civilians had to get a special permission to travel for an emergency purpose. Of course, I could not obtain such a paper. Yet I knew that I could not possibly miss the opening of school and fall down on my first real job. I explained my situation over and over again and made a nuisance of myself. Finally, the station master, irritated and wanting to get rid of me, said angrily, "All right, miss. Here is your ticket for the soldiers' train. It leaves in two hours." Excited and happy, I went to the train. It seemed terribly long and packed to capacity, but as I began to lose hope of getting on, an arm stretched out of the window and picked up my suitcases, and I heard a soldier say, "Take the seat on this bunk before it is occupied." Inside, I looked around me—all soldiers, no other civilians.

The train started moving. I pressed myself into the corner and pretended to be asleep. As night approached, a soldier took down my bag with the blanket and pillow and said, "Take the lower bunk. We'll manage!" Some of the men sat up all night, and two of them took turns on the upper bunk.

We traveled this way for nearly four days. I thought only of my job, and it never occurred to me that there was anything unusual or risky in a young girl's being alone with hundreds of soldiers on their way to the front. Perhaps my very innocence was my best protection. I do not recall hearing one ambiguous word from those simple souls, and nobody so much as touched my arm. They treated me with great friendliness, carried my luggage, brought me hot water for tea. We talked about their villages, their families, their fears—only too well founded, as they were soon to find out. Some were very depressed, others more cheerful, but all were wondering, "Why war? Who has attacked Russia?"

There was no answer to that "Why?" I was as little informed as they. The people knew nothing of what was happening. As we crossed Russia, from north to south, one plea, one word cut through the air, again and again: *"Ga-ze-ty! Ga-ze-ty!"* (A newspaper! A newspaper!) Wherever it was possible to get the newspapers at a train stop, the soldiers ran out and bought several copies for me. First I read the news to them, and then they rolled the newspapers into a tight bundle and threw it out of the window as we passed a village and heard the desperate cry *"Ga-ze-ty!"*

Finally I reached Stavropol and said goodbye to the soldiers, who went on to the Turkish front.

TEACHING IN STAVROPOL

Stavropol was built in the North Caucasus in the first half of the eighteenth century as a fort to defend what was then the southern frontier of Russia. It was an administrative city rather than a commercial or industrial one, and had some 50,000 inhabitants of various races; though Russians predominated, there were many Armenians, Tatars, Jews, Georgians, Kalmyks.

The school had two male teachers and one woman teacher besides me. All three of them, much older than I, had taught there for several years and felt themselves a part of the school and the city. Lacking any experience, I felt very insecure and threw myself into the work, determined to do well. Friendship with Esther, the older teacher, was most helpful; we rented rooms from the same family and spent many evenings discussing school work. I taught in two classes—the first grade, with seven-year-old children, and the fourth, the highest.

Almost all the children came from poor families, so we had a special closet for clothing and shoes donated by well-to-do families. We had to distribute them most tactfully and inconspicuously. Many of the children were very proud, and some refused to accept anything, even a light coat when it was raining, despite the suggestion that they might bring it back the next day.

The children, particularly those in the first grade, captured my heart very quickly. Some were adorable. Even now, nearly fifty years later, a few are as vivid before my eyes as they were then. A little boy from the slums, with dreamy eyes and the natural bearing of a prince; another, tiny and ever smiling, like an angel dropped from the sky; several girls, lovely and neatly dressed; a boy of eight, serious and mature beyond his age. For my birthday the following year, this boy sent a card to me in Irkutsk (I remained only one year in Stavropol) with a single phrase: "I wish you would live forever." I cannot think of anything more touching and more heartwarming than this card.

Being young, I often could not maintain the demeanor of a serious teacher and laughed along with the children. One day I tried unsuccessfully to explain the meaning of the word "wicked." Finally, to approach that word at least halfway, I asked that little angel what his mother said to him if he did something wrong. He got up and, looking at me with his innocent eyes, said, "Gangster" (in Russian, *"arrestant,"* a jailbird). It was so unexpected that I could not stop laughing for a long while.

The fourth grade was more difficult. There were some boys of thirteen and even fourteen, husky and strong. During the recreation period, they ran and played in the school yard, often fought with each other and at the sound of the bell, rushed into the classroom still full of excitement. To calm them down, I would read or talk in a very low voice so that they had to stop talking, rattling pages, or moving their desks to hear. Only when complete silence was re-established, would I raise my voice and ask questions.

Elementary schools like the one in which I taught had the same teacher for all subjects—Russian, arithmetic, geography, history, botany, zoology, and so on, all of which, of course, were taught within narrow limits. The fine municipal museum of natural sciences was very handy, and we often took the children there for a demonstration of a particular topic, such as the manufacture of linen from the flax seed to the weaving of cloth. Outdoor excursions were a regular feature of the school program.

Of the two male teachers, the younger was witty and intelligent, and both Esther and I liked him; I still remember some of his jokes. The older was a tall man with gray hair, who could not handle the boys, and often Esther or I rushed to his aid when he lost control of the class.

Though we were very busy, the war was ever with us. We had to clear the second floor of the school for war prisoners from the Austrian front— about fifty young officers and soldiers, some with arms in slings; the badly wounded were hospitalized. Many people stood on the sidewalk watching them march into the school, but there was no special animosity in the crowd.

After the end of the school year, I visited my friend Manya in Witebsk, then went to see my half brother in Archangelsk where I encountered the "white" nights, on which the northern lights enabled one to read and write without a lamp. From there I went home to Irkutsk, at the urging of Mother.

YOUNG DREAMS

All that and more was the life of many young college graduates from St. Petersburg and other universities. Inside was another life, a personal life of dreams, unrealized desires, and maturing awareness of what was to be the decisive factor in my life.

Some excerpts from the diary I kept in the last years before meeting Wolik, the only one I still have from that period, may illustrate my hopes and fears.

In my heart there are songs, joy, and peace, something radiant and great. To bury my head into the boisterous, agitated grass and kick up my feet, laugh ringingly and happily, smile at everything and be happy, happy . . .

Much free time for thoughts, and I abandon myself to them. They are so quiet, so peaceful. None of the sadness, none of the resentful pride as before. Perhaps this is because the hopes left me, those sweet, little creatures that chirped so gaily and laughed, fluttered so lightly and thrust themselves forward so swiftly and eagerly at every chance . . . But their departure has not left me empty and cold. I am serene and calm, I no longer dream of the future . . . I do want happiness, do want fulfillment, but these desires do not torment me any longer . . .

The sun is bright, the day is clear. The silvery, dressed-up trees speak of purity and beauty. The avenue is like an enchanted kingdom, the branches of the trees look like fluffy wings of the paradise birds. . . . Why I am so sad? Where are the songs that filled me during the summer?

. . . There are two souls in me—in one there is darkness and such a cutting pain, in the other there is innocence, and serenity, and the cheerful laughter of a child. When I listen to the first, I wish to wander, wander in the world until I am exhausted and absorb, like a sponge, the new, the unknown, and so spend myself. The other soul sings and calls to live and be happy. To which should I listen?

I walk in the streets and seek my knight. It seems to me that I would recognize him at the first glance. I walk and seek him, the noble and strong, one who lives dreaming of my smile, who could never, never forget me! Where is he? He is mine, mine, yet he is not with me! I give my time, my words to others, but somewhere, far away from me, he suffers because life without me is darkness for him. How can life be bright for him without me? I would like to sit down at the piano and play, so that soft, sad sounds of music merge with those that are now in my heart. If they could reach him, tell him about me, bring him to me . . .

The school takes all of my time, my thoughts, my interests. There is no opportunity to be quiet and feel myself. The main thing—the sense of insecurity: Will I handle the work well? Can I give the children something worth-while? The school has hold of me . . . I am wrapped up in my work . . . I live its life, its worries, its problems. The children are becoming ever closer to me. My feeling of inadequacy for the job is fading. I begin to hope that everything will work out . . . Yet I know—I could never fill my life with the school, the school only. Dissatisfaction and sadness will remain with me. I need happiness, love, songs, and fairy tales! Without them there is no life!

Saturday morning. My day of rest . . . but there is no rest for me. I am sick at heart. This sadness does not keep me from chatting gaily, laughing infectiously, and working, but it is always inside me. I live as in a dream. I walk, I talk, but I sense this is not life but a dream. I hear so much praise, such exciting words about myself that sometimes, just for one short moment, I wish I could think that way of myself. I am told how lovely life is because of me; "In your eyes is the sun," says V. But if all this is true, if I am really so attractive, beautiful, understanding, then why am I so lonely, why have I not brought happiness to someone, why have I not met greatness and nobility but have always seen weakness and littleness? . . . If all this is true, I could make a real knight happy, a real hero! . . . I want something enormous, immense . . .

Like a fly in a corked-up bottle, my troubled thoughts turn round and round . . . Life and death seem equally senseless, equally needless, and equally terrifying—one by all that I know of it and the other, by its mystery. Yet when darkness thickens around me, when I feel so very sad, then death stretches its arms toward me and smiles so softly, so tenderly, that I feel drawn toward those arms—to take them and deliver myself to their power . . . I am at the crossroads between life and death. I have not turned away from death and have not really joined life. I laugh at the dangers of life, I can fight them cheerfully and bravely, brush aside its attacks, lightly and thoughtlessly, but I know what nobody knows—I want heavenly, immense happiness, bottomless love, I want absolute sincerity and truth, complete absorption of another being's soul, I want beauty, I want unbounded joy that chokes me in its madness. Without this, there is no life for me. Nothing else would satisfy me. In this, in the impossibility for me of any other way of living is my delight and my torment . . .

I almost perished yesterday at Lake Baykal. I was sitting at the edge of a sharp, rocky precipice, with Baykal lying below. Suddenly, at the very top of the mountain, an enormous boulder broke loose and began to rush downhill at full speed toward me. There was no room for me to escape. In those seconds or minutes while it was falling, I saw only two alternatives—either to be crushed by the boulder right where I was or to be thrown by it into the lake. In either case —death! But a few yards from me the boulder made a sharp turn, almost touched my feet, and fell down over the edge. Following it, another stone, somewhat smaller, rushed down and also avoided me. I was not scared—there was no time for it. I only looked in bewilderment and with some curiosity at the threat to my life. The friends with whom I had made the trip were terrified but were too far from me to even try to do something. Then I forgot what happened, was calm, and laughed a lot. But at night, in bed, when I was resting from boating and hiking, the picture of the frightening boulder, the precipice, Lake Baykal, began to float before my eyes, and I became frightened. I wanted to hide myself from that nightmarish picture, forget it, to force it to disappear, to dissolve the horror that pressed on my heart. Yet it stayed on and held me in its grip, until my thoughts took a more cheerful turn. Again I had been exposed to peril but fate had saved me. It meant that I was needed for something or somebody. I wanted to believe that I was saved for one who sought me, dreamed of me. Or was this only a warning, and will something worse happen?

With all my changing moods and dreams of love, I was completely ignorant of and uninterested in the "sex problem," now so dominant in the lives of teenagers and even younger children. While I was abstracting material for some books to be recommended for popular consumption, I happened onto a tiny brochure with the intriguing title "What the Child of Four or Five Should Know." It introduced me, a college junior, to the facts of life, but made no particular impression on me.

In Irkutsk, before Manya arrived and I met Wolik, I formed a rather close friendship with an older woman named Olga Yogel, wife of a successful lawyer. There could not have been a greater contrast than that between us two, but I liked her and she, most surprisingly, clung to me as though she needed me—needed, at least for a time, as she once said to me, to be in an atmosphere of purity and inner honesty. When Olga was very young, she had been married to a rich old man; when she could not stand the marriage any longer, she had taken her umbrella (it was a rainy day) and left him. When I knew her, she lived in a common-law marriage, not having obtained a divorce. This was a rather frequent occurrence in Siberia. She had an intelligent and affectionate husband and two adorable small children. The children were fond of me and wanted to address me by *ty* (thou), as they addressed their parents, instead of *vy* (you). When their mother forbade it, the little rascals made up a name for me using *ty*, "Tyshka," or the diminutive "Tyshonchik." This is untranslatable, but it was a mark of endearment and showed that our relation was particularly close.

Her house was a meeting place for the intellectuals and artists of the city. She was neither plain nor especially attractive, yet there was some come-hither in her—in her voice, her smile, the way she talked, her bearing. I do not remember how we met, but we were drawn to each other almost immediately. We made several boat trips together on the Angara River and Lake Baykal; in the evening she used to ring our doorbell or knock at my window, and suggest taking a walk along the river.

Once, as I understood much later, she evidently wanted to unburden herself by telling me that one of her friends, the head of a Government agency, had been transferred to southern Russia and was bombarding her with telegrams to follow him. Probably I seemed a complete idiot to her, because I sincerely could not comprehend why he would expect her to do such a fantastic thing. She did not feel it necessary to go into the details for a college graduate of twenty-two and was baffled by my lack of understanding. Perhaps it amused her, perhaps she liked me for this. Incidentally, Olga was among those who tried to dissuade me from uniting my life with Wolik's.

My changing moods continued until new feelings burst into my life with hurricane force. When I was least expecting anything to happen, Wolik appeared on the scene. In a flash, I realized that what he brought to me was more than I had ever dreamed of.

3. *Year of Crisis: 1917*

ON THE THIRD DAY of my trip to Petrograd to meet Wolik's mother, I was overtaken by the Revolution, which broke out unexpectedly. My first impulse was to go back to be with Wolik, but I learned that the railroad tracks had been destroyed at various points to keep the Tsarist troops from moving against the revolutionary capital, and so if I tried to get back, I might find myself marooned somewhere. As it turned out, those precautions were unnecessary; from the first day, the army was on the side of the people. So I continued the trip to Petrograd, the sure place from which I would be able to get in touch with Wolik. All I could do was to read the newspapers, talk with other passengers, and watch the countryside and the people's reaction as we crossed Russia. This was Wolik's second revolution, but my first. I was thrilled and wanted to be a part of it, but realized my political unpreparedness. I felt that I had to learn fast.

WOLIK'S FAMILY

The excitement around me drew my thoughts away from Wolik's family. I had been somewhat uncomfortable at the prospect of meeting them after Wolik's enthusiastic letters about me. He had shown me a letter to his mother that he wanted me to give to her. Among other things, he wrote:

> All these years when I thought of you, I had a feeling of guilt, guilt at having brought you so many worries, much pain and sadness, never happiness . . . But my life was such that I had no happiness to share with you. I knew how little joy there was in your life but I myself was so poor in joy that I had nothing to offer you. But now when I am indescribably happy and rays of the sun permeate my whole being, I want to join you with this happiness so that the beams of my radiant sun will touch your head . . . I feel that my sweetheart, with one word, one smile, one look of her wonderful eyes, can make one happy. I wish not only that she bring you the message of my happiness but that she enter your life and illumine

it. I believe this will happen. Miracles occur in the world, and my darling, with her innocence and sunny love, is a miracle.

Who would not be afraid to face the mother of her beloved after such an introduction? Fortunately, when I reached Wolik's family, my arrival was like a ripple on the surface of an agitated sea. Nadya's husband had been appointed by the new authorities to the Commission investigating the crimes of the Tsar's ministers; Wolik's older brother was also attached to the new Government; and most important, Wolik's exile was over, and a telegram from him announced he would arrive in a few days. Everybody was in a turmoil, happily so, and there was little time and desire to look over Wolik's "sun."

I had met Wolik's father. His mother was very different—more practical, more conscious of conventional patterns of life, rather inclined to worry about what might happen (though many of her worries never materialized), but very thoughtful, sweet, tactful, and loving. She and Father were not too congenial but lived in harmony. Mother sighed when he returned from his customary summer trip to Europe with a load of new books and the news that more were on the way. She disapproved of his passion for collecting, declaring that there was no room left for additions; he responded good-naturedly, yet never changed his habits. He was what people expect of a scholar—extremely absent-minded, occasionally funny. He was frequently tapped for loans by acquaintances and distant relatives, and when he gave over the money he also gave the borrower a little slip indicating the amount lent. When someone laughed at this practice, he replied, "Isn't it reasonable? I may forget, but they would not want to forget that they owe me money."

The entire family accepted me with warm friendliness, but the times were not conducive to quiet talks to bring us closer together. Events on all sides were so stirring that even when Wolik arrived, his mother and brothers, who had not seen him for twelve or thirteen years, felt that he belonged to the Revolution and the country rather than to his family.

We stayed with Wolik's family until I found an apartment, and I saw more of him than they, largely because I spent my days in the Tauride Palace, the center of the democratic forces and the heart of the Revolution. There, I occasionally got a glimpse of him. Usually he returned home at night very late, when everyone but me was sound asleep. There were also troublesome nights that he spent at the Palace.

THE COUNTRY IN TURMOIL

It was a mad time. Early in the morning, Wolik would leave in a hurry to attend a meeting of the "Star Chamber," at which five or six persons discussed the political situation and arrived at all the important decisions. After this, Wolik would prepare the formulation of the adopted policy. Then he would rush to the Tauride Palace to participate in the session of the Executive Committee of the Petrograd Soviet of Workers' and Soldiers' Deputies, or to address the plenary meeting of the Soviet, or, if necessary, to go to factories or barracks where a dispute had to be settled or a crowd to be addressed. He was coeditor of *Izvestiya* and wrote daily editorials and articles. Often when he was having his dinner long after midnight, the telephone would ring with a message urging him to return to *Izvestiya* or to go to the barracks to quell a sudden flare-up, or to do something else. He ate twice a day—a steak for breakfast and a meal at night. All my efforts to make him aware of the sandwiches that I stuffed into his coat pockets were unsuccessful; either he brought them back or someone else ate them.

My life, too, was abnormal, going from meeting to meeting, without rest, with growing consciousness of the situation, growing political maturity, oppressing worries for the future of the country, and constant anxiety about Wolik. He went into the lion's den several times—to speak to the sailors in Kronstadt, to address riotous meetings. I could not even suggest that I go with him, but I found an understanding soul in O. P. Goldenberg, who was invariably kind and helpful. He sensed my worry when Wolik undertook dangerous missions and understood my desire to be there. Several times he got permission for me to buy a ticket. In Kronstadt, I was in the violent crowd of sailors when Wolik spoke to them, but did not let him see me lest he be afraid for my safety. When he went to Helsinki, Finland, to address a regional convention, I surprised him after the meeting, and we had a few hours together, though we returned to Petrograd separately.

As in Irkutsk, we never thought or talked about the material side of life, but everything worked out satisfactorily. Whenever Wolik gave an educationally important speech, it was reproduced not only in *Izvestiya* but as a separate pamphlet by the publishing house Kniga, which frequently took down his speeches. The royalty was one cent or occasionally only half a cent per pamphlet, but the edition of 200,000 or 300,000 copies was fully paid for in advance. I did some newspaper work—not too interesting but not tiring and within the Tauride Palace; I, too, was paid for it. We rented a five-room apartment, and Wolik's father gave us a check that covered the costs of furnishings.

I matured politically, though not necessarily under Wolik's influence—he had no time for himself or for me. The Revolution educated me through all that I saw, read, heard. The demagoguery of the Communists—their lies and shameless charges against the democratic leaders—was revolting, while the extremists on the opposite side, the right wing of the Constitutional-Democratic Party and the conservatives—with their clichés in judgment, political blindness, and inability to understand that those who wanted to fight the Communists actually were their best allies—made one despair of the future.

From March to July, we spent only one day together, when we went to Terioki, where Wolik's father had a large and beautiful estate. But even that Sunday ended in anxiety. We relaxed a little, took a walk along the beach, had meals with the family. Wolik had to return to Petrograd by seven o'clock, but Mother begged me to spend a few more hours with them. When I reached the city at midnight, the first thing I saw was the large headline in the newspaper: WOYTINSKY WOUNDED IN AUTOMOBILE ACCI-DENT. The paper did not give the name of the hospital to which he had been taken. Should I go to the Tauride Palace for information or go home and call from there? By the time I started frantically calling one place after another, Wolik appeared at the door with a bandaged head but, of course, smiling and assuring me that his injury was slight. Didn't I think the bandage very becoming?

Then came the July days, with the first serious attempt by the Communists to seize power. I realized at once the danger of the situation, locked the apartment, and went to the Tauride Palace, where I spent several days and nights. It looked like an armed camp, and I watched the agony of the Revolution and then its slow and uncertain victory over the destructive forces. Wolik was in personal danger every hour of those tragic days, but I am sure he never was aware of this, being completely absorbed by one thought only—to crush the dangerous assault on what was still the only hope for survival of the democratic regime in Russia.

Indecision and disunity within the democratic forces made the prospects for the future darker with every day. Wolik could not continue to work at the pace he had set for himself, and frustration depressed him more than fatigue. I, too, was disheartened. The political situation in the capital looked hopeless. A casual meeting offered him a chance to change his field of activity, and Wolik accepted the offer to go to the Northern Front as Assistant Commissar of both the Provisional Government and the Executive Committee of the All-Russian Soviet of Workers' and Soldiers' Delegates, on condition that I could go with him.

The wives of military personnel were not allowed to follow their husbands, but a few exceptions had been made for members of the High Command. Permission was obtained for me, and I was appointed Wolik's personal secretary. The final formality was to obtain papers showing our "official" marriage. On the way to the train Wolik was to take for Riga, we stopped at the office of the civil rabbi to have our marriage legally confirmed. The rabbi, a quiet, dignified man, hesitated, saying that he did not know either of us personally and, who knew?, perhaps each of us had been married to somebody else. Just as we were beginning to cast about for ways to prove that we were indeed married to each other, the door of the study opened, and who should walk in and greet me most happily but the young teacher from Stavropol, now the executive secretary of the rabbi! In a few minutes, he assured the latter that my word was my bond, and without further delay we got the papers enabling me to join Wolik at the front.

RIGA

A week after Wolik left for Riga, the headquarters of the Twelfth Army on the Northern Front, I followed him. Riga, a very old city, once a member of the Hanseatic League, had been ruled intermittently by the Teutonic Knights, a Catholic bishop, and after the Reformation, by Poland, Russia, and Sweden. It changed hands many times until, early in the eighteenth century, Russia defeated Charles XII of Sweden and took final possession of it.* In our time, Riga was a lively city. Situated on both banks of the Dvina River, it had a mixed population, partly Russian, partly Latvian, partly German. Close at hand were sandy beaches stretching for miles and attracting thousands of summer guests from the western part of Russia—beaches, by the way, that we heard of but that we never had time to visit.

Wolik plunged into his new work, no less demanding than that in Petrograd but more satisfying. Danger awaited him at every step, particularly in the rioting regiments, which were not uncommon at that time, and from German shells. He was constantly traveling on highways under fire. One day, looking for some paper in his drawer, I found his request to the Army Headquarters for an award to his chauffeur, who had driven him under German shelling.

With his great capacity for understanding the point of view of others, his straightforward approach to problems and people, and his overriding concern for the future of Russia, he tried to impress upon both the Command and the soldiers the need to re-establish discipline in the army on the basis of mutual trust and to be prepared to defend the new democratic Russia against the enemy.

He knew how to talk to the soldiers, who were tired, distrustful of the officers, rebellious against the war and the years spent in filthy trenches, and wanted to go home to their villages. But he also knew how to talk to the officers, bewildered, scared by a revolution that had pulled the rug out from under their feet and had destroyed their authority and self-confidence.

I saw little of Wolik, not much more than in Petrograd, but I was his official secretary and so he called me more frequently than before. Occasionally he wanted me to take some confidential or secret papers to Army Headquarters. My appearance there invariably caused a commotion; never before had a woman asked to enter that sacred place! The guards, always new, would leave me standing and rush inside for instructions, and at each door there were again questioning, undisguised surprise, and even contempt implying that that was how low Russia had fallen with all these revolutionaries in power!

To fill the long days and ease my constant anxiety for Wolik's life, I began to lecture on Russia's history and economy to the soldiers and the general public in the People's House. Also, I established a close relationship with the Executive Committee of Soldiers' Delegates of the

* The history of Riga did not end there. In 1917, during World War I, it was taken by the Germans; then after the defeat of Germany it became the capital of independent Latvia, was again occupied by Russia at the end of World War II, and is now within the Soviet Union as the capital of the "Soviet Socialist Republic of Latvia." This occupation has not been recognized by the United States.

Twelfth Army (called Iskosol, for short). These were intelligent, courageous men, nearly all of them decorated for military valor, many of
them volunteers, true patriots of their country and the Revolution
which, they passionately hoped, would vindicate the Russian people's
old dream for freedom. Sensing their admiration for Wolik, I felt a natural friendship for them. It was harder for them to accept me on equal
terms and to deal with me in Wolik's absence at the front. Gradually I
gained their trust and with some of them, particularly with J. Kharash,
developed a lasting friendship. When any of them accompanied Wolik
on trips into the lion's den, I felt a little better.

THE FALL OF RIGA

Early one morning the telephone rang. I heard Wolik say, "Yes . . .
All right . . . I am coming." He told me that Army Headquarters had
summoned him and left in a hurry. Not suspecting anything unusual, I
worked on a lecture scheduled for that afternoon. I heard bursting shells
and explosions, but these were an everyday occurrence and I gave no
thought to them. When I went to the People's House, it was closed;
there was no notice on the door about cancellation of the lecture. I
turned to go home when a car stopped near me, and Wolik's assistant
jumped out of it to say, "If evacuation becomes necessary, I will take
care of you." Before I could say anything, a soldier appeared from nowhere and shouted, "Get on with the car, there are wounded soldiers in
the next block." They disappeared, leaving me completely confused.

Shortly thereafter, police told me that sewer pipes had been broken by
the shelling and the area was closed. I made a detour, finally reached the
place where we lived and called the Iskosol. Then I learned about the
German breakthrough in the front line, Riga was under direct attack,
Wolik was at the front, they did not know where; there was no communication with the front. What should I do? I decided to go to the Iskosol.
I had a better chance there to hear from or about Wolik.

In the Iskosol the telephone was ringing all the time, and shells were
exploding all around us. The German long-distance artillery had chosen
that building as its main target. Everybody was excited and busy, and I
felt almost a nuisance. I found a corner and sat there for endless hours,
with the unconcealed question on my face, "Where is Wolik?" Now and
then one of my friends would stop and say, "Sorry, we have no news for
you. Do not worry, he is safe!"

I learned later that Wolik had driven under constant shelling, hearing
the distant booming of the artillery, to division headquarters. The
ground on both sides of the road was smoking from frequent explosions. When he finally reached there, he found that the place had been
hurriedly abandoned: three telephone instruments were hanging on the
wall. Where had the office gone? There was no one to answer that question. Then he saw an officer arriving on horseback with an emergency
report. He, too, did not know that headquarters had retreated. There

were two roads: should he take the one to the left or to the right? The
chauffeur called Wolik's attention to a woman with a child:

> At first I did not notice that woman. She stood so motionless that
> from a distance I took her for a post. I ran to her. "Mother, do you
> know where the officers went? You understand? There were soldiers
> and a general here. Where did they go?" The woman was beside a
> cart loaded with a heavy peasant chest, a basket with chickens, a
> bench turned upside down, a home-made cradle, a hooked rug. The
> disheveled nag, half-harnessed, stood with lowered head . . .
>
> The woman, some forty years old, was poorly dressed. A girl of
> about ten hugged her knees with her head buried in the folds of
> woman's skirt. The woman, pressing her hands against her head
> with both arms in the air, stared into space with eyes full of horror,
> standing motionless, like one dead. There was not a trace of blood
> in her gray, wrinkled face. Perhaps, she was Latvian and therefore
> had not answered. "You understand Russian?" I asked. No answer.
> I faced her directly, but she did not see me. "You, little girl, say
> something. I won't harm you." I took the child by the shoulders and
> tried to force her to look at me. She did not cry, did not beat me off,
> but clung even more desperately to her mother's knees. Seeing her
> thin, tanned neck tighten and her hands tremble, I could feel the
> terror in the child's heart. The mother did not drop her arms even
> to defend the girl but continued, with hands at her head, to stare
> into space . . .
>
> "We must leave," the chauffeur urged me. Shells exploded al-
> most at our feet. "I shall take the left road," said the officer, and
> rode away. I tried again, but in the woman's eyes, blinded by fire
> and explosions, was such horror that I, too, became frightened. I
> looked at the map and said to the chauffeur, "Start the car. Let us
> also go to the left. What about them?" I motioned toward the
> woman and child. "Where with them?" he laughed. I understood, of
> course, that we could not burden ourselves with a woman and child
> mad with fear and did not insist.
>
> Five minutes later the road entered a forest. No shells . . . We
> felt safe again, but I could not forget the woman with the mad eyes,
> the little girl whose face I had not seen, only her thin neck and
> trembling hands. "We should not have left them there," I said to
> the chauffeur. "They will be killed." "That is right, killed," he
> agreed, and after a while he added resignedly, "War!," as if this one
> word explained everything.*

About three in the morning, Kharash came to talk to me. Riga was to
be abandoned to the Germans in a few hours, the last trucks with evac-
uated nurses were about to leave, and he wanted me to go with them. I
begged him to let me stay with Iskosol, my only link with Wolik, but he
insisted, saying that, as soldiers, they would leave with the army at the

* "V Pokinutoy Derevne" ("In the Deserted Village"), *Borba* (Tiflis), 1918.

last moment, while I, in the city with the Germans, would be unable to join Wolik until the end of the war. So I went to the last truck, so crowded that we all had to stand during the entire retreat, from Riga to Wenden.

The road was packed with retreating soldiers—some still marching as a unit, in good order, others just walking away. Several times I heard them shout to the nurses. "Always better treated than us poor fellows. Having a nice time, eh?" Nobody answered from the truck.

We drove and drove until we reached Wenden, the new headquarters. I tried unsuccessfully to locate Wolik, but nobody knew where he was. For several days, I walked aimlessly in the streets of that strange little town, inquiring, grasping every chance to find out about him, returning at night to the school building where we took refuge. Then walking one day, I suddenly saw a car with Wolik and some officers. We were together again. He was near exhaustion from sleepless nights and trips from one sector of the front to another, and I, too, was not in the best of condition!

We left for Petrograd the same day—Wolik in the army car, and I by train. There a new excitement waited for us—the mutiny of General Kornilov, the Supreme Commander.

Much has been written on this tragic event, which crushed all hopes of maintaining the army as the defender of the front. How could anybody persuade the irate soldiers to obey the commanding officers when the Supreme Commander was a traitor who wanted to arrest the Provisional Government, "put an end to the Revolution," and assume dictatorial powers?

Though the mutiny was easily put down by the efforts of the workers and the refusal of the soldiers to fight against the democratic forces, the damage, magnified many times by the Communist demagoguery, was enormous. The gates were now wide open to the other extremists, who were no less the enemies of the people's freedom, the Communists.

In those critical days, Wolik was again the troubleshooter—visiting barracks in the capital and the workers' districts, talking at meetings, reporting to the plenary session of the Soviet, and telephoning all day long. His satisfaction with victory faded as soon as he returned to the front—this time to Pskov, headquarters of the Commander for the Northern Front. There he was confronted with the impact of the general's mutiny on the soldiers, the backbone of the army. All those months of patient, difficult work, at the risk of his life, had been wiped out by the Command's senseless attempt to exercise power they no longer possessed. Still, Kornilov's threat to court-martial Wolik for defending the soldiers helped him preserve some vestige of authority. But even this fact, spread through the armed forces with all kinds of embellishments, was not enough to outweigh the soldiers' loss of trust in the Command and the Government, which did not take energetic measures against the rebellious General.

IN PSKOV·

Wolik's office as the Commissar of the Northern Front was in a large building, formerly a high school. A few rooms were used as living quarters, and we settled down in one of them. Again, Wolik was often away, and I was alone with the staff inherited from Wolik's predecessor, V. Stankevich. It consisted of several officers and two privates; strangely enough, both the latter were poets—one just entering on his career, the other, Sasha Cherny, a well-known and popular poet in Russia.

Meals were served from the officers' canteen. When I went to the table for the first time, I sensed that my presence, as a woman and the wife of the "boss," made everybody tense, including myself. Yet the men tried to talk in their habitual way, with risqué jokes and equivocal allusions. Unaccustomed to such conversations, I was uncomfortable and annoyed, particularly at Sasha Cherny, from whom I would not have expected such behavior. I went to two more meals and then apologized for my desire to have my meals in my room. Cherny came to "explain," and I expressed my surprise at his pleasure in such jokes, adding that I did not want my presence to force the men to be gentlemen. He was very embarrassed and offered to influence the group, but I continued to take meals in my room. Nevertheless, Cherny and I became good friends, and from time to time he came to chat or to read a new poem.

Much of the confidential information from Wolik to the Army Headquarters in Pskov and the Central Headquarters in Mogilev continued to pass through my hands. I often asked the army telegrapher to come to the office to send direct wires over the equipment installed in the room next to ours. The staff continued the routine work of recording army news as they did before.

When Wolik happened to be in Pskov, he frequently had visitors— military representatives of the Allies, higher officers of the Army, delegates of the soldiers, journalists, and so on. I disliked the visits from Russian generals, harbingers of some dangerous assignment for Wolik. They always complained of the impossibility of handling the soldiers and asked for his help. I knew that they were in a most difficult situation, created by the Revolution, which they hated and which had destroyed everything they cherished—loyalty to the throne, their authority over the soldiers, their prestige. Yet when I heard them begging Wolik to come to their regiments and introduce some order in them, I could not help feeling that they were asking him to endanger his life in order to safeguard theirs.

There were some commanders whom Wolik sincerely respected. They understood the change and were willing to accept the new conditions in good faith. There were also outstanding commanders with whom Wolik established relations of mutual trust and friendship. One, General Skalon, had such faith in Wolik's integrity and superior qualities of leadership that he believed that the country would accept him as the

head of the Government if he showed a willingness to undertake this trying job. Unfortunately, the majority of the commanders who came to
our office seemed like squeezed lemons—frightened, feeble, unfit for rough
living in times of war and revolution.

Some visits were rather amusing. I recall a French general who appeared to complain against abusive allusions to the French Government
in the Communist newspaper *Okopnaya Pravda* (*The Truth of the
Trenches*). Wolik explained that Russia was in a state of revolution and
that *Pravda* used much stronger words about the Russian Government.
But the general persisted, "This does not concern us. You may accept
such abuses, we do not. I have noticed the absence of discipline here.
When I came into the hall, your orderly did not get up, so I said to him,
'I am a general of the French Army and expect to be treated accordingly.'
And what happened? He got up, saluted, and took my coat." He gave
Wolik a look of triumph, sure that if Russian generals assumed the same
posture, army discipline would be restored easily.

THE LAST DAYS IN PSKOV

News from Petrograd, from the front, from everywhere, was distressing. I
cannot remember one cheerful moment. Though Pskov is one of the
oldest cities of Russia, with an exceptionally interesting, dramatic history, and has a kremlin, old churches, and ruins of old walls, it never even
occurred to me, much less to Wolik, to do any sightseeing, as would have
been natural in other circumstances.

A weak government, irresolute democratic organizations confronting
falsehoods, fantastic charges by the Communists . . . seemingly no end
to the war . . . postponement of the elections to the Constituent Assembly . . . disintegration of the Army . . . Against this background,
Wolik's dogged efforts to save what could be saved, to inspire civil
courage and the will to defend free, democratic Russia. I remember the
last meeting in his office with the representatives from the three armies
on the Northern Front. I listened from the neighboring room. The reports were almost monotonous in their hopelessness and despair: distrust
of the officers, disobedience of the soldiers, fraternization with the enemy,
the growing strength of the Communists, who promised to end the war
immediately and distribute the land, their slogans "peace, bread and
freedom!" Wolik spoke last, summarizing the situation. I yearned to hear
him say something to break the vicious circle, but he represented both
the Executive Committee of the All-Russian Soviet and the Provisional
Government, and so held to their line. Perhaps there still was a chance
through a bold reshuffling of the Government (as Wolik suggests in
Stormy Passage), through bold reforms, perhaps even immediate withdrawal from the war, as the War Minister himself dramatically suggested.

Nothing of the sort happened, and the Communists started their
armed attack against the Provisional Government. Their leaders had
been abroad when the Tsarist regime was overthrown, but were now here

in Russia to overthrow a democratic government. From the Winter Palace, the seat of the Government, came requests for reliable troops to crush the *coup d'état,* but there were no more reliable troops. That the Government was unaware of the situation on the front spoke for itself. At best, some regiments declared themselves neutral, meaning that they were waiting to see which side ended up on top. The Commander of the Northern Front, General Cheremissov, took the same ambiguous position.

Wolik decided to fight with what forces he could assemble, a unit here, another there, hoping that the Communist forces in Petrograd were not too imposing. He sent wires in all directions, contacted army committees, talked with soldiers' delegates. There was some response. He did not give up hope and continued to organize armed resistance to the usurpers of power against and over the people, though news about the arrest of the Provisional Government had reached us already.

That evening several soldiers came to the office to ask Wolik to attend the joint meeting of the local Soviet and delegates from the troops stationed in and around Pskov. He left with them at about seven o'clock. The teletype operator left, too. None of the staff members had appeared that day. Only Sasha Cherny came in, said, "Everything is finished. Russia is lost," kissed my hand, and went out. I walked through the rooms, decided not to look at my watch, then looked. Time seemed frozen. I stared out the window. The street was dark. I did not know where Wolik was, where the meeting was. I counted the minutes but gave up. Eleven o'clock, midnight—still no Wolik.

About one o'clock, steps sounded outside. I rushed to the door, and threw it open. There was a young officer asking for Wolik; he had an important report. When he heard my reply, he slumped into the chair, closed his eyes, and fell asleep at once. I shook him, tried to tell him the situation, but he was so exhausted that he opened his eyes for only a second, then closed them again. I could not possibly give up my only chance to find Wolik, and I shook him again and again until he got up from the chair and listened to me. I implored him to go to the meeting and take me with him; I could no longer stand the uncertainty. After a while, he agreed to go to the meeting but refused to take me. I insisted so strenuously that finally he gave in, saying, "All right, we shall go together. But remember, there are thousands of excited, hostile men. I shall leave you at the entrance, in back of the crowd. No matter what you see, you must promise not to show yourself. One scream from a woman, and anything might happen to you and to your husband." I promised, and we set out. After crossing several dark streets in one, then another direction, we reached the theater. The officer left me at the door. The theater was packed. All the seats were occupied, and the galleries and aisles were jammed with armed soldiers.

From where I was, I could see the stage. Wolik was sitting at the table and a Communist orator—a civil engineer, I was told later—was going from one end of the stage to the other, screaming abuses against Wolik as the one man responsible for all the bloodshed on the Northern Front. If Wolik had told the Government about the human losses there, the orator shouted, the war would have been stopped long ago. But no, Wolik was one of those who got rich from people's suffering. And what was the Commissar doing now? He read the copy of Wolik's appeals to resist the *coup d'état,* appeals to military units to arise in the defense of that miserable government. There were shouts of indignation from all sides.

Then Wolik got up, confirmed that he was organizing the defense of the democratic government against those who would usurp power, reminded the crowd that elections would take place soon and that the Constituent Assembly alone, representing the will of the people, not just of the garrison of Pskov or Petrograd, would decide the fate of Russia. The crowd was silent, and Wolik, apparently hoping to take it by surprise, left the stage and started down the central aisle toward the door. The crowd was stunned until, as he reached the middle of the hall, somebody shouted, "Hold him! He is going to send more troops to Petrograd!" Another shouted, "Kill him!" Several soldiers rushed to seize him, a few others tried to hold them back but were pushed aside. Realizing that his attempt to slip out had failed and that he would be safer on the stage than in the middle of the hostile crowd, Wolik went back on the stage and said loudly, "I believed that I had answered all your questions, and I wanted to go back to my office, where I have much work to do. But evidently you want to put more questions to me. All right, I shall stay a little longer."

Wolik sat down, but this time the chairman had summoned soldiers with fixed bayonets to stand behind him, indicating that he was under arrest. The engineer had resumed his abuse of Wolik and his activities in the war, when the chairman announced that a delegate from Luga, a city between Pskov and Petrograd with a much larger garrison than Pskov, wanted to say something. The Luga delegate got a thunderous ovation, but his first words stunned the crowd: "I am here to convey the greetings of my Division and to find out what is going on in Pskov. But I have seen what just happened and shall not even talk to you. I was in the penitentiary with Commissar Woytinsky. I know how he fought for the freedom of the people when you were crawling under the tables and did not know how to blow your noses."

The mood of the audience underwent a dramatic reversal. At a sign from the chairman, the soldiers behind Wolik disappeared. Some soldiers said loudly, "We have nothing against the Commissar. We know him, he is all right." Wolik said good-naturedly to the Luga delegate, "I am glad to see you here after so many years, Nikolai. But this was just a family squabble." The Luga man spoke a few minutes longer, then turned to the crowd and said, "I have things to discuss with my old pal. So long!" and signaling to Wolik to follow him, he left the stage.

I rushed out, hoping to see Wolik, but I was afraid to call out to him and he did not see me. I saw him and the Luga man get into a car and disappear.

The city was dark. I could not remember the way back to the office and walked and walked in different directions until I saw the light in the deserted office building that I had forgotten to turn off. I went to my room, not knowing what to do. Around five o'clock, there was a knock at my door; several soldiers asked for Wolik. I said that he had gone to their meeting and had not returned. I pretended that I expected them to tell me where he was, but they said nothing and left.

IMPENDING DEFEAT

When nobody appeared in the office that morning, I collected all the secret documents, maps, and plans and went to deliver them to Army Headquarters. If the democratic government was re-established, as I hoped, I did not want to have the military accuse Wolik, a civilian, of having abandoned secret papers to the curiosity of the soldiers and possibly of the enemy. This time, Headquarters looked different. I went in without any questioning, and saw boxes and files strewn on the floor amid a scene of frightening confusion. An officer took the documents from me, and I returned to the office to await instructions from Wolik. Since our office remained the only center from which armed resistance to the Communist *coup d'état* was directed, visitors began to converge from all sides. It was the natural place for the members of the Iskosol— Kharash, Tumarkin, Kuchin, Likhach, and others. Representatives of various political groups came, along with delegates to the Soviets in various neighboring cities, and Victor Chernov, an outstanding member of the Socialist Revolutionary Party and a former member of the Provisional Government. Despite my anxiety for Wolik, I had to take care of them all—to feed them and arrange for sleeping accommodations. They had no place to go, and all were friends dedicated to the same cause.

Late one evening I was called to Army Headquarters: Wolik was calling, and the other line was dead. This was his first call to me since I had seen him leave the meeting, and I wanted to tell him that nobody had reported for duty and that his assistant had disappeared. Not wishing the teletypist to know of whom I was speaking, I used an expression of Sasha Cherny in his parody of that man: "The dejected crow flew away." The teletypist told me, "I know of whom you are talking."

What Wolik wanted of me would have seemed unbelievable only a few weeks ago: I was to ask General Baranovsky, who had been a member of the staff at the Front, whether he would accept appointment to succeed Cheremissov as Commander of the Northern Front. While I went to talk to the General, Wolik would wait for the answer.

The General's face could not have shown more disgust as I approached him with Wolik's question. This was probably the final humiliation for a man in his position: At night, inside Army Headquarters, a woman offering him, in the name of her husband, the position of the Commander of the Front! Still, such a proposal was not a thing to toss aside just because it came almost casually. The General took a rigid military position, saluted, and said, "Report to Commissar Woytinsky that I shall be glad to serve in such a capacity." Wolik transmitted this news to Kerensky, who signed, in Wolik's notebook, the order releasing Cheremissov and appointing Baranovsky to succeed him. As Wolik said in *Stormy Passage,* removal of Cheremissov was my last official act in Pskov.

Several soldiers came to Wolik's office to inquire about him, but I sent them away with one story or another. Despite the presence of many people in the building, the days seemed endless. I could not reach Wolik, and he could not get in touch with me. Then rumors began to spread that resistance had been broken, that the troops sent by Wolik had capitulated, that the Communists had taken Gatchina, the last place held by the units from the front. Finally, a telegram from Wolik told me that he had been arrested but was safe and that I should not worry. He was taken to Petrograd.

I wanted to go there immediately, but how? The railroad tracks had been torn up. There were still two cars, but I knew all too well that each of the people around me was in mortal danger and that the only chance to escape was by car. I could not use a car for myself. The Iskosol friends showed their warm feelings toward me. First they suggested I drive to Petrograd with a chauffeur. I refused, explaining why. They consulted among themselves and then suggested that two of them and I take one car and drive to Petrograd with false papers identifying us as delegates to the Commission on Elections to the Constituent Assembly, so as to pass the Communist posts along the highway. I agreed to this, and set out. At the outskirts of Petrograd, we said goodbye to each other, never to meet again.

It was after midnight, but instead of going to our apartment I went directly to Smolny, where the Communist Soviet center was, to find out where Wolik was held. There I insisted so energetically on being admitted that I not only was told of Wolik's whereabouts but was immediately permitted to see him for fifteen minutes. Wolik was in a large room, with five or six others who had been arrested. My arrival awoke them, but they did not mind, understanding my desire to assure myself that Wolik was as safe as he could be in the circumstances. When my time was up, I left, but not before obtaining permission to come next morning for an hour. Wolik, of course, tried to dissipate my worry and told me again and again that he was not in any danger and that his only trouble had been the thought of my anxiety.

THE FORTRESS OF PETER AND PAUL

A few days later, Wolik was transferred to a solitary cell in the Fortress of Peter and Paul, a dungeon famous in the history of the Russian freedom movement. Here many martyrs of that movement had spent most of their lives, and many others had perished. Twenty-minute visits were permitted twice a week, with guards standing near by.

Wolik's mother and Nadya came to visit me frequently, eager to get my mind off my anxiety, and invited me to go with them to the concerts and the theater. They were used to Wolik's being in prison, but I was not. To me, the whole world was centered in the cell where Wolik was. I talked, read the newspapers, walked the streets, listened to what people were saying, but all this was on the surface. Inside, I was with Wolik, saw only him, thought of him, talked to him.

The three agonizing months that Wolik spent in the Fortress were of great importance in our personal life. We had hardly begun to live together when the Revolution burst upon us with the elemental force of a hurricane. Our love, so serene and blissful, became a source of anxiety, sleepless nights, constant worry, became subordinated to something bigger than ourselves.

Now everything else had been crushed, but we two remained, free to think of ourselves. We wrote to each other every day. In one letter, Wolik wrote:

> . . . How wonderful that I can see you when I close my eyes! Sometimes you do not come at once, I must wait a little. Then you are there and look at me with wide-open eyes, deep as the sky, pure as the sky, beautiful as the sky . . . I see you most often in the black velvet cap and the fur coat, sometimes in the black suit with the white-brimmed hat, sometimes with the blue scarf amidst the trees, your face touched by the sun . . .
>
> You remember, darling, how you told me at times that love occupies a smaller place in my life than in yours? I never objected, because inside of me I felt this was true. Yet during this month in the cell I have realized that this is not true. In my life, too, love for you is all, it has filled my life and outgrown my heart . . . You are all my life, all my world. Without you, without your love, I could not live a single day. Never, never have I felt it so deeply, so sharply, so clearly as now . . . Do love me always even if I am not worthy of your great innocent love. Do love me, my beloved, though I am not capable of giving you as sunny a love. Do love me though this love brings you not only happiness but also pain.

And from my letters:

> I love you. I am full of admiration, of pride in you. I am under the spell of your great heart, your great mind. I love your dimples, your charming, infectious laughter. I hear it now in my ears and feel it even more clearly in my heart, such a young, enchanting, healthy laughter . . . I embrace you for your wonderful letters. You are right—these are not letters, but a caress, as tender as the touch of your eyelashes at my face, as hot as your kisses . . . Ah, but I want

to brag now—you did get "hooked," my dearest love. I did tie you to me and for good, though you were afraid of love and could not give "a guarantee for the future" . . . Do not write that you feel guilty, you who gave me such a burning, intoxicating joy of love and life, you, my wonderful, fearless knight. Guilty of what? Of having ignited a whole world of bliss and joy in the eyes in which you had seen only sadness before?

Both Wolik and I were on friendly terms with Dr. Manukhin, the prison physician. A liberal intellectual, a friend of Gorki, and a well-known figure in progressive circles, he had been appointed to the Fortress by the Provisional Government when the Tsarist Cabinet was arrested. He acted as our postmaster; every time he paid a call to Wolik's cell, he carried out a letter for me and mailed it; also, he delivered my letters to Wolik. Once when I visited him to ask about Wolik's health, he said to me, "The only time I relax in the Fortress is when I am in your husband's cell. We talk about all kinds of things, and his good spirits and humor give me a lift. Unfortunately, everybody else is so depressed . . . I arranged that some prisoners should have their walk in the yard at the same time as Wladimir Savelievich. I hope this will help."

He was thinking of the members of the Provisional Government. They were not cowards or weaklings, but they had never been in politics before, had taken their posts for prestige or out of patriotism, and had found themselves in a situation for which their lives had not prepared them. Their wives and mothers frequently called me up to share or seek some prison news, and I felt their anxiety was well founded. Two among these men, Shingarev and Kokoshkin, outstanding intellectuals with moderate leanings, needed hospital care. After long negotiations, they were taken to a private hospital. But the day they arrived, a group of soldiers and sailors broke in, tore them from their beds, and lynched them. This was "spontaneous indignation" over the release of "people's enemies."

The impact was very strong, and the new Government was accused of arranging the "spontaneous" lynching. I went to Dr. Manukhin and begged him to help me save Wolik from torture. I asked for cyanide, assuring him that since I did not hesitate to give it to Wolik, he could be absolutely sure that Wolik would take it only in the utmost extremity. I begged him to act not as a doctor but as a friend, and to understand my faith in Wolik. He told me to come next morning, when his receptionist gave me a little white package. On my next visit to Wolik I pressed it into his hand with this little note:

You are strong, my knight, and I give this to you without fear. Take it when there can be no other escape. I know you will not do it before—you hold two lives in your hands. But do know that I shall follow you with a happy smile. My torment is only that they may raise their hands against you . . . I hope this will never happen, but we must be ready for everything . . . How good it is to be with

you in my thoughts! I become so excited, hot joy overflows my soul.
I see your lovely, sweet smile and feel with all my being that you are
with me, that you love me. I have come into this world only to meet
and love you, and I began to love life only after I found you and
your love.

All I want is that we shall be calm, that we do not worry too much,
needlessly. Most of all I want this for you, and I beg you, my love, to
think only of the boundless joy with which you have filled my life. I
bless not only Arshan and Angara days but also the days of torment
and worry because these were torment and worry for you. Not only
in the past but also in the future shall I willingly accept all the hardships if I can be with you, love you, and have your love.

Returning home, I found the letter from Wolik, mailed a day before
by our medical friend:

Today, my darling, we learned of the murder of Shingarev and
Kokoshkin. So terrible! Yet the day is so bright, so sunny . . .

A storm of madness and bestiality is over us. Our love is like a
flower in the field under a heavy wind, a roaring storm. Will the
storm sweep us out of existence, destroy us? Or will we survive? I do
not know. But one thing I do know: In you is the achievement and
the justification of my life, in you my happiness, my pride, my joy.
Through all the hardships, through pain, agony, even through fail-
ures I was going to you. I reached the highest point in life when I
met you, fell in love with you, when my soul merged with yours . . .

Two months later, at his release, the first thing Wolik did was to pull
that little package out of his pocket. We immediately destroyed it. Some
fifteen years later, I met Dr. Manukhin at a public gathering in Paris,
and he asked with a broad grin, "No more need for those unhealthy
packages?"

On my next visit, Wolik told me that some soldiers in the Fortress had
been so shocked by the lynching of Shingarev and Kokoshkin that two of
them had come to him and disclosed that there was an underwater tunnel leading to the Neva River and that, in the event of an attack on him
and his friends, they would lead them to the tunnel. I went to Abram
Gotz, of whom I wrote earlier. He was in hiding and his wife bedridden,
but he was ready to help me plan Wolik's escape from the Fortress via
the tunnel. We discussed all the ways to get the right boat and to
synchronize it with the time when Wolik and possibly somebody else
could appear at the end gate of the tunnel.

Maxim Gorki, the popular Russian writer, whose opinion counted with
the Communists and, most importantly, with Lenin, wrote the latter asking for Wolik's release. From the Southwestern Front, not yet in the hands
of the Communists, came a resolution demanding his release and carrying a great number of signatures.

Then I learned that the trial of a moderate Socialist and the treasurer of the Executive Committee of the All-Russian Soviet, L. M. Bramson, had been scheduled. I went to the trial. Communist power had not yet been consolidated, and except for arrests and occasional assassinations, there was no real, all-pervasive terror, such as spread through Russia later. Most of the opposition newspapers had been suspended, but some still appeared with criticisms of Communist rule. All Government employees were on strike to protest the *coup d'état*. This transitional state of affairs was evident in the conduct of the Bramson trial. The "judges" were confused and embarrassed; only the chairman of the court spoke, and he was rude, repeating over and over again, "I shall take vigorous measures" against the protesting public, or giving the order "Clear the court!" Nobody moved, and the guards, surrounded by spectators who made them ashamed of their role, were confused and tried to defend themselves by saying, "We are ordered . . ." Taking advantage of the situation, we remained in the court room.

The charge against Bramson was that instead of delivering the funds of the old Executive Committee of the All-Russian Soviet to the new Government, he had turned them over to the organization fighting the latter. Several witnesses testified, and though the chairman cut off each of them at some point, some succeeding in saying more, some less, all testified to Bramson's democratic past and his honesty and integrity. Some compared the new regime with the Tsarist days, when, too, Bramson had been in disfavor. The high point of the proceedings was the courageous speech by Bramson himself, who accused the Communists of usurping power under false promises to bring peace, freedom, and bread to the people. The result was that the court did not dare to sentence Bramson and limited itself to expressing its moral disapproval. Bramson was free to leave the court.

This trial gave me the idea of trying to get Wolik before the court. I was sure I could easily get many workers and soldiers in St. Petersburg to testify about his revolutionary past and his years in prison for his efforts to make Russia free. I went to the Ministry of Justice to get information on his case. Because all Government employees were on strike to protest the *coup d'état*, the building was empty except for a lone guard, the Minister, and his Deputy. The last two were members of the left wing of the Socialist Revolutionary Party who had supported the Communists from the beginning.

I knocked at the door of the Minister, Mr. I. Schreiber. In answering my question, he called Wolik "comrade." I interrupted him sharply, "My husband is not a comrade of you and your Government." He spread his arms helplessly and said, "If you talk this way . . . Anyhow, your husband's case is in the hands of Comrade Schreider, the Assistant Minister." He sent me to him.

Schreider told me that Wolik might have been liberated except that the Fortress garrison might become so indignant over his release that his life would be imperiled. Still under the impact of the lynching of two members of the Provisional Government, I was outraged by this official hypocrisy and I said savagely, "Oh yes, his life will be in danger if you repeat what was done with Shingarev and Kokoshkin. If you incite the mob and stand by to watch the murder, anything can happen. But give me the order for release, and I shall have not the slightest fear of any so-called spontaneous indignation from the garrison. He will walk out with me safe and alive."

He said shortly, "I will visit the Fortress tonight, and we shall see what can be done."

He did go there that night, entered the cell of Wolik and his friends, and reached out his hand in greeting. All of them held back their hands. That was the end of that story.

THE SECOND BLOODY SUNDAY

The session of the Constituent Assembly was to open on January 5, 1918 (old calendar). Not even the Communists dared to cancel the elections. They had claimed, among other pretexts, that they had overthrown the Provisional Government because the latter would not hold elections. Despite the suspension of the opposition press, especially in the provinces, and the curtailment of free meetings, the will of the people was unmistakably clear: The Communists received only about 25 per cent of the votes; nearly all the rest had gone to the moderate Socialists.

People gathered in the streets to head for the Tauride Palace, the seat of the Assembly, in order to greet the arriving delegates and to show the feelings of the capital's populace. The Communists were prepared: They placed machine guns on the roofs of tall buildings close to the Tauride Palace. As soon as we came under them, the machine guns began to click. We continued on, though some marchers were hit. Shells began to fall on all sides, and many were wounded, many killed. We tried to take cover for a few minutes, but as soon as the shelling stopped, we reassembled. Then the machine guns started cracking again, and did not cease until the demonstration was broken up. I know I was not too brave, or I would have been among the victims. If Wolik had been with me, it would have been different. Emotionally, my hatred was so great that I was ready for anything so far as I was concerned, but I could not leave Wolik alone in the Fortress . . . And so when other people scattered and left the streets, I did the same. I do not remember how many were killed or wounded, but a historical parallel is interesting. Shelling of a peaceful, unarmed demonstration has occurred twice in the Russian capital—on Bloody Sunday, January 9, 1905, by Tsarist troops, and on January 5, 1918, by Communist troops.

Wolik's letter was waiting for me on my return home. He asked me not to join in the demonstration without him. It was too late, but I felt I had demonstrated for him and, in my thoughts, with him. I wrote to him that I had gone, adding:

You told me yesterday that now you know what it means to worry about the beloved. I know this only too well. If I did not have to worry in Irkutsk, I have had my full share of torment and fear for you since last February. While you talked to me yesterday, I thought of the long, sleepless nights when I listened to every rustle on the stairs, every movement in the hall, to the noise of passing cars. Nights when I stared into the darkness of the streets and waited for you; nights when I went to bed, then got up, opened the window. Sometimes I fell asleep, but even in sleep I felt when you approached the house, knew almost without fail when you returned. Do you recall that I always opened the door before you rang the bell?

I remember how I worried when for the first time you came home late in the morning. I was so upset, I walked aimlessly about the room, tried to be calm but could not; horrible pictures moved before my eyes . . . And Riga! Your trip to the rioting regiment, the days of retreat . . . Sheer nightmare! I do not remember a thing except that all the time I kept my hand close to my heart—I was afraid it would break . . . Then Pskov, your trips to the front. I was never free from worry, even when you were with me. But the worst were the last days when you left for Luga. I shall never forget those ten days. In that atmosphere of general anxiety, general excitement, at times superseded by hopelessness, all kinds of rumors were born, false but frightening rumors. I was afraid to listen to them, afraid to hear something about you, afraid to look at people who came for fear of reading the terrible news on their faces. I was afraid to think, to ask, being sure that we would be swept out of existence . . . There were people about me from morning till morning; nobody slept. There were all sorts of things to be done. Everyone was surprised at my "calm," balanced mood, my apparent lack of fatigue. I had to reassure people, talk to the delegations, answer the telegrams, negotiate . . . I do not know from whence came the strength to do all that—I thought only of you . . .

The Constituent Assembly, the old dream of the progressive movement and the Socialists in Russia, was dissolved the very day it convened. After that, the gates were wide open to civil war, terror, and anarchy. A week later, I wrote to Wolik:

Life is oppressive. The news lies like a heavy stone on one's soul. No gleam of hope . . . Before one's eyes pictures of violence and senseless cruelty, pictures of incredible savagery . . . The quarrel of the sailors over the leather jacket on the lynched body of Shingarev, the senseless murder of the artist Valua after he was robbed . . . Hatred, beastly hatred of everything that is great and noble . . . The shameless conditions of the peace treaty with Germany and the complete indifference on the part of the people. . . .

Nadya told me that she had received many presents this month. I bragged and said, "I, too, have had wonderful presents—twenty letters from Wolik."

Wolik, too, was depressed and disheartened:

I think of the destruction of the values that were at the base of the political struggle and created so much enthusiasm. To me, that destruction is the most telling, the most terrible expression of the disillusionment in which we find ourselves. *All* the ideals, *all* the political values of democracy are humiliated, desecrated, vilified—the rule of the people, free elections, the republic, freedom itself, the Constituent Assembly. Everything is reflected in the distorted mirror of Bolshevism in so wicked and ugly a light that it arouses disgust and scorn . . . Perhaps I would have felt this less painfully, less sharply, if my attitude toward political life were, as behooves a person in politics, to look at everything with a cold mind and firmly relate all special situations to a definite, unchangeable, once-and-forever established evaluation of the historical process. Such, for example, is the attitude of Tseretelli, and in this is his strength. He is organically incapable of doubting the Revolution. But I cannot calm my doubts by logical arguments and well-composed conclusions and thus reaffirm the shaking evaluations. In recent days, I have talked about this with the friends in the Fortress. Most of them agree with me, though some find my formulations too sharp. But even when they agree, their attitude toward the events is different from mine—they *see* the disaster, I *feel* it. To them the catastrophe is something that happens *outside,* to me it is *inside.*

You remember, I wrote once about "epos" and "lyricism." "Epos" is struggle in all its forms, of which the highest and purest expression is political heroism. "Lyricism" is the personal, inner life, and its highest expression is love. Before I met you, my life was only "epos," without any "lyricism," and I felt myself unneeded, superfluous in the world. Arshan and Angara are "lyricism" without any addition of "epos," and they have been the happiest days of my life. The eight months of the Revolution have been a test period for our love. I am apparently incapable of achieving a synthesis of "epos" and "lyricism"—the bustle from outside had invaded our life and deafened me. But now "epos" has shown itself to be a bloody farce, ugly, unnecessary, while the beauty of "lyricism" shines with renewed brilliance as the uniquely true eternal force of life.

4. Defending Georgia

In every letter we planned what we would do when Wolik was free again. We hoped that we would then have several months for ourselves—as Wolik suggested, to live with "the sun, the sky, our love, and without people around." Finally, on January 16, 1918, he was told that he might be released shortly. After a few days of waiting, I could no longer contain myself. I decided to go to the Fortress, though it was not the regular day for seeing Wolik. I was told this at the office, but before I turned to leave, one of the soldiers whispered to me, "Wait! Your husband and some others will be released shortly." About an hour later, Wolik and five or six of his friends came out. We walked quietly and calmly through several courts. Several soldiers looked at us with curiosity, but there was no sign of "spontaneous" indignation over the release of the "people's enemies." Finally, we were outside the Fortress. Not a droshky in sight, and all of the men had suitcases with books and clothing. I suggested they wait, and ran for several blocks, finding first one droshky, then another, and finally one for us. One friend, Bruderer, a Swiss born in Russia and a member of the Socialist Revolutionary Party, had no place to go, and so we took him to our home. (Later, during the civil war, he was killed by Kolchak's officers in Siberia.)

We had one day of bliss—together again! Mother and Nadya came to share our happiness. I bought tickets for *Faust* with Chaliapin, whom Wolik had never heard. But in the trolley, I began to be afraid. Several people had recognized him. I heard his name spoken and did not know if these were friends or enemies. In the opera, our seats were in a front row, and we found ourselves among sailors from Kronstadt. The moment we sat down, I saw agitation about us, heard Wolik's name, then, "How did he get out?" One man rose from his seat, saying, "I shall check with Smolny." I was terrified. As soon as the curtain went up and Chaliapin appeared, I pulled Wolik's arm and we left.

Early next morning, Nadya came to tell us that she had learned via the grapevine that Wolik was to be rearrested; some important Communists disapproved of his release. Where could we go? We called up his Aunt Rose, who owned a library open to the public. She lived in the same quarters, situated at the corner of two streets. The entrance to the library was on one street, to her private rooms, on the other. She suggested barricading the door between her own rooms and the library with a large wardrobe so that we could stay with her unnoticed.

WE GO TO GEORGIA

Several days later, Tseretelli let us know that a military hospital train with Georgian soldiers and officers was leaving for the Caucasus and asked whether we would go with him to Georgia, which was under the control of the Mensheviks. We decided to take this opportunity. Wolik disguised himself so well by shaving off his mustache, cropping his hair, and putting on patched soldier's trousers, a soldier's torn coat, and a military cap that, on opening the door to him, I did not recognize him and became frightened when he asked in an assumed voice for the whereabouts of Wolik. I carried the papers of an army nurse.

The trip took about three weeks instead of the normal two days. Again I was crossing Russia—not alone among soldiers, as I had done at the outbreak of the war, but with Wolik, my heart overflowing with joy that he was free and safe. We both despaired at what we saw around us. At each station, there were soldiers in coats without shoulder straps, soldiers selling cigarettes and matches, selling bread, selling shoe laces and wax, soldiers with bags on their backs—everywhere soldiers who had deserted the front and had been drawn into the vortex of speculation with the protection of appropriated rifles and even machine guns. The same soldiers who had been so humane, so decent, toward a defenseless girl less than four years before now looked like outlaws, rough, arrogant, hateful. They descended on our train at nearly every stop, searched for arms which nobody had, confiscated whatever they wanted —all this "in the name of the Revolution." There was no point in asking them to show the search warrant: They had none and needed none. Who could the passengers be but "the people's enemies" running away from the center of the revolution toward the south, where the opposition was concentrated? At nearly every station, we saw trains carrying soldiers and machine guns, carrying cannons to the villages "just in case." The ghost of civil war faced us at every turn with blood, hatred, senseless violence, spiteful speech and action. Russia was crisscrossed by fronts.

At some stations, we were held up for eight or ten hours for a check of our papers and a search; at others, we waited until the men from our train loaded wood into the locomotives. At each station, there were long negotiations; we elected a committee to carry them on. Our ambulance car had some alcohol, and the committee used it to treat the station authorities in order to get the green light for our train. There was no law, no rule; at any station, we might be arrested or attacked as "counterrevolutionaries" at the whim of a soldier, a station master, anybody, or we might be left in peace.

Once our train started to move before our "guests" had returned to their offices, and a telegram went ahead of us to hold the train that had "kidnaped" the revolutionary commissars of the station. Our train was shunted to a siding at the next station and surrounded by machine guns. We were ordered to alight. The "misunderstanding" was clarified when the revolutionary heroes appeared, safe but tipsy. At another station, we found everybody upset by rumors that the Cossacks were approaching, ready to attack. The soldiers and officers in our train were told that they were to be armed to march against the Cossacks. The alternative was for them to be arrested, and the train to be requisitioned. After a consultation, our committee agreed under the condition that women, children, and sick (Tseretelli and the two of us were to be counted among the sick) would be protected until the return of our men from battle. Negotiations went on for hours, but when it came to supplying the men with arms, the station authorities decided it would be much safer to let our train proceed. We went on, changing our routes to avoid large cities, retracing our itinerary here and there. South of Rostov, our train was finally requisitioned or "exchanged" for several passenger cars and a safe-conduct to Tuapse, the nearest port on the Black Sea and the terminal of the railroad.

Tseretelli's friends met us at Tuapse and took us to their house for the night. To get to Georgia, we had to go by ship. Although the Black Sea fleet was in the hands of the Communists, it was still safer to be passengers on a boat than to try to cross the Caucasus, with its many fronts. We hesitated; sailors were raiding the ships and the shores. They fired on the coastal cities and towns, arrested the mayors, imposed ransoms, took hostages. Yet Tseretelli's friends suggested that we should disguise ourselves as best we could and entrust our lives to the pirates if we wanted to reach Georgia. They assured us that paying passengers had not been mistreated.

We embarked in the morning and went down to the cabin, intending to stay there until we arrived at Batum. But the ship stopped at Sukhum, a lovely subtropical city. Wolik and I could not resist the temptation and, with other passengers, went ashore. We had been there less than an hour when Sukhum was suddenly bombarded from the sea. We rushed back to our boat only to learn that the salvos had come from it! How safe could we feel in the hands of that crew!

Finally, we anchored in the harbor of Batum, underwent inspection of luggage and papers, and were on the mainland, in Georgia. We again breathed the air of freedom!

IN GEORGIA

That same day we reached Tiflis (now Tbilisi), a city with a very long history. During the 1,500 years of its existence, it has been subjected to many rulers—the Khozars, Huns, Byzantinians, Persians, Mongols, Arabs, Turks-Osmans, Turks-Seldjuks, and since 1799, the Russians. Above Tiflis towers the monastery of St. David, built in the sixth century, a popular attraction for excursions.

Though we were still in Russia, we encountered much in Transcaucasia that was new to us—languages, costumes, customs. Apart from the Russians, there were three main national groups in the area—Georgians, Armenians, and Tatars. There were also Ossets, descendants of a Samaritan tribe who spoke an Iranian language, Abkhasis, Adzhars, and other small tribes. Walking in the street, one might suddenly meet someone who seemed to have stepped out of an ancient carving, such as an Assyrian with a spade-shaped, long, wavy beard.

We were met with great friendliness, even more, with real warmth. Many political leaders had known Wolik or had heard of him, and our friendship with Tseretelli, who was universally loved and admired, meant a great deal to the Georgians. Invitations came from all sides. The festive ceremonies at the dining table were novel to us. Meals were often served in the garden, and the garden path was decorated with roses strewn along it. There were roses everywhere—men wore them in their lapels, soldiers had them on their rifles, fruit stands displayed them, even the butchers stuck them into the hanging carcasses. At table, the very light domestic wine was served as water is served in northern areas. The host noticed that we did not empty our glasses but only sipped from them and had ordered the wine served to us in horns, which we had to empty. When Wolik did not permit his horn to be refilled, the toastmaster, who had been offering one toast after another, was very much disappointed. He sighed and said resignedly, "Then we shall all drink water."

Transcaucasia, and we with it, was undergoing a difficult time. It had not recognized the Communist *coup d'état* in Petrograd and had its own government, consisting of representatives of the three main nationalities. Unfortunately, these were united only in their refusal to accept the Communist seizure of power, and they disagreed on many other essential points—most importantly, on foreign policy. The Tatars, Moslem by religion, leaned toward the Turks, traditional enemies of the Armenians. The Georgians, too, felt themselves in imminent danger, abandoned by the new Russian Government without arms in face of the powerful Turkish army.

In the nearly eight months we stayed in Tiflis, one dramatic event followed another. Russia concluded a peace treaty with Turkey under which it ceded to that country two Armenian districts and the port of Batum. This new situation sharpened the tensions within the Transcaucasian government, which then dissolved Transcaucasia into three independent republics—Georgia, Armenia, and Azerbeidzhan. We were closely associated with Georgia, its fortunes and troubles, its main party, the Social Democrats, and its political leaders, Tseretelli, Jordania, Chkheidze.

To prevent the entrance of Turkish troops into Georgia, the government asked Germany, the ally of Turkey, to take over the safeguarding of the Georgian railroads. The German soldiers came, and though they did not interfere in any way with the internal politics of the country, everyone felt their presence as an occupation force. Soon Germany was defeated by the Allies, the Germans left quietly, and the British, in turn, occupied Georgia. Meanwhile, civil war in Russia became more and more violent, and Georgia was menaced by both extreme political parties—the Whites and the Reds.

"Epos" again took hold of us. We could not be in the center of Georgia's turbulent political life without becoming involved emotionally and intellectually. The fate of Russia troubled us very much, and we maintained as close contacts with events in the North as the conditions of civil war permitted. Of course, all our earlier dreams for ourselves had evaporated. We started working a day or two after our arrival— Wolik as chief editor of *Bor'ba* (*Struggle*), the official Government daily in Russian, and I as its executive secretary.

Jordania, President of the Republic of Georgia, whose apartment was on the same floor of a Government building as our office, came in occasionally to tell us the latest news or suggest an editorial. We had an assistant editor, Datico Sharashidze, and a literary critic, Leo Kremer. Datico, intelligent, well-bred, with a certain subtlety in his attitudes and a shyness toward Wolik, provided most helpful, intimate knowledge of Georgian politics and personalities. He was a good writer but could not be pressed to do a rush job when the necessity arose. Leo was brilliant; some of his literary essays were exceptionally good. Though he was a son of a governor of a large province in the east of Russia, he looked like a little clerk; nothing in his appearance betrayed his education or talent. His trouble was that he drank, and his constitution apparently could not take what a person with greater physical stamina could easily have handled. This failing created many awkward situations.

One morning, for example, a visitor asked for the editor of *Bor'ba*. He was directed to Wolik. He sat down and said, "Yesterday that window, mister!" "What?" asked Wolik. "The broken window, don't you remember?" "What are you talking about? I don't remember anything." Gradually it became clear to Wolik that Leo, completely drunk, had broken the window in some shop and afterward had fallen asleep on the sidewalk. When the police arrived, he identified himself as the editor of *Bor'ba*, so that the shop owner was sure that he was talking to the right person. His claim was settled, but though we laughed to hear Wolik tell the story, the incident was rather embarrassing for an official newspaper. Leo's wife was a proud Georgian girl, and his little boy was charming. We became very good friends and hated to see Leo's salary wasted while the family needed it badly. Yet we could not suggest that it be paid to his wife—she would have been more deeply offended than he. Several times he promised me he would go straight home with his pay, but next morning his guilty smile told me that he again had squandered the money.

The four of us worked very harmoniously. Wolik carried the heaviest load. I handled administrative and financial matters, gradually acquainting myself with the intricacies of a daily paper. Most of all, I appreciated the fact that in this work Wolik and I could be together. Like any newspaper, *Bor'ba* provided not only excitement, anxiety, and pressure but also amusement. Once a woman came in with a letter that she wanted us to print. I read it; it was nothing but gossip about her neighbor. I told her that *Bor'ba* was a political daily and had no space for personal affairs. She insisted belligerently, and I tried again to explain why we could not publish the letter. Furious, she tossed at me, "This is your vaunted freedom of the press!" and slammed the door. An old man once opened the office door when I was alone, said loudly, "Nobody in!," and left.

INTERLUDES OF PEACE

Despite the heavy pressure of work, we had moments of pure "lyricism," when we escaped for a few days from Tiflis. The scenery of the Caucasus overwhelmed us—majestic mountains piercing the sky, mysterious canyons, sparkling waterfalls, luxurious vegetation, a wealth of sun-kissed flowers. Late in July, we went to a resort, Borzhom, and fell under the spell of its severe grandeur. Steep mountain walls covered with dense forests surrounded us and hid us from all that was dark and painful in the world. We felt that in that closed amphitheater of precipitous peaks, peace returned to us, peace that we had not known during that long, agitated year. Peace, but not that jubilant merriment that filled us in Arshan! It was not easy to throw off the thoughts and worries about what was happening around us, to isolate ourselves from the rest of the world.

Our favorite walk in Borzhom was to the waterfall. We would sit there listening to its murmur, watching its frolics. In my diary I wrote:

> Mermaids danced to the unceasing music of the running, jumping water. I saw them very distinctly—their long hair fluttering in all directions, their smiling, lovely faces, their frisky, playful leaps. With fantastic ease, almost without touching the stony bottom, they ran down, while on the top appeared new chains of dancers. I saw them embrace one another, heard them clicking their hands in tune with the music . . . I watched them until my eyes got tired . . .
>
> I closed my eyes for a minute—and the waterfall changed completely. Now I saw riders, rushing, hurrying so as not to be late. I heard the clatter of swords, the thud of horses, and the bugler who played his bugle luringly, as if he put his heart into it. It seemed as if a powerful, menacing army had darted out of the mountain's cleft. Confident of its invincible strength, it advanced cheerfully, laughingly, against the enemy. That movement was so enticing, it lured one into its stream so strongly that I wanted to join it, to jump on a horse and ride ahead with that fearless host!

In those few restful days in Borzhom I again became young and breathless with happiness; again people called me the "sunny girl," and one elderly man whose name I do not even recall blessed me for the "cheer you brought into my life." When we came back, some acquaintances asked me on the street, "How are you?" At my unthinking "Splendid," they stopped surprised and said, "This is the first time in my life I have got such an answer." At home we were again full of laughter, and Wolik was unceasing fun!

About a month later, Jordania asked us to go with him to Abbas-Tumani, a small resort in the mountains. The winding road climbed in wide zigzags through the darkness of a dense forest. As we drove up and up, the trees became smaller, even crooked, and then with one long curve we were on a wide stretch of grass. The air was invigorating. We were told that it was considered healing for persons afflicted with tuberculosis. Before the Revolution, that area had belonged to one of the grand dukes and had been closed to the public. Now the abandoned buildings had been transformed into a retreat.

We spent about ten days there—time enough to transform our amicable relations with Jordania into a real friendship. To me, it was natural that he showed much more interest in Wolik than in me, and I was perfectly satisfied to listen to their talks without sharing in their stimulating conversation. Yet without my noticing when, how, and why, Jordania began to sense that Wolik and I were not separable and, little by little, he built up a special attitude of friendship and great courtesy toward me.

Two more couples came to the retreat: We had our meals together. In the evening, too, Wolik and I were with the others, because the bedrooms did not have electric light and it was impossible to read in them. Though we relaxed and had fun in Abbas-Tumani, I did not bring back from that stay as much buoyancy as I did from Borzhom.

In Abbas-Tumani, I did nothing of consequence except prepare three meals a day for the crowd (visitors for Jordania came unannounced every day) and manage the household so as to provide some degree of comfort and even official decorum amid the most primitive conditions. Wolik did what he liked best, sat outdoors, facing magnificent scenery, and worked either outlining a book or article or writing that very book or article. While there, he wrote a short novel* that reflected his mood at the time, a mood that recurred from time to time in which he felt a deep, painful awareness of the lack of understanding between the "people" and the intellectuals. In that novel, he wrote of a young revolutionary idealist, willing to sacrifice his life and to endure hardships for the freedom and well-being of the people. He described his humiliations in prison, his suffering from the lack of true contact with people around him, the cold indifference of the populace in the area to which he was deported, and then his last days before execution, filled with despair from the realization of how little he had achieved and how little happiness there had been in his life.

There was much in the mood of the novel's hero that occasionally took hold of Wolik himself. It was present in him subconsciously, and

* *Na Poslednem Etape (At the Last Station)* (Berlin: Mysl', 1922).

when a situation was conducive to low spirits, it moved into the area of consciousness. Nobody else noticed it, but I recognized it instantly. At the first danger signal, it was a challenge for our love to meet head on, to fill every moment with its radiance so that everything else would appear of no consequence. In Abbas-Tumani, the clouds disintegrated rather rapidly.

THE TSAR'S "LIBRARY"

We got another chance to be alone during a week we spent in Zinandali, at what had been one of the Tsar's estates. I do not know whether the Tsar ever visited that modest palace, but the wine it produced was well known in Russia. In contrast to Abbas-Tumani, this estate was situated in a more accessible region. The main building, located in a beautiful English-type park with acres of well-kept lawn, had large rooms with balconies from which the view stretched to the horizon.

We were alone and needed to be alone, to feel our closeness and the continuous fusing of our beings, and to draw strength from this closeness in order to face the uncertain and troubled future. To be alone, at least for a short while, in order to feel the full intensity of our love, to drink from that vivifying, life-giving source. We walked along the alleys lined by cypresses, basked in the sun on the lawn, sat in the evening on the balcony to watch the gold-covered mountains during the sunset. The southern sky is dark at night, almost black, but the stars shimmer the more brilliantly, and the fireflies, millions of them around us, seemed the brighter. There were no newspapers, and we had taken only two books of poems with us. Wolik knew many poems by heart, some of them ten or more pages long. I loved to listen as he recited them in the quiet of the night.

We were the only guests. The manager of the estate was the old appointee, probably opposed to the Socialist Government but glad not to have been fired. So he was courteous and tried to please the unfamiliar new owners. He showed us around and asked whether we would like to visit the Tsar's library. Intrigued, we said, "Yes, of course!"

Next morning, he came to take us there, accompanied by a friend of his. We walked for a while and reached a building with slanting sides covered by sod and reminiscent of an old-fashioned ice house. The front door, crossed by iron bars, looked impressive. The manager unlocked it with an enormous key, and we entered a long, dark corridor. When our eyes got used to the darkness, we saw, on both sides, shelves full of wine bottles. A few minutes later, we found ourselves in a large, windowless room, with a round, conference-type table in its center and huge, comfortable leather armchairs. This was the Tsar's "library"—a wine cellar with bottles of wine from different vintage years!

A butler brought a basket with the bottle of wine ordered by the manager after an animated discussion between the two men. He poured a little in the huge glasses on the table. Wishing to be pleasant, Wolik and

I each took a sip and said with satisfaction in our voices, "Very fine wine, indeed!" Both men gave us killing glances that replied clearly enough, "Such ignoramuses now rule the country!" Realizing the depths of our downfall, we said nothing more and observed the unfolding of the ritual. The manager lifted his glass and, holding it high in the air, breathed in its bouquet and declared contentedly, "You can just feel its age, its gray hair, so to speak." He put his glass down without having touched it with his lips. Then the other man repeated the motion, said, "Right you are," and recalled the special features of various harvest years, the quality of this or that type of grape. The conversation shifted to particularly successful blends, the two connoisseurs, or "degustators," as they were called in Russia, completely forgetting our presence. We felt out of place and waited impatiently for a fitting moment to interrupt the reminiscences without appearing rude.

From the "library," we drove to the vineyards on the mountain slopes. The manager called a foreman and said something to him. Soon two workers appeared with a simple wooden table, which they covered with grape leaves. Then on each leaf, they put a different bunch of grapes—round, long, pink, purple, green, black. I do not recall exactly how many different bunches there were, perhaps fifteen or more. In the center was a huge bunch, every grape larger than a walnut. We were told that the fruit was not edible but purely decorative, to be used as a centerpiece on a dining table.

ON THE INTERNATIONAL FRONT

Probably the days in Zinandali were our sunniest days in Georgia. When we returned to Tiflis, an unexpected task awaited us. The government of Georgia had obtained permission to present the country's case to the Versailles Conference, in order to obtain the recognition of its independence by the Great Powers, and had decided to provide the heads of the Georgian delegation, Tseretelli and Chkheidze, with a well-documented record of its foreign policy. Time was short, and Wolik was asked whether he could prepare such a report within two weeks. He thought that, working as a team, we could do this if we had the full cooperation of all agencies and the printing houses.

We worked day and night, reading thousands of documents—resolutions, records of meetings, telegrams, speeches, official declarations. Our purpose was to make a selection that would show the essential features of Georgia's foreign policy, with all its drama and urgency, beginning with the Communists' seizure of power in Petrograd in November, 1917. We did not withhold a single item of importance because it was secret or controversial, nor did we change or delete a single word. Instead of a typist, we engaged an elderly couple in our block to copy our material in longhand. They had lost everything they possessed and, not wanting to accept charity, were only too happy to do the job. Reading and checking their work was a little more time-consuming than handling typewritten pages, but they kept pace with our work, and seeing their friendly smiles was worth something, too!

The documents selected formed a book of more than 500 printed pages. To publish it quickly, we used three printing houses and they worked in three shifts. Though the fonts of type they used were different, the book, ready ten days after we had started, made a great impression because of both its content and the speed with which it had been prepared. Jordania immediately asked us to join the delegation to the Conference.

Our trip to Paris was interrupted by visa complications at Constantinople. They were supposed to last only a few days, but months passed before we were informed finally that the French Government did not care to admit us. It was as blind politically as those today to whom any liberal, any Socialist, is a Communist. We planned our time as soon as we realized that we would have a long stay at Constantinople. Wolik began to write a book on Georgia and articles for *Bor'ba;* I translated chapters of the book into French. Outside our hotel, we walked in history. Constantinople is one of the four pillars of Western civilization, along with Athens, Rome, and Jerusalem. We fell under the spell of the city, with its superb location, its magnificent mosques including the wonderful St. Sophie, the walls around the city, the fortresses on both sides of the Bosphorus, the colorful markets loaded with beautiful handiwork.

No sooner had we returned from Constantinople to Tiflis than we were asked to join the Georgian delegation to Italy. We did not want to repeat our tedious visa difficulties, and agreed to go to Rome only if the Italian Government would express its desire to have us come. This was arranged, and despite some annoying incidents on the way there, we reached Italy safely as the guests of the Italian Government. Wolik was the economic consultant of the delegation, and my work was in the field of information and the press.

Italian journalists considered Georgia an exotic land and regarded nearly every Georgian who came to Italy as a prince. They refused to believe that I was not a princess, since my black hair and dark eyes fitted their image of an Oriental princess. Several asked me why I insisted on pretending I was not. Russia, of course, was a savage land, and when I happened to mention Siberia, the first question was about bears. Though there may still be some people even in advanced countries who do not know much more about Russia, and especially about Georgia, I was surprised, and tried my best to explain the complexities of the political situation in those countries.

The reporters wrote of me as a Georgian princess, and their story reached my family in Russia in a distorted version, causing them great worry. I learned of this when, after many years during which we could not communicate, we succeeded in re-establishing contact. Mark, my older brother, then wrote me how happy he was that I was alive. "Some idiot from Tiflis told me," he said, "that Wolik had married a Georgian

princess, and he did not know anything about you. From this we concluded that you must have died and that Wolik had married for the
second time."

At the receptions given our delegation by the members of the government, Wolik was always surrounded by a crowd interviewing him, asking his opinion on the future of Russia, of the world. Being an exotic
curiosity and the first woman in a diplomatic mission, I got my share of
attention. We did not speak Italian, but nearly everybody spoke French,
so there was no problem of communication.

Italy was in a state of bewilderment—emotional, intellectual, political. Economic conditions were chaotic. We met many people, from
members of the Government and leaders of political parties to academic
people, businessmen, journalists. Our general impression was that, despite the decades of parliamentary government and the high cultural
level, the Italian people could easily become a prey of demagoguery.
The political parties were split into several factions; mutual recrimina-
tions and rumors poisoned the air. In which direction would the Italian
ship turn?

In leisure hours, we went sightseeing. The charm of Rome, of Italy,
was irresistible. That comparatively small country has filled the museums of the whole world with products of its art, yet it still possesses
an inexhaustible supply. Rome fascinated us, and this fascination is as
vivid to me today as it was some forty years ago. We spent much time
in the Forum, reliving Roman history from period to period; we visited
the Vatican many times to see every part of it without haste; we climbed
the narrow, winding stairs in many churches to see Rome from the
steeples, and never tired of it; we went to the museums, strolled
through the streets, rested on staircases and at fountains.

MY FIGHT FOR LIFE

When climbing and walking, I felt some pain in the stomach but believing it nothing serious, I did not mention it, not wanting to worry Wolik
or keep him from enjoying Rome. The pain was worse on his birthday,
which we started with a visit to the Sistine Chapel in the Vatican, after
which we went to the home of Italian friends for lunch. I held out until
we returned to the hotel.

Then began a months-long fight for life—operations, a struggle between hope for recovery and despair, discomfort, anguish. I developed
peritonitis and underwent a major operation; a relapse, with a recur-
rence of peritonitis, making another operation imperative, then several
more.

This was a trying time for both of us, but particularly for Wolik. It is
always more painful and heartbreaking for the one who must watch
helplessly when a loved one suffers. Wolik spent the whole day in my
little hospital room, returning to the delegation only for the evening conferences or emergency meetings. It was hot, there was no air condition-

ing, of course (I do not remember if there was even a fan), and a hospital could not provide the refreshments available in a hotel. Wolik worked at a table put in specially for him, prepared the reports for the delegation and the government in Tiflis, wrote articles for *Bor'ba* and the Italian newspapers. This work was frequently interrupted by the doctors and nurses who changed my bandages, took my temperature, and so on.

Wolik brought me newspapers and magazines, beautiful books on Italian art, flowers, and all kinds of amusing curios that he could pick up on the way to the hospital. To stress his complete confidence in my recovery, he brought me lovely scarfs, embroidered blouses, silk for dresses. He made plans for trips to various parts of Italy when I would be strong enough for travel and sightseeing, read me descriptions of various cities and their museums. He filled my day with every possible kind of care and attention that his loving heart could suggest. To divert me from sad thoughts, he pantomimed for me the meetings of the delegation, read poetry, drew amusing cartoons.

Some excerpts from pencil-scribbled notes in my diary tell of my feelings and mood:

> When I see with what anxiety and fear Wolik opens the door to my room in the hospital, I want to cry . . . I want to live; with all the strength of youth and love, I want to live. But even stronger than this desire is the fear of leaving Wolik alone in the world. I feel so clearly that he cannot live without me, that he will not be able to stand the loneliness . . . If I were alone and Wolik's worried eyes were not looking at me with such grief and such boundless love, I could have stopped that suffering long ago. For what do I endure these pains, this agony? But for even a moment I cannot think of that while Wolik is beside me all day long with his tenderness and care. Even though I am motionless in bed, he is not completely alone, he still hopes to see me well again. Can I destroy this hope? I am ready to take anything that may come for his sake, but it is so hard to accept the illusion of his hopes, the uselessness of my agony . . .
>
> Later. I have just reread pages shining with happiness and joy of our love . . . I am thankful with all my heart for the happiness I have found in life and am ever ready to pay for it with my life . . .
>
> They have begun to treat me by exposing me to the sun, and this has revived my faith in recovery. The sun will help, will heal me; I always loved it. I have often been called the sunny girl, told that I was full of sun, that it shone in me. Now I turn to the sun and hope to get back to health and life with its help.
>
> Early morning . . . I look back at the life lived with Wolik . . . In it is that perfect merging of which I always dreamed, in it I see complete purity, happiness, and love. Though I now am suffering so much for my dearest, I do feel a certain pride. With all my heart,

77831

I know that with nobody else would Wolik have been as happy as with me, that only with me has he found shining, boundless, complete happiness! . . .

My dearest, my wonderful Wolik, forgive me all the pain, all the grief that I have brought to you, and remember only our happy days together . . . I am fighting but I am so weak and I fear that I shall be beaten. I love you so much, and yet I cause you so much distress. I myself must inflict upon you that terrible sorrow . . . No, I must, I must recover. Wolik is entitled to happiness more than anybody else in the world . . .

To fill the long days and months in the hospital, I learned Italian and read a great deal, though reading in a horizontal position was not very easy. Various patients from other wards visited me, and our low-voiced conversations did not bother Wolik in his work. The visit of the Queen to the hospital was a special event. She had been born in Russia and so was immediately told of the *signora rusa*. We chatted in Russian, while the head of the hospital and the staff stood respectfully at her side. Much more interesting was one of the nuns who took care of me.

MADRE ELENA

The hospital personnel consisted mostly of nuns supervised by the Mother Superior, but there were also practical nurses—young girls from the villages. Nearly every one of the latter attached herself emotionally to one of the nuns who, to her, represented the most ideal image of godliness. My room was in the charge of a young nun, Madre Elena, and Giuseppina, a practical nurse, who worshiped the nun. Even in her austere garb, Madre Elena was an attractive girl. She had delicately chiseled features and was swift-moving. One could sense that she had a lively temperament, suppressed by her own will and the restrictions imposed by the order. I do not recall how long Madre Elena had been in the order before my arrival, but within the months of my stay there I noticed that her face was losing color and that she occasionally showed signs of fatigue. Giuseppina never ceased to worry about her, and it seemed to her that her idol was overburdened with work much too rough for her frail constitution. When she saw Madre Elena scrubbing the stone floor, she could not help running to me with tears streaming down her face. Yet she did not dare to show any sign of her feelings and worry to Madre Elena, who was too proud ever to complain.

One day Giuseppina told me that Madre Elena's sister had come to the hospital to bear a child and wanted to see me before she left. The sister was shocked by the change in Madre Elena's appearance and was trying to get the Mother Superior to permit her to have a physical examination by a male doctor. She told me that Madre Elena had always been considered very delicate but that the family could not keep her from taking the veil when her mother died. Giuseppina was torn between the happiness of seeing Madre Elena every day and worry that if the nun continued in the hospital, she would collapse under the strain of the heavy work. I found out that Madre Elena belonged to a rich and aristocratic family and that she had not yet been ordained so that her deposits would be returned to her if she left the order. The sister came twice to talk to me, but Madre Elena never said a word about the situation. By that time Madre Elena had had the medical examination, and it had clearly established incipient tuberculosis. A further stay in the order, with its austere diet and heavy work, would inevitably result in a severe deterioration of Madre Elena's health. On the basis of that finding, the order permitted her to withdraw.

Madre Elena was still running around with the thermometer and other hospital paraphernalia as if nothing had happened. Then one night, about two o'clock, when she was sitting beside my bed, she burst out, "I don't understand Mother Superior! If I am to leave the order, I should be permitted to think of growing my hair and other things." I knew then that, in her thoughts, she was already outside. She left quietly with her sister and brother-in-law a night or two later. For about a year and a half she wrote to me, complaining that she could not find her place in the world and felt useless. To cheer her up, I replied that she could serve her God by taking care of poor children, of whom there were plenty right where she lived, that she had enough education to be a good teacher and, with her warm heart, would inspire them to develop the best in them. I sent her some stories by Leo Tolstoy and other books to cultivate her interest in real life, and also urged her to think of her health. Gradually, our correspondence began to slow down; there were longer intervals between our letters, and when we moved to Germany in the early fall of 1922, I lost touch with her completely.

I began to get better, but I was very weak. I had lost some thirty or thirty-five pounds, and when I was permitted to get out of bed, my feet would not hold me. Soon thereafter Wolik took me to Frascati, and also took Giuseppina, whom the hospital gave a leave of absence. She wheeled me up to the roof of the hotel, helped me in and out of bed, brought my meals to the room and so on. To change from the hospital to a hotel meant a return to life, an end to gloomy thoughts, and it delighted me to see Wolik's eyes again smiling, twinkling, to hear his jokes, his young laughter.

My strength returned little by little, and every day I could walk a little farther in the room. When Jordania urged us to go join the Georgian legation in Paris, the incision was still not completely healed, yet off we went.

IN FRANCE

We stayed in France for about two years. We wanted to shake off the dust of the hospital, the drugs, the bandages—in short, to forget all the anxieties of the past year and be young and happy again. Wolik was concerned about my physical debility, and I did everything I could to make him forget it. The most important thing to us was, to my mind, to perk up emotionally, to restore the gaiety that once overflowed our hearts, to feel our inner harmony.

We both started working at the Georgian legation. Wolik took over the press office, and I was his assistant. The work consisted largely of providing the French press with information about the situation in Georgia, whose independence was threatened by Soviet Russia, and of strengthening its support by the Western powers.

By chance, we found a most unusual apartment in Paris. It was the second floor of a three-story house that had once belonged to the Minister of Education and had been inherited by his daughter and son-in-law, both professors at the Sorbonne. Our floor had been used for entertaining. There was a huge living room with thirty-two comfortable chairs, a large buffet table, and on one side of the room, a full-sized billiard table. A master bedroom with an adjoining bathroom, a big kitchen, a butler's pantry, a long hall, and the maid's room completed the apartment. I recall that when the editor of *Le Temps* entered our living room, he stopped at the door and said, "I haven't seen such a living room in any apartment in Paris." We had a maid who lived in, so that my household duties consisted only of discussing the daily menu with her.

In addition to the work in the legation, Wolik published a book, *La Démocratie Géorgienne,** and wrote articles for the French press. I registered at the Alliance Française to improve my French and obtain its certificate.

In comparison with Italy, postwar France gave an impression of being deafened, prostrated. It seemed that her people could not stretch out their wings, they were still stunned. Of course, France had suffered enormously during the war, which had decimated its youthful population, destroyed entire regions, filled the air with hatred. Mothers had lost their sons; wives, their husbands. Inflation had ruined the "little" people, those who lived on a fixed income. The people bitterly resented that incredible fortunes had been piled up by war profiteers, unscrupulous businessmen. These contrasts created instability, strengthened by the intoxicating arrogance of victory. Deservedly or not, everybody snatched at the fruits of victory, wanted to have a good time at any price, for *"Le boche payera!"* (The German will pay!)

The French press disappointed, even shocked us; we found corruption, cynicism, everywhere. While visiting us, the editor of one of the largest newspapers in Paris turned the sheets of his paper and said, *"Tout ça est plus ou moins payé"* (All this is more or less paid for). Then looking at the back pages, he added, "Of course, when you take a room in a hotel, you pay more for the one that overlooks a lake or the sea than for one with windows on the back yard. Isn't this so, monsieur?"

* Paris: Librairie Alcan Lévy, 1921.

Ignorance about Russia was pathetic, except among a small group of Socialist parliamentarians who were better informed and were at least interested in what was happening there. Georgia was a kind of phantom, and we had to explain the Transcaucasian maze on many occasions, with a great deal of patience, feeling afterward that we had achieved nothing. Once, after dinner, the guests in a French house urged me to tell how we had left Russia. I tried to be as brief and matter-of-fact as possible, and the reaction of the listeners climaxed in the excited question, *"Et vos bijoux, madame?"* (And your jewelry?). None of the ladies in the room could think for a minute that I might not have had jewelry to save and that that was the last thing to worry about anyhow.

In the legation, we continued to live with the problems of the little country whose freedom we were defending against terrible odds. There was a moment when it seemed that perhaps it would manage to steer its ship of state between the Scylla of the Communist menace and the Charybdis of the world's indifference to its fate. As a result of intensive diplomatic work by the Georgian Government and its representatives abroad, the Great Powers recognized its independence *de jure*. At the celebration of this news in Tiflis on February 4, the representative of Soviet Russia congratulated the head of the Georgian Government on its country's formal entry into the group of independent nations. This gesture did not keep Soviet Russia from moving its troops against Georgia a few weeks later, and it was easy, of course, for the colossus of the north to crush the Georgian army. The Soviet Government occupied Georgia, and its elected government escaped to Paris.

The main purpose of the legation's work then became the rallying of public opinion against the occupation, of encouraging protests by various parties and groups against so blatant a violation of the principle of self-determination. But that little country, a little oasis of freedom and civilization in Transcaucasia, was too remote; it meant nothing on the chessboard of world politics, and the Great Powers, anxious to establish a modus vivendi with Soviet Russia, let Russia swallow the little nation.

We continued to work with our Georgian friends. Our salaries, like those of everybody else, were cut to the bone. Though we had a year's lease on the apartment, its owners sympathized with Georgia and let us cancel the lease. We moved to a very modest, banal apartment near the Bois de Vincennes. The landlady, who owned the house and rented the apartments furnished, could not understand why we needed a desk, "Monsieur always has a desk in his office. Who wants one at home?" When I insisted, she said, "I would even buy a desk for you, but there would be no use for it when you leave." Apparently, nobody was expected to work at home.

Since leaving Russia, we had tried again and again to get in touch with our relatives, but with no success. Then we got a letter from Wolik's mother; she was in Terioki, Finland, where his father had recently died during the occupation by the German troops. She was trying to sell the estate before leaving for Paris. Considering the political instability in Russia and Finland and wishing to have Mother with us for at least some years of peace and rest, we urged her to forget the estate (or "burn it," as we suggested) and come to us. She did sell Father's fine library, with its many handwritten books on parchment and old maps, to a German library, but could not find a buyer for the real estate. Finally, she gave in to our urgings and came to Paris. She had aged but was still active. We were very happy to have her with us and glad that we could give her the comfort she needed. She derived much pleasure from being with Wolik, from whom she had been separated for so many years by prison and exile and whom she had seen only occasionally during the revolutionary months of 1917.

Our work involved some traveling, mainly to the Socialist congresses to present the case for Georgia. The chief Georgian delegate was Tseretelli, but he always asked us to go with him. At such congresses, we met all the leaders of the European Socialist parties, and established cordial relations with some of them. Some had visited Georgia before its occupation, on the invitation of the Georgian Government, and so were rather well acquainted with the situation there. They came out openly against Soviet imperialism and demanded the liberation of Georgia. When the British trade unions held their convention in Brighton in 1921, Jordania, Tseretelli, and we went there, together with Camille Huysmans, the well-known Belgian Socialist, whom we had met before at the congress in Brussels. In England, we became acquainted with all the Socialist leaders and were invited to the home of Sidney and Beatrice Webb. It did not occur to us then that later we would be called the "Russian Webbs" or the "American Webbs." Though I have great respect for their work before their trip to Soviet Russia, where they failed completely, I do not think that our life and their "partnership," as they called their marriage, were as similar as some people believe.

It was unbelievable but true: Less than a year after I left the hospital, Wolik and I were in Saint-Gervais, in the French Alps, for a summer vacation. We hiked in the mountains as if that nightmarish year in Rome had never been. Wolik was again his old self, happy, enjoying the scenery, full of fun. As before, he insisted that I had three pairs of eyes (at least, for him): brown, green, and gray. Every morning he carefully inspected my eyes to find out which color they would be that day. He loved the gray eyes best of all and expected the day "with gray eyes" to be especially cheering. Once when we were waiting in line for tickets for the cable car taking us to the Mer de Glace, a Frenchman behind us, wanting to please Wolik by paying me a compliment, said to him, "Your daughter is charming." Furious, Wolik replied with polished courtesy, "So sorry to disappoint you, monsieur. She is my grandmother."

Wolik was doubly happy in the Alps that year because he had nearly given up hope that I would ever again be able to hike, perhaps even to walk. That I was in the seventh heaven is only too understandable. Here is what I wrote in my diary:

The sun is lighting up everything with such dazzling brilliance that all that depressed my heart has evaporated into thin air, and again there are smiles inside, smiles of joy and bliss. Under the window roars a stream, and its incessant, exuberant noise tells of the power of living, awakens courage in me. The water rushes amid the dense fir woods, it has carved a bed for itself and rolls down with mad bravery. Bravery and work, these are an enormous force, and the century-old firs make way for the stream and let it run. Noisy and twisting its way, it whirls at full speed, sparkles in the sun, and carries wonderful freshness from the mountains.

Around us are the mountains, majestic, powerful. But there is no mystery in them such as we saw in Arshan, no menace and austerity as in Borzhom. No, they look festive, dressed up, shining; they come down in soft, gradual slopes, down to earth and the people, and turn into plowed-up fields, multicolored houses, verdant groves . . . One of the mountains is already our friend. Over our house we see a formidable rhinoceros—his broad snout, his paws pushed down, his powerful fangs turned up. He has stretched himself over the top of the mountain and looks down, lazily, indifferently, on the people in the valley. On the opposite side towers Mont Blanc, and our rhino looks at it and, in the whole valley, admires only its snow-white crown.

Today we left the house very early, and our first greeting was to the rhino. We could hardly recognize him—suffused by sun, he appeared friendly, touchingly friendly. It seemed as though he was laughing, with his huge awkward body basking in the warm sun rays; even his horn, despite its fearful strength, seemed transparent and thin.

We entered a trail; the rhino disappeared. One's foot slipped, but somewhere, not far from us, water murmured, and we hurried, sensing that we were going to discover new beauty. What beauty! In a deep cleft, between two mighty rocks, water thundered and ran down to a deep bow, there breaking to a thousand sparks, breaking with voluptuousness. From that bow, it pressed on like a stormy force and rushed down to the valley. With the water, freshness reached the valley, such invigorating freshness in these hot days!

The Georgian legation in Berlin needed Wolik's help in preparing a paper. I did not want to leave Mother alone as she did not feel well, so Wolik went by himself. On his return, he brought news from many Russian refugees and the offer of publisher I. Grzhebin to put out his memoirs in three volumes. There were other offers, too—to teach at the university, and so on. Wolik's impression was that life in Berlin was more stimulating and promising than in Paris. We discussed this alternative among ourselves and with Mother. She preferred Germany to France as it was closer to Russia, to which she wanted to return because her only daughter, Nadya, with whom she always had been very close, was in Petrograd. All three of us spoke German as well as French, and so we decided to move to Germany.

5. Success and Defeat in
Germany: 1922–33

LATE IN THE SUMMER of 1922, we said goodbye to our Georgian, Russian, and French friends in Paris and left for Germany. We had decided to take a few weeks' vacation along the Rhine before going to Berlin, and so we settled Mother in a nice boardinghouse in Godesberg and, with knapsacks on our backs, started out on our hike. We stopped at ancient castles on both sides of the Rhine, crossing it by steamboat. The countryside was beautiful, almost unscathed by the war, but the people were badly shaken and disturbed. Signs of occupation and foreign troops were everywhere. There was intense hatred of the French, British, and Americans but, strangely enough, not of the Russians. We bought something from a farmer and, when he heard that we were from Russia, he said, "Oh, the Russians! They are smart. They don't pay their debts!"

IN BERLIN

We found rooms in a private house for Mother and ourselves, and began to look around. Events from outside were crowding in on us— wherever we looked, we saw signs of agitation, bewilderment, antagonism, desire for change. The very foundations of normalcy had been shattered by the war, the revolutions in Russia, Germany, Austria, the changes in the political structure and ethnic situations all over Europe. Only self-centered people could go back into their shells and live as if nothing had happened. We, Wolik in particular, could not shut ourselves up in our own life in the midst of excited, stirred humanity. We had not yet cut the umbilical cord that held us to Russia; our ties with Georgia were strong, too, and we felt involved, intellectually and emotionally, in what was happening in Italy, France, Germany. It was difficult to maintain the serenity of our personal life amid a turbulent sea.

Wolik felt the urge to write down his experiences during the revolution of 1905 and his prison years—not piecemeal, as he had done before in articles, but in finished form—and also to describe what he had lived through in the second revolution in 1917. He had an offer from a publisher, and plunged himself into the work. Everything was still fresh and vivid in his memory, and he was writing for Russian readers in his rich, colorful Russian, knowing that historical, political, and literary allusions and references and the political names in his story would not require explanations and footnotes. His two volumes, *1905* and *Woe to the Defeated,** published under the common title *Years of Victories and Defeats,* had excellent reviews and brought us many enthusiastic letters. Unconsciously, Wolik revealed himself in those books as he was—young, fearless, braving dangers and giving himself without reservation to the cause he believed in, as hard as steel toward the oppressors but as soft as wax toward all who had suffered, full of humor, knowing no self-pity. I read and reread his manuscript, and Wolik supplemented it by telling me many other stories that he had to omit for lack of space. In his memoirs, *Stormy Passage,* Wolik had to sacrifice many parts of those two volumes for the same reason. They bring the reader only to World War I, while *Stormy Passage* ends in 1960.

Meanwhile, I had been deeply impressed by Stefan Zweig's drama *Jeremiah,* an exalted outcry against war, and wanted to translate it into Russian. I wrote to Zweig asking permission to do so if he had not already given it to someone else. I also wrote to Maxim Gorki, then in Czechoslovakia, with whom Wolik had long been on good terms, told him briefly of the drama's content, and inquired whether he could and would arrange publication of *Jeremiah* in Russia. Zweig sent me a very gracious letter saying that it would please him very much to have his drama published in Russian, and Gorki replied that he would do his best and if publication of *Jeremiah* as a book should prove impossible, he would try to arrange to have it printed in the Moscow magazine of which he was editor. *Jeremiah* was partly written in blank verse, and Wolik helped me to bring out the exact meaning of the text while preserving its poetical form. Gorki liked the translation and tried to have it published in Russia, but failed, largely because, as he explained to me, the religious framework and the numerous appeals by Jeremiah and the people to God were unacceptable to Moscow.

No country in the world had ever experienced the kind of inflation Germany lived through in the early twenties, particularly in 1923. We rented a beautiful five-room apartment in Berlin, furnished and equipped with silver, linen, china, and even portraits of a succession of generals in an old military family. It belonged to two spinsters, only descendants of that family. They wanted us to keep their maid, whom they did not wish to dismiss and could not afford to maintain; moreover, she was to remain as a kind of a watchdog over their property. For the rent, they suggested alternatives—either a flexible rent changing each month according to the value of the mark on the stock exchange or an annual lease at one United States dollar per month. We signed the lease to the satisfaction of the ladies, who invited us to stay with them in Thüringen on our summer trip down to Schwarzwald.

Under the contract, the publisher of Wolik's memoirs first paid him

* *1905* and *Na Ushcherbe Revolutsii* (Berlin: Grzhebin, 1923 and 1924).

in English pounds on the first of the month, but later he suggested paying in German marks the equivalent of a certain amount of American dollars, according to the situation on the stock exchange. It made a substantial difference whether that amount was paid in the morning or in the afternoon, when the new quotation of the German mark was announced. When the maid went to the market, I urged her to spend all the money I had given her, but she could not understand why and often would surprise me a day or two later by returning what she had "saved" by careful shopping; by then, that money was worthless.

Many businessmen were as bewildered as our maid. We became friends with a businessman who had a magnificent villa in a fine residential section of Berlin. Offered a fantastic sum for it in paper marks, he sold it and took a down payment, the remainder to be paid in six months. When that time arrived, he could not buy a loaf of bread with the money he received. One heard of such manipulations all the time. Many shrewd and unscrupulous people acquired much real estate in the city, while naïve people still clung to the mark, insisting, "The German mark will always be the same," and lost everything they had. The middle class was ruined, while Germany was swarming with tourists buying whatever they saw right and left. Hatred of foreigners therefore became nearly general, though in reality it was largely the national profiteers of inflation who dispossessed the middle class.

Then, as if by magic, the mark was reevaluated in a day; on January 1, 1924, its value was set at 4.2 marks to the United States dollar. Reeducation of the people to a sound currency took time but was accomplished with great skill.

RETURN TO SCHOLARLY WORK

Both of us were deeply stirred by the trial of the twelve Socialist Revolutionaries in Moscow and the sentence condemning them to death. Many of them were our close friends; all were of heroic stature and uncompromising in their beliefs. Representatives of their party abroad asked Wolik to write a pamphlet on this trial and the life story of the condemned, who together had spent a total of more than 100 years in Tsarist dungeons because of their fight for the liberation of the Russian people. Who could write about it without living with them, suffering their agony, feeling indignation, even revulsion, against the new oppressors of Russia, no less cruel than the Tsarist tyrants had been? Again, past and present merged for us, and "epos" came back into our life with all its invincible strength. The pamphlet was published in five languages simultaneously.

From the day of her arrival, Mother had said that she wanted to stay with us for a while but that later she wished to join Nadya who, she felt, needed her more than we. We understood her desire but worried that, because of her delicate health, life in Leningrad would be too hard for her. Yet she was determined, and all we could do was to help her make her preparations. Finally, the day of departure arrived, and we took her to the port of Stettin, where she was to board a steamer going to Leningrad.

At the wharf, Mother, as a passenger, was separated from us and was occupied with passport and custom formalities. Wolik was directed into one room, I into another with the rest of the women. To my horror, I saw that everyone was being searched. Apparently, it was suspected that money or jewels were being smuggled out of Germany by transfer to passengers at the last farewell. I was scared, because I had a few English pounds with me—all our wealth—in a little sachet that I always carried inside my brassière for fear of theft. If discovered, they would be confiscated, and how could we convince the port authorities that this was not money to pass on to Mother, money we had earned and on which we lived, exchanging a pound or two from time to time? The laws against smuggling money were severe at that time, as I recalled from occasional stories in the newspapers. I pushed the little sachet inconspicuously from the front to the side until it was under my left arm. When my turn came, I went into the examination room dead of fright. A woman detective pushed her hand over the front of my body from throat to legs, repeated the motion on my back, and let me go.

Mother reached Leningrad safely and was very happy to be with Nadya, but very soon her health began to be affected by the austerity of life there, to which her physical constitution had not been accustomed. She wrote to us frequently, never complaining. After less than two years, she died on a day on which her doctor had given her a clean bill of health.

Perhaps it could have been a break with "epos" when, during the Christmas season in 1923, Wolik and I decided to shift from politics to scholarly work. Though it may seem that this decision was made abruptly, on the spur of the moment, actually it had been growing on us for some time. We went to Marienbad, Czechoslovakia, to spend Christmas in the mountains. On the train, we discussed our future plans. Wolik had finished and published the two volumes of his memoirs; he had the third volume in draft form, but Grzhebin, his publisher, was in financial difficulties and could not undertake new publications. I was through with *Jeremiah* and several other smaller translations from Kellermann and other German writers that Gorki had asked me to do for his magazine.

I strongly urged Wolik to return to academic work, which he had started so brilliantly as a teen-ager. He began to take stock of his knowledge of economics and statistics and, as usual, made notes on his pad. By the time we reached Marienbad, Wolik had a rough draft of an outline for his next study. It was no less than a plan for a seven-volume survey of international statistics. All through our stay in Marienbad, Wolik worked on his outline. Before he put anything on paper, he liked to walk from one end of the room to the other, telling me the new ideas he had formed during the day's coasting and hiking. I listened quietly, and then we discussed the whole plan again and again. We had some small savings that would carry us through several months of modest living, and decided to start working on that project immediately after our return to Berlin, without waiting to make an arrangement for its publication.

With this prospect in mind, we wanted to take full advantage of our two weeks in Marienbad. The weather was excellent and the scenery breath-taking. The forest was an enchanting world of silvery, feathery trees, with icicles hanging in the air and glimmering under the sun. Everything—the road, the houses—was covered with snow, here pure white, there deep blue, blue as the sky. We hiked to our heart's delight, braving the forest without a plan or a map but with a compass in Wolik's hand; we coasted down the twisting long mountain road carved between the trees, joined others on toboggans rushing down with incredible speed. Not a thought of the past or the future! We were one with the sun, the snow, the dressed-up trees, and we breathed in new freshness, new strength, new enjoyment of life together.

We spent several evenings with Maxim Gorki, who then lived in Marienbad. He was very critical of the Soviet Government at that time and made biting remarks about some of its leaders, so that we were on common ground in conversations with him.

DIE WELT IN ZAHLEN

On returning to Berlin, we organized our work. The best international statistical library was in the Prussian Statistical Office. Its librarian put a large table at our disposal, introduced us to his staff, and we began the task that kept us nailed to that table for the next five years. From the beginning, the title of the project was *Ves' Mir v Tsifrakh (The World in Figures)*. We thought of publishing it in Russian, since the Soviet Government was then admitting various books in Russian from abroad, particularly scientific books.

Das Berliner Tageblatt, a newspaper with a large circulation in Germany, was printed by the Rudolf Mosse publishing house, which had recently opened a Russian-language branch. Mr. Schkliaver, the head of that branch, believed that he could get the company to agree to include the survey in its list, despite its unusual size and character. After working for three months, no less than twelve to fourteen hours a day, without taking off Sundays or holidays, we had the rough penciled draft of the first volume, with penciled sketches of charts and an outline of the survey. Mr. Schkliaver wanted to have a look at the material, and Wolik gave it to him reluctantly. Several days later, we learned that that unkempt, hardly readable draft had been forwarded to Professor V. I. Bortkiewicz, the recognized authority in the field of statistics, who had a complete command of the Russian language. We were upset but could do nothing about it— the draft was in his hands, and he refused to meet the author before he passed judgment on it. Though we had little hope that anything would come out of this first attempt, we continued working and began to consider other possibilities for the publication of the survey.

We received the thirteen pages of comments by Bortkiewicz, and found them critical, almost pedantic. He did not overlook even the absence of an accent on some vowels in German or Swedish names. The last, thirteenth, page summarized his opinion: "The statistics presented in the volume not only cover the present time but also present a large number of historical series. It is therefore not to be feared that the survey may become outdated and lose in interest for readers . . . An adjustment [for German readers] will hardly be necessary, since the content is kept on an entirely international level. The fact that Russia is treated more extensively than a non-Russian might have treated it might ensure a larger distribution of the survey."

To us, this last page seemed like a drop of honey politely offered to sweeten the critical tone of the comments. But when Wolik went to pick up our draft (we did not have a copy, since we had no typewriter), Mosse's chief editor beamed at him and said, *"Wir werden kaufen vierzehn Kätze in einem Sack"* (We are going to buy fourteen cats in a bag), meaning that they would publish the seven volumes in both Russian and German. What luck! Wolik, a foreigner, totally unknown in Germany, a country with highly developed statistics, had been given an unexpected, even unhoped-for chance to show what he could do in producing an extensive, individually planned survey!

Another marvelous feature of this project was the part Professor Bortkiewicz played in it. We learned later that he had been the terror of all German publishers, most of whom had ceased to send him their statistical publications for comment. Not that he was mean—actually, he was just the opposite. He was the embodiment of scientific integrity and honesty; when he wrote a review, he was concerned not with the author but with his literary product only, and he gave a sincere appraisal. The only trouble was that it was extremely difficult to satisfy him, to reach his level. He was called the "Pope of Statistics," also "Die Leuchte" (The Luminary). After Mosse had accepted the project, Wolik went to see Bortkiewicz. Apparently, he appraised Wolik at once, because at that first meeting he agreed to become the official editor of a series of statistical books to be issued by Rudolf Mosse. Actually, the series began and ended with our survey, *Die Welt in Zahlen* (*The World in Figures*), and its supplementary volume on Germany, *Zehn Jahre Neues Deutschland* (*Ten Years of New Germany*). For German scholars, the fact that Bortkiewicz for the first time had associated his name with a project was a guarantee of both its exceptional quality and the scholarly status of its author.

For Wolik, the continuous contact with this great scholar provided a most valuable opportunity to check each thought, each statement, against the judgment of a much more mature thinker. Of course, Bortkiewicz was not entirely on the giving side; he sincerely enjoyed working with Wolik. They met every week to discuss a chapter, or to plan the next chapter or volume, or to go over comments on the part he had finished reading. He prepared additional documentation which he considered interesting and applicable, and also he would evolve some mathematical problems in theoretical statistics, which they would try to solve, each in his own way—Bortkiewicz by geometry and Wolik by algebra.

Knowing of my part in this project, Bortkiewicz wanted to meet me, and gradually we came to see him, and his sister Helen, who lived with him, rather frequently. In the beginning, I felt awed in his presence and was very shy. He inspired great respect, and I also felt some reserve in him not easy to break. Yet under his formal, proud, almost stiff appearance lived a suppressed desire for fun, friendly banter, and light, restful conversation. Once the ice was broken, he sent us jingles, sometimes two pages long, funny charades in Russian, French, German, and even Latin; he invited us to write charades or jingles at his home, or to a restaurant, or to hear poetry read by mutual friends. I have scores of such notes from him and wish I could translate them into English. Nobody who knew Bortkiewicz from his behavior at the university or from his writings, so highly technical that he could never distribute all ten of the reprints he received from a journal, could realize how much wit and fun he had in him when he let the bars down.

In our relations with Bortkiewicz, gratitude, respect, pleasure at ever closer contacts with him, merged into a warm friendship. On his side, there was a real fondness for Wolik and appreciation of his mind and character, and great courtesy toward me, which did not prevent him from constantly teasing us, together and separately, and from challenging us to competition in wit, storytelling, or jingles.

How can I describe and evaluate those five years of work on *The World in Figures?* We were at the library by nine in the morning and worked without interruption until it closed at half past five, at lunchtime munching dry homemade sandwiches (there was no cafeteria near by and it was not proper to take a Thermos bottle with coffee to our centrally located table). We had neither a typewriter nor a calculating machine. Wolik drew all the charts, and I colored them with seven different pencils. From the library we went home, had supper, and worked until eleven or even midnight. Some of our friends called it "slave labor." Yet we loved it for the new horizons it opened to us, for the fascination of our expanding knowledge of the world, but most of all for keeping us close to each other in every thought, every interest, for making us one not only emotionally but also intellectually. In the morning, when we were about ready to go to the library, Wolik used to say, "Let us go to plow Shakespeare" the expression reportedly used by Edmund Kean, the famous British performer of Shakespearean roles, when he was about to go on stage.

Many times, then and later, we were asked about the mechanics of our joint work, because there are very few examples of such complete and harmonious collaboration. We achieved it without any effort on either part, but we never put into words what made us tick in our work nor can I explain it now. I remember that Eric d'Acosta, introducing us to an audience in New Delhi, said that he had urged us unsuccessfully to give a talk other than the one scheduled, that is, to explain how we worked together and how we could produce an amount that no two people in India could possibly match. All I can say is that it was easy, natural, and never created any tension between us. Perhaps our individual attitudes had something to do with this. There was no problem of competition. I never questioned Wolik's intellectual superiority, and all I wanted was to assure his success. For his part, Wolik had an exaggerated opinion of my abilities and felt that it was only because we worked together that they did not come to the fore as much as they deserved.

With the appearance of the first volume of *The World in Figures,* Wolik made his mark. He was at once recognized as a first-class statistician. The reviews were unanimous in recognizing his pioneering work in international statistics, the high quality of the interpretive text, the scholarly standard of the selected tables and annotations, the originality and lucidity of the multicolored charts, but above all, his ability to make the figures speak, to make them come alive.

Our first reader of the printed book was rather unusual, to say the least. The night the first volume appeared, we were to dine with my cousin, in whose house Professor Albert Einstein had an apartment. In appreciation of my cousin's unfailing readiness to oblige him in every way in which a landlord can be obliging, Professor and Mrs. Einstein graciously accepted his invitation to dinner once a year, after which some of the finest musicians, such as Piatagorsky, played informally for him. Dinner that night happened to be one at which Einstein was present. We had never met him before and did not know that we were going to meet him then. I brought the book as a token of courtesy to my cousin. Professor Einstein happened to notice it before returning to his apartment, glanced through its pages, and said to my cousin that he would like to look at it at his leisure. Next morning, he called up to say that the book had kept him up until two in the morning; he could not put it down. He wanted to know more about Wolik and invited us to his apartment.

Professor Einstein, by his friendly, unaffected approach, put one at ease very readily. His first wife was a gracious and intelligent lady. Einstein greatly enjoyed the after-dinner musical performances arranged for him by my cousin. On one occasion, he ran down to his apartment, brought back a small violin made for him by a Japanese admirer, and played several pieces.

Some time later he sent us tickets for his report to the Kaiser Wilhelm Institute. This was a solemn occasion. Scholars from many countries, many of them mathematicians, physicists, or astronomers, filled the huge lecture hall. While he was speaking, one could have heard a fly move through the air. I knew that I could not grasp the full meaning and implications of his report, and did not try to concentrate on it. All my attention, nevertheless, was on the speaker—on his way of presenting his report rather than its content. He spoke softly, meditatively, giving the impression that he wanted to make his theory understood, but he made no effort to convince his listeners of its correctness or to use oratorical pressure. Wolik told me later that he followed the speech up to a certain point but then lost contact, either because of a momentary distraction or because of insufficient knowledge of modern mathematics.

When Einstein finished, he turned to both sides of the hall and asked if anybody wanted to comment on his talk. There were no challengers. He looked around and inquired almost shyly: "Are there any questions? I would be glad to answer them." Again silence. He smiled and said with some regret in his voice but also with a kind of childlike relief, "This means, then, that I am dismissed." The audience gave him an ovation.

During the dinner served afterward, Professor Einstein stopped at each table to say a few friendly words or make an innocent joke in a happy, carefree mood. This is how I still remember him; we never met again.

We delivered the manuscript of the successive volumes at the promised dates, though at times the work seemed to exceed our strength. While we were correcting the proofs of the second volume (Labor), for example, updating the tables, text, and charts, and while Bortkiewicz was reading and discussing the third volume (Agriculture), suggesting changes here and there and the use of additional material, we were already working on the fourth volume (Industry) and trying to follow all new publications and new statistical information on at least those three volumes of nearly 1,100 printed pages, plus filing any occasional documentation within our reach for the last three volumes, on commerce, transportation, finance, and culture—all this for some sixty countries, with material published in many European languages.

When new material became available, we replaced full-page tables and the corresponding charts and text with new tables, charts, and text, or we added new countries to our international tables, while the manuscript was in the hands of the printer, or even in galleys or page proofs. All these changes were made in handwriting, and nearly each page looked like a hard puzzle. Moreover, when Wolik was not satisfied with the layout of a table (though the manuscript was set in the best German printing house, the Bibliographisches Institut), he remade a page or two and asked to have his layout followed. Yet the publisher acted with good grace, and though he complained occasionally that we treated him like a stepson, he never interfered or raised the question of cost.

Only the first two volumes of the Russian edition were released, because in Russia importation of books was no longer permitted.

The World in Figures was not the only work with which we were occupied during those busy years. Wolik wrote a book, *Sily Sovremennogo Sotsialisma* (*The Forces of Contemporary Socialism*), which was the outgrowth of our large survey, and another book on the unification of Europe, which appeared in German in Berlin under the title *Die Vereinigten Staaten von Europa* (*The United States of Europe*) and then in French in Brussels. In 1926, a United States of Europe impressed many as the dream of a visionary; today it is close to being realized. Also, Wolik published many articles on international topics in various economic and statistical magazines and trade-union periodicals, as well as many articles on current issues in various newspapers. We collaborated on all these writings in our usual manner and also prepared jointly a rather substantial survey of health conditions in the world.

In addition, I prepared a booklet on the municipal problems of metropolitan Berlin, published in 1929, and worked on another project, which was never published. The Russian branch of the Mosse House had asked me to prepare textbooks on arithmetic for the first four grades of Russian elementary schools. I accepted and acquainted myself with the new Russian textbooks in that field. But by the time the page proofs of my four textbooks were ready, it had become impossible to export books to Russia. Thus there was no sense in printing them in Germany. Not willing to accept defeat without a fight, I sent the manuscript to a teacher I had known in Russia, suggesting that it be offered directly to the Government publishing house in Moscow. To my surprise, the manuscript was received favorably, and many of its features were commended as "novel" and "original." It was thought, however, that I should adjust the text to what they then called a "complex method" (I did not understand this then and could not explain it now), in accordance with printed instructions in use there. I had no desire to put more work into those textbooks, particularly since their publication was not entirely sure. Wolik used to call such projects *"nashi korabliki na more"* (our little boats on the high seas). Some returned to our port after a successful voyage, as new editions or translations or with requests for new articles and projects; others sank for one reason or another. In that terminology, my "little boat" with the textbooks on arithmetic was lost on the high seas.

Our work for Mosse also included, within the series of Bortkiewicz, a special statistical book on Germany alone, *Zehn Jahre Neues Deutschland*. This was a rather easy project. We had collected much of the material during the work on *The World in Figures,* and in any case to work and write about a single country with readily available documentation was relaxing after constantly searching for any kind of data on scores of countries, many of which provided the most rudimentary statistics or none at all.

The World in Figures was much more successful than we had dared to hope and was generally accepted as the first basic work on international statistics. The general response was summarized in the following state-

ment by the well-known statistician Robert Kuczynski in his review in
Finanzpolitische Korrespondenz:

> When one sees how a single scholar has created an international
> encyclopedia that by far overshadows what has been produced in
> this field by the International Statistical Institute or the League of
> Nations with their much larger means, skepticism again revives
> about "organized" scientific production. Of course, it would have
> been contrary to the habits of those institutions to draw a genius
> like Woytinsky into their work.

Wolik's reputation spread first in Germany and German-speaking
countries—Austria and Switzerland—and also in Czechoslovakia, The
Netherlands, and the Scandinavian countries. It continued to spread
throughout Europe and even reached Japan. Up to the present time,
I have never met a German statistician or economist who has not at
least heard of *The World in Figures* and Wolik's name. Sometimes a
German admirer appeared in most unusual circumstances. We were
leaving Quito, Ecuador, for Santiago, Chile, at about five in the morning.
Shortly before the departure of the plane, the United States cultural
attaché arrived and shouted, "Woytinsky, Woytinsky!" Suddenly a man
who was taking care of passengers at a little airport counter left his
customers, ran to Wolik, and bubbling from excitement, said, "Are you
the author of *Die Welt in Zahlen?* I never dreamed I would meet you.
I am so glad, so glad. I still have all your seven volumes. I wouldn't
think of leaving them to Hitler!" He embraced the surprised Wolik
and ran back to his customers.

BAVARIAN INTERLUDE

In the summer of 1925, we decided to spend several weeks in Obersdorf, the terminus of a small mountain railroad in the Bavarian Alps.
In the train, we remarked how pleasant it would be to rent a room with
an unobstructed view of the mountains. We arrived around four in the
afternoon, checked the luggage, and went to look for a suitable room.
To our surprise and dismay, Obersdorf was overflowing. No place to
stay! In one house, the landlady told us that she had rented even the
bathroom for that night. Indeed, tourists were wandering about in
droves; at every boardinghouse, inn, hotel, we found people asking for
rooms and behind us came others. Finally, one innkeeper suggested
that we go to the neighboring village, some two or three kilometers
away. He thought that some of the farmers might take in tourists, at
least overnight. We followed his advice, but none of the farmers, still
resentful of the years of inflation they blamed on the city people,
wanted to accept intruders from outside.

While returning to Obersdorf, we decided to take the train down to
the valley and stop at the first station, Sonthofen, which was still high in
the mountains and a somewhat larger town than Obersdorf. There we

resumed the search. No luck—everything was occupied! Disappointed and even angry, we went back to the station intending to return to Munich and change our summer plans. Alas, the station was closed; the next train was scheduled for six the following morning.

All we could do was to go to a restaurant where we thought we could sit through the night by ordering something from time to time. But at eleven o'clock, the waiter announced, *"Polizeistunde!"* ("Police hour," meaning closing time), and began to turn the lights off. We had to leave and decided to find a church and sit there. It, too, was closed.

By now, it was completely dark, and it started raining—not too much, just a drizzle, but we needed a roof. The last resort was to go to the police and ask their hospitality for the night. This really was the last thing we would normally do. Our friends in Berlin had tried to dissuade us from going to Bavaria, then the nest of German reactionaries associated with many White Russians to whom the name of Wolik, a Socialist, would be anathema. But we had no alternative, and we also thought, Who in this little town would know Wolik's name? But where was the police station? There was nobody to ask, all the houses were shut, no lights anywhere. We walked in one direction, then in the other —no police building! Suddenly we heard footsteps, listened to determine their direction, and almost collided with a man in the darkness. We asked him how to reach the police station. He told us and then asked, "Has anything happened? Why do you need the police station at this hour?" We told him our predicament, and he said, "I am a salesman and spent the whole day in Munich. A friend brought me back in his car. I do not know whether my wife has rented the two rooms we use for the tourist trade in the summer. Anyhow, we have comfortable chairs in the living room where you can wait until the morning train."

Relieved and delighted, we walked with him to his house. There he left us in the living room and, on returning with two pillows in his arms, said, "Well, the rooms are rented, but make yourselves comfortable in these chairs." We thanked him profusely. Hearing the foreign accent again, he asked, "From what country do you come?" "From Russia." "Russia? That's wonderful." Seeing our perplexity, he explained, "You see, I was a war prisoner in Russia for two years. Everybody treated me well. I learned a few words in Russian. I would go up to a man and say, *'Papirosky?'* (Cigarette?). He would look at me, see that I was hungry and poor, and give me a couple of cigarettes, and sometimes money for a meal. I would knock at a kitchen door, and when a woman opened it, I used to say, *'Ya vas lyublyu'* (I love you). She would understand that the poor devil wanted to ingratiate himself and would ask me who I was, then feed me, and occasionally give me her husband's old shirt, coat, or shoes. When I came back, I promised myself that I should repay the first Russian I met for the help I got in your country. And now you are in my home. Tomorrow I shall vacate a room for you, and you will stay right here. I must tell this to my wife."

He kept his word, and we spent two weeks in his house. Moreover, he and his wife had a grocery store, and so a food problem did not exist for us. Of course, we paid for everything. It was fantastic luck to meet that night the one German out of a million—or perhaps one out of *all* Germans—willing to open his arms to strangers simply because they came from Russia! We had a wonderful vacation hiking in the Bavarian Alps, exploring all the trails and peaks, and talking in the evening with our hosts about the situation in that area and in Germany in general.

WOLIK'S BROTHER KOLYA

Kolya, Wolik's younger brother, showed me great affection and consideration. When we had been in Petrograd, the arrival of an enormous basket of flowers was a sure sign that Kolya had come to town. If we had had a chance to live for some time in the same place under more or less normal conditions, close contact with Wolik, whom he worshiped, and with me would have done Kolya a lot of good. He had a craving to be loved, and though he was rather awkward in expressing his feelings, he was drawn to us as though to a magnet. He could have been an excellent family man despite his occasional moodiness, but he was unlucky; his wife was a neurotic person, always complaining and very pretentious. I never met her but that is how other members of the family described her, and Kolya's references to her sometimes showed that he was not happy. Moreover, by taking on more obligations and work than even his iron constitution could bear, he strained his heart and so ruined his health.

Early in the 1920's, Kolya surprised us around six in the morning by knocking at the door of our bedroom in Berlin and shouting, "Get up, get up, you sleepyheads!" We were with him in a few minutes. He had come to buy two lumber plants for Russia, one in Germany and the other in Sweden. Yet, with all this responsibility, he was afraid of his own shadow. He was dying to be with us, yet scared to death by his temerity in coming to see us. We discussed how we could spend a little time together in a neutral place. I suggested meeting Sunday at Spreewald, a small resort not far from Berlin, often called the German Venice. There the Spree River breaks into two hundred or more arms, which meander through uninhabited woods. One can hire a gondola for a day-long trip through the narrow canals. This is a one-way trip, however, and once begun it cannot be interrupted. Both Wolik and Kolya approved, believing that there we could be together in the wilderness, away from watching eyes. Alas, we did not guess the power of terror over a citizen of the Soviet Union. We met at Spreewald, hired the boat, and started the trip in a cheery mood. An hour or so later, other boats began to appear, and Kolya was gripped by the fear that someone might be observing him. Nothing we could say reassured him. Terrified, he looked around, and his eyes fell on a pile of blankets for use in the event of rain. He grabbed one, pulled it over his head and stayed under it for the rest of the day. Instead of looking at our dear Kolya, we saw only the big tiger that decorated the blanket. We were miserable and felt guilty at having imposed such an experience on him, but who could have anticipated his reaction? That was how we saw him for the last time.

PAUL AXELROD

Paul Axelrod, one of the founders of the Russian Social Democratic Party, lived in Berlin at that time. His frail body housed an indomitable spirit. He was a man with an exceptionally keen analytical mind and absolute integrity. He hated Communism intensely for its debasement of the high ideals of humane socialism to which he had devoted all his life. Wolik had met him at gatherings of European Socialists and had known of him, of course, since 1905. I met him in 1921 in Paris, where he visited us frequently and a warm relationship gradually united us. He was then about seventy years old.

Axelrod's friends and followers attempted to persuade him to write his memoirs, which would be of great historical significance for the study of the beginnings of the Russian revolutionary movement. He did not have the strength to do so, and Wolik offered his help.* He would talk freely, and Wolik would take down his story and shape it. Axelrod was unusually exacting. He checked and rechecked every word for its meaning and its possible interpretations and implications, and often came up with new thoughts about a part already edited and approved by him, after which he and Wolik would edit again for the ninth time. It was a labor of love for Wolik, and he showed a touching patience. He was sincerely interested and knew that the old man would not have been able to do it without him. Sometimes Axelrod's uncompromising attitude toward some expression amused Wolik, but he always succeeded in finding a satisfactory substitute.

We had a very large apartment in Berlin, and Axelrod stayed with us for some time. However, this did not turn out to be a very felicitous arrangement. The old man felt lonely when we were away for the whole day at the library, but accepted this absence *nolens volens*. However, sometimes when we wanted to go out in the evening, we felt his disappointment and occasionally some slight resentment. This limited our freedom to some extent, for out of our affection for him, we then would spend several evenings at home to make him happy, until the next time he found himself alone. Moreover, some of his visitors did not feel too comfortable in our presence, or perhaps even in our home when we were absent.

A favorable solution appeared when a distant relative of his, who had come to Berlin from Switzerland, proved willing to live with him in a separate apartment and to take care of him. Then our friendship flourished without any strain. We often visited him, and he loved to

* Axelrod's memoirs appeared in Berlin under the title *Thought Through and Lived Through* (in Russian, *Perezhitoe i Peredumannoe*).

listen to stories about our trips and other experiences. Occasionally he listened with much attention and then sighed contentedly and said, "What a nice story! You've told it to me before, but I enjoyed hearing it again." During wanderings in the mountains, we usually sent him some humorous jingles, which he loved to show his friends. It was touching to see his pride in Wolik's successes, his deep attachment to him and also to me, or rather to us as one.

Axelrod followed political developments in Russia and Europe avidly, but his strength began to wane. We had no illusions, seeing that he became weaker every day, though he clung to life and fought death with all that was left of his will and temperament.

MOUNTAINEERING

We could not have worked continuously under the constant pressure of deadlines for returning galleys and proofs, for delivering material to Bortkiewicz and manuscripts to the publisher. We probably would have broken down if we had not varied our pattern of life. Our system was to work for ten months, sixty to sixty-six hours a week, and then disappear for two full months without leaving an address for forwarding mail. We would take the train to a mountain resort in the Tirol from which we intended to start the ascent to the peaks. From thereabouts, we sent a suitcase or two to the place we expected to reach in eight or ten days. We packed our knapsacks with sweaters, extra shoes, slippers, and other clothing and paraphernalia, loaded ourselves with camera and field glasses, put on hob-nailed mountain shoes, took ice picks, and off we went from one mountain refuge to another.

Our initial point might be Krimml, or Zellensee, or Innsbruck, and from there we would hike, ascending a mountain or a glacier from one valley and descending along its slope to another. Only once did we hire a guide, and that was on our first ascent, which happened to be that of the Wildspitze, when we knew nothing of that fascinating sport. The guide cut ice covering the steep slope for footholds and held us on his rope. Afterward, we went climbing and crossing glaciers alone. The usual plan was to start the ascent around three in the morning so as to be able to reach the top, there to rest, enjoy the scenery, and take pictures, and then to make the icy part of the descent before noon, when the thin ice bridges formed over the crevasses during the night would melt. More often than not, we were not alone on the ice; ahead and behind us, we would see other climbers, some more and others less experienced than we were. Once after we climbed the Gross Venediger, a popular glacier and comparatively easy to negotiate, we had to stand in line for a view from the top!

In the mountain shelters, lights were off and everybody was asleep by nine or ten o'clock. Still, it was not too pleasant to get up in the chilly room at two in the morning, have a quick breakfast, and start the ascent in the darkness. But this was the safest way, of course, and it somehow cheered up both of us when Wolik said, securing his knapsack and taking the ice pick: *"Pobredem, Markovna, pobredem!"* (Let us move on, Markovna, let us move on!)—as the exiled priest Abacum reportedly used to say to his wife, Markovna, while taking his crook and urging her to get up.

Wolik's passion for the mountains was extraordinary. The high-altitude air intoxicated him, the panorama of mountain ranges filled him with a yearning to cross other valleys, climb other peaks. Perhaps no other scenery gave him as strong a stimulus and as complete enjoyment as that of the mountains; his love for them was insatiable. We usually spent July and August in the mountains, and on our return, Wolik already had a plan for next year's trip. Of course, his pleasure would not have been so great if I had not shared his enthusiasm. In that again we were one; fortunately, we were both healthy, strong, not easily fatigued, unafraid of the risks connected with mountaineering, not subject to the dizziness that keeps many from that sport. At first, it was rather hard to climb with fully packed knapsacks, but once we learned to walk at a steady pace, we could climb up to three thousand feet in a day without too much strain on the heart. I even used to say that apparently I had no heart at all.

When we returned to Berlin from our first adventure in mountain-climbing, we were so exhilarated that we had to share our passion with friends who never ventured beyond a near-by lake or a popular resort. We turned our apartment into an exhibition gallery, covered its walls with enlarged photographs of mountains and charts showing various points we had reached; we hung up our alpine shoes, ice picks, knapsacks, field glasses, cameras, arranged the equipment for picnics in the Alps on a little table; spread, on another table, the things we carried in our knapsacks. Wolik felt that we needed a commercial. He took two huge pieces of cardboard. On one of them, he sketched a man with a nearly idiotic expression on his face, sitting before a volume of *The World in Figures*. The caption said, "I have not read this book!" We hung this drawing in the entrance hall. In the last exhibition room was another drawing, showing an intelligent-looking man, a real intellectual, pointing to *The World in Figures* and saying with an air of complete satisfaction, "I have just finished reading it."

The high-altitude sector of the Tirol, too rocky and cold for farming, had become the domain of the German-Austrian Alpine Society, but all its accommodations were open to everybody. Each member city of the society had built a hostel that bore its name—Dresdener Hütte, Berliner Hütte, Frankfurter Hütte, Innsbrucker Hütte, and so on. Some were large, comfortable houses with separate sleeping accommodations for men and women and single rooms; others had only wooden boards with thin mattresses for ten or twelve men or women; still others, like the Berliner Hütte, almost reminded one of a hotel. Naturally, we preferred to have a cubicle to ourselves, no matter how small or modest, but in the final analysis, this was irrelevant. The scenery, the wonderful mountain air, and the physical excitement of climbing were important; nothing else mattered. The general rule was that no matter how crowded the shelter, no one was turned away after dark. Hot food, of a rather primitive but filling type, was available. We liked the atmosphere in those shelters. We were surrounded by husky youngsters; all the talk centered on problems of climbing—mountain weather, the quality of the roads and trails and so on; in the evening, somebody played the guitar if one was available, somebody sang. Here or there a hiker was too boastful or had poor manners, but all in all, this was a pleasanter crowd than one could expect to meet in a swanky resort.

One cannot spend months hiking in the Alps without occasionally exposing oneself to unforeseen dangers. We were not so adventurous as to look for perils, but we encountered some just the same. I recall, for example, one early morning when we reached a large open field; we intended to cross it and start the ascent of a glacier. Suddenly we heard a heavy tramping, and out of nowhere, a large herd of cattle came stampeding toward us. No one was with the cattle. We looked around; there was no place to hide—no house, no tree. To start running would be more dangerous than to stand still. We stood, rooted to the spot, for what was only a few minutes but seemed endless.

Another time, we set out on a climb described as perfectly safe. When we were high up, we found ourselves on a path so narrow that our knapsacks almost touched the rocky wall. We walked one behind the other, not daring even to turn our heads. The path was covered with slippery snow that had fallen the night before, and there was nothing to hold onto. When finally, drained and exhausted, we reached the top, we saw next to the refuge a huge roll of steel cable. It was, as we learned later, to be secured along the path over which we had just come.

After hiking for six successive summers in the Tirol, we wanted new horizons. We went to the Dolomites and descended from them to Venice; we hiked in the Pyrenees, the Swiss Alps, the French Alps, in Norway. These were wonderful summers, full of sun and fun. We had many delightful experiences in meeting the people of those countries. I remember with pleasure the days we spent with a farm family in Norway. Our system in that country was to cross a glacier on foot, descend to the fiord, take a boat to the other side, and hike across the next glacier. One afternoon, just as we reached the foot of a glacier and were about to start climbing, Wolik sprained his ankle. To go on was out of the question. We looked around; there was nothing except, at some distance, a single large house, almost a manor. We walked to it, showed Wolik's foot, and asked for hospitality. We had picked up a few Norwegian words, which we sprinkled with English, occasionally known there, but in the main we resorted to gestures understood the world over. The old mother, apparently the head of the clan, nodded graciously and showed us to a small room, immaculately clean and adorned with homemade rugs. We stayed there for two days, until the swollen ankle had subsided.

This was a farm family—mother, married sons and their wives, three unmarried daughters, and in-laws. It was harvest time, and, of course, we did not want to burden them with caring for us. After the very copious breakfast, all of them went to work in the fields, and we moved slowly out of their view, lay down in the shade, and hoped that they would forget about us until supper. But around noon, one of the women hustled back to the house to prepare lunch for us.

Food was plentiful, and so was the hospitality. After the evening meal, we "talked." When a difficulty in communicating arose, everybody laughed, and one of the men patted Wolik on the shoulder. Even after everyone else was indoors and ready to go to bed, the old mother was still in the yard, putting the tools away, checking, sweeping. When we left, the whole clan assembled to shake hands and wish us well. We wanted to pay for our room and board, though we could not pay for their friendly hospitality. The old mother refused: Their house was not a hotel, and she could not take money from occasional guests sent— she pointed to the sky—by God. Finally, we compromised by putting a donation in the alms box for the needy of their community.

Of course, there were contrasting experiences as well. We came down to Venice from the Dolomites with knapsacks on our backs and asked two boys, about ten or twelve years old, to direct us to the nearest hotel. They offered to accompany us. We walked some ten or fifteen minutes, chatting with them. The older, a very handsome, well-dressed boy, told us that his father was a lawyer and described other members of what appeared to be a middle-class family. We registered at the hotel, and I went out to thank the youngsters for the help. I was still holding a bouquet of mountain immortelles gathered, not without risk, that very morning. I offered it and a box of candy to the boys, but they shook their heads and the older one said, *"No, signora, soldi!"* (No, lady, money!)

It is strange how memory retains some insignificant impressions while losing more important and telling ones. I can see us returning after a difficult, all-day hike in the Swiss Alps to our hotel in Pontresina. It became dark, and we realized that we still had two hours to walk. We decided to stop at the first opportunity to get supper or at least a snack. Soon we spotted a little restaurant and went in, our hob-nailed shoes clattering on the floor. Inside the dimly lit dining room sat one couple, evidently English, she in a low-necked, long black dress, he in a tuxedo and patent-leather shoes. The contrast between them and us was so funny that we laughed all through the meal, composed a jingle about it, and addressed it to Bortkiewicz.

In France, in the Pyrenees, we decided to make the village of Gavarnie our headquarters for hikes in the Cirque de Gavarnie, an imposing amphitheater of sheer cliffs with a magnificent waterfall. The owner of the one hotel in the village showed us a room that had a beautiful view over the Cirque but said that he could take us for one day only.

"Is this room reserved for someone else?" we inquired.

"Oh, no," he replied, "I have several other empty rooms, but I rent them for one night only."

This was something novel, and to our question "Why?," he said, "You will not be satisfied with my cuisine, and the room is rented with board."

Knowing the excellence of French cuisine, we tried to persuade him that we had simple tastes, easy to satisfy. He repeated that he never accepted patrons for more than one night, but finally broke down and agreed to let us have the room.

On the second day, we learned the reason for his policy. Around noon, each day, three buses filled with tourists drew up; the tourists lunched at our hotel, then went with guides to the foot of the Cirque, "grazed" there for a couple of hours, returned to the hotel, dined, and left. The guests were always new, but the menu was always the same, and the owner felt that this repetition of meals was too much of an imposition for anyone to stay at his hotel. We assured him that his menu was so well chosen and diversified that we could want nothing better. He beamed, let us stay, and every once in a while would say with a mysterious smile, "I have something special for your dinner tonight." Then he would solemnly serve us a pheasant or something equally spectacular. After a two-week stay and many unforgettable hikes, we parted the best of friends.

LOURDES

On our way back from the mountains, we visited several cities. Our strongest impression was of Lourdes. We had read Zola's novel about that city and heard much debate about it, particularly from several medical friends. We had also heard a moving story from a French doctor, an agnostic, a cynic even, who told of hearing through the thin walls of his room at Lourdes the pathetic sobbing and praying of a crippled woman, appealing desperately to the Supreme Power after all human power had failed her.

The day was hot; the sun knew no mercy. We walked from the station along the street leading to the grotto. The stores on both sides displayed cheaply made religious objects—rosaries, crucifixes, statues of the Virgin. The city was full of pilgrims: We were told later, some 40,000 Irish pilgrims had congregated in Lourdes that day, which happened to be Ireland's pilgrimage day. We reached the shrine, saw the subterranean church, saw thousands of crutches hanging on the walls, mute testimonies to "miracles" occurring after bathing in the pool or otherwise during the pilgrimage to the Blessed Virgin. The crutches reminded us of Anatole France's skeptical remark that he would rather have seen the crippled legs discarded after healing.

Exhausted by the heat, depressed at seeing about us so much human wretchedness—distorted faces, twisted limbs, the blind, the epileptic, women with legs that looked like heavy barrels, the sick on stretchers, the sick on crutches, the sick crawling or moving in little boxes on wheels—we sat down on a bench in a small square near the Basilica. We wanted to rest and to consider whether to leave Lourdes right away or to stay longer. Next to us sat a rather young woman, a typical middle-class housewife. Answering some casual remark of hers, I mentioned that we might leave the city shortly. She exclaimed with astonishment, *"Comment, madame? Vous voulez partir sans avoir vu les miracles?"* (What, madam? You want to leave without having seen the miracles?) There was no doubt in her mind or voice that miracles would happen. This aroused our interest, and we assured her that we would stay to witness them.

Shortly thereafter, the pilgrims began to flock to the Place du Rosaire. We followed the stream to the circular Basilica towering over the square. On both sides, its broad ramps seemed to embrace the entire square like enormous arms. We were early and found a good spot on the left slope, high above the square. Nurses and relatives rolled stretchers on which lay the sick or crippled, arranging them next to one another, close to the walls below the ramps. Under the burning sun, the pilgrims gradually filled the square, leaving only its center unoccupied, for the priest. He appeared and began to pray in a ringing voice that reached every corner of the square. When he shouted, *"Seigneur, faites guérir nos malades!"* (Lord, heal our sick!), the crowd knelt, many cried, some kissed the ground, others stretched their arms to the sky. He repeated over and over, *"Seigneur, faites guérir nos malades!"* and the crowd repeated his appeal with fervor. Then he shouted, *"Seigneur, ayez pitié de nous! Seigneur, faites votre choix!"* (Lord, have pity on us! Lord, make your choice!) A kind of delirium gripped the praying pilgrims. The air was filled with imploring voices trying to reach the sky, to penetrate the invisible barrier, to touch the Lord, to reach Him with their supplications. There was no escape from those loud, pleading, clamoring voices, from the ecstasy that gripped the kneeling crowd. The priest continued in a voice that seemed to grow stronger and ever more insistent, *"Seigneur, ayez pitié de nous! Seigneur, faites votre choix!"*

From our position, we could see the cripples try out their limbs, checking them, hoping that the Lord had chosen them for His mercy. Even more pathetic were the mothers, who examined their crippled or sick babies on stretchers, touching their legs and arms with infinite love, praying for a miracle. Their despair, their resignation, was painful to watch; they seemed crushed. What now? Where to turn? We were shaken by that concentration of faith, hope, and misery. Who knows, it might have taken months for some of these sick people and their families to prepare for the trip to Lourdes and get here, only to return more miserable than before, bereft of their last hope. We saw one sick person, then another, breathe his last; the nurses quietly covered them with blankets and rolled the stretchers away. A woman next to Wolik said, "They are lucky! The Lord chose them to stay with Him. They died in ecstasy." The mass continued.

We asked what happened next, and were told that a procession of pilgrims would come to Our Lady of Lourdes at the Place du Rosaire at night, to thank Her for the miracles performed. We had not seen any miracles, so we decided to see the procession at least. It was indeed a sight! The night was pitch-dark; only the brilliant stars glowed in the sky. The crowned statue of the Virgin, on an invisible rock, was illuminated and seemed to float in the air. The spire of the Basilica was flooded with light. The pilgrims began to arrive, each with a lighted candle. They ascended the ramp at the right, with the glowing tapers in their hands, singing *Ave Maria*. They crossed the Basilica, came down the left slope, and zigzagged endlessly from one end of the square to another. This group was not praying, unlike that in the afternoon; it was passionately serenading the Blessed Virgin, singing *Ave Maria* again and again. Scores of thousands of tapers danced in the air, flickered in the darkness; from above, the crowd looked like a winding serpent with millions of flaming eyes. The serenade was still resounding as we left the square and went to the railway station.

OUR WEEKEND RETREAT

Our sedentary life stimulated a yearning for physical activity, and our love of nature intensified the desire for outdoor relaxation. So, over the years, we took up various sports, one by one. Every time we could take a few hours for ourselves, we hiked in the forest at the edge of Berlin, the Grunewald. We skated on the Wansee; the ice was occasionally rough, but the frosty air, the blue sky, and the feeling of free space around us more than compensated for its unevenness. One winter we went to the Austrian mountains, ordered shoes and skis made for us, and initiated a new adventure. Though we never mastered this sport very well, we fell in love with it and tried to squeeze in a week or ten days every winter for skiing in the Riesengebirge, Czechoslovakia, or elsewhere. We usually arrived with skis and knapsacks containing the essentials, skied from the station to the hotel hidden in the snow-covered forest, loved every minute we spent there and, most of all, the last part of the trip— skiing down the hills straight to the station. We returned home with ventilated lungs, tanned faces, and a fresh supply of vigor.

While hiking near Berlin, we discovered a village with one rather large and several small closed-in lakes and thought that it might be a good place for summer weekends. On the shore of one of those small lakes, accessible to shore owners only, we saw a flower garden, and inside the garden, a modest cabin. The woman who owned it, a flower grower with a market stand in Berlin, twice a week took her flowers to the city to sell. The cabin, consisting of one large room, was unfurnished and without electricity, but was charmingly located. We offered to rent it for the summer months if the owner would put in electricity, give the place a coat of fresh paint, and furnish it with the bare essentials. We would provide the rest. The cabin was connected with the lake by a tiny bridge, to which a boat was tied; these became "our lake" and "our boat." Every weekend we brought something to make the cabin more livable—china, an electric plate, pots and pans, warm blankets; we had folding chairs and a table delivered, and brought old sweaters, bathing suits, robes, linen, books, and writing supplies for ourselves and frequent guests. Gradually the cabin began to look like a modest but comfortable weekend house. Of course, Wolik told our friends that it was equipped with Oriental luxury. For swimming, we went to the larger lake, across the woods, but for boating we used our peaceful, quiet lake, on which we were frequently alone. After that year, we took an annual lease and became so fond of that little place and its opportunities for outdoor activities that we hated to have to close it in winter for lack of heating facilities. We went there as late as November, hiked the whole day, had a hot meal while the hot-water bottles took the chill out of the otherwise freezing bedsheets (an electric blanket would have been ideal!), and slept like kittens.

In our leisure moments, Wolik was fond of inventing humorous-sounding new words. He loved, for example, to stretch himself out on the grass in a clearing and bask in the sun. In Russian, a clearing is called *lujaika* (a diminutive from the word *lug*, or meadow), and he substituted the letter *e* for *u*, making it *lejaika*, a nonexistent word yet attractive-sounding, with a clear meaning—a place to lie. When I said that I loved his dimples (in Russian, *yamochki*), he replied with a twinkle in his eyes, *"Yamochki ot Emmochki"* (using the diminutive of Emma and implying that the dimples came from smiling at me).

By the fall of 1929, nearly six years after we started *The World in Figures*, all seven volumes and the supplementary book on Germany had been published. We celebrated the occasion with Bortkiewicz and several other friends. By that time, Wolik had acquired such recognition in Germany that he had several offers for future work, including one from the Board of the General Federation of Labor Unions (ADGB, in the German abbreviation) to head their statistical department and advise them on economic policy.

WORKING WITH THE UNIONS

We knew, of course, that the German unions had no special regard for intellectuals in general and that very few worked for and with them. The ADGB would never have thought of turning to Wolik if his reputation had not been so thoroughly established in Germany. Yet labor was always closer to Wolik than any other group because he believed in its basic idealism and decency and because he considered labor the underdog. After discussing all aspects of ADGB's offer, we concluded that he should give that opportunity a try.

Financial considerations never played an important part in our life. Satisfaction from work in both the scientific and the political sense always prevailed over all other advantages. Moreover, we always earned more than enough for our way of life, except perhaps during one short period after our arrival in France from Nazi Germany, and so we could always be on the giving side. This made us indifferent to the material aspect of any offer of work. We discussed such propositions primarily from the point of view of their significance, interest, and political acceptability. Wolik never accepted work just to make a living. We always had *korabliki,* our little boats on the high seas, with an outline of a project, or a manuscript of a book or a series of articles. There were also unexpected requests for literary work, participation in some institutional project, lecture series, and so on. We accepted some and refused others that did not offer any intellectual appeal.

While discussing ADGB's offer and, generally, our future plans, I raised a question to which we later returned many times, that of emigrating to the United States. True, we were successful in our work and well off in Germany, but we did not feel congenial with the Germans and so did not want to become German citizens. For different reasons, we did not think of acquiring French citizenship either, and it was totally unrealistic to think of returning to a democratic Russia. Therefore, I suggested that we should reorient our thinking toward the United States where, I felt sure, we would be more at home than in any European country. Wolik was totally unresponsive to this suggestion. It seemed imprudent to him to leave the country and even the continent where his work was recognized and valued and where we had many friends and professional contacts for an entirely new environment where we might or might not achieve as much. There was validity in his reasoning, and we decided Wolik should accept work with the ADGB.

Thus, joint work on a large project from morning till night was interrupted for the time being. Work with Bortkiewicz also came to an end, but not our friendship and intellectual contact. As for us, we continued, in a sense, to work together in our usual fashion. I began the German translation of Wolik's two volumes of memoirs, published several years before in Russian. Wolik took a very active part in this by expanding the text with additional material to make it more understandable to Germans not familiar with all shades of political attitudes in Russia and to incorporate various experiences that had since gained in importance in his mind. I edited the translation with a German friend, a true polyglot, Friedrich Schlömer, and both volumes were published in Berlin, the first in 1931, the second in 1933. I also wrote on women's work and municipal problems, and we wrote other articles together.

For about three and a half years, Wolik worked with the General Federation of the "Free" (Socialist) Labor Unions, which included about 80 per cent of all organized workers in Germany and was very influential in the country's political and economic life. Wolik had to deal with the Board of the Federation and the leaders of the individual unions. They were able, intelligent people but without much education; the only other intellectual in the office was Lothar Erdman, editor of the ADGB's monthly magazine, *Die Arbeit*. Wolik was treated with great respect, but he never established a close personal relationship with anyone in the ADGB. We hardly had real social contact even with Erdman, though Wolik was very fond of him.

Generally speaking, we and the German intellectuals were not too congenial. Despite Wolik's scholarly success (and there was no trace of animosity or jealousy in their recognition of a foreigner), we felt rather lonely in Germany and in all the eleven years spent there we did not build up even one real friendship with a German family, though we had, of course, many good and pleasant acquaintances.

Our only real friendship was with Karl and Louise Kautsky from Austria. Wolik had met them in Rome, to where they had gone with other leaders of the European Socialist parties before leaving for Georgia, and Louise had visited me in the hospital at that time. I cannot remember when we met again in Berlin, but we soon became very good friends, and Louise stayed with us when she came to Berlin from Vienna, their permanent home. She was a lively, refined person with fine bearing. She was completely unpretentious, and it was easy to feel comfortable with her on all occasions. Moreover, she had a gay disposition and could tell many stories. Usually we would invite some of her many friends for dinner, and she used to say, "Life at the Woytinskys' after they've had a party costs nothing. They could feed another group with what's left." Every morning, she received a letter from Karl, which she read to us at the breakfast table. He wrote of his work, his sons, this and that. I recall one part of a letter in particular:

> Last night, I was working quietly in my study, when I heard a light knock at the door. Without raising my head, I said, "Come in." Would you believe it, an angel flitted in, dainty, all white, with two large wings. Without a word, she began to circle the room, fluttering her wings and clapping her hands. I watched, spellbound. Have you guessed who that angel was? Our little Mary [their maid], ready to go to a masquerade. She wanted to show me how she looked and to wish me good night.*

In the beginning of Wolik's work with the ADGB, he concentrated on the improvement and reorganization of statistics and on writing articles for the union periodicals and lecturing. That year, we got into the habit of Sunday walks in the woods, often with some of our Russian friends, or enjoyed skating or playing tennis. During the years when we

* When Hitler was about to enter Vienna, the Kautskys fled in one of the last planes to Amsterdam. Karl soon died there, and Louise fell into the hands of the German Gestapo and was taken to a concentration camp in Germany. There she discovered that her younger son, Benjamin, arrested earlier, was in the neighboring camp for men. Louise died a natural death—that is, not in the gas chamber.

were working on *The World in Figures,* it never occurred to us to regard Sunday as a leisure day, and so it was novel and pleasant to plan
something special for each Sunday. That day, of course, was different
for us from the Sundays of many families in Berlin, as described by a
friend, a social worker: "Everybody expects Sunday to be different and
pleasant, but as the hours pass and the day is as dull as the others, people become resentful, begin to quarrel, find fault with this and that,
nag at each other, and all kinds of troubles result."

Occasionally, our Sunday walk in the Grunewald had a funny ending.
One Monday, Wolik went to a barber to have his hair cut. The man
looked at him, laughed, and then explained: "I saw you yesterday in the
woods and said to my wife, 'That gentleman needs a haircut.' "

There was a large Russian colony in Berlin, mostly refugees from
the new regime—representatives of various political parties, from the
extreme right and the monarchists to the leftists among the Socialists.
Our friends were largely among the moderate Socialists, but there were
several among the progressive intellectuals without party affiliation. In
general, we maintained a broad spectrum in our contacts with people.
Some of the friendships deepened in the course of years, particularly
with one family. Contacts with relatives in Russia were few and sparse.
I heard occasionally from my dearest childhood friend, Manya, of whom
I have spoken.

APPROACHING DOOM

That peaceful time, when Wolik was working predominantly on methodological statistical problems, came to an end. As the German economic scene began to show ominous signs of an approaching depression,
Wolik's role in the ADGB and the orientation of his work underwent a
radical change. His reorganization of union statistics enabled him to
show the growing stresses in the German economy. With his acute
responsiveness to any increase in unemployment, Wolik became alarmed
when neither the Government nor the political parties realized the impending danger. He sounded a warning as early as 1930 in several articles, and from that time until the Hitler regime was installed he led a
passionate fight against unemployment and depression. His whole being
—mind and heart—was engaged in that fight.

From 1930 through the first quarter of 1933, Wolik published scores
of such articles in various periodicals, mostly in Germany but also in
the Scandinavian countries, The Netherlands, Austria, Czechoslovakia,
in the organ of the International Labor Office, Geneva, and so on. He
published a book on the dangers of deflation and the methods of com-
bating it as an international problem, *Internationale Hebung der Preise
als Ausweg aus der Krise.** Finally, he fought for the policy of public
works and deficit spending in Germany itself, when it became clear that

* *The International Rise of Prices as the Solution of the Crisis* (Leipzig: 1931).

there was no hope for any international action. (Later, the United States adopted a similar policy in the New Deal.)

Wolik did not just theorize about the danger of mass unemployment; he felt it in his bones. At an impressionable age, in his youth, he had lived in close contact with the unemployed, felt their worries and suffering, saw good, respectable men demoralized, reduced to thievery and drunkenness, saw them seized by a spirit of violence, of hatred for an indifferent society. Telling of his experiences during that early period, he once said, "How can I forget Peter, a fine, skilled worker, intelligent and levelheaded? One morning, he came to my office greatly agitated and broke down. 'Is this right, tell me, is this right? My only child has become a streetwalker.' What could I say to him when he cried like a child?" In the Germany of the 1930's, he continued the fight he had begun in 1906-7 in St. Petersburg. He saw the sword of Damocles hanging over Germany at a time when its leaders were mostly concerned with the integrity of their country's currency.

While Wolik enlisted the support of the ADGB and its monthly, *Die Arbeit,* opened its pages to him, the Social Democratic Party opposed the unorthodox solutions he recommended to combat the depression. Its press attacked him without giving him the opportunity of defending his opinion. This unfairness angered him, and he fought back with sharper words than he would otherwise have used. The ADGB gave him its moral support, but it was not a fighting organization. Its leaders were decent men, but sedate, unimaginative, and hesitant, and they wanted to put off the fight "until the appropriate moment." The ADGB would not oppose the SD Party, with which it had been allied, and especially not Rudolf Hilferding, the Social Democratic Party's recognized authority on finances.

I did not know Wolik in 1906-7 when, singlehandedly, he fought for the unemployed against his party and all other forces in St. Petersburg. Therefore, I cannot compare his emotions then with his mood in the 1930's, when again he led a lonely fight against both the party he was closest to and against the orthodox economists and official Government policy. Wolik felt frustrated. His ideas, now familiar to all students of economics, then appeared revolutionary, almost fantastic, the brain storm of an egghead who, in the terminology of this country, had never met a payroll. The tepid support offered by the ADGB was based mostly on political considerations; they could understand the danger of mass unemployment, the only thing they really understood in that controversy. But in the theoretical controversy about economic measures to counteract the depression nobody in that organization was equipped to take a forceful stand. All the influential economists within and without the Government held that the depression had to run its course and that the time-tested measures of low wages, low interest rates, and low prices would automatically bring about the desired reversal in the business cycle. The same conviction prevailed in the Social Democratic

Party, which in combination with the unions could exert considerable influence on Government policy. There was a nearly unanimous front against Wolik. Yet he was sure that he was right, and he continued to fight, hoping against hope that he could breach that front.

Wolik became unhappy, depressed, often moody. His usual cheerfulness, even his gentleness, were gone. At times, he was nervous and irritable. I tried to cheer him up in every way I could, often without showing my intention or letting it become too evident. Occasionally I confronted him with a mirror and asked, "Can you recognize 'our gentle Wolik'?" He could not help laughing, and we could again chat light-heartedly. He always liked gay, amusing things, bright colors, all sorts of toys, so I would divert his gloomy thoughts to merrier things by decorating the dining table with bright flowers, bringing in a book on art with colorful reproductions, asking him to solve a Japanese wooden puzzle, or showing him some unusual toys. All this helped but, of course, for only a short time. Perhaps Wolik needed me more then than at other times; I do not know. I do not know because most of the time, if not all the time, we did not feel like two separate beings, and subconsciously or unconsciously our feelings and reactions merged to such a degree that when more blood was needed in one heart than in the other, the transfusion was automatic.

A helpful diversion came with an invitation to present a paper at the International Conference on Population in Rome. In that large conference of statisticians and demographers from most European countries, our *World in Figures* was universally known. As a result, Wolik met with great respect, almost awe, and even I shared in the recognition, from not only the German delegates but also the delegates of the Scandinavian and Low Countries in particular.

In addition to the interesting meetings, Rome itself was always an inspiration to Wolik. At every successive visit, he discovered a fountain, a statue, a little street, previously overlooked, and he never failed to spend several hours in the Forum, one of his favorite spots.

The Governor of Rome invited the members of the Conference to an alfresco dinner at his palace. This was just the thing for Wolik: guards in medieval uniforms at the entrance, torchbearers in gay-colored array guiding us through the dark garden, the broad terrace of the palace with an unparalleled view over the illuminated city, a visit to the Governor's museum, open only on exceptional occasions. I do not believe that any delegate was more susceptible to that magnificent combination of history, pageantry, and beauty than Wolik.

Next morning, when Wolik was attending some methodological discussion, I decided to pay a visit to my favorite Venus of Cirenaica in the National Museum. The first time I had been there, I had sat in the rotunda, which she occupies, for an hour or more, and on returning to the hotel, had surprised Wolik by my failure to notice the absence of a head on that statue. This time, I again sat down and enjoyed that perfect incorporation of a woman's beauty. The Italian guard looked at me rather suspiciously for a while. Finally, he came over and told me that he, too, loved that Venus above the other sculptures in the museum and was glad when it was his turn to be on duty here. We chatted for a few moments, and in a sudden display of good will, he gestured for me to approach the statue. After convincing himself that nobody else was around, he suggested that I pass my hand over the statue. I did, following every curve, every tensed muscle. Then he leaned toward me and said, "Marvelous, isn't it? I will tell you who taught me this. One day I was on duty here when two gentlemen came—one old, with gray hair, the other much younger. They spent a lot of time in the rotunda and talked in a language I did not understand. It was almost closing time, so I went in, and I saw the old gentleman touching the statue just as you did. I went up to him and said that it was not permitted to touch the statues. Then he said, 'Give me your hand, and you will learn something you have never known.' He took my hand and let it move slowly, slowly over each curve of the body, which I had never noticed by just looking at it, and added, 'You must touch every muscle, follow every movement of the body, if you want to appraise how fine the statue is.' And, *signora,* you will never guess who that old gentleman was. It was Rodin, the famous Frenchman!"

We went back to Italy again that year, first to Venice, then to Capri, known the world over for the beauty of its location, its luxuriant vegetation, glorious sunrises and sunsets, and unforgettable scenery. Immediately, Wolik insisted that I wear a red skirt and a white blouse (very suitable there, by the way) and got himself two white suits and bright ties. He was in such a gay mood that it seemed as if he had come out from under a heavy weight pressing down on him. He chatted merrily with the boatmen who took us to the grottoes, played with children at the beaches, again was full of fun and youthful energy. We went on long walks; Wolik took many still pictures and I shot moving-picture film.

Yet that world of sun, blue sky, and blue sea also had much poverty, filth, slums. An old woman kept her fruit shop open till midnight. One evening when we stopped to buy fruit, we noticed two little children sleeping on rags spread over some rotten produce. On my questioning, the old shopkeeper said that she had to keep her grandchildren around till closing time, when she could take them home; their mother was in the hospital. I was afraid to think of the kind of home they lived in.

On our way to Berlin, we had to change to a different train. We found a compartment with several empty seats, put our suitcases on the rack, and sat down. Suddenly a little bag fell from the rack to the floor, hitting an old lady's leg in its fall. She began to cry and complain of the pain. Everybody offered something to quiet her. Then one passenger asked, "Whose bag is it?" No one acknowledged ownership. After a while, another man came in and took a seat. Several agitated passengers started to tell him that his bag had fallen and hit the old lady. Greatly embarrassed, he began to apologize in most humble terms, until he suddenly realized that the criminal bag did not belong to him. Then he straightened up, gave us all a haughty look, and declared, "This is not my bag. I withdraw all my apologies, and the matter is closed." I know it was not polite to laugh, but we just could not hold ourselves in and laughed again and again.

We returned to Berlin refreshed and in good spirits. Alas, the economic situation there had continued to deteriorate, unemployment was growing unabatedly, and with it the extremist tendencies—Communist and Nazi—were acquiring more and more followers. Again Wolik plunged into the battle for measures to counteract the depression. He lived that struggle twenty-four hours a day. He saw the catastrophe coming nearer and nearer, realized only too well what Nazism would bring to Germany and the world, yet was helpless to prevent the disaster. The political climate was becoming unbearable. In both the Reichstag and the Prussian Landhaus, the Communists and the Nazis voted together against the democratic government, each counting on seizing power. Yet even in the face of this, what still remained of the democratic forces could not assume the initiative in taking measures against depression and joblessness and thus regain the people's confidence. That confidence had been shattered. I remember standing on the sidewalk in the center of Berlin one day when a Nazi demonstration invaded the streets. A young worker passing by shouted defiantly, "Four months without work. Nobody cares. Must I starve?" We were sitting on a volcano, and the Government and the major democratic parties seemed to be paralyzed.

That period, particularly the year 1932, was the most trying time in our personal life. Wolik was close to despair, and I no longer could cheer him up. "Epos" took full possession of him. The narrow-mindedness and mediocrity against which he had to fight exasperated him. The lukewarm support he got here and there was not enough. He wanted action, wanted to see the results of the policy he was trying to push through. He felt it was the only sound policy in the circumstances. But his hope of achieving any breakthrough in that situation was fading.

I felt that Wolik needed to get away, at least for a while, from this atmosphere of perpetual tension and preoccupation. Fortunately, a suitable occasion presented itself. We learned that Wolik's friend Andrea Caffi was in Paris. Wolik had told me much of him, and he always hoped to find him again and re-establish that friendship of his youth.

CAFFI

I grasped this opportunity and insisted that Wolik should go to Paris to see Caffi. I did not want to go with him, as he suggested, because I thought the impact would be much stronger if they found themselves together without me. Wolik did not wish to have me stay in Berlin alone, and I agreed to spend those few days at Sylt, a resort on the North Sea.

From his train to Paris, Wolik wrote me:

> I am thinking only of you. Andrey will want to know everything about you, and I shall have to describe you to him. But you know how little I value the power of words in such cases. Yet I do like to talk with myself occasionally and to form sentences that I may use later or, more frequently, not use at all. Thus I started to describe my Emmochka to myself. And can you imagine, I did not find one shortcoming, one doubtful feature, only the best and all in superlative degree. The portrait is truthful but not at all artistic, not convincing. If, in the interest of artistic plausibility, I had to reproach you with anything at all, it would be that you are too wonderful, too upright, that you love me too much. With all my efforts to find faults in you, I could not think of anything else.

After meeting Caffi, Wolik wrote:

> We met very warmly, but my first impression was sad. Evidently, twenty-four years do not go for nothing. Andrey has changed very much, his face is unhealthy, puffy. The impression his clothing and his room give is not only of carelessness but also of great need . . . We went down to a restaurant. Andrey told me that in recent months he has had only cold food in his room. Yet his intellectual life is as brilliant and rich as before; all his remarks are highly refined, deep, broad-minded. The years past have left no impact on our personal relations. We talked as if we had parted only a few weeks ago.

In his second letter, Wolik added:

> We lunched and dined yesterday in a miserable restaurant next to Andrey's hotel; he has a swollen foot and cannot walk. He confessed that it was the first time in months he had had a hot meal and had sat at a table with a tablecloth twice the same day. Here is real need. Yet his room is crowded with classical Byzantine writers, notes for a large work on the evolution of Hellenism in the world history; his speech is as sharp and sparkling as in his youth.

The day Wolik left for Paris, I had sent a letter to Caffi telling him how glad I was he existed and describing Wolik's gloom and frustration. I wrote that I was sending Wolik to him in the hope that he would recover his youthful spirit from this meeting and bring new strength from the contact with his best friend. In return, I got this answer from Caffi:

> I am deeply touched by your letter . . . but I cannot conceal the sad truth from you. I believe . . . that Volodya [as he called

Wolik], because of the heavy pressure from his crucially responsible work and the nightmarish European situation (with his vivid description of much I did not know, he made me realize the abyss toward which we are rushing), really needs to "tighten the inner ties with life," as you wrote. I would add that he needs to breathe air less filled with impending storm and, in general, to get a little respite.

By the way, I found Volodya a stronger and greater personality than I expected from my memories of the time when he was in the formative period. Frankly, I ascribe to you the greatest credit in this shaping—particularly in that sensitivity, gentle humaneness, which has so fully survived, in his endearing modesty, uprightness, sincerity. I did not know what to admire more: his manly courage in all situations, the straightforwardness of his well-thought-out direction, or that touch of sadness that does not permit bitterness, his smiling judgment, with a surprising leniency toward weak people and a warm appraisal of those barely adequate. All this against the background of his life experiences, all this when he is forced to act in an alien environment, fully aware that reason can expect nothing but thorns.

Yes, I do somehow feel what Volodya needs, but no matter how indulgently he smooths over his impressions in Paris, you should know what he found here—something from a shipwreck and atmosphere of an almshouse. He could ascribe much to my occasional invalidism, but, of course, he realized all that comes from an irreparable decadence. This is most deplorable, because never before have I wanted so much to be able to give something positive to this meeting, after twenty-four years' separation, with the best friend I ever had. I thought sadly of this today long after he plunged into the "underground kingdom" [the subway]. Of course, as a friend he will accept much and try to explain in the best possible way . . . but there was disappointment. Personally, I got a great deal from this meeting (including the more exact measure of myself). Thank you from the bottom of my heart . . .

Next he wrote a letter to both of us, part of which I quote:

That you, Volodya, see the futility of many efforts of which you could actually be proud and that you are so acutely aware of 1) the dawn of Europe and her impending fall into an abyss and of 2) the stubborn hostility of man (and the mass of humanity, in general) toward reason elevates you very much in my eyes and makes you very close, worthy of love . . . The despondency of the last year which nothing can expel expressed itself in you in a certain gentleness in which shadings of tired resignation merge with some great anxiety . . . You once threw at me the life of Pericles, who ended his life in darkest sorrow, as proof of what you were saying. Indeed, he lost everybody he loved, was undeservedly insulted and slandered by those for whom he had long been leader, benefactor, and idol; he saw clearly the abyss into which his life work—the power of Athens—was to fall. And yet, the Age of Pericles was, and remains, radiant, and he got the highest enjoyment from the contact with the sensitive, refined Aspasia, from the great discussions with Anaxagoras, from feeling the imperishable beauty of the creations of Phidias, from the brilliant political successes (not personal but of his system, which has become the pattern for humanity) achieved by the power of his genius—all this could not be obliterated by the terrible sufferings in the evening of his life.

Most probably, for the "sadness of Volodya" the best help can come from Emma. However, whatever the warmth of friendship can do, I hope, he will find it in me, at any moment . . .

Later I shall write again of Caffi. What saddened me then was that we were not much better off than we had been. Wolik went back to his work, and the old wheels began to spin again in the same direction. Some gleam of hope came when he gained the very important support of Albert Thomas, Director of the International Labor Office (ILO). On his visit to Berlin, Thomas made a date with Wolik, had a long discussion with him, and asked him to write an article on the depression for the ILO's monthly magazine, published in three languages. On returning to Geneva, he wrote Wolik about the promised article, saying that he would see to it that it was published prominently and without delay.*

As the depression deepened, the idea of public works began to spread. Several economists, mostly young and therefore little known and without authority, shared Wolik's view that the chief enemy was deflation, and not the inflation feared by the Government and the Social Democratic Party. They wrote articles to that effect and spoke about it in theoretical discussions, but none of them tied his professional reputation to such views as unreservedly as did Wolik, to whom any theoretical alibis in such a fight had always been distasteful.

Yet he did find two allies, with whom he worked out the outline of a plan for halting the depression. These were Fritz Tarnow, the head of the German carpenters' union and a member of the ADGB board, and Fritz Baade, an outstanding economist and a high-ranking Government official. Their plan became known as the Woytinsky-Tarnow-Baade Plan, or the W-T-B Plan. Coincidentally, these three letters were well known to every newspaper reader in Germany: The German press agency Wolff-Telegraphen-Bureau used the same letters.

The Plan was the most articulate piece of economic thinking to appear in Germany during that time. It sharply attacked the policy of deflation, which was bringing the country closer to catastrophe with every passing month. It advocated large-scale public works, at the price

* "International Measures to Create Employment: A Remedy for the Depression," *International Labor Review* (Geneva), No. 1 (1932).

of deficit spending and controlled inflation. The only political force that could activate the Plan and rally the working masses around it was the Social Democratic Party, but in a decisive meeting with the leadership of the trade unions, it refused its support. The door was now open to Hitler.

Wolik was in a state of perpetual gloom. Even at home, he could not think of anything else. Returning from the office, he went straight to his desk to write another article. Requests came from all sides, and he did not refuse any opportunity to express his opinion, even when it came from a rather unimportant tabloid, or to rebut attacks on the W-T-B Plan. All in all, it was a nightmarish year!

Though I was fully on his side, I decided that the situation was beginning to make such inroads on our personal life that I must call Wolik's attention to it. Perhaps excerpts from the letter I wrote then would express my feeling better than I can describe it now:

> This last awful year I have suffered for you, for myself, and for our love. Most of all for you. I would be so happy if I could help you in any way, brighten your spirits. I feel so terribly sorry for you and am so terribly sad to see your gloom and not be able to help you. You said, "There can be no help in such a situation." I could not agree with this, and thinking of you and what I could do for you, I began to check the role of "lyricism" in your feelings now . . . You once told me that the "tone" of love may be brighter or duller, depending on one's emotional state, but that its substance is unchangeable. I have felt depressed when its "tone" was lusterless and happy when it revived and sparkled, but have lived in unshakable security that such a great harmonious love as ours is stronger than life and death . . . When I began to realize that in a difficult time like now not only do you not seek a foothold in lyricism but it cannot even offer you any help, I began to be alarmed. This alarm appeared and vanished because you told me repeatedly that you were giving yourself as fully as before, with all the love of which you were capable. Again I reproached myself that instead of thinking of you, I thought of our love and myself . . .
>
> This whole winter you have been so sad . . . Why? Why do you lose your poise at each reverse? Why is it that important to you? Isn't it much more important to preserve a great, healthy feeling inside you? Haven't you now reached a point at which the superficial and irrelevant are pushing the main, the fundamental, into the background, if not ousting it altogether? . . . But, Wolik, my dearest love, I told you quite recently that if you cannot give me that great love that alone is acceptable to me, I would say as in Irkutsk, "This is too little for me." Then you assured me that you loved me more than yourself, more than your life, and at seeing your eyes veiled with tears, I forgot everything in the world . . . I know you are sure of my love, but love is like a plant—to grow and be storm-

Emma Woytinsky's parents.

Emma Woytinsky as a college student, preparing herself for a career as an educator.

W. S. Woytinsky as a student at the University of St. Petersburg, 1904. He was at
this time already the author of a book on
economic theory, *Market and Prices*.

Emma and Wolik in Siberia, 1916; these two pictures were taken on the day of their engagement.

Помнишь, любимая, Ты не разъ говорила мнѣ, что въ моей жизни любовь занимаетъ меньшія мѣста, чѣмъ въ Твоей жизни? Я никогда не возражалъ, такъ какъ въ глубинѣ души соглашался, что это такъ.

А за этотъ мѣсяцъ я убѣдился, что это не такъ. За этотъ мѣсяцъ я убѣдился, что и въ моей жизни любовь - всё, что любовь моя къ Тебѣ заполнила всю мою жизнь, переросла мою душу.

Дѣточка моя ненаглядная! Ты - вся моя жизнь, весь мой міръ. Въ Тебѣ - вся моя радость, весь свѣтъ мой. Безъ Тебя, безъ Твоей любви я не могъ бы жить ни одного дня.

Excerpts from two letters written by Woytinsky in the Fortress of Peter and Paul, Petrograd, where he was detained by the Communists after his unsuccessful resistance to their November, 1917, *coup d'état*. (The longer excerpt was dated Nov. 30–Dec. 1, 1917; the shorter one, Dec. 3–4, 1917.)

Я шелъ къ высшему доступному въ мірѣ счастью, а думалъ, что иду на муку. Но даже, если бы къ жесточайшимъ мукамъ я долженъ былъ придти черезъ любовь къ Тебѣ, я пошелъ бы этимъ путемъ, отдалъ бы за Твою любовь жизнь и душу.

The Woytinskys hiking on the Höhenweg (Summit Trail), Schwarzwald, Germany, in 1923. Their first experience of crossing a snow-covered summit awakened a passion for mountain climbing in both Emma and Wolik.

At Krimml, Austria (1927), one of the Woytinskys' starting points (the others were Innsbruck and Zellensee) for mountaineering during six summers (1922–27). They spent eight to nine weeks each summer in the Tirol, hiking from one mountain refuge to another and climbing one glacier after another.

On a glacier in the Tirol, 1927.

Descending from a glacier in the Tirol; rest after the descent, which always had to be complished before noon.

The Woytinskys explored Canada in 1937, after their first cross-country trip in the United States (in 1936). These pictures were taken in Laurentian National Park, which was then in the first stages of development; the accommodations were primitive, the tourists few.

At their home in Washingt[on]
in 1955, the Woytinskys e[njoy]
some of the travel films t[hey]
took on their numerous tr[ips]
throughout the United Sta[tes]
and abroad.

The Woytinskys enjoying [the]
flowers of their Washingt[on]
garden.

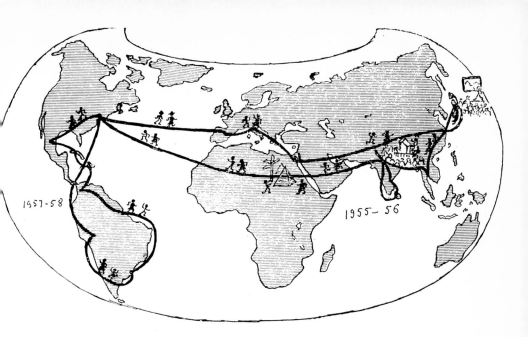

is map, which decorated a Christmas
'd sent by the Woytinskys to their
ends, shows the route of their two lec-
'e tours—to the Far East in 1955–56
d to Latin America in 1957–58.

ie Woytinskys arriving in Cuzco,
ru, in 1957.

W. S. Woytinsky (1957).

Emma S. Woytinsky (1953).

resistant, it must get nourishment . . . This nourishment, in our case, can come only from a loving, intimate contact of souls, the oneness of our feelings, the desire to be better, more perfect, in the eyes of the beloved. If, despite all the hardships and agonies we have lived through, we were able to preserve our young, beautiful love, we would be just as happy as before. There is nothing in the whole world I would not do for you, no love is stronger and brighter than mine, no pride greater than my pride in you, no devotion more constant than mine. I am sorry if I am making you unhappy. The aim of my life has been to be the source of love, tenderness, happiness, for you . . . The awareness that you are mine, that you love me, fills me with pride and triumph, and the thought of our years together makes my heart beat faster . . .

Here are excerpts from Wolik's answer:

I look at your picture, your happy, bright smile, and am writing to you, my dearest, dearest love. I know why you are sad, why your happiness has lost some of its luster, and I know that it is not in my power to help you . . . because I am too dull, too pedestrian for you. I love you with all my heart, but it is not the love worthy of you, not the love of which you dreamed. Yet I do not possess more to give you . . . I am like a poor man who has unexpectedly found a hidden treasure, joy and happiness . . .

. . . My gentle, sweet, innocent darling! How often have I been afraid in caressing you that my caress was not gentle enough, that I was hurting you . . . Always—in Irkutsk, in Arshan, on the Angara—I was embarrassed by my lusterless, colorless words . . . I remember how strongly I felt this when you read to me what you had written in your diary about the forest, the river, about us . . . As long as you love me, as long as the sun of your love shines on me, you will be sad because we are not equal, because of the contrast between me and the brightness and resonance of your soul . . . My love, I am not guilty before you. No matter whom you would have loved, this sadness would have come. There is no love worthy of you, nobody is worthy of you in the world. It is not that the Great Love of which you dream is not realizable but that your dream of a beloved who would be equal to you and worthy of you is unrealizable. You know, I have told you this many times that I love you more than myself, more than my life. This is all the love I can give, all the love I am capable of.

WE LEAVE GERMANY

Suddenly the situation in Germany became explosive. By the end of January, 1933, Hitler was appointed Chancellor, and shortly thereafter he took all power into his hands.

To us, this meant a complete break with Germany. Beginning with

February, 1933, our Russian friends had left for France, one by one. Many urged us to do the same, especially since Wolik had been in a much more exposed position than any of them. But we both felt that Wolik could not possibly work with the trade unions for three and a half years as an adviser, friend, and companion-in-arms whom they had supported as best they could, and then desert them in an hour of peril to think of his and our safety. We knew what we were risking by staying, but we did not even discuss it, knowing that no other way of dealing with the situation was morally acceptable. Moreover, we still thought that the unions might oppose the Nazis, and this, too, obligated us to stay.

A little before May 1, the traditional Labor Day in Europe, Hitler's Secretary of Labor asked the General Federation of Trade Unions and all the affiliated unions to participate in the joint "celebration" of Labor Day and march with the Black Shirts, thus demonstrating the labor movement's "unity" with the Government. The board of the ADGB convened. They were broken men, aware of complete defeat, of the ignominy of accepting that invitation. Wolik was the only one opposed to joining in that parade. He said that their fate was sealed anyhow and that the only thing they still could do was to preserve the honor of the union movement and the dignity of their own convictions. The rest of the board voted unanimously against his single vote to accept Hitler's invitation. Wolik resigned, said a few friendly words, and left.

He telephoned from the office, and by the time he arrived home, I had packed his suitcase and had found out about the next train to Switzerland. I insisted that he leave without delay; of the two of us, he was in immediate danger. It was imperative to get him out of Germany. Wolik objected vigorously, but I implored him to agree for the sake of both of us. Finally, I went with him to the station, watched the train leave, and returned home.

I could not sleep that night for fear the police would come for him or that the Nazis would apprehend him on the train. Around five in the morning, I decided to get up and to ride back and forth in the subway or walk the streets until Wolik's train reached Switzerland. I made the bed and was ready to leave when the doorbell rang. My heart fell. I opened the door; a policeman asked for Wolik. I said that he had left for his office early to have an hour or two before everybody else came in so that he could finish something from the preceding day. He looked at me suspiciously, and I said reassuringly, "My husband can come to the precinct after his office hours, if you wish. I shall tell him." Just then the telephone rang. In those troubled days, it was customary to alert everybody of the arrest of a friend or acquaintance or a physical attack on them. I picked up the receiver, said pointedly, "I have a visitor," and hung up. In the meantime, the policeman walked through the whole apartment—a liberty unthinkable in the Weimar Republic! Fortunately, Wolik was not there, and the straightened bed did not reveal that I had been alone that night. After many more questions, he left; I alerted the last remaining Russian friend in Berlin and went out. On my return, I found Wolik's telegram—he was safe!

Before leaving Germany, I had to close the accounts of a small group known unofficially as the Political Red Cross. Our activity consisted in collecting money to help political prisoners in Soviet Russia—Socialists as well as Baptists or those of other religions—regardless of the character of their political "crimes." Political Red Cross groups had existed in Tsarist times in almost every Russian city when money, books, and food packages usually could penetrate prison walls without too much difficulty. Such a group could continue this old tradition in Soviet times only because our intermediary was Mrs. P., the wife of an outstanding Russian writer. Because of his exceptional position in Soviet Russia, she enjoyed certain privileges, such as permission to visit some prisoners and send packages to them. This solved the most difficult problem of all—how to deliver what we collected to the inmates of Soviet prisons and concentration camps.

Collecting money was time-consuming but not too burdensome. We organized one or two events a year, with dramatic or musical performances followed by dancing. We rented a hall, hired one or two musical bands, and had a lottery, with prizes contributed by many stores and our own donations. The buffet, too, was donated by us. The income from tickets usually more than covered our expenses for the hall, musicians, waiters, announcements, and so on, while receipts from the lottery and the buffet, booths with fortunetellers, the artistic programs designed by sympathetic painters, and similar attractions brought in substantial sums. We also received money contributions, and the artists who performed on the stage donated their services. In general, the attitude toward our purpose was friendly, and the Russian colony in Berlin cooperated very willingly.

It so happened that I had headed our last ball on New Year's Eve in 1932, and so had in my hands many bills, receipts for payments, and some cash. To clear the accounts before leaving Germany, I took all these to our treasurer, Mrs. L. M. Bramson. She was alone, and we were sitting in the dining room, with our papers and money spread on the table, when the doorbell suddenly rang. We had the same thought: Police. She told me to go to her bedroom and wait there. Yes, it was a policeman. He inquired about Mr. Bramson and, noticing the money and account books, asked what she was doing with all that stuff on the table. She said that her husband was away and would be back shortly; in his absence, she was busy with her monthly bookkeeping. Then the policeman shifted to more serious matters. Did they often have meetings in their apartment? No, their last party was a long time ago. No, the policeman insisted, he was not asking about a party but about political meetings of subversive people, of Communists, which reportedly they had had quite frequently. Sensing malicious denunciation, Mrs. Bramson became both panicky and excited and said that the only people who would falsely accuse them in order to get rid of them must have been the persons living below them; when she moved about her apartment over their heads, they were annoyed by her heavy step and often knocked on the ceiling with the broomstick.

I heard all the talk from the bedroom, but could not see the policeman's face. My friend told me later that his expression of surprise at her quick apprehension clearly indicated that her suspicion was well founded. She again reiterated that they never had any political meetings and never met or were visited by a Communist. The policeman, embarrassed, got up, said he would return to see her husband, and left. I came out of hiding, but both of us were shaken at the thought of what might have happened if he had searched the rooms and found me.

At my own place I had to face SS men collecting money for the Nazi Party. Afraid not to give and hating to give, I tried to look most innocent when saying that their Führer had forbidden foreigners to intervene in the internal political life of Germany and I would be afraid to disobey his order. They assured me that there was no danger in helping their Führer's party, but I could not be convinced. The safest thing, I insisted, was to act correctly, even though I was sorry to disappoint them. In a trolley or the subway, I could not read as I once did. I would not touch a Nazi newspaper, and carrying anything else was too provocative. So I looked down at the floor as everybody else did. There was tense silence except when boisterous, laughing Nazis entered the car and filled the air with their insolent remarks.

I stayed for two more weeks, tying up loose ends, trying to collect money due us from the banks, publishers, magazines. Though I knew that the Nazis had confiscated the second volume of Wolik's memoirs, which had appeared three days before Hitler came to power (and was burned later, with other books, in a public auto-da-fé), I went to the head of the publishing house, the Büchergilde, to see if I could obtain some payment of royalties for the first volume. He refused to pay, saying that he would make himself liable to arrest if he did. I could not ask him, or anybody else, for that matter, to run such a risk. All in all, I collected 2,000 marks (about $450).

The next problem was how to take the money out of Germany. It was forbidden to do so, but everybody tried to, so as not to become a public charge in the country to which they fled. I knew that Wolik was already in contact with the Swiss unions and general magazines and had published several articles in Switzerland, but I wanted to keep those few dollars for us instead of leaving them to the Hitlerites. I asked the advice of a friend who had a Rumanian passport and so felt more secure than the others. He promised to try to convert my money into two large bills, each one for 1,000 marks, but warned it might take a few days.

In the meantime, I paid taxes in advance for the year 1933, so as not to have troubles on that account, and arranged with movers to pack everything in a van on a given day to be shipped when I sent for it, and paid them in advance.

Two days before I expected the packers, there was a commotion on the street; trucks loaded with uniformed SS men were congregating in the next block, known as the artists' and writers' colony. They surrounded the block, put guards at all exits, and began a systematic search, apartment after apartment. From the window, I saw books being carried out and loaded on the trucks and some people being led out by the SS men. What if they moved on to our block? I glanced at our bookshelves —all sorts of "subversive" books that the Nazis would love to burn. Would they take just the books, or me, too? I must get rid of the books, but how?

Our block, like the others, was a complete square, with a paved yard inside. In its center was a roofed stand for trash cans. I took a wastebasket, filled it with books and pamphlets, covered them with trash, and went downstairs. Once in the yard, I was terrified. There were hundreds of windows in that six-story apartment block, and it seemed to me that from each of them somebody was spying on me. Anyway, it was possible for someone to do just that. Under the roof of that stand, I felt even more frightened. At any minute, another tenant might appear with trash and see me. I lifted the lids of several huge cans. Some were filled to the top; I could not use them. Then I found some half-filled ones, threw my stuff into them and took trash from other cans to cover my books, all the time looking around to see if anybody was coming. Half dead from fear, I repeated this trip three times, calling myself a coward and reminding myself that Wolik thought I was fearless.

Down the street, the search continued until about dark, then all the trucks left; our block was not on the list.

On the eve of my departure, I went to say goodbye to a German family with whom we had been on friendly terms for several years. The man, a Jewish lawyer with a large practice, did not approve of our leaving Germany. Why? Just because of Hitler? *"Es wird nicht so heiss gegessen wie gekocht."* ("Food is not eaten as hot as it is cooked.") "Hitler won't last forever. Moreover," he added reassuringly, "though it is a shame that you did not become naturalized here, there still are some small states where the Socialists still hold power and could arrange citizenship papers in no time." I looked at him incredulously: How could one be so naïve as to suggest citizenship in Hitler's Germany? "Well, well," he concluded, "I realize that you have made up your mind. You Russians are nomads, always on the go."

Many Germans, like that lawyer, could not grasp at once the full meaning of the impact Hitler's regime would have on every facet of life. Extreme reactionary measures, yes, they expected this; but upsetting the entire government system, returning Germany to the religion of the Middle Ages, making bestiality the law of the land—impossible!

Finally came the day of packing and departure. My train was leaving at around eight in the evening. The movers left, and I waited in the apartment for the friend to bring me the large bills. He came, I tied the two bills in the corner of a handkerchief and, without thinking, opened one of the two suitcases I was taking with me. It contained only two tennis rackets, each rolled up in a bathrobe. I put the kerchief with the money into the pocket of the robe on top. Not until I was sitting in the train and saw seven other passengers in the compartment did I realize to what danger I was exposing myself. If the Nazis should discover the money, they would arrest me and I might never see Wolik again. And for what? That miserable money. What a fool I had been! But I could not change anything. I had to sit quietly and pretend to be calm so as not arouse any suspicion. All the people around me might be Nazis.

We reached the border early in the morning. German customs officers, accompanied by SS men, entered our compartment. When my turn came, one of the customs officers pointed to the suitcase with the rackets and robes. I took it down, unlocked it. He looked in and asked, "What is this?" I said, "My husband is vacationing in Switzerland. We are going to play tennis and swim in the lake." He pulled out the robe, shook it, and stuck his hand in a pocket. My heart pounded dreadfully, and I didn't breathe. He slipped his hand out, and I knew that that was the empty one. Then he turned to the next passenger. I closed the suitcase and calmly put it back. Then the Swiss customs officers appeared, and shortly thereafter I was in Wolik's arms!

6. Our Last Years in Europe

AGAIN WE WERE in Switzerland. We knew most of its cities, had climbed its mountains, and hiked in its valleys. It is not an exciting country intellectually, but after the tension in Germany, we needed to have a civilized atmosphere, needed to see good-natured, smiling people, to hear people talk without hatred in their voices. I remember how impressed I was by a most insignificant incident: Two young men collided on their bicycles; both alit, they exchanged a few words, shook hands, and parted. I looked at them and thought that in Germany there would have been violent cursing, perhaps a fight; there, everybody's nerves were strained to the breaking point.

Little by little, the German nightmare began to fade, though its aftermath reached us every day, in one way or another. Hilferding, the chief culprit, so to speak, in the defeat of Wolik's W-T-B Plan, arrived, sought Wolik out, and in a long meeting, tried to persuade him to work on a joint survey of the depression in Germany. To put it mildly, Wolik was surprised, and of course refused, saying that he had been interested in fighting the depression, not in describing it.

Again I raised the question of moving to the United States, this time more insistently. Wolik was not willing to consider it even as a possibility. I suggested that we should at least keep it in mind in our future discussions. Thus, the choice was between Switzerland and France. Wolik was ready to accept either, but I felt that life would be dull in Switzerland, a beautiful but rather philistine country. Wolik did establish contacts with the Swiss trade unions and helped them to prepare a plan for work adjusted to their country's conditions. But opportunities there for a man of Wolik's caliber were very limited. I was glad when technical difficulties developed in regard to our permanent stay in Switzerland, precipitating a decision to settle in France.

IN PARIS

We went to Paris and after a few weeks in a modest hotel, found a lovely modern apartment with a large living room near the Porte de St. Cloud.

I ordered the movers in Berlin to send the van with our furniture and other belongings to Paris and at the same time asked our "Rumanian" friend to take care of all necessary arrangements. A few days later, he informed us that new permits from the tax office were required. He had been told in that office that we had run away without paying the taxes and the permit would not be given, but he understood that a bribe might help. I wrote back that all taxes had been paid a year in advance but he should hand out bribes and act for us generally without worrying; we approved beforehand anything he did. Then came a telegram that the van had left for France. Our friend's subsequent letter made everybody laugh. He had gone to the tax office, put two large bills on the desk of an employee, who thereupon had prepared the requested license; he then put the permit in his pocket, casually picked up the two bills, and left with both permit and bribe. The dumfounded employee had not dared to say or do anything in the presence of others.

Immediately after our arrival in Paris, Wolik got in touch with Léon Jouhaux and his General Federation of Trade Unions (CGT). The latter had organized a committee to draw up an economic plan. Soon the well-known economists invited to participate began to drop out, one by one. Wolik and Jouhaux jointly prepared Le Plan du Travail (Plan for Work), based largely on the ideas in the W-T-B Plan, Wolik's analysis of deflation and the policy to combat it advocated in his previous writings, with adaptations for specific French conditions.

In contrast to the situation in Germany and Switzerland, Wolik was little known in France, though everybody pretended to have read his books and know of his reputation. Nevertheless, the Statistical Institute of the University of Paris asked him to write a special report on the world economic situation. One of the largest newspapers offered to publish a series of his articles, displaying his first essay on the front page with his portrait. As before, Wolik continued to write for foreign magazines—Dutch, Danish, Czechoslovakian, and so on.

Since our joint work took only part of my time, I enrolled at the École des Hautes Études for postgraduate studies. I concentrated on economic conditions in the United States and prepared two reports—one on American agriculture, the other on the causes of the depression in the United States.

In Paris, we had a large circle of friends, actually five different circles that were not congenial and seldom met but with each of which we had common intellectual interests and with some members of which, very warm personal relations. We had French friends, political and academic; Russian friends of various political orientations except the two extremes (the Whites and the Reds); Georgian friends, made in our work with their embassy in Paris and our stay in Georgia; German friends, refugees from Hitler; and Italian friends, refugees from Mussolini.

We were busy as usual, but we also had time to follow political and

economic life in Europe and elsewhere. We attended important meetings, went hiking on Sundays, alone or with friends. There were a few
friends whom we saw rather often—Tseretelli, Garvy, Caffi.

I want to say more of Caffi because of Wolik's friendship with him
since their youth. Such a friendship can take and overlook much more
than one made in later years, as I know from personal experience with
my childhood friends, Tema and Manya, of whom I shall write later.

Wolik's and my attitude toward people were nearly always the same,
with perhaps occasional shadings of difference. But with Caffi, it was
different. Before he and I met, we had heard much about each other
from Wolik, and expectations were high on both sides. Perhaps too
high. I recognized at once Caffi's superior intellect, his enormous knowledge of the humanities, and his great sincerity; there was also a touch of
the artist in him. Yet there was much that I could not take. His judgments
about people and about the political situation, and his ideas on how to
change the world seemed arrogant and unconvincing to me; they led
nowhere. He was skeptical of everything in a typical French fashion; no
social order satisfied him; he saw falsehood, cupidity, cynicism everywhere and in everything. He dreamed of a fraternity of superior minds
and ideal characters to rule the world. This was his ideal, noble yet
childish, but there was no childishness in him, which might have
made such an attitude more readily understandable. As a matter of fact,
his attitude was not a product of bright faith in the best of man but
the result of bitter disappointment and the intellectual beating he had
taken during a life of hardships of all sorts. His appearance also disappointed me; in Wolik's youth, he might have been charming, but
I met a man who slouched, was careless in his dress, and was fully spent.

Caffi came to see us often, and this was the only instance in our life
in which Wolik and a guest went into the study after dinner and I did
not join them. I was sorry not to be able to come closer to him, to show
more warmth, to establish a real friendship with him. I did not even
try, because it would not have worked. Both of us were sincere, and any
pretense would have been detected. Wolik never reproached me for
this, but now I bitterly reproach myself. I have reread Caffi's letters—
they are so sparkling, yet so confused. But what torments me now is that
in some of his letters there is a heart-breaking sadness and resignation.
Why, why did I not feel his need for warmth, for friendship? I cannot
read the following lines in his letters without pangs of conscience and
a feeling that I failed not only him but also Wolik:

> What you say about my being abandoned is unfortunately true,
> and apparently things will get even worse. The guilt is all mine, in
> my nature, which not only no longer attracts anyone but somehow
> puzzles and at times even bores; in my bewilderment in the face
> of life. I have missed all the opportunities I might have seized; al-
> ways, inevitably, I feel myself guilty, condemned in advance.

When we left France for the United States, Wolik's correspondence with Caffi continued but rather irregularly. The war ended it, and then in 1945 we suddenly received, through a Russian friend, the horrifying news that Caffi had been arrested in Toulouse with other Italians during the war and tortured (I tremble to think of this, he was so feeble). We sent him money and packages immediately. In his last letter, on March 26, 1945, he wrote that he and his comrades had been sleeping on the floor in the torture chamber of the "militia," and added:

> But otherwise, the last years have been less horrible for me than for many others. In 1940, I did not want to leave Europe,* and now I am waiting for an opportunity to return to my so-called native land. I may still be capable of doing something . . . Your packages are really touching, impressive—and the wrapping! We have forgotten it exists . . . But the greatest admiration was for the soap, real sudsing soap, without sand. Europe is almost as much of an invalid as I am. But inveterate rascals do not capitulate too easily. As to myself, I cannot promise anything. But Europe someday will run amuck and arouse the indignation of her virtuous saviors . . .

We later heard that Caffi died in Italy, but could not find out under what circumstances.

We stayed in Paris for seven or eight months, but I cannot say that we established close contacts with the French. Perhaps our active attitude toward politics and life in general irritated the skeptical French. For our part, we felt disappointment at what appeared to us to be a national inertia, a desire to retire into one's own tiny shell and forget the rest of the world. In one cabaret, we heard an actor singing, to the audience's applause, that all that the French people wanted was to live *"chez nous, avec nous, entre nous"* (at home, with ourselves, among ourselves). Academic and political life in France gave us an impression of provincialism, of musty, stuffy air. Political instabilty was then the most stable feature of the country. Yet the French were not dismayed. A friend, a successful businessman in Paris, assured us there was nothing to worry about. When the situation reaches the boiling point, he told us, *"un type viendra"* (a chap will come) who will take things into his hands and arrange everything. Probably Charles de Gaulle personifies this *type.*

Another characteristic that surprised and even depressed us was the complete lack of interest in anything beyond France, or even beyond Paris. A professor of French literature who visited us rather often once revealed in a conversation about summer vacations that for forty years he had gone to Bois Colombe, almost a suburb of Paris. Walking in the little towns around Paris, we saw the high brick walls that separate one

---

* He referred to a chance to go to the United States with other political refugees from Nazism and Fascism, a chance given by President Roosevelt's instructions to consuls to give visas to a rather large number of persons on a list wired from Washington. Caffi was on that list.

house from another. Though we, too, loved privacy, those walls seemed rude, unfriendly, saying sharply, "Keep away!"

These impressions and various small incidents discouraged us, but generalizations are always a risky affair. Moreover, some of our sophisticated friends loved France dearly, praised its superior culture, its refinement. Maybe we were just unlucky in not having experienced these.

Unexpectedly, Wolik received an invitation to attend the annual convention of the International Labor Office (ILO) in Geneva, where the most urgent problem of the day—unemployment—was to be explored. He was the only participant who had prepared a paper on this subject. It was an immediate success, and the ILO asked him to expand the paper into a full report. This was a *korablik* that found its way to our shores, and we received it with much appreciation. Wolik worked on this study into the winter of 1934. When he delivered it, he suggested another survey, on the social consequences of the depression. His report, "Three Sources of Unemployment," met with warm approval by F. Maurette, vice director of the ILO, and Henri Fuss, head of the unemployment section. Maurette was very happy to have the other survey done under the auspices of the ILO.

We began to work on the new project, and soon found that it would be more practical to move to Geneva, where the library of the ILO and much of its unpublished material would be at our disposal. In March, 1935, we were ready to say goodbye to France. Again we discussed moving to the United States. Wolik was as opposed as before. At one moment he even said reproachfully, "You must not raise this question again. I have a definite foreboding that there we would sink to the bottom" (*poydyom ko dnu*). This expression *poydyom ko dnu* became a classic humorous reference during our life in the United States. Wolik himself joked about it occasionally and laughed infectiously over it. But in 1935, this was not a joke to him, and though I came back to this solution several times, I felt he must not be pressed to accept it. Finally, we compromised: Wolik said that work with the ILO would be his last attempt in Europe, and I suggested going to the United States for one year with the understanding that if we were unable to find fully satisfying, inspiring work there we would return to Europe.

IN GENEVA AND OXFORD

With this decision in mind, we went to Geneva, rented an apartment across the park, Perle du Lac, with a view of Mont Blanc from our windows, and within walking distance of the ILO.

Our routine was to work all day in the library, returning to the apartment for lunch. Many people in the ILO knew Wolik or knew of him, and we soon built up friendly relations with several families within that organization.

Perhaps the brief interlude in Geneva would not be worth mentioning except for the insight it gave us into the life of an international organization superimposed on a closed native community, without any contact between these two societies, like two liquids in a container that always remain separate. Neither before nor afterward have we lived anywhere without an immediate contact with the people around us, as we did there. In Geneva, there seemed to be no "people" around as far as the ILO (and, for that matter, the League of Nations, too) was concerned. Some of the members of those two world organizations had lived in Geneva for ten or fifteen years or even more and had no relationship whatsoever with the native population. I asked jokingly several times, "Where are the Swiss? Have you ever met one?" We felt as if we were living on a cruise ship—there were only the passengers and the crew, and within that group special circles were formed which, again, lived like closed communities. There were many interesting people from various countries, but somehow life seemed almost unreal. The League of Nations was another cruise ship, with no contact with the Swiss and only a few social contacts with the ILO passengers.

I do not know whether this pattern is valid for other international bodies or whether specific Swiss conditions had something to do with it. Anyhow, I hoped that Wolik's temperament and his whole being would rebel against that comfortable but insipid life, and I am sure that they would have if we had stayed in Geneva longer.

There were compensations, of course, and I enjoyed them as much as Wolik did. The work on the new book was stimulating, and I had no doubt that if Wolik continued to work with the ILO, he would always be as independent in his work as he had been all his life and would choose his own line of research.

Mountaineering was also a great attraction; we took advantage of every opportunity to spend a weekend in the Alps. In general, we could live closer to nature in Geneva than in a big city, like Berlin or Paris.

As a matter of fact, right after our arrival we established a rather close relationship with nature as represented by a swan family. Our first evening in Geneva we crossed Lausanne Street from our apartment and walked into the park. On the shore of Lake Geneva, we saw a swan sitting on an open nest. The March wind was rough, the temperature low. Suddenly we saw the mother swan get up and slowly stretch her wings back and forth; clearly she was freezing and was trying to warm herself. Where had she learned to do that, in what book? The male swan took her place to protect the eggs, but did so gingerly, apparently afraid he would crush them. I sought out the park custodian to inquire if something could be done to keep the mother swan warm during the nesting period. He explained that swans preferred to rough it while nesting. The year before, the city had built a little house, warm and with all conveniences, for a nesting swan, but she would not move in and had violently resisted attempts of the park workers to carry her there.

We visited the swan family on the way to and from the library every day. The mother swan looked dirty from the rain and the wind and badly needed to make her toilette if she cared at all about the impression she made on passers-by.

Then one day the big event occurred. We found the mother with four little swans roaming about rather hesitatingly but with unmistakable curiosity. I happened to have a loaf of white bread with me, and threw a few small pieces to the little ones. The mother swan disapproved of this food; she picked up every bit of it in her bill and flung it beyond their reach. She was very busy trying to bring some order into the situation, and pushed the blood-stained straw into the water. When we returned, mother swan was nearly finished with her own cleaning up—her feathers were silvery white—but she was still picking up a bit of dirt here and there. The family was reunited—the father had returned, perhaps from a trip for food. The little ones were trying to enter the water, the parents were watching carefully and barred the way if they ventured too far out.

A day or two later, we saw the mother swan lower her right wing to the ground and the little swans climb on top of her back. She closed both wings over them and then cruised majestically on the lake. Wolik called it a "first-class boat trip." Very soon we witnessed a lesson in diving: the father dived first, then the mother, perhaps seven or eight times, until the most courageous of their fledglings decided to take a chance and make the risky move. The parents watched, then encouraged him to try again. Gradually, one by one, all the little swans were diving, while the parents by their own example showed them, patiently but firmly, the right way to go down and come up.

The ILO friends knew of our interest in the swan family and called them the Woytinsky swans. Frankly, they were much more interesting to us than many "passengers" on the ILO cruise ship. It even looked as if the swans recognized us; when we approached their area, they swam toward us, even from a distance.

One morning, on the way to the library, we saw the father swan knocking furiously at a boat anchored close to the gate of the park. When we came closer, we found that the boat had chrome sides. The swan saw his reflection in the bright metal and evidently thought that some stranger was invading his and his family's territory. He fought him vigorously, but the stranger would not fly away. We were late for an appointment and could not linger, but at lunchtime we returned and found the situation unchanged. Worrying over the health and the mental safety of the swan, I looked around, found the park keeper, and insisted that he do something. He brought a large piece of burlap and threw it over the boat. The "enemy" disappeared! The swan was bewildered for a moment, unable to understand where the stranger had gone. Then he turned around and swam off in the opposite direction. We were still discussing the situation with the park keeper when the father swam triumphantly back, followed by his family. He had brought them back from the hiding place where they had been waiting the whole morning. Well, if we did not make contact with the Swiss in Geneva, we were, at least, in close touch with the Swiss swans.

Early in the summer, it became clear that Maurette and Léon Jouhaux had failed in their efforts to ensure a permanent key position for Wolik in the ILO (as the spokesman for the labor group). Wolik then suggested, rather reluctantly, that he had no objection to moving to the United States. His lack of enthusiasm is clear from his letter of September 23, 1935, from Brussels, where he was attending the International Congress of Econometricians and had presented his paper on three sources of unemployment:

> My dearest love,
>
> Returning to your letter, I want to stress that if I have been boorish in recent days, this is not your fault at all. My low spirits are connected with moving to the United States. For me, the departure from Europe is acknowledgment of defeat. This acknowledgment is humiliating. To other people I may say something else, but I can neither deceive myself nor change my mind. This cannot be helped, this is a matter of feelings.

Nevertheless, I was happy, most of all for Wolik, because of my hope that he would find a broader field for his talents in the United States than in any place in Europe. Somehow I was sure that our life in America would be fuller and richer than in Switzerland. Some of our friends, while sorry that we were about to leave, felt that we had made a wise decision. Our Belgian friend, Henri Fuss, ended his letter by saying, *"Je me demande d'ailleurs quel est le pays que vous ne trouveriez pas enchanteur avec tous les dons d'enchantement que vous portez si heureusement en vous-mêmes"* (I wonder, indeed, what country there is that you would not find enchanting with all the gifts of enchantment that you so happily possess in yourselves).

We decided to spend the last two months in England, mostly for the sake of the language. We went to Oxford where our friend, Jacob Marschak, was teaching at All Souls College. He and Marianna, his wife, planned to go to a Belgian resort for six weeks and offered us their house, in which they left their two children, Anne and Tommy, with the housekeeper.

Wolik wanted to write several articles in English and have them edited. I needed English lessons. Marschak recommended Mr. Candliff, a teacher with a fine reputation. We called him up and arranged to visit him. At the gate to his house was an arrow indicating a little building inside a small garden. We went to it, knocked, heard "Come in," opened the door, and on a high stool in a library filled with books on all sides, saw Mr. Candliff, a dwarf, with a highly intelligent, sensitive face and two tiny legs that dangled helplessly. Naturally, we tried to show no surprise or other reaction and began to discuss what hours he could give us, the purpose of work with him, and so on. Subsequently we saw him regularly several times a week and had increasingly long talks about everything—politics in general, Russia, colonialism, philosophy, poetry, and what not. Sitting on his high stool which was on casters, he moved himself about in the large library, and refused any help from me when I showed readiness to bring the book he wanted from the desk or the shelves. Gradually we became fond of one another, and both he and we enjoyed the meetings.

Mr. Candliff tried to persuade us that America was not the right place for people like ourselves (he meant, of course, Wolik). What would we do there? We should stay in England, where we would find kindred souls, appreciation, and surely, opportunities for the right type of work. Of course, he was not successful in his efforts, and he had to resign himself to our departure. He sent us a warm farewell letter telling how much the meetings with us had meant to him and ending by saying that if we should not meet again in this world, he hoped we would meet in the next one. We were touched by this expression of sincere friendliness.

Then a few hours before our departure we got a letter from him that left a bitter taste in our mouths. He had discovered that one of his dictionaries was missing and asked if we had not taken it by mistake. All we had time to do was to send a brief note saying we had not, but it hurt us that he could think it possible, even for a moment. We did not meet him again in this world, and how could we prove by meeting Mr. Candliff in the next world that we do not take books of others "by mistake"?

MANYA

Manya was my closest and dearest childhood friend. I do not recall how and when we met, or how we became inseparable. Probably this happened after the collapse of my plan to run away with Ada, but now I feel that Manya had always been with me. Probably we were drawn to each other at once. She was more heavily built than I, had a freckled but very attractive face and a winning smile, and when she laughed, I heard bells ring. One glance at her face, and there could be no doubt of her inner honesty. She held herself erect and gave the impression that she was equally upright inside.

We were completely sincere and frank with each other in everything; we both wanted to share happiness and not to be shut out when a depressed mood overtook one of us—any other attitude would have been "imperfect" friendship. I called her "Vesnyanka," from the Russian word *vesna* for spring, because there was something charmingly fresh and cheering about her.

In high school, Manya was one grade behind me, but we were together during recesses and most of the time after school. Parting in the evening was a long-drawn-out affair: we walked back and forth from my home to the place she boarded, always finding something important to discuss at the last moment. I do not remember what we talked about so intensely—probably happenings in school, books we read, our dreams and plans. Our family backgrounds were very different, and we felt instinctively that there could be no intimacy between our families.

Manya came from Velizh, a smaller town than Polotsk, where I lived. There was no high school in Velizh, so her mother let her stay with some distant relatives in Polotsk. Manya's father had been dead since her early years. Her mother, owner of a textile store, was an energetic woman with a sharply defined, puritanical attitude toward life. There was something straight but unyielding in her, and perhaps she could not or would not express her love for her two daughters. Manya's sister, Rebecca, was considered a beauty and was very spoiled, but to Manya and me her beauty was too sensual and therefore of no great appeal. When she was very young, Rebecca had married a rich man, much older than she, but she had soon left him. When I met her, she was already divorced. Manya was critical of her sister's vanity, and though she did not express her disapproval openly, Rebecca must have sensed it and was resentful.

Of course, Manya and I were different, too, but this strengthened our bond instead of weakening it. She was more realistic than I, stood with both feet on the ground, and had a more secure vision of her future. In contrast, I was swayed by undefined but alluring dreams of dedicating myself to something big, something extraordinary of which I really had no clear notion. I had not found my niche but wanted it to be as big as the world. Despite this difference, or because of it, a glance, a moment of silence, a touch of the hand, was enough to convey what each of us felt or thought, or to sense the other's reaction to what one of us said, did, or intended to do. Imperceptibly but unerringly, we were in constant communication.

During our college years, we became separated and saw each other only in summer, and even then not every year, since my family had moved to Irkutsk, in Siberia. Our correspondence, however, was very active. Then Manya met her destiny in Isaac, a very talented, warmhearted man, and she wanted us to meet. I graduated from college that year and went to Witebsk to see them. It was sheer alchemy. We were together only one evening, and Isaac and I at once felt bound by a brother-sister feeling. I remember the stirring I felt when he began to sing a lovely Russian song, turning to me, as though embracing me in their love and friendship. Next morning, I left, happy for Manya, happy for myself.

A month or so after World War I started, Isaac was sent to the front, without even having seen Manya to say goodbye. I received several wonderful letters from him and his photograph. In the last, brief letter, written before a battle, he said, "We are going somewhere . . . somewhere from which I may not return . . . I leave Manya to you. She needs you. You are stronger than she . . ."

I was teaching in the Caucasus when Isaac's relatives learned of his death at the front. I knew that the same bullet had killed Manya. A decade later, she wrote to me, "Today is ten years since Isaac passed away. I should have made an end to myself then. All my attempts to create a

tie to life [she meant the child she bore several years later, who died]
have led to nothing. I am exactly where Isaac left me."

As soon as school closed, I went to see Manya in Witebsk. Those were
sad days. One night I was awakened by the sound of her moving in bed.
She could hardly say a word; she had taken poison. It took all the
strength I had to bring her back to life, and afterward we never talked
about it.

Manya and I were together for the last time when she came to Irkutsk
and saw Wolik and me join our lives into one. Then for five or so years,
events in Russia made it impossible for us to keep in touch. In 1922, we
found each other again and could exchange letters. Manya was the head
of a large kindergarten. In various ways, her letters told of her weariness
of life; her only desire was to rest, to have quiet and privacy—things that
did not exist then and perhaps do not now in Soviet Russia. Fatigue and
infinite loneliness: "There is not a single day in all these years that I
would want to relive. All of them, whether occupied or empty, carried
with them a feeling of dismal, unbearable loneliness." And in another
letter: "I have only one all-devouring wish—either to make an end to
this wretchedness and have a normal life or to do away with everything."

She could tell me in only a few words that she had borne a little girl,
fathered by a Norwegian nobleman, a first-class intellectual. Why they
did not marry, why "he had to leave, and I insisted on it," where and
how he died, she could not write. Every letter was full of loving descriptions of her child, Galya. She loved her desperately but wanted Galya to
have more links with life, to be loved by us. She was afraid that we
might get to love other children before her Galya had a chance to win
our hearts. "For the first time in life I am jealous," she wrote. "When
Galya is particularly lovable, I have an overpowering desire to grab her
legs and throw her over to you. I so want her to have your love, your
care." The child was constantly told of us and dreamed of us as of invisible friends. She showed everyone the dolls, stuffed animals, and clothing we sent her, and when someone asked if she had brothers or sisters,
she replied defensively that she had Aunt Emma and Uncle Wolik, who
loved her very much.

Manya sensed unerringly that in the circumstances in which she lived,
she could not bring up Galya as she wanted to, could not provide her
with a normal, healthy environment. She was occupied from early morning till late at night—not only with work in her institution but with
commissions, meetings, and various other inescapable obligations. Both
she and Galya were often sick; there was a lack of everything, but most
of all, of the peace and normalcy essential for the sensitive, delicate child
that Galya evidently was. So Manya wanted and hoped to bring her to
us and thus assure her a loving, inspiring, and normal environment.
Strenuous efforts on both sides to achieve this failed. Then Galya developed an infection and died.

Manya sank into boundless despair. She bitterly reproached herself
for everything that might have been different. I suffered with her but

was not able to reach out and help her across the insurmountable barrier. It was clear to her, she wrote me, that her life had had only three dangerous attachments, vulnerable to a stroke of fate: "You, Isaac, and Galya." She had lost the last two, and she and I could not be together. I, too, reproached myself, and still do, for not having tried harder, for not having been insistent enough. Perhaps I should have pressed more in every direction. At the time, it seemed that we did everything possible under the sun.

When, afterward I asked her if another child would not help her, she answered: "Am I thinking of a child? No, I cannot. A horror grips me, a feeling that I have committed a crime. I gave Galya all of myself and also the love of my mother who adored her, but this proved not enough to keep her alive!"

Yet in her loneliness and despair, Manya did begin, after a year or so, to think of creating a new tie to life; for her, this could only be a child. She was clear about it: "Need for a child out of love for Galya? No, only out of the horror and emptiness of life around and inside me. Only this. I shall never have a child like Galya. No! As her father was to me after Isaac, so another child will be after Galya." Later she wrote, "When I have another child, this will prove my almost criminal irresponsibility."

In 1926, Manya wrote that I had guessed right, that she was expecting a baby. I knew the identity of the father, or thought I knew. Though she assured herself and me repeatedly that she could not possibly love the child born out of despair, she did love the boy with all her heart and with a fierce determination to keep him alive. Her life was hard: "I am alone, always and everywhere alone . . . I love my child and hate my life with all my strength . . . It would be such an incredible happiness to have you here . . . Perhaps I would catch your vigor, your healthy cheerfulness . . . Emmochka, I am so tired, so deeply, so thoroughly tired . . . I cannot breathe any more." She described her little boy, Sanya: "He is charming, with a constant smile on his face. Yesterday in the trolley somebody thought that he was a girl. When he protested, a woman said, 'You are too beautiful for a boy!' And another woman looked back as she got off and said, 'How can such beauty exist?' "

Again Manya felt that the only safe haven for her child was with us. The link between Manya and me was as strong as ever, and she had unshakable confidence in Wolik and loved him for what he was to me and for himself. We wanted to have both Manya and Sanya come to live with us. It would be too cruel to let her continue in that terrifying loneliness without her chief link with life, her child. But again, how could we achieve this?

Sanya grew up hearing about us, about life with us, about all the wonderful things that life with us would mean. We sent him presents, toys, books, clothing, food. He dictated letters to us, "I want to go to you. I love you, I want to be with you!" One day when he was about seven, he said to Manya, "I think all the time of Aunt Emma and Uncle

Wolik." Manya wrote, "Just got your parcel, but the best, the real, present could be only you yourself. How can I tell you what I feel? It is not enough for me that you are so endlessly dear to me. I want to do something for you. I want you to feel some special happiness coming from me to you, to add more joy to the cheerful smile on your picture."

Our correspondence continued after we left Hitler's Germany for France. Many letters reached me in Paris, and we still hoped that somehow, some miracle would unite all four of us. In one of her letters, Manya said, "I would gladly accept an existence of half hunger for Sanya if he could live with you and Wolik." Then we left for the United States. Very soon after we arrived in this country, at the beginning of 1936, we received two letters—one from Manya, the other from Nadya, Wolik's sister. Though they lived in different cities separated by hundreds of miles, both used the same formula: "As soon as I have an apartment, I shall let you know my address." This could mean only that we were not to write until we heard from them. Some twenty-five years have passed, and no letter has ever come from either of them. We were afraid to write. We, in complete safety, did not dare to expose them to the danger of contacts with a foreign country. No matter how personal and nonpolitical our letters would be, the recipients still could be accused of treason or anything else as perilous. Were we right? I always felt that we were. But now, rereading Manya's letters again and again, letters full of such desperate love of her children, love of me, I no longer know. Perhaps it would have been better to take the risk, to have done our utmost even if it was dangerous for them; perhaps we could have succeeded. These are heartbreaking thoughts and feelings.

7. Our Life in the New World

LEAVING EUROPE was not like leaving Russia. When we went from Petrograd to Georgia in 1918, we were going from one part of Russia to another. When we left Georgia, then independent, for Rome, we expected to return when our work was completed. But leaving Europe for the United States in October, 1935, was a deliberate plunge into the unknown. One must remember that to Europeans, the United States then and now are two different countries. When I looked for a guidebook to the United States in London, there was none in the bookstores. At Cook's Travel Bureau, I was offered tiny leaflets on New York, Chicago, and Niagara Falls. "This will be about all you will care to see there," said the clerk.

The United States has always been more popular in Russia than elsewhere in Europe. Every schoolchild knew *Tom Sawyer* and *Huckleberry Finn,* and every schoolchild cried over *Uncle Tom's Cabin.* The stories about the West by James Fenimore Cooper, Bret Harte, and Zane Grey were in every library. Even the books of the British writer Mayne Reid about the American West were popular reading among Russian children. Jack London was, of course, a must. The favorite volume in the series of great world statesmen was *From Log Cabin to the White House,* on Lincoln, by Avenarius. The naïve image of America that attracted so many to this country is described with warm humor by a popular Russian writer, Wladimir Korolenko, in his story "In a Strange Land": A Russian peasant emigrates to the United States, finds his way about, and tries to induce two of his relatives to follow his example by writing them: "Liberty is great in this country . . . Lots of land . . . Men with heads on their shoulders and good hands are respected and valued. Even I, Osip Lozinsky, was recently asked whom I wanted to choose as the chief President of the whole country, and I voted like everyone else. Although, true, the results were somewhat different from what I and my boss desired, I liked at least that I was consulted on the matter. In a word, Liberty and everything aplenty." This letter, according to the story, causes great excitement in the village. "Osip Lozinsky has become rich in America and is an important man, so important that they even asked his advice as to who should be made President . . . If even Osip was consulted, then imagine how far others could reach, for we have brighter heads than Osip. Moreover, there is liberty, liberty, LIBERTY!"

Wolik and I were fairly familiar with American literature since World War I, having read, mostly in the original, the novels of Sinclair Lewis, Ernest Hemingway (*A Farewell to Arms* was our favorite), Dos Passos, Upton Sinclair, and others. In *The World in Figures,* we constantly used American economic and statistical data; my postgraduate work was on the American economy. On the political side, we had followed the development of the New Deal with great interest.

With all this background, we nevertheless had no clear idea of how our life would shape up in the New World. Neither of us had the slightest fear about making a living. We never had had any; even in Irkutsk, with all the odds against us, we lived comfortably and were able to help our friends. We were strong, healthy, adaptable, and had too many skills not to be able to earn our livelihood. When Wolik gloomily predicted *my poydyom ko dnu,* he meant something different from barely making a living. He feared a lack of opportunities for scholarly work such as he had had in Europe, perhaps the necessity of accepting work that, though lucrative, was devoid of scientific or political interest. He reminded me of our great poet Pushkin's saying—"Inspiration is not for sale, but a manuscript can be sold"—and he sadly asked himself and me, "Will I be forced to trade in inspiration?" I answered resolutely, "Never! If this proves to be the America to which I am urging you to go, we will return to Europe."

It was disappointing that none of our Russian friends approved of our decision. Some were evasive, others showed their surprise and regret quite openly. One friend who lived meagerly, preoccupied with making ends meet, said feelingly: *"Ot khoroshey zhizni ne poletish!"* ("One does not take to the sky if life is good!")

My main hope was that we would leave behind us the atmosphere of hatred and spite that pervaded every speech, every move, about us; that we would find peace, serenity, a climate of good will in which "lyricism" could blossom again, in which Wolik could live and work, expanding his superior abilities and enjoying inner satisfaction from both life and work. Most of all, I wanted, for his sake and mine, to leave the "epos" of Europe, and I felt intuitively that we would breathe free air in the United States.

The sea was stormy; we were sick and spent most of the time in bed or on deck chairs. We arrived in New York late in the evening of October 9, 1935. The customs officer checked our luggage and, seeing a box with old Russian coins, declared, "You must talk about this to the chief." We showed him that our declaration listed the coins, and told him that they had only a sentimental value, being from the collection of Wolik's father, and were not for sale. But he insisted that we have it checked, and I suggested that Wolik go to the customs office. The Negro porter said, "Let *her* go! Let *her* go!" So I went and straightened out the situation. When I returned, the porter said, "You see? I knew she would get him to agree. The women never pay, but the men always do. They earn the money and don't argue like women." This was our first practical lesson in the United States.

Our destination was Washington, but we stayed in New York for nearly two weeks, curious to see that gateway to the New World. The hustle and bustle, the skyscrapers, the noisy crowds on Broadway, the cars filling every street—all this deafened us as it deafens any newcomer entering the United States at New York. We were impressed, excited, but glad to leave for Washington.

There we felt immediately at ease. We arrived Tuesday night. The next morning Wolik went to the Central Statistical Board, and Thursday morning, the telephone rang: Wolik was asked to come to take the oath of office for work with that agency. Evidently Wolik had impressed Stuart Rice, the chairman of the Board, with his knowledge and experience in the short time that they had spent together, despite Wolik's English, which was then wholly inadequate.

What we could not know was that Wolik had arrived at a strategic time: The Social Security Act had been promulgated two months earlier, and at the time of our arrival "it was evident that sound statistical data would be needed immediately to set up the administration of the new Social Security Act." But the available data "were largely geared to the problems of the past rather than to the current situation and future needs. . . . Almost overnight it was necessary for him [Wolik] to learn the intricate provisions of the new and untried Social Security Act of 1935, and to master the mass of accumulated statistics adapted to a previous era in order to develop a basis for the administration of the new legislation. This was a challenge not only of an intellectual nature but also of a practical character that would appeal to the social reformer."*

Wolik "sank" not to the bottom but into this challenging work with the energy and excitement of a man hungry to see the results of an important task. I was enormously relieved. To keep our life full and rich, to bring its "lyricism" again to a full-grown fruition, now depended only on us, and we did not need to worry in this respect.

FIRST IMPRESSIONS

In a few days, we found a bungalow with a small garden. The first Sunday, we went to explore the neighborhood. Very soon we found ourselves in the woods, pushing our way deeper and deeper into "wilderness" until we reached a little stream crossed by a bridge, with a building that looked like a power house. On the other bank was an inviting path. Was that area closed to the public? We hesitated, but there was no familiar "Verboten" sign. We took the path on the other side of the

* Perlman, Jacob, "An Architect of Social Security," in *So Much Alive* (New York: Vanguard Press, 1962), p. 91.

stream and shortly thereafter found ourselves in a clearing, in front of a big public building with a guard at its gate. I went up to him and asked, "Is it permitted to walk here?" He replied, "Can't you see the sign?" I looked. The sign said "State Property." Clearly we were in the wrong. But the guard interpreted the sign for us: "State property! That means it belongs to you, to me, to everybody. Why shouldn't you walk here?"

Since Wolik worked in his office, I decided to use my time to acquire a more intimate knowledge of American history and political life. Coming from Germany, where one had to register and pay for admission to the National Library, I asked at the entrance to the Library of Congress where the registration desk was. Nobody understood what I wanted, and I was sent to the main reading room. Still without an admission card, I waited at the door. Finally I went in and asked an attendant at the main desk where I could register. Surprised, he asked, "For what do you want to register?" "To get an admission card. I want to work here." "Order the books you need and go ahead!" Observing that I hesitated to follow his advice, he added, "You are welcome. Our library is open to everybody!" The attendant would have understood my attitude if he had known that once Wolik had forgotten his admission card and was not permitted to enter the reading room in the National Library in Berlin, even when he told the attendant that more than a dozen of his own books were on the reference shelf and many more were in the stacks.

A few days after our arrival in Washington, we were invited to visit a family that lived in a comfortable but unpretentious house at the edge of the city. The host occupied an important position in the Government. We were amused and surprised when he proudly displayed his new library of do-it-yourself bookshelves: ordinary boards extending along the walls and separated and supported by bricks between them on both ends and in the middle. It was indeed a practical arrangement, but to us, a library always meant solid bookcases and shelves, a huge desk, and comfortable armchairs. To see a high-ranking official show off such primitive bookshelves with genuine satisfaction and to hear the approving remarks of the guests was a lesson in the informality of American living, which far exceeded what was considered simple style in Russia!

TAKING ROOT

It is hard to recall how we felt during our first years in this country because, it seems to me now, we found ourselves at home here at once. We accepted everything, the good and the bad, the wonderful features and the shortcomings. We loved this country for its wonderful features and regretted its shortcomings, but emotionally we were attached to both. Uppermost to us, of course, was the freedom, the security of freedom, the absence of fear in everybody. After our experiences in Russia and Germany, nothing in the world was sweeter than the air of freedom here. The genuine friendliness of the people, the informality, the openness and hospitality, so similar to the hospitality of the Russian people; the feeling of space, of elbow room, again so similar to that in Russia—we felt all this from our first days in the United States. Never, for a moment, did we think of adjusting ourselves; we were naturally at home! We soon established friendly relations with many intellectuals in Washington; many became warm friendships in the course of years.

Of course, not everything was clover. A few weeks after Wolik started working, he found himself in a fight. In the middle of November, he began to report in memoranda to the Central Statistical Board that the next decennial census (of 1940) must shift from occupational to industrial classification in order to conform to the industrial development of the country and to provide its expanding social legislation with necessary data. Though he tried to preserve as much as possible of the existing methodology and material, the vested interests were angered that a foreigner, in the country less than a month, dared to suggest basic changes in the census schedules. A private institution, long known for its work in the field of the U.S. population, asked Wolik to write an article for publication on the occupational structure of the U.S. population, then rejected it because it contained criticism of the U.S. censuses.

But Wolik did not worry at all. He was in his element. He gave himself wholly to the work, and had no doubt that he was offering the right methods. His masterful handling of the material not only was recognized by specialists but inspired admiration and respect. In fact, some officials in the Social Security Board believed that if Wolik had come earlier, he could have helped in shaping and improving the Act of 1935.[*]

Under these conditions, the controversy did not trouble Wolik. On the contrary, he was animated and gay, and enjoying the excitement of expanding his own knowledge of this country while doing work for which he was eminently prepared. Moreover, his proposals for adjusting the decennial censuses to the needs of modern life and the new legislation were adopted, in one form or another, during the formulations of the 1940 Census, in which he participated.

To meet people and have the opportunity of practicing English, I joined the American Association of University Women. The very first day, I attended a drama group because Pushkin's *Boris Godunov* was on the program. My English was atrocious, but I forgot myself and intervened when that play, which is on a par with the best plays of Shakespeare, was treated rather flippantly. Nobody was irritated by the way I abused the language (as undoubtedly would have been the case in France), and to my surprise, I was asked to give a talk on Pushkin at the next meeting. A few days later, the group studying the United States economy elected me its chairman. In both cases, I accepted. The first assignment forced me to work on the language, and the second, on various aspects of the American economy with which I was totally

[*] See *So Much Alive,* pp. 88-112.

unfamiliar. In addition, the need to conduct the meeting and talk rather frequently helped me to overcome, to some extent, the shyness that I still feel on addressing an audience.

I spent much time in the Library of Congress. As in every large library, I had the feeling that all the knowledge of the world was at my disposal there. All I had to do was to go to the shelves, reach out for that knowledge, and plunge into it. I swallowed book after book on American history and political life, read the voluminous biographies of Thomas Jefferson, John Marshall, Andrew Jackson, Sam Houston, Woodrow Wilson, and Lincoln, and novels on regional life, stories of pioneer hardships and adjustments, and so on. Because of the personality of President Roosevelt, I was particularly interested in the role of the Presidency in the United States and sought elucidation in books on this subject. Nothing impressed me more than Woodrow Wilson's speeches on constitutional government, and specifically on the President of the United States. Some of his formulations were so sharp and meaningful that they became engraved in my memory, and I often returned to them later. For example, "The President is at liberty, both in law and conscience, to be as big a man as he can. His capacity will set the limit," but "he has no means of compelling Congress except through public opinion." Also, "Let him once win the admiration and confidence of the country, and no other single force can withstand him, no combination of forces will easily overpower him." And, "If he rightly interpret the national thought and boldly insist upon it, he is irresistible." Written in 1908, before Woodrow Wilson became President, these observations are as valid today as then.

We were very much interested in the workings of the New Deal and its various agencies, read many of its publications, heard controversial judgments about its aims and the results of its activities, as well as about various Government officials most clearly associated with President Roosevelt. We were more inclined to listen than to express any opinions until we could become better acquainted with all sides of the situation. On the other hand, people we met here showed an entirely different attitude as soon as the conversation touched Russia. The assurance with which everybody or, at least, most people spoke about that country was occasionally irritating, and several times I broke off the discussion by saying that since we had left Russia some seventeen years ago, we really knew very little in comparison with those who had never been there and therefore could have an unbiased opinion. This needling remark was an answer to some persons' dismissal of our statements about conditions in Russia as reflecting "the natural grudges of the refugees from that country who have lost everything." When I think of the confused attitude toward Russia at that time, I am less surprised now than I was then, because I see in the press and hear over the radio how many misconceptions still exist of what Russia was and is.

While we found much in common between Russians and Americans, there were, of course, clearly different attitudes in some respects—for example, toward the theater and art. Love of the theater and theatrical art in all its forms—drama, ballet, opera, comedy, and so on—has long been a distinguishing characteristic of Russian life. In my youth, every respectable provincial city had a permanent theater, and the theaters of St. Petersburg and Moscow and their great artists were—and are—known the world over. Many people who admire the present theaters in Moscow talk about Soviet art without realizing that this is Russian art, which has a great tradition and has always occupied an honored place in the hearts of the Russian people.

The great Russian artist had a home in Russia, a roof over his head, in contrast to the American artist. One who had been accepted into the Moscow Art Theater, for example, stayed with it for good. This was his home, where he belonged. He would never think of leaving it to play somewhere else, as do artists in this country, even the greatest and most appreciated; they may play this season in one theater, the next season in another. In Russia, the artists grew with their theaters, which had studios and schools for all kinds of experimentation with new ideas, new scenery, new methods.

We had to see to believe that the capital of the United States, peopled by Government and diplomatic personnel, had no permanent theater or beautiful theater building. We experienced another shock when we heard the director of a WPA art project say that there were teachers of art in this country who had never visited an art museum. Today the situation is totally different, of course, but that statement stunned us.

The uniformity of speech in this country surprised me. In Russia and also in Europe, a store clerk, a porter, a flower woman, spoke differently from a teacher, a doctor, a lawyer. Not that the latter necessarily used more beautiful language. Often the simple people, even the Russian peasants so much abused in the foreign literature as nearly illiterate savages, expressed themselves in a more colorful, striking way than middle-class or even professional people, whose language might be more stilted or bookish. But, essentially, there was no stereotype in conversation, and stock phrases were seldom used. The first thing I noticed in the United States was the repetition of the same expressions, whether I talked to a worker in a garage, the head of a Government office, or a professor. "Will see you," "will be in touch with you," "looking forward to seeing you," "enjoyed every bit of it," "you bet," and so on and on, rang in my ears the whole day. I began to write down such typical expressions, and the list kept on growing: "Too good to be true," "never a dull moment," "they sell like hot cakes," "a hot potato," "one of those things," and so forth.

Another difference was that, in contrast to Russia, where literary quotations and references to characters in classical novels and poems were common in conversation and writing and where the contact between life and literature was close, almost intimate, here nobody or almost no one referred to a poem or used a literary personality for characterization. I am not referring to official speeches prepared by ghost writers, which are often filled with high-brow quotations and references for prestige purposes, *pour épater les bourgeois* (to impress the uninitiated), but to everyday conversation or casual writing in a newspaper. This is what made the oral or written language in Russia picturesque, full of allusions and even wit, and what I missed here.

One example may perhaps stress the contrast very clearly: Almost every sentence from the play *Gore ot Uma* (*Woe from Wit*), written in 1825 by the greatest master of Russian dialogue, Griboedov, has become a part of conversational language, referred to constantly in one combination or another, such as "How can one neglect a man that's a relative!," "Can't you for your outing a little further round go scouting?," "Thrice blessed is he who believes; believing warms the heart," "All calendars are liars," "Something and a view," and so on. In translation, these expressions may appear dull, but in the original, they are very effective and readily remembered.

Except for occasional references to Shakespeare and possibly the Bible, one almost never hears a quotation from any writer or poet so well known that a phrase or an expression from his works comes to mind naturally. The same is true with respect to literary types. In Russian conversation, references to Oblomov, Khlestakov, Sobakevich, Plushkin, Nozdrev, Akakiy Akakievich, Ivan Karamazov, Lenski, Tatyana, Dyadya Vanya, "a lady *agréable* in all respects," and "a lady simply *agréable*," "Mitrofanushka" and so on are used to characterize people and are immediately understood. And in this country? Except for Babbitt, Topsy and Pollyanna, I never heard any such references, and even these were pulled out of memory to show me that some literary characterizations were in use. Again, characters from the Russian folklore such as Ivanushka-Durachek (Ivanushka the Fool) and Ilya Muromets (one of the heroes of the Russian epic) are living personalities to a Russian, and references to them are meaningful and evoke a clear notion of what one means.

Also in constant use were quotations and references to characters in literary works of foreign writers, such as Shakespeare, Goethe, Mark Twain, Ibsen, Balzac, Hamsun, Maupassant, Daudet, Dante, Zola and so on. Tartarin de Tarascon, Topsy, Tom Sawyer, King Lear, Hamlet, Lady Macbeth, Nora from *A Doll's House,* and Nana were no less alive to Russian intellectuals than some of the national literary characters.

Mention of even so comparatively inconspicuous a character as Gogol's Korobochka conveyed an immediate vivid impression. One day, Wolik returned from a visit to his dentist in Washington and said, "I just met Mrs. Korobochka, or rather overheard her conversation with the dentist while waiting in the reception room." Then he tried to reproduce the conversation: "Have you made up your mind about the front tooth that I think must be pulled out?" "Yes, Doctor, I know you told me this but I spent last Sunday at my sister's and she said that when a tooth is pulled out it won't be there any more and it cannot be put back.

That is just that." "Yes, of course. So what is your decision?" "I just don't know, Doctor, what to decide. I think all the time of what my sister said." "Well, it is up to you, and if you don't trust my judgment, you have the privilege of consulting another doctor." "No, Doctor. I trust you, I do trust you but you can see the other side of the story. I would lose the tooth forever, just as my sister said. She is a very practical person and has always handled the family affairs." "Look, Mrs. So-and-So, I am busy and have no time to talk about your sister. Tell me, do you want this tooth pulled out or not?" "Doctor, how can I say that I want the tooth pulled out? Of course, I do not want it taken out; that is not a pleasure." "All I am saying is that in my opinion it must come out, and now make up your mind: yes or no?" "Please, Doctor, give me time to consider the matter. This is a very serious thing. Just as my sister said—" Here the doctor was called to the telephone and on his return he shut the door to the room.

As Wolik was telling the story, I saw Mrs. Korobochka very clearly, a short, fat woman with a round face and dull, expressionless eyes. She seemed stupid, but there was a purpose in her talk—to postpone the unpleasant decision, and above all to postpone the inevitable event—the parting with the tooth.

It would almost be un-American not to have a story to tell about a car. We never had a car before, but we bought a used Chevrolet almost immediately after our arrival, got permits to learn to drive, and engaged an instructor. At that time, there were no registered instructors in Washington, and the AAA school of driving did not exist. I do not recall who recommended the instructor to us, perhaps the car dealer. Anyhow, he was a simple soul, and I had difficulty in understanding what he wanted of me. "Disengage the clutch!" How could I when I did not know what the clutch was? "Shift to high gear!" He did not explain what the gear was and what "high" meant! Everybody knew that, everybody but me.

After two lessons, I got a textbook on driving from the library, and everything became clear as daylight. I told this to the wife of an official we met; she laughed, thinking it too funny for words. At the next party at her home, she introduced me by saying that I was learning to drive from a book. That *was* funny, but I kept on using the book. Anyhow, before I got my license after ten lessons, I had a day in court.

In the last part of November, heavy snow fell. Then, as now, heavy snow caused traffic jams in Washington, and over and over the radio broadcast an appeal to the public not to use a car unless it was absolutely necessary. The instructor refused to come. The car, completely snowed under, stood in front of our house. The next day I noticed a ticket on the window. Unfamiliar with such ordinary facts of life, I was told by the neighbor that it was notification by the police that the car was overparked; District law did not permit parking for longer than eighteen hours. A passing policeman had readily seen that the car, with all the windows hidden under the snow, had not been moved.

This was my first collision with the police, and I took it rather seriously. I went to the designated precinct to explain the situation, but the police officer cut me short. "Pay the three-dollar fine, and if you are not satisfied, tell the judge your story." Irritated by his brusque tone, I replied haughtily, "Yes, I shall tell my story to the judge, and he will understand what you do not understand," paid the fine, and left. I had never been in any court before (except at the trial of L. M. Bramson in Petrograd) and regretted my words as soon as I closed the door. Yet I could not possibly go back, and so next morning at nine o'clock I was in the courtroom. My case was called at four in the afternoon. By that time, I had become so interested in the proceedings that I had almost forgotten why I was there. Anyhow, I had learned something about how to answer questions.

After the policeman gave his report, the judge asked me if the car had not been moved at all. I confirmed this. "Why not?" asked the judge. "There was nowhere to move the car," I explained. "To the left is Massachusetts Avenue, where the car would have interfered with traffic. On the right, Maryland begins, and I did not want to park my car in another state." The judge sighed and said, "Why didn't you move the car just a foot or two?" "But, Judge, I have no license to drive, and the instructor did not want to come." "The case is suspended; get your three dollars back," was the court's decision.

That night in writing to the friends in Paris, I mentioned the court experience. Under my signature, Wolik wrote, "Emmochka is modest as usual. She gave a brilliant speech. The judge was spellbound." I laughed and added, "You know Wolik. He is joking, of course." There was hardly space for more words, but Wolik managed to add, "Joking? And why did the newspapers print her speech, and the cameras never cease to click?" I gave up, and Wolik teased me all evening about my "triumph" in court.

The funniest footnote to this story came five years later. Several friends from Paris came over to settle in this country. Once one of them complained about his difficulties with the English language. To encourage him, I said that every newcomer has language troubles, only to hear, "Not you, though! I know of your speech in court right after your arrival." Neither of us said anything, but afterward we laughed like children. No, they did not know Wolik!

MEETING THE UNITED STATES

To get the feel of the country, we decided to drive across the continent to the West Coast. Perhaps a matter-of-fact undertaking to an American, this trip was an exciting experience for us. We were delighted to travel in complete privacy, alone in the car. Coupled with this was the pleasure of being independent of train schedules. We started very early, with the car ready and waiting for us. Side trips, changes in plans, stops of undetermined length being possible, we felt that we could go any place, follow any sudden whim. After nearly thirty years in this country, it is difficult to describe the fascination that took hold of us on that first trip. Later, we crossed the country on six other trips to the West and loved each of them, but we knew what we would encounter on the way, and there were few surprises. Yet the trip during our first year here, by a way of traveling new to us in a country with whose scenery, life, and people we were totally unfamiliar, remained unforgettable.

Friends in Washington could not believe that so soon after our arrival such inexperienced drivers as we were would contemplate crossing the country by car. Yet, we went the very first summer here, braving all kinds of unusual situations and repeated troubles with our second-hand car. We christened it with an untranslatable, endearing name from a Russian fairy tale, "Konyok-Gorbunok," a kind of hunchbacked magic horse that took his rider in a few strides across mountains and seas. I remember, in particular, a sharp climb somewhere in Colorado on a narrow weather-beaten mountain road, with us on the edge and what seemed like a precipice on the right side. We could not turn back and we climbed on, hoping against hope that we would get to the top before a car appeared from the opposite direction. But one came, collision seemed inevitable, and we became tense. Then we noticed that the driver in the other car was smiling at us encouragingly and making a friendly gesture with his hand. Oh, if so, we could also smile and greet him! Whether or not it will be believed, the fact remains that our magic horse understood the situation, shrank to let the other car pass by, and then resumed its previous size. I saw or felt this happen, and if it is not true, then how did we pass each other without colliding?

In our childhood, America had been to us the land of endless prairies, mysterious mountains and canyons, powerful rivers, the land of red Indians, fearless pioneers, hunters, and gold-seekers. In Europe after World War I, America meant the noise and vanity of the cities, skyscrapers, the Chicago stockyards, Ford plants, the vulgarity of Hollywood—soulless, mechanical culture.

When we were planning our first trip, we sought to find the America of the forgotten children's books. We followed the pioneers from east to west, across the fertile valleys and endless prairies to the America of Western marvels. And there were so many of those marvels.

The America we wanted to bring to life from our memories began as soon as we left Missouri and Kansas behind. Everything began to exhibit gigantic dimensions. We drove over beautiful roads along dense, fragrant forests at altitudes at which even moss does not grow in Europe. We saw a crater more than a mile wide that a meteor had once created. And the Grand Canyon! It took us by surprise. We were driving in an evergreen forest with a dense undergrowth when all of a sudden the earth opened its inside to us. Before us, or rather below us, fantastic mountains grew out of the earth's entrails. Pyramids, castles, towers, appeared on all sides. Our eyes did not look up, as usual, to the sight of the mountains, but down, down . . . And this depth, this inside of the earth, was painted so brightly, there was so much gold and purple that it seemed as if flaming rock boiling under the earth's crust had broken loose, and all the mountains, castles, temples, were only tongues of fire. Suddenly a cloud moved over the sun, and all that mysterious world became silvery white, then turned soft blue. Was that symphony of colors real or a mirage?

What was more natural than to want to enter that magic world? Next morning we descended to one terrace after another, while the rocks around us were continuously changing their colors and shapes. Down, down, to the road that seemed to run over the earth's spine! Finally, we reached the Colorado River, the creator of all these wonders. True, it took millions of years. We crossed the hanging bridge, took a few more steps, and saw a narrow green valley, with Phantom Ranch at its entrance.

Then the Bryce Canyon in Utah—again this inside of the earth! Yet the impression it gave was so different from that of the Grand Canyon. None of that infinity, of that forcefulness as at the beginning of the world's creation. Beyond that split in the earth, there were forests running up to the horizon and soft green hills.

The Bryce Canyon shimmered in all the colors of the rainbow. At our arrival during the sunset, all shades of pink, red, orange, turned into such an orgy of bright gold that one's eyes begged for mercy. When we got used to those wild colorings, odd shapes began to appear and become recognizable. To the right was a fortress with walls of red stone and golden spires. We took a narrow path into that fantastic world. Which way should we turn? To the right, where amidst the statues, Queen Victoria stood on a high ledge in her long-trained dress with her ladies in waiting? There could be no mistake, the likeness was remarkable. Or to the left, where we saw a gigantic organ? Or to board that huge ship ready to take off? Whose fantasy had created that enchanting world? The prosaic answer was: the water, the wind. What water? No sign of a river! The water from rain or snow disappearing in the fissures within the earth. In Bryce Canyon, this work is not yet finished. Here and there we saw "workshops," from which, in some thousands of years, new statues, new palaces, new temples, will rise. Have patience, such marvels are not produced in a hurry.

We understood the name Painted Desert when we drove across it one day, then another, dizzy from its inexplicable charm. The air, the ground, the sky, the mountains on the horizon, the sandy hills around —all this was a flowing gamut of purple, crimson, pink.

The marvels of nature gradually merged with marvels of human creation. On our next trip we saw, in the midst of the desert where thorny cacti bristled and man could not live, crystal-clear, deep-blue Boulder Lake, created by men who had blocked the flow of the Colorado River, raised its level above that of Niagara Falls, and filtered its muddy water. One has to drive for hours in a desert that is choked by burning heat and feel as choked as the desert, then come on the blueness of that lovely lake, to appreciate the daring and the beauty of that technical wonder.

From a forest full of plant and animal life, we drove into the Petrified Forest. On the ground, trees were strewn around as if broken by a storm. We could see the inner structure, but the living substance has long since changed to stone. We touched a thick stump—cold, hard stone. We walked among the dead trees, touched them here and there—nothing but stone. The forest stretched for miles, without a single live tree—about us only stones that millions of years ago had been living trees.

Wildlife fascinated us—the shy elks that came to the camps for food, the deer we met occasionally along the highway, the slow-moving and sometimes almost immobile moose, and most of all, the bears. The latter were everywhere in the Yellowstone and other Western national parks. It was real fun to watch and photograph them. We sat at a picnic table, spread our food on it. A bear of respectable size, attracted by the smell of the food, stationed himself not far from the table and waited. Waited for what? Would he jump on the table and grab the food, scaring us? No, he waited for us to throw some food to him. Yet the rangers insisted, this must not be done. Fortunately, several cars passed, and the bear, disappointed by our stinginess, rushed to the highway. Another time we saw a bear take up a strategic position on the highway. When a competitor appeared, he chased him up the tree and walked round and round, thus giving me a chance to film the scene. We saw, for the first time, sugar cane growing, cotton and tobacco fields. Every day brought something new. Throughout the trip we did not see a horse, until we went to the annual Spanish festival in Santa Barbara, California. On the highway, we noticed several trucks carrying horses to it. They really epitomized the role of the motor vehicle in the United States, where even horses use cars to go places.

In Santa Barbara, it also was demonstrated to us that the car is truly a domestic animal, just as familiar to American children as a dog or a cat. That little town was all dressed up; nearly everyone on the street wore a Spanish costume. We drove round and round in search of a vacancy in a parking lot, but the town was overflowing. Finally, we saw a "Parking" sign on a tobacco stand. The salesman directed us to his back yard, where his son would show us where to park the car. The boy, about nine or ten, was the authority on the lot. He pointed to a place. I realized that if we took it we would have to wait to leave until everybody else had moved out, and asked if we could park in front of the sidewalk so we could leave immediately after the parade. The boy cast one look at the spot and said indifferently, "If you wish, but you'll break your muffler when you go."

The diversity of the scenery charmed the passionate photographers in us. Wolik took slides, I made movies. Accordingly, each of us had a different way of taking pictures. Wolik was after an unusual composition, and spared neither time nor effort in seeking out the best possible angle; he climbed hills, got over fences, walked great distances back and forth. I had to use my camera in a hurry, before the action was completed, though I also photographed scenery by slowly turning with the camera in my hand and thus obtaining panoramic pictures. We took turns in driving; if I was at the wheel and Wolik noticed something to his liking, he would say, "Please, stop and look! Something big is happening in the sky!" It might be an unusual cloud formation or the sight of sun rays piercing a dark cloud or a glowing sunset ball. Wolik was very responsive to every change in the scenery, overlooked nothing.

All in all, however, our deepest impressions came from the people we met. If they had been unfriendly, boorish, or simply reserved, the whole tenor of the trip would not have been as bright, gay, and charming as it was. But everywhere, we found hospitality, sincere friendliness, an unselfish desire to be helpful when our second-hand car occasionally caused trouble. This was before the Presidential elections in 1936. At our stops at gas stations and restaurants, people noticed our car license and said naïvely, "When you get back to Washington, tell the President he's swell." We laughed and replied, "We will give him your greetings as soon as we return." If somebody raised political questions, we answered cautiously that we had been in this country too short a time, or that, as foreigners, we did not wish to enter political discussions. "Foreigners? All of us came from the Old Country."

We stopped at several CCC camps. Their posters invited visitors. It was good to talk to those animated youngsters, hear about their life and work, their plans for the future. One boy, a typical product of a big city, not too developed physically but with bright eyes and delicate features, told us, "Before I came here, I had never been in a forest, had never seen a sunrise. All I expected was to become a clerk in a drug store. I don't want to go back to city life any more. I talked to the ranger, and he promised to keep me in mind."

We thought of the young people in Germany during the depression—no hope, no future, nobody cared. The contrast was striking—Germany followed Hitler, America followed F.D.R.

The whole country was open to us. We entered a city—gardens, gardens without fences, not hidden behind tall, impenetrable walls, as in France. As we drove along the fenceless streets, all the cities seemed to merge into one continuous colorful rug, and the cities seemed drowned among flowerbeds and lawns.

Green America? Full of flowers? Smiling? Populated by friendly, hospitable people? Yes, this is how we saw the United States even in that depression time. Love of nature, a sense of freedom, friendliness, are more characteristic of America than Europeans used to consider its salient characteristics—love of material success, money grabbing, practicality in every move.

Our impressions rather surprised some of our American friends. They could not understand the special fascination that America's seemingly unlimited space, the wild beauty of its scenery, the informality in its life, the freedom in its very air, hold for those who have passed through the crucible of hatred and mutual suspicion in various countries of Europe.

EXPLORING THE HEMISPHERE

Though our work load, particularly Wolik's, was always heavy, we made time for travel in order to satisfy our unquenchable interest in this country and its neighbors.

In the United States, our great love has been the West. In all, we went there seven times, each time selecting new points to see and new places to stop. We crossed all the states and stayed for days or weeks in some of them. Long hiking trips, such as we made in the Tirol, from one mountain peak and shelter to another, are not possible in this country but we hiked as much as we conveniently could. For example, we hiked twelve miles up in the Sierras to the Mountain Bear Farm, met a bear in the forest, followed the ranger's advice to make a noise and thus scare him, and slept in a tent among the majestic peaks. We walked on the Columbia ice fields in Western Canada, hiked in Olympic National Park and the Grand Teton, in Yosemite and Glacier National parks. In the East, too, we made many ascents in the Adirondacks and the Smoky Mountains, climbed Mount Washington, and made many trips in Nova Scotia and elsewhere in Canada. All our impressions of people were favorable. Perhaps we were just lucky, but I cannot recall a single unfriendly gesture toward us. Indeed, we never expected one.

During our trips, then and later, we often met small craftsmen here and there and liked to see their work. They, in turn, responded warmly to our appreciation of their skills. In Oregon, for example, we stopped at an exhibit of myrtle-wood products along the highway. Beautiful bowls and trays were on display, but nobody was attending to the business. We selected a large slab, artfully polished on both sides, and looked around for somebody to pay. An old man came out and was pleased by our selection: "This is my favorite piece, but nobody appreciated it. I am glad you like it enough to take it home." We talked for a few minutes about his work, and he told us of his disappointment. "These tourists, they come, walk around, and leave. They don't care, don't understand that one works not only with his hands but also with his mind and heart. Sometimes I cannot make myself stay in the store when I hear the door open."

He took us inside his workshop, showed us his logs of myrtle wood, told us what he was going to make of them. From another room, he brought a very thin cup and saucer made of myrtle wood to show the delicate work involved in making them and said with pride, "I selected the finest grain to make this present for my wife on her sixtieth birthday!"

Another time, we stopped in Pisgah, N.C., at a pottery shop deep in the woods. The owner was a real artist who was trying to create special colorings of the Chinese and Venetian types and refused to sell the pieces he liked best. I asked for permission to film him while he was working at his wheel. Pleased by our interest, he made a vase for me and invited us to see his "museum," the products he kept for himself.

In Honolulu, we discovered a small plant making articles from monkey-pod wood. The owner, a retired Army officer, showed us around. Without hesitation, we chose a coffee table with three "hearts" on top. He was sorry. "This is my showpiece. It is not for sale." We bought two bowls, and Wolik asked about the technique of processing and polishing. The owner led us into the workshop and demonstrated each step in the process. In that half hour, a contact was established by that mysterious something that brings people together. We promised to come again before leaving for the mainland. When we did, the first thing our new friend said was, "If you wish, I will let you have the table. It will be in good hands, and I shall try to find a similar piece for myself."

In Mexico, we stopped at a small glass plant, with one worker and two boys of eight or nine as helpers. As soon as the man noticed that we were watching his work with interest, he picked up some glass and signaled to us that something special was on the way. He puffed and blew again and again and finally presented us with a rooster of intricate design.

We have many such things at home, of no value to others but reminders to us of the people who made them, often in a surge of good will or gratitude for our appreciation of their work.

In our travels through many years, we observed the development and growth of tourism and the tourist industry in this country and Canada. At the time of our first cross-country trip in 1936, there were some decent tourist camps, but we often had to stay in primitive cabins, barely furnished, without electricity. The bath and toilet were often outside the cabin in one central building serving the camp. Gradually, cabins began to improve, and we could get them with all the conveniences as a matter of course. Then the motel business appeared on the scene, and now it has reached proportions that surprise the economist with its profitableness and the demand for it. It also made us wonder as tourists about the practicality of those elaborate furnishings, beautiful rugs, TV sets, and telephones, when one usually arrives rather late and leaves early, yet has to pay for unneeded luxury. In any case, the motel *is* a good institution, and it is a big relief and convenience on long trips to have the car at the door and to feel all right in any travel dress.

We visited Canada for the first time in 1938. We drove along the Gaspé Peninsula, took a boat across the Saguenay River, and hiked in the Laurentian National Park, then just beginning to be developed. After a few years in the United States, the contrast was striking. There were very few cars on the highways, and on Sundays we saw nothing but little carriages taking people to church; the churches were almost encircled by such vehicles. Twice we saw on the road a little carriage drawn by a dog —in the first was a boy with a milk bottle, apparently going to a store; in the second, an adult. In every village of French Canada we saw children, children of all ages everywhere. We bought a hooked rug from a woman surrounded by children. Wolik asked her, "Are these your children?" She answered, "Yes, sir. Sixteen of them." Wolik wondered, "Why so few?" She straightened herself up and said proudly, "Sir, I am only thirty-two."

At one camp we met a professor from Vancouver with his family. He had been transferred to the University of Montreal, and they were visiting that part of Canada for the first time. Neither of them could speak French, and it amused us to serve as interpreters for them in their own country. They traveled with us for some ten days, stopping where we stopped until we took the road to the Laurentian Park.

We were troubled by certain aspects of American life which we could not overlook during our trips across the country. We visited various Indian reservations and saw the Indians around them. Some reservations were so commercialized as to make an unfavorable impression. An Indian at the Taos pueblo in New Mexico asked one price for letting me photograph him as he was and another if he changed to a traditional Indian costume. He was surprised when I did not care to have any picture of him. At some reservations, the Indians looked pathetic when they sat motionless for hours, their heads down, without exchanging a word or lifting their eyes. Their pose seemed to say, "We are doomed. What is the use doing anything?"

We were in the Mesa Verde National Park, in Colorado, when a group of rangers arrived. We learned from them that next evening various Indian tribes were to assemble and perform dances to celebrate the end of certain work for the Park Service and to show their appreciation for the good wages they had earned during that summer. Next evening, everyone staying at the lodge, rangers and tourists, drove out to the open field where the Indians set up a huge bonfire, using whole trees for that purpose. We parked at a distance and formed a semicircle, as directed by men in charge. When it was totally dark, the dances began to cheerless, monotonous music. First the dancers, almost naked and painted white, circled the bonfire, gradually quickening their steps. Then they jumped across the fire, one after another, danced around it and again leaped through it. Whether it was a dance of purification by fire or had another meaning, we could not find out.

For the next dance, a little girl of five or six appeared, looking rather scared. The dancers circled around her. We understood that she represented a bird that each dancer tried to catch. There was nobody to explain the symbolism of this dance, and as I sat there on the grass, I felt that there was no bridge of understanding between the Indians and ourselves. Nor was there the fascination of beauty that requires no explanation but carries one along.

A few days later we spent a day in the Indian school in Phoenix, Arizona. Children of various tribes—Navaho, Zuni, Apache, Ute—were educated there. They had no common language until they learned a little English, which made communication among them possible. None of the teachers spoke any of the native tongues. The children in the first grade had pencils and paper for drawing, material for weaving and the like. I looked at one drawing—a horse in full motion, very well done. When I praised the drawing, the boy on whose desk it lay, evidently understood, if not the words, then the friendly tone. He blushed and, pressing his hand against his breast, said proudly, "Me!"

In the higher grades, the children spoke English, and the classes resembled those in other schools. After lunch, the head of the school suggested that a youngster from the top grade take us through the rest of the school. Our guide, a Zuni boy of sixteen, was knowledgeable and tactful, and we discussed various problems connected with the life and future of Indian children. Yet when we asked him if he wanted to return to his tribe after he graduated or take up some occupation outside the reservation, he was reluctant to go into the matter, and we did not insist.

The best answer to the problem of the Indians, it seems to me, was given by the teacher in a Cherokee village. We talked about her school and the children, the attitude of the parents, and the like. At one point she apparently discerned a shading of curiosity in my question, because she looked straight at me and said sadly, "We are people, just people, no more and no less."

Another aspect of American life that seemed to us to contradict the impressions of fairness, general friendliness, and the sense of equality that we had witnessed under many conditions was the Negro problem. We faced it in Washington and everywhere else. Actually, this is more a white American's problem than a Negro's. Though it is not possible to legislate good will and fairness in human relations, we felt that the American people had enough of these qualities to free themselves of this sad heritage from the past. Every one of us can cite many cases of ugliness in this area, and we witnessed our share of uncivilized, even brutal incidents. Yet nothing hurt me as badly as seeing on the television screen a lonely little Negro girl on her way to school braving two packed rows of shouting, screaming teen-agers. How I wanted to see at least one of them break loose from that wall of hatred and join her!

LATIN AMERICA

The New World fascinated us, and we wanted to see its southern part, the Latin countries. We made a modest beginning by driving to Mexico via Laredo, and after having stayed in Mexico City, Taxco, Cuernavaca, Toluca, Puebla, Lake Patzcuaro and other places, we crossed to Guadalajara and entered the United States at El Paso. This was a wonderful trip. In its guidebook, the AAA warned tourists not to leave their cars in the streets (we asked ourselves where one should leave the car?), and we understood the warning when we arrived in Mexico City. The hotel manager suggested that we leave the car in the garage and use taxis instead. But in the small towns and villages when we wanted to visit a church, a pottery shop, a school, we had to leave the car in front of it. Small boys immediately offered to watch our car—for a tip, of course. I was already sick at seeing how American tourists were ruining Mexican children by accustoming them to stretch out their hands for tips. So I would say, "No, thank you. The Mexicans are a very fine people, and nobody will touch our car, as you will see yourselves." The boys were surprised, but the car was safe. We always had hard candy for the children in our pockets but never tipped them. The Americans were surprised, too, but the system worked.

Despite all the warnings of the dire things that might happen to our car, what really happened was a source of continuous fun. On one of our first days in Mexico, Wolik bought a big sombrero that struck his fancy. Soon thereafter he had had enough of it and wished to get rid of this inconvenient article. In nearly every store or museum, he put it discreetly in some corner and tried to leave without it, but no sooner did he step out into the street than somebody ran after him: "*Señor, señor, su sombrero!*" He had to bring it back to the United States. The climax came when we were back in Washington and began to unpack our purchases in various Mexican shops. Among them, we discovered a package that we had not bought. Apparently it had been put into our car by mistake. Somebody must have been complaining about having been cheated, but we could not undo somebody else's mistake.

We liked Mexico very much—its museums, art galleries, historical monuments, old churches—but everything that appealed to us as tourists because it was picturesque and colorful, such as the native markets, could not make us overlook the unhealthful conditions in which the people lived and the poverty wherever we turned.

The best part of that first trip to Mexico (we returned several times and saw much improvement) was the children. They were charming, immediately responsive, and very attractive physically. Some of them would have had to be washed with strong chemicals to make them really clean, but their bright eyes shone happily just the same. At the Pyramids of Tiotihuacán, not far from Mexico City, we found a visiting group of schoolboys about eight to twelve years old, with a tall, fat teacher. One of the boys shyly asked Wolik if he would let him look through his field glasses. Wolik put the straps around the boy's neck and handed him the glasses. Before we could say a word, the entire class lined up, with the monumental teacher last in line. Each boy handled the binoculars carefully, and they went from one to another until the teacher returned them to Wolik. The delight of the children who had looked for the first time through the binoculars was great, and at our departure they cheered us, shouting, "Goodbye, *americanos!*," to the great surprise of tourists who had arrived later.

We stopped in many villages, went into the schools, talked to the teachers, looked at children's notebooks. Remembering the extravagant use of paper in schools in this country, we were impressed to see that not a line was skipped or wasted in those notebooks in shifting from one year to the next.

Driving was rather complicated, because the roads were not only for motorists but also for everybody else—pedestrians, often carrying heavy, cumbersome loads on their backs, donkeys, cows, fowl. One had to be on the alert every second, though the Mexican drivers, used to those conditions, seemed not to worry at all. We saw several accidents on the road, and once we had to take in injured people—a woman covered with blood, with a broken nose, and a girl of about seventeen whose dress was also spotted with blood but who, as we found out later, had received a shock but had not been injured. We explained that we had only enough gasoline to reach the next village or town (it was Sunday and at every filling station we had heard the same "No hay," meaning there was no gasoline). It impressed us that the woman controlled herself, never moaning. When we reached the first village and stopped the car at the central plaza, the girl jumped out and told the people what had happened and that we had no more gasoline. From nowhere appeared a can with gasoline and the tank was filled; the injured woman was carried away on a stretcher; everybody saluted us in the friendliest manner, and we drove on.

We left Mexico with a desire to come back, but decided to read and learn more about that country before we went again.

Our next trip to Mexico (and several other Latin American countries) was by air. In Mexico, we wanted to see the great monuments of the Mayan civilization—Chichén Itza, Uxmal, and others. The marvel that is Chichén Itza has been described many times, and this name invokes a sense of grandeur and also regret that that vast area with a brilliant civilization was abandoned to decay for reasons yet unknown.

The week we spent in that area was full of excitement. We climbed the tall, imposing pyramid only to discover that the descent on its ninety narrow, abrupt stairs was more difficult than the ascent. We examined every carving, every stela, spent hours admiring the endless columns, trying to understand the meaning of their symbolic designs. We spent almost a whole day at the Caracol and then explored the near-by jungle, full of mysteries and undiscovered monuments. It was quite an experience to grope in the jungle and see statues emerge suddenly—here a warrior, there a head of a woman almost covered by dense vegetation. We also discovered there a large, half-preserved stone building, beautifully carved, with many small cells or rooms without windows except for openings to the jungle. We were told later that once this had been a huge dwelling for scientists, each of whom had a separate room. Wolik declared immediately that if he had lived in Mayan times, he would have had a room in that building. We went back to select "our" room and photographed it several times. We hiked for hours every day—to catch a view of the Caracol from different angles, to visit the ball court, in which the acoustics were such that, standing at its opposite ends, nearly 500 feet apart, we could hear each other though we talked in low voices. We stayed several days in a cottage of the Hotel Mayaland in a gorgeous garden, then spent a day at the Uxmal ruins, with the imposing Casa del Gobernador and its well-preserved carvings and bas-reliefs.

From Merida, we flew to Guatemala and fell in love with that beautiful country and its people. At that time, Guatemala was not as overcrowded with tourists as it is now, and the ways of life were still simple and somewhat naïve. When we registered at the Hotel Tsanjuyu on Lake Atitlan, the owner (or manager) said, "We have two kinds of rooms—at seven and at eight dollars a day with board." I asked, "What is the difference between them?" He replied, "Frankly, I cannot see any difference." We laughed, and I said, "Will you, please, show us the room?" He took us to a large, comfortable room with a balcony overlooking the lake and huge bowls of calla lilies on two tables. Wolik decided, "We like this room. Is it your eight-dollar one?" "No, this is the one for seven dollars."

The lake was glorious, and it was an unending pleasure to look at its green shores, the beautiful blue sky with ever-changing clouds, the majestic, lofty mountains, and the gorgeous flowers of the tropical highlands. Breakfast was served on a balcony overhanging the lake; we dropped bits of bread into the water and watched the fish rush to pick them up, fighting among themselves. We visited on foot most of the villages around that landlocked lake, some days walking from fifteen to twenty miles, villages at which the boat rarely stopped and where few if any tourists ventured. Each village had distinguishing costumes for both men and women. In San Antonio, if I remember rightly, a woman wanted to sell me pink embroidered cotton pants for Wolik. I said that he could not wear them where we lived. She asked innocently, "Aren't they nice? Our men love them."

The climax was Chichicastenango—in its own way as fantastic, as overwhelming, as the Grand Canyon had been. We were there on a market day. The huge plaza, flanked by two imposing churches, was packed. I wished I had two or three pairs of eyes—everything was breath-taking, exciting, magnificent. The men's costumes were no less interesting than the women's. Chichicastenango men wore black woolen shirts and shorts, both embroidered with large red roses. All the colors were represented not only in costumes but also in goods spread either on modest stands or laid out on sheets covering the ground. There were excellent textiles, silver jewelry, basketry, various spices, and so on. We watched the behavior of the people. A customer stopped before some article he wanted to buy, greeted the seller, looked over his selection most carefully, turning it in all directions, asked the price. The seller never hurried him but waited patiently. Some onlookers stopped by. The polite attitude prevailed until the end, whether or not the article was bought.

Suddenly and without the slightest warning, a tropical storm broke out, and the downpour forced everybody to seek a roof. There was a substantial market building with regular stands inside. Everybody collected his wares rapidly and rushed there. We watched with interest that there was no pushing, no rudeness. Those who were closer to the building got in and filled it. The remaining people, caught in the pouring rain, covered their goods the best they could, stood quietly, silently, waiting for the rain to stop.

Market day is also the day of religious services. In that village, this was a wondrous experience. Many broad stone steps led to the Church of St. Thomas (if I am not mistaken). On those steps was a built-in altar to the old Indian gods, and Indian priests with red kerchiefs on their heads prayed before the burning hearth and scattered incense over the believers. The air at that side of the plaza was full of smoke. There were people everywhere—on the steps, near the fire, in front of the steps on both sides. Officially, Guatemala is a Catholic country, but those services were of a distinctly pagan nature, as was also the service inside the church.

The church was empty from the portal to the altar except for the statues of Christ and the Virgin along the walls, and a wide path of flower petals stretched its whole length. On both sides of that strip of flowers, kneeling Indians held burning candles, one for each member of the family and every living creature in the household, perhaps a pig, a dog, a cat, a chicken. A priest moved along the flower line, blessed the Indians with holy water and prayed for them. A lay brother carrying a bowl walked quietly behind him, stopping in front of each Indian, who dropped a coin or two in the bowl. Thus both religions had their day.

There was a great commotion at the close of the market. Unsold wares were packed up, stands were disassembled and loaded on the merchant's back. I filmed a scene that I had never seen before nor have I seen since: One woman packed her goods into a large bundle, then pulled up the poles that held up the stand and tied them together, strapped her child on her back, turned her table upside down and placed it on her head, grabbed the bundle in one hand and the poles in the other, and walked away. Another time, we saw a family of four trudging along the mountain road. The father, a man of forty or more, was carrying an old woman sitting in a chair strapped to his shoulders. It was too pathetic a sight for photography, and we felt the family would have resented it if we had tried to take a picture. The sight of men, women, even children, carrying loads of all weights and sizes, without turning their heads to look around or stopping for rest, was so common that after a few days one ceased to wonder how they did it.

From Chichicastenango, we went to a mountain where, we were told, the Indians prayed to the idol Turkah. There we found a woman priestess with a red kerchief on her head. She was chanting something in her Quiché language, and moving between several crosses in the ground and the idol, she burned candles in front of him and then moved back and forth again between him and the crosses. The curator of the church museum in Chichicastenango was philosophical about it. "I don't blame them. They take no chances. We finally gave them our statues, and now they pray to both ours and theirs."

The Mayan Inn, at which we stayed in that village, was, to our taste, the finest place imaginable, though one should not expect to find all modern conveniences there. Each room was distinctly different and contained old Spanish furniture. The dining room was very attractive. An Indian waiter dressed à la Chichicastenango was assigned to each room to take care of everything. Our Pedro served us as waiter, guide, and interpreter. In the evening, we listened to marimba music in the lovely garden of the inn, then walked a few yards and were again in the central plaza.

For the first time, we were in a country with a primitive economy where even what is considered waste in an industrial country represented desirable, valuable manufactured goods. Jars and bottles that the poorest families in the United States would throw out were proudly displayed in the markets of Guatemala; sandals and shoes had soles made of discarded automobile tires; water was carried in large American cans that once held gasoline or oil. Native artisans made most other goods—blankets, clothing, other textiles, silver articles of all kinds, pottery, basketry, and so on. We could verify many of the statements about a primitive, not fully monetized economy given in books on economics by observing rather closely the economy of that little country.

The village people of Guatemala were tillers of the soil, transport workers, and merchants, all rolled into one. Perhaps trade takes no less of their time than working the land. They spend a night or a day walking to market, sleep anywhere waiting for it to open, stay until dark, then trudge back home. Marketing is not only business but also a social affair —meeting people from neighboring villages, perhaps meeting relatives, exchanging news and worries.

The country was poor, but the people with whom we talked showed no envy of their wealthy neighbor, the United States. On the contrary, many praised their way of living as more pleasant, less frantic. Even a young man who worked as a chauffeur for our hotel on Lake Atitlan for $50 a month and a room for himself, his wife, and child, was not complaining, though he had a diploma from New York University. When I said that he could have a better job in the United States, he replied, "You cannot give me the sun and smiles of our country. There you live too fast for us."

We traveled mostly by bus, though we had been warned in Washington never to do that but to use instead a private car. We preferred the bus because it let us see how the native people traveled and behaved in that crowded, rickety, creaking vehicle. The bus stopped where somebody wanted to get in or out. No matter how crowded it was, new passengers were admitted. Nobody protested; on the contrary, those inside pressed closer to one another, or took a child on their lap, or pointed to a bag on the floor as a possible seat—all this quietly, courteously, as the thing to do. When the road was bumpy, as usually it was, the bus jolted and rattled and we were thrown against one another and shaken up, but we survived. For longer trips, as in crossing Guatemala to reach Quezaltenango on its western border, we traveled by air.

Most of all we liked to hike in Guatemala. The scenery was beautiful, the plant life lush and colorful, and the people were friendly, the children gay, winning us without trying. We visited village schools, talked to teachers and pupils. With the scantiest means at their disposal, both showed much ingenuity in decorating their simple buildings; they kept flowerbeds around the school and some maintained a kind of zoo for a few wild animals and birds caught in the forests covering the mountains.

In Guatemala City, we were deeply impressed by the *Casa del Niño* (Home of the Child). We stumbled onto it one day by noticing a sign on the building and asked permission to visit it. That institution takes children of preschool age for the whole day, thus freeing their mothers for work (mostly selling in the markets). The children change to clean aprons on arrival, play, have their lunch, rest in beds after lunch, swim in the pool. They also get medical care. The *casa* we visited had a dental office and an operating room, the latter with a broad inscription over the door: "Erected by the Jewish Community in gratitude for friendship shown toward them by the people of Guatemala."

The director of the *casa* said that they followed up their children through the elementary school, helped the able ones to get into high school and even to college. She showed us the register. For each child, there was information on weight at certain dates, age, earnings of the parents, mostly mothers (unregistered marriage is very frequent in Latin America), usually a dollar or so per week. Those who could, paid up to half a dollar a month. In exceptional cases, the *casa* accepted a rich child. The director showed us one: a pale, unsmiling, timid little boy, son of rich parents, who had tried unsuccessfully to break through his complete withdrawal into himself. Finally, they begged the *casa* to accept him for a trial. We were told that after two weeks of inner isolation, he had smiled for the first time and said two words to a little girl. There was hope that he would defrost in that gay, animated *casa*.

When we were there, Guatemala City had four *casas*, with more than 1,200 children. There was a permanent medical service—a director, deputy director, five medical doctors for the children, medical service for the parents and also for prenatal consultations. We spent two days in two *casas* to see their work and learn about their history.

Like every other effort of this type, this work had begun on a small scale, attacked by some, ridiculed by others, with predictions that it would soon collapse. Yet, entirely on a voluntary basis, it was carried on with courage and devotion. After a while, it won such recognition that even the government offered its participation and financial support. The founders of the one *casa* then in existence were glad to have a sound financial basis, but after a short time (I do not remember whether it was a year or several years), it withdrew from the arrangement because the government wanted not only to help but also to control the life of the *casa*. In our time, the *casas* had become an established national institution, spreading from the capital to other cities—for example, Quezaltenango.

The existence of the *casas* is due to the dedicated work of a group of intellectuals organized as the Sociedad Protectora del Niño (Society for the Protection of the Child), and is supported by donations in kind by merchants, producers, and others. The budget was minute, and we marveled at how much was achieved with infinitesimal financial resources but evidently great human resources, great in the spirit of humanity.

Years later, in 1958, we were again in Guatemala, during a lecture tour to fifteen Latin American countries for the Department of State. Visiting the U.S. Embassy in Guatemala City, I asked the cultural attaché about the *casa del niño*. "*Casa del niño?* What is it?" he asked. Incredible! Neither he nor anybody else in his office, after years in that small city, had ever heard that name. This showed us that there was no contact between our cultural representatives in that country and the intellectuals in the capital, since they, too, evidently had never tried to get in touch with or interest the Embassy in the *casas*.

Our strongest impression from our stay in Honduras came from Copan, the city of Mayan ruins. We flew to it from Tegucigalpa, since the road was reportedly very bad, almost impassable. The airplane, an obsolete U.S. Army training plane, had no seats because its main purpose was to carry produce from the villages to the cities, and goods from the cities to the villages. Three chairs were hooked in for us and one other passenger and one belt was provided. The flight was exciting. We almost touched majestic mountains and crossed several beautiful valleys. The plane landed at the airfield, that is, a pasture; the only indication that it was an airfield was a little shed. The plane took off immediately, and we had to walk for a mile or more to the village. We had been told to ask for Marina, who had rooms to rent. She showed us a large room with two bedsteads with mattresses but no pillows or sheets, a stool with a bowl and a pitcher, and two tiny night tables. Since there was nowhere else to go, I asked meekly if she had anything better, but she replied, "This is room No. 1," indicating it was her best. We took it, and she promised to give each of us a sheet. But that was unimportant—we had come to see Copan!

We left our overnight bags, went to the ruins, and were immediately in another world. What a world of magnificence and advanced civilization it must have been! The hieroglyphic stairway, with Mayan history engraved in its marble steps; the temple on top of a hill surrounded by imposing statues; the ball court, with seats for the spectators; the altar engraved on all four sides, showing the first scientific world conference of astronomers around a table with instruments in their hands; the jaguar stairway, with two monstrous jaguars engaged in fight; many, many stelae representing statesmen, warriors, and priests and one representing a woman. Each recorded the history of its time in hieroglyphs; one had been erected every twenty years. It was enchanting, and it held us, alone in that enormous area, from the early morning till dark, when we tore ourselves away only to return at sunrise.

At Marina's, we waited on the little porch for the men to return for supper. She was pacing the porch, trying to calm the crying baby in her arms. I asked the age of the child—four months. "Was your boy born here, in the village?" "Oh no, I flew to Teguci, stayed in hospital there. Two days after he was born I flew back." She looked very proud when I commented, "There are few boys in the world who have been in the air on their third day of life!"

At suppertime, we were pulled back rudely from this last word of modernity. The washstand was at my right elbow, and as each man washed and shaved himself, drops of water rained on me. But Copan was worth all its inconveniences, so I ignored them and chatted with the people around.

Next morning we revisited the ruins, again admired the stairway, the temple, the statues and sculptured heads, carefully examined the altar with the astronomers, who had kindled Wolik's imagination and in whom he sensed kindred souls. Then we reached the "airfield" and while waiting for the plane, watched the peasants come out of the woods with heavily laden donkeys. They, too, were waiting for the plane, to ship their bags of coffee and get bags of salt. Two eras, the donkey age and the airplane age, met there and cooperated in a most natural way.

We took an immediate dislike to Nicaragua. After registering at a hotel, we took our cameras and went out to see the capital, Managua. We had gone barely a hundred yards on the broad main avenue when a car stopped alongside us and the man inside said in good English, "You must not take pictures here. Better leave your cameras at the hotel." We did not know anything about special rules on picture-taking in Nicaragua, decided that we did not have to obey some stranger's advice, and continued to walk. Shortly thereafter we noticed a booth on the sidewalk; a soldier came out of it and said, "No pictures!" Later we stopped before the statue of President Roosevelt at the end of the avenue, and opened the cameras, thinking it would be asinine to forbid Americans to photograph their President, but another soldier appeared: "No pictures!" We mounted the steps leading to a broad terrace on which the palace of Nicaragua's President is situated. An officer came to inform us again that we could not take pictures. Wolik tried to explain to him that Managua is a flat city, that the only chance to take a picture of the capital was from an elevation, and that he had his back to the palace. "No, picture-taking is forbidden." We returned to the hotel, telephoned the airline office, secured seats on next morning's flight to El Salvador, and did not leave the hotel that evening.

In El Salvador, we were struck by the sharp contrast between wealth and degrading poverty. Such contrasts exist everywhere, but it seemed to us that nowhere else were they so brutally exposed as in that small Latin country. Besides the gates of a beautiful villa with huge, gorgeous grounds, we saw a filthy tent with no fewer than ten children, some of them naked crawlers, while dirty, poorly dressed adults sat and chewed something—a picture of the most abject poverty. We asked ourselves how could people, not only the poor but the rich, live that way? We saw similar scenes again and again. And the market! Nothing but a hotbed of infections and diseases of all sorts!

Fortunately, we found improvement when our lecture trip took us to El Salvador again, but there, as in all other Latin countries, the road of progress is long and difficult.

Perhaps the most civilized country in Latin America was Costa Rica, almost a serene, quiet place after Nicaragua and El Salvador. We happened to be there on Costa Rica's Independence Day. On its eve, we saw a fine ballet performance in the National Theater, a miniature replica of the Opera House in Paris. When the Guatemalan dancers appeared on the stage, we were glad we could recognize the costumes of every village in that country. The next day, we watched the parade of school children on the main plaza of San José. We spent about a week in a little resort, Catilina, actually a plantation with accommodations for guests. It was the rainy season, and the rain usually started around noon and persisted until night. So we got up around four or five in the morning and had a day's hike by lunchtime; then we stayed inside the cottage or on its roofed porch. It was a pleasure to be among Costa Rica's courteous, civilized people. We loved the abundance of flowers, particularly the wealth and variety of orchids, and we planned to come back for a longer stay. Alas, that never happened.

WORLD WAR II

We sensed the approach of the war, heard its furtive, menacing steps, each bringing the inevitable explosion closer and closer. We knew that it was hopeless to appease the tyrants and were heart-broken when we heard over the radio how the English had cheered Neville Chamberlain for his declaration that he had brought them "peace in our time." Yet we also knew how strong was the desire for peace at any price in France and England alike. We were skeptical when Léon Jouhaux, passing through Washington on his way back to Paris, replied confidently to Wolik's question about whether the alliance treaty with Czechoslovakia would be disregarded: *"Pas par un pays comme la France"* (Not by a country like France). Alas, after the confession of weakness that was Munich, there was nothing to hold Hitler back. When he signed the treaty with Stalin, there was everything to push him toward further conquests.

We hung on the radio every free minute, but all the news was depressing, catastrophic. Occupation of Poland by both Germany and Russia, of Belgium, destruction of Rotterdam, Germans everywhere. I recall a little incident from that period. I stopped at a grocery and asked the clerk for asparagus. He did not understand, so I pointed to the vegetables and then asked, "From what country are you?" "From Greece. And you?" "From Russia." The boy suddenly said, "Why are you attacking my country? You must not help the Germans." I replied resolutely, "I agree with you. I am ashamed that Russia is lending itself to helping

Germany destroy your small country." He was pleased and, giving me the bag with the asparagus, said, "Two more, two more." I did not understand. "What?" "Two more asparagus, and tell the Russians not to fight us."

Then came Hitler's attack on Russia the night of June 21, 1941. Wolik tells in *Stormy Passage* how surprised our neighbors were when he predicted that the picketing at the White House against U.S. aid to "imperialist" Great Britain would be halted and that the strike in munitions plants would end at once. "Why? What is the connection?" was the naïve question. We watched many leftists discover overnight that Stalin's pact with Hitler had been a clever maneuver on his part to gain time for better preparation to fight Hitler, though nobody suggested the same reason for Chamberlain.

The morning after Hitler's attack, I was questioned by the staff of the Committee on Social Security (where I was working on Wolik's project of the Social Science Research Council) about what I expected to happen in Russia. When I said that Hitler, though easily successful in the beginning, à la Napoleon, would be defeated, they were incredulous. One of the staff members said, "What do you mean? Our Army staff predicts that Hitler will occupy Russia in six weeks." I replied, "I am not a military expert, and the Army staff knows better than I about the preparedness of both countries. But I know a little of Russian history and the Russian people, and I see no reason for them to exchange Stalin for Hitler. They are of the same breed, but Hitler is a stranger, an invader, and to him the Russians are *Untermenschen* (subhumans). They will fight and they will throw him out." When they laughed and said, "You still have your Russian patriotism," I answered only, "If the American troops were coming with Roosevelt and the banner of freedom, the story would be different."

We were very much interested in the 1940 elections and were sure that President Roosevelt would win. Wolik suggested a slogan to combat opposition to the third term: "Which is more important for the country, a good President or a good precedent?" We both joined in informal pools on the election result among friends and both of us won.

Then Pearl Harbor, and Germany declared war on the United States. This country was again in a world war, this time fighting on both oceans. Russia became an ally, and the shift confused everyone, or nearly everyone. The democratic countries were fighting one dictatorship and helping another.

As is only too well known, people moved from one extreme to the other—from considering Russia an illiterate, backward country to an unreserved admiration for Russian resistance, enthusiasm for the Red Army and Stalin. With my Russian name, I was constantly exposed to the expression of such sentiments. When I presented a check to a bank teller, a letter to be registered at the post office, I was told about the magnificent Red Army. In a trolley, an ordinary middle-class woman reading the newspaper turned suddenly to me: "Isn't the Red Army grand?" I replied, "Well, they are fighting invaders with their backs to the wall. But why don't you admire the GIs who travel nearly five thousand miles to help the Russians?" When she said, "The Russians have a wonderful leader. Look at this picture of Stalin," I could not restrain myself: "He is a menace to Russia, to this country, and to the world. You should be glad that we have a great war leader here." She replied spitefully, "Oh, that man in the White House!" and turned away from me.

This universal enthusiasm for the Red Army here and in England is pretty much forgotten now, but then there were few who knew enough of Russian history to evaluate the situation correctly and foresee the future. I recall that I was nearly ostracized for not being enthusiastic about Russian policy.

BATTLE OF THE PROJECTIONS

Almost immediately after the United States entered the war, Wolik started to study the future of the postwar American economy and prepared, as early as 1942, his first analysis, "Economic Perspectives, 1942-46." This was followed by two revised and expanded mimeographed reports for 1942-47 and 1943-48. At that time, pessimistic predictions of what would happen when 12 million men were demobilized were on everybody's lips. It was commonly predicted that unemployment of 10 million to 15 million was inevitable.

No wonder, then, that Wolik's survey, indicating expansion of the American economy after the war and comparatively easy absorption of demobilized soldiers by the peacetime economy, appeared fantastic. In his own agency, the Social Security Board, a colleague asked to comment on Wolik's survey wrote, "Not since I came out of the Perisphere at the World's Fair in the summer of 1939 have I seen so bright and cheerful a picture of the 'world of tomorrow' as that presented by Mr. Woytinsky in his report." Wolik's views were attacked by both economists and politicians, who had already planned the Government's postwar policy in line with the gloomy prospects. The only man on the Social Security Board who shared Wolik's views and supported him was Ewan Clague. The Board itself was not on Wolik's side, but he was left free to circulate his "Economic Perspectives" and to defend his point of view in various departmental conferences.

Wolik was unswayed by this opposition to his views. He had not adjusted the facts to fit his political views or theories, but had analyzed them as they were and, checking his estimates several times, he could not find any flaw in them. I, too, was confident and did not worry about the developing controversy. The work of an independent mind, especially when it is combined with great knowledge and an ability to express ideas, inevitably becomes controversial. But when Wolik wanted to publish his analysis and to have his findings and estimates discussed publicly, even a most important U.S. economic magazine did not dare to challenge the widespread appraisals and wrote that it had to reserve its pages for more commonly accepted opinions.

A friend, a well-known economist, told me that when he came to Washington for the first time, he wanted to meet Wolik and made the appointment for the next morning. But that morning one of Washington's newspapers carried an editorial about the prospects for the American economy after the war, all of them on the gloomy side, and added as an afterthought that there was one foolish economist who believed instead that the American postwar economy would absorb the demobilized armed forces and there would be no unemployment of consequence. The economist expected to find Wolik hurt or irritated since the allusion was unmistakable, and was surprised to note his good spirits. Wolik laughed and said to him, "I am made now. Lots of people will be curious to know what that fool is saying."

Professor William Haber, of the University of Michigan, told me that during that controversy on postwar perspectives, Wolik came to his office to discuss the outlook. Immediately thereafter, Professor Haber went to a staff meeting of the Office of the Director of Mobilization and Reconversion at the White House, where the same problem was the main topic for discussion. He remarked that while he did not share Woytinsky's views, he felt it his obligation to report them. When he was asked to go ahead and outlined Wolik's reasoning and predictions, the reaction was, "Are you out of your mind?" When he told me this story, Professor Haber concluded, "History proved your husband correct and almost everyone, including myself, quite wrong."

Something in this attitude of the economists, a kind of snobbish arrogance implying that his views were not worth consideration, provoked Wolik's fighting spirit. At the 1944 meeting of the Economic Association in Chicago, Wolik, who had always been good-humored, sharply accused the economic and statistical fraternities of being intolerant toward anyone who dared to express independent views and of using their influence in the Government and in the press to close avenues for public discussion of opposing views. Even I had not expected such an outburst of resentment; evidently it had grown in him gradually.

Once his economic projections were fully vindicated, his analyses no longer were brushed aside. Business organizations, Government agencies, magazines, and newspapers suddenly discovered him, and the press opened its columns to him. *Life* magazine asked him to present his views and sent an artist, who spent almost a full day at our home, talking to Wolik and sketching the curve of the development of American economy as Wolik visualized it for fifteen years ahead. When we arrived in Chicago for the Christmas meetings in 1947, the issue of *Life* with Wolik's article and portrait had just reached the newspaper stands. Many met us waving the magazine. This was Wolik's day, with congratulations from all sides.

The interesting thing about that article in *Life,* which could not be known then, was that Wolik's curve of the development of the American economy predicted all the recessions that followed between 1947 and 1962. Even in 1958, Wolik continued to receive letters about that curve from business organizations and economists in this country and Canada. His reputation was no longer questioned, no longer controversial.

Wolik was modest and unassuming. He had no thirst for fame, but he knew that he could have given more than he was asked to or had a chance to give. Had he been born in a free society or had Russia maintained the freedom it acquired briefly in 1917, he would have shone in all his greatness. Despite the ten years he spent in prison and exile and even without the support of his native land, he stood out wherever life took him—in Germany as in the United States. That his native country did not know how to make better use of him and his great store of knowledge and understanding was more its loss than his. When the first volume of *The World in Figures* appeared in Germany, Robert Kuczynski, a noted German statistician, wrote in his review that it would have been out of character for the League of Nations to get hold of such a genius as Woytinsky and thus raise the standard of its own work. With even greater justification, this could later have been said of the United Nations, because in the interim Wolik had become a world-famous economist and statistician. That no university honored itself by honoring him bespeaks the expediency of many university honors. Wolik did not need recognition, but he would have been glad to give even more than he did.

Wolik was not eager to give personal advice unless urged to express his opinion, but at the national or world-wide level he tried to make science accessible to the masses, to make statistics an instrument of education, and to make economics understood and used for practical decisions. He greeted warmly every step that others made in this direction and never resented it when others appropriated his ideas, even his writings, without giving him credit; the spread of ideas was the only important thing to him. Sometimes he did feel frustrated when a right decision he was advocating was defeated. Because of his belief in humanity, in the public spirit and intelligence of people, he was an optimist, but as Paul Webbink wrote in *So Much Alive,* his "optimism was not the empty, vapid cheerfulness of a man who retreats from the ugly facts of the world, but the natural courage of one who had partaken of the many vicissitudes of life in the first half of the twentieth century, in many different parts of the world and for many different reasons."

His purpose as a social reformer was to lift the educational level of the masses, enrich their knowledge of past and present, strengthen their sense of human dignity, of "belonging" to their nation and humanity. To him, a higher standard of living meant not only improvement of material living conditions but also more leisure, broader education, greater ability to use the acquired knowledge to fulfill creative activities. During the war he envisaged an imaginative use of many facilities built for war purposes— use of surplus ships as floating universities to carry students and teachers to other shores for better understanding and communication with peoples beyond the country's borders, use of surplus aircraft as flying schools, and so on.

MY WORK DURING THE WAR

While Wolik was absorbed in the problems of the domestic economy, I was working on international economics in the Economic Warfare Board (later the Foreign Economic Administration). My assignment was to study and evaluate Germany's supply and need of various raw materials important for the war effort, and her available resources for obtaining them. I worked first on various textiles, later on metals and minerals. Our sources of information were wholly inadequate. Sufficient to say that my copy of the *German Statistical Yearbook* for 1938 was in constant use, moving from one room to another. Occasionally I was in the difficult situation of having two analysts come to me, each insisting on using that book immediately. Why it never occurred to us to photostat it, I do not know.

In connection with this work, I was made an alternate member of the pre-emption committee. The United States pre-empted certain goods, like tungsten, from the markets of the several remaining neutral countries in Europe, such as Spain or Portugal, so as to keep them from Germany if it was believed that it needed them.

In five years of Government work, I had only one project that interested me very much—a study of the German supply of alloys needed for the production of quality steel required by the specifications of modern arms. I was lucky in working on this in association with Dr. Augustus Kinzel, a first-class specialist in metallurgy, a man of great knowledge, imaginative thinking and—strange as this may sound, perhaps even to him—some congeniality with me. He was a dollar-a-year man working in support of the war effort, and came to my office once a week from New York. As I learned after the war, he was also engaged in the Manhattan Project.

This is not the place to describe how we made our estimates of Germany's war industry. Speaking personally, I learned a lot and have preserved pleasant memories of this period. Steel technology had been unfamiliar to me, but I had to understand it and acquaint myself with the different properties of various alloys and their possible interrelationships and substitutions. As always, I plunged into the basic sources, but I would not have been able to digest the complicated material except for the invaluable and always friendly help I received from Dr. Kinzel. I prepared a list of questions for each meeting with him and enjoyed, almost esthetically, his lucid, brief, yet conclusive answers. Like all other outstanding persons, he never showed his superiority toward a novice in the field in which he was a master but shared his knowledge with patience and courtesy.

When the report was ready, I went to see him in his New York office at the Union Carbide Corporation. I waited while he read it from beginning to end. After his approval, I turned the report over to my division chief. Next morning he called me in and said, "This is a darn good report." Unfamiliar with this slang, I was upset and stopped two colleagues in the hall to find out what "darn good" meant.

This was Friday. On Saturday, we used to work until one o'clock; afterward I went to buy groceries for the next week, then an important and time-consuming affair. When I returned home, the telephone was ringing. "Where have you been?" I was asked, "We have called you many times. You must come back to the office right away. The White House has asked for your report, and you have to proofread it. It must be there tomorrow."

On Monday, it was decided that Dr. Kinzel was to fly to London and discuss these findings personally with the British Ministry of Warfare. Of course, every VIP on the Economic Warfare Board suddenly was found to have been associated, in one way or another, with this report by a modest analyst. I would have been pushed out of sight except that none of them could answer the technical and statistical questions that would be raised in the conferences, so I was asked to attend.

It was something to see the surprise of the conferences of metallurgical experts on Germany's munitions industry when a woman appeared to give "expert" explanations. I particularly recall a meeting in the Pentagon with General Armstrong in the chair and twenty or more officers in attendance. My assignment was to report on the properties of vanadium, German needs for it, and the substitutes available to her. When I entered the room, everyone turned to get a look at the "specialist" in vanadium and I began my report in a trembling voice.

On another occasion I had to discuss the German situation in non-ferrous metals with the engineers of a large American corporation in New Jersey. The meeting had to be early in the morning, and I reached a New York hotel late in the preceding evening. The trip had been decided upon that same day, giving me no time in which to get in touch with any of our friends in New York, so I decided to go for a stroll along Broadway. At one corner, I saw a line extending from a theater and thought that this would be a good way to spend the evening. I joined the queue, waited until my turn came, then asked for a ticket for that night. Without lifting her eyes, the girl in the ticket booth said, "Tickets on sale for the last week in April." It was now mid-November. As I turned away, I glanced at the billboard: *Oklahoma!* At the meeting the next morning, the engineers were amused at my "provincial optimism."

Except for work with Dr. Kinzel, those years were rather disappointing, perhaps because I had to work with people of small stature. Nevertheless, I would not want to have missed them. I really believe that to understand the operations of the huge government machinery in this country, one has to be inside, even as a small cog. No amount of telling can make one "feel" how it works, and being inside during the war made for greater awareness in many ways. Somehow, it also gave a feeling, perhaps unjustified, of being a part of the war effort.

OUR JOINT WORK

Of all the work we did jointly or separately, we liked best the two international volumes *World Population and Production* and *World Commerce and Governments,* a project accepted by the Rockefeller Foundation, administered first by Johns Hopkins University and later by the Twentieth Century Fund, and financed by the Rockefeller Foundation and the Twentieth Century Fund. The Fund published both volumes. In a way, this work took us back to the years when we worked on *The World in Figures* in Germany.

We had thought about this project ever since we came to the United States. During our summer trips, we discussed it, added more and more topics to be included but relegated it to a time when both of us would have given up Government service. As soon as the war ended, we began to think more seriously about it and drew up an outline. Securing the support of the Rockefeller Foundation did not take much time, and in November, 1947, we began to work on it officially. First, we planned to have one volume of some eight or nine hundred pages. The material, however, continued to expand, and we decided on two volumes. The final product consisted of two volumes comprising nearly 2,200 pages, some 800 tables, and more than 500 charts and maps.

We divided the entire content of the study between us in accordance with our inclinations and abilities. Wolik took the theoretical sections on population, national income, systems of national economy, finances, taxation, trade and tariffs, and so on. I wrote the more descriptive chapters on world agriculture, metals and minerals, individual industries, transportation. We treated each topic on a world-wide scale, but also gave much attention to individual countries.

Wolik and I had totally different ways of going about this work. Broadly speaking, he knew the field he intended to cover in each chapter, could plan it at once and start writing. He read a great deal on each topic, but what he read only supplemented what he had already known before he started, filling in some gaps or adding more recent statistical material.

Not having Wolik's enormous store of knowledge, I worked differently. Some chapters which I had to write concerned subjects with which I was only slightly familiar or not familiar at all, such as the technology of the chemical industry or the techniques used in extracting and processing petroleum. What helped me was my long-established habit of working in libraries and my ability to find the necessary documentation. I could not possibly have prepared the outline for these chapters at the start, as Wolik could for the chapter on national income. First, before I could organize the chapter, I had to familiarize myself with the history of each industry, its technical development, its national and international sources of raw materials, the output in various countries, the industry's financial and organizational problems, and so on. Compilations on the subject never tempted me; I always plowed through the basic works of outstanding experts in each particular area. It required a real effort to understand their technical language, and I checked myself again and again in order to be absolutely certain about the meaning of each term. I had to have the content of the chapter more or less complete in my head before I could sit down to write. However, once I knew what I wanted to say, the writing was comparatively easy. I was often surprised to find how much one can learn in two or three weeks of intensive work! Wolik teased me by remarking that I lacked the ability to pad the text, saying that this was an important element in the works of experienced writers and orators.

Though we worked independently of each other, the study was a joint task. We helped each other constantly through consultation and advice, in the search for material, with comments on every chapter, and in checking statistics, proofreading, and so on. We had no outside help except a librarian in a Government agency who typed for us nights or Sundays. We mailed the drafts to her, and she returned the typed copy by mail or occasionally brought it. Wolik, an excellent and imaginative draftsman, made most of the charts, and we also used some charts from Government publications. I drew up most of the tables. The study continued to grow and expand beyond the time originally contemplated for its completion and beyond the funds provided by the Foundation and the Fund. This did not deter us from finishing the project, and we worked for more than a year without salaries.

We gave all our time to the work. We talked about it when we went to bed at night and when we woke in the morning. Our stop sign came at eleven o'clock at night, when I turned on the radio to hear the news. Even then, Wolik was occasionally not ready to call it a day. We tried not to interrupt each other's work. If I wanted to consult Wolik on something before a mealtime break, I asked for an "audience" or for "extra time." We knew no Sundays or holidays, and friends were careful not to call unnecessarily. We worked steadily for seven years. It was hard but exciting work. It strengthened our unity. We lived and worked in our own world, and because of the loving harmony in which that work had been conceived and carried out, the end product, our two volumes, gave the impression of complete unity. Nevertheless, of one thing I am completely sure: Wolik could have prepared both volumes without me in perhaps ten or more years, instead of the seven years that it took the two of us; I could never have done it without him.

Much of the work we put into those two volumes cannot be seen. We started the project when postwar data for almost all countries were fragmentary and for some, not available at all. Each successive yearbook of the United Nations, of the Food and Agriculture Organization, or individual countries substituted new data for those we had previously used. This forced us not only to change the data in many tables but also to adjust the text referring to those tables and to change the relevant charts. In a number of cases, we made such changes several times. Moreover, new information was reaching us all the time, and we tried to update the content of each chapter. In some instances, new documentation entirely altered the picture, and we had to rewrite the entire text. Only those who have worked on similar projects can appreciate the amount of such lost or "wasted" work.

In one respect, the work on our two international volumes was psychologically more taxing than that on *The World in Figures*. A year after we had started to work on the earlier survey, the first volume appeared; then one or two volumes appeared every year. It was easier to continue working in an atmosphere of universal recognition that grew with each volume than to work here for six years before the first volume appeared. It began to look as if the book would never see the light of day. There were so many delays in publication, probably most of them justified but nevertheless exasperating.

In addition to the Library of Congress, we used many Governmental libraries in Washington—those of the Departments of Agriculture, Commerce, and the Interior, and of the Federal Power Commission, Tariff Commission, Bureau of Public Roads, and several others. The United Nations and many of its agencies, such as the Food and Agriculture Organization, the International Labor Office, Commissions for Europe, Asia, Latin America, and others, provided us with their reports and yearbooks, monthly publications, and many monographic studies. Our home library was very helpful; moreover, a telephone call to almost any Government agency or Congressional committee was sufficient to obtain any publication we needed.

Nevertheless, we felt the need for additional information, and wanted to discuss various problems, especially those concerning the recovery of Europe after the war, with specialists in individual European countries. With this in mind, we made a four-month trip to Europe in 1950.

POSTWAR EUROPE

This was our first trip to Europe after fifteen years in the United States. On the one hand, we could not help looking at the European scene with new eyes, "American eyes"; on the other, we keenly felt our European background. The charm of Europe was a part of us—everything was familiar, and we had a nostalgic desire to revisit various spots.

We started with England, and were shocked at the amount of destruction still to be seen in London five years after the end of hostilities. Whole streets were fenced to cover the rubble behind them. Yet we were pleasantly surprised at the change noticeable in the people. We had been in England several times before and had had the impression that people were reserved, withdrawn into their shells, though, of course, very polite. With all this, they maintained some air of conscious superiority that it was difficult to penetrate. In 1950, in contrast, every person we called up (many of whom we had never met) wanted us to come to his home for the evening meal. Food was still rationed, and we felt uncomfortable about accepting the invitation, particularly because we were very conscious of the plenty in this country. A little incident showed us how regulated food distribution still was in England. We were buying a newspaper at a stand in a railroad station. A woman with a boy of seven or eight stopped to pick up a magazine. Seeing candy on the stand, the boy began to beg her to buy him some. She tried to reason with him but finally gave in, carefully tore off a coupon, and bought three minute pieces of candy.

Other chance experiences that we might not have noticed before our life in the United States caught our attention. We stopped one day at an eating place where the tables on the first floor were occupied. The waiter showed us to the second floor. There, as we waited, we saw the waitresses fill their trays with dirty dishes, and walk down the stairway holding the tray in the air. They went down to the first floor, then to the basement, where the kitchen was, and then returned with fresh trays of food to the second floor. We thought immediately that an elevator or a dumb-waiter would be such a simple solution. From the window of the bus taking us to Piccadilly, we saw a sign in a shoe-repair shop: "Shoes repaired in two weeks," and laughed. "With such a sign in his shop, this man would be out of business in two weeks in the United States," we thought. It was April, the weather was rather inclement, and it made us uncomfortable to see old women on their hands and knees scrubbing the sidewalks in front of large department stores with brushes.

We admired the nation's resolute spirit in undergoing a painful transition in its world position, adjusting itself to a more austere way of life than its people had known before, and this with calmness, dignity, and confidence. We were very much impressed by the remark of a professor of economics who had invited us to his home: "We have accepted many sacrifices, but there are compensations. We are proud that no British child was hungry during the war."

We had several interesting meetings in London, Oxford, Cambridge, obtained a lot of documentation, got many internal and mimeographed reports, and left convinced that "there will always be an England."

We crossed the Channel and were in France. The very first words of the proprietress of the small hotel on the Left Bank facing the Louvre showed us that the French spirit had not changed. Having learned that we came from London, she exclaimed, *"Les anglais, ils sont fous!* [The English, they are crazy!] They are still rationing. When will they begin to live? We shall never understand them." Yes, this was France, all right!

Yet there were also new faces and a new mood in France. We were very much impressed by Jean Monnet and the team of economists working on his plan. Our meetings with academic people were much more pleasant and encouraging than in former times. Some of them were fully aware of what American help meant to France. One professor told us, "The French workers eat American bread but believe that you are helping only the industrialists. You should put more pressure on employers to raise wages and salaries." When we asked what the reaction would be to such interference with domestic affairs, he replied, "No matter what you do, you are accused of all sins!" He invited us to his home. I cannot describe the embarrassment we felt when we found that this professor of the Sorbonne and director of a large museum lived in a poor section of Paris in a fourth- or fifth-floor walk-up. The study in which he and his wife received us was crowded with books, and there was just enough space for the two extra chairs and a little service table.

Since we covered different topics in our international survey and our schedule abroad was extremely heavy from the very beginning, we visited particularly outstanding people together but otherwise made separate appointments. Wolik called up a high Government official in charge of estimating French losses during the war as a basis for reparation demands. He suggested a meeting at his home in the evening. When Wolik rang the bell, his wife opened the door and exclaimed pathetically, "My husband has just come home from the hospital, where he had a serious operation. He needs rest, and we have visitors, visitors all the time." Completely confused, Wolik began to apologize and started to leave, when the host appeared at the door; saying, "Please come in. I want to talk to you. This is important. My wife is worried, but I will be all right." He kept Wolik for nearly two hours, showed him the working tables, maps of destroyed areas, went into many details, was animated. Wolik tried to shorten his stay, but could not break off the man's explanation. So passionate an interest in one's job was something novel in France.

In the meantime, I had meetings with representatives of the French food and textile industries and obtained their publications. They were cordial, but rather surprised to have to talk with a woman on such dry matters. Wolik and I rushed from meeting to meeting, from topic to topic, trying to see as many people as possible. Whenever there was a chance for an hour of leisure, we enjoyed just being in Paris, walking along the Seine, or visiting a museum.

The destruction the Germans inflicted on The Netherlands was ghastly—the devastation of the central part of Rotterdam at the beginning of the war, and the opening of the dikes and flooding of a large part of the precious land by salt water before the final retreat. To this was added the terror during the occupation. No matter what the topic of conversation, the effect of the war colored it. Memories of what the country had undergone were still fresh and painful. We met an outstanding engineer in Amsterdam, who, with his wife, took us on a cross-country drive one Sunday. At one place, they pointed to a monument and told us that it had been erected by the nation in memory of the township's entire male population—adults and even baby boys—which the Germans had executed to avenge the killing of a Gestapo member there. During the last months of occupation, the Dutch, cut off from American supplies, were starving; this obviously rich couple told us that their two boys had rummaged for food in garbage cans of the German army.

In Rotterdam, we spent much time in the building center, where the plans for the city's reconstruction were displayed along with large photographs showing Rotterdam before the bombing. Wolik was particularly interested in the problem of urban reconstruction because it belonged to his chapter on cities. The head of the center was apparently glad to find a visitor so well informed and interested in even the details of the city's plans for rebuilding. He gave his time liberally and provided Wolik with various maps and all kinds of documentation.

In the agency for central planning, Wolik discussed problems of national income and economic recovery. Another problem that was causing great concern in The Netherlands was the rapid growth of the population, particularly in view of the loss of Indonesia, which used to absorb part of the population surplus. In the meantime, I had several conferences with officials in the Ministry of Agriculture and tried to obtain information on land reclamation, the dairy industry, and agricultural production in general.

In all our meetings with Government officials, business and labor leaders, and economists, we felt their great concern about the future of their country. There was also a sense of determination, of firmness, a sense of unity in the Dutch people. They did not speak of it, but it came to the fore unconsciously. It was clear that they all saw as their first task the necessity to restore the national economy, to bring the country back to its position among the European nations, to its prewar high standard of living.

Despite the leaders' anxiety, the people did not seem to be gloomy or dejected. On the contrary, the country looked at its best, and there was a light-heartedness in the air. The impressive dresses of the village belles in the North and the boys happily scampering around the boats in a fishing village seemed to assert that the people wanted to forget the past and look to the future.

Love of flowers was evident everywhere. In Amsterdam, we admired the artistic and original flower arrangement in every flower shop; in the villages, every house had lovely flowerbeds in front, and the windows were filled with potted flowering plants. In Aalsmeer, we went to see a flower auction, something we had never seen before and which, to our knowledge, was unique. Seats for the brokers were arranged in a semicircle, with the rows raised one above the other. At each seat was an electric button that connected with the auctioneer on the dais. We saw a farmer roll in a cart filled with bunches of lilies. The auctioneer lifted one bunch to show it to the brokers, while the farmer's price appeared on the electric board. Bargaining by the brokers followed, each price appearing on the board. The last broker who pushed the button bought the contents of the cart. Another cart was rolled in. We were told that the brokers rely on the uniform quality of the flowers they buy. A farmer who cheated would be disqualified from participation in the auction.

We wandered through several huge halls filled with flowers—potted and cut, all prize specimens, each more beautiful than the last. Wolik asked what happened to the flowers sold in the auction. "Oh, they are taken immediately to the airport, where planes are waiting to fly them to Australia, the United States, London, anywhere."

Animals in The Netherlands receive the same loving care given the flowers, and they appeared clean and healthy. Driving past a meadow, we caught a glimpse of a farmer bent over a newborn calf; he was feeding it milk from a bottle.

In July, 1950, we returned to London, in order to attend the World Power Conference. At the registration desk, we were handed the envelopes with the program and invitations to special events. Both of us were interested in the subjects to be presented—Wolik for his chapter on energy, and I for those on coal and petroleum. Atomic power was a new and revolutionary factor, and many sessions were devoted to discussion of its technical aspects and economic implications. Wolik was particularly eager to attend the meetings on this subject.

Among the invitations was a dinner scheduled for the opening night at the British Museum of Industry. The card specified evening dress and decorations. Before we left for Europe, I had asked whether evening clothes would be needed and have been told that formal dress had been a war casualty. Conscious of weight limitations in air travel, we were relieved to learn this and did not take formal attire. Wolik had only a black suit and I, a three-quarter-length black dress. We decided to ignore the discomfort of not being properly dressed rather than forgo the opening-night dinner. In the museum, we sat with a Canadian engineer and his wife and chatted pleasantly from time to time. Of course, I was conscious of being dressed differently from other women, but Wolik was unconcerned. His attention was concentrated on the museum's exhibits of old machinery—original specimens of the first printing machines, first locomotives and railroad coaches, and the like. He was animated and turned my thoughts to the beginnings of the Industrial Revolution.

Our next invitation was to a dinner at the Guild Hall. Naturally, we were eager to see the Guild Hall in all its splendor on such an occasion, formal dress or no formal dress. We stood in line at the entrance, along with British ladies in long evening gowns and men with ribbons and medals covering their breasts. This seemed a kind of make-believe prewar world, and the people who glorified in it seemed out of line with current realities. If we felt any discomfort in breaking the rules on the invitation, it was worth it.

By now, we had had enough of those formal occasions, and passed up the third invitation, by Herbert Morrison to a dinner in a fancy restaurant, to see *Venus Observed,* by Christopher Fry. The next day at a luncheon at a friend's house, I was recounting our experience. One of the guests, the daughter of Sir Stafford Cripps, was amused. "Didn't it occur to you," she asked, "that in all probability all that gorgeous evening dress had been rented? Who of us has clothes like that now? We used up everything we had during the war, when men's tuxedos were recut to make women's suits."

A professor of medicine and his wife took us for a Sunday picnic to the country, some distance from London. As we were walking, we passed two girls, and one of them said: "Look! That must be Einstein!" We were used to having Wolik taken for Einstein, and several reporters mentioned the likeness in describing Wolik's appearance. But when the professor asked with some curiosity in his voice, "Which of us could those girls have had in mind?" Wolik looked at him and quickly replied, "Your venerable appearance and my unkempt hair created a composite picture of Einstein."

Italy seemed to have come out from under the triple pressure of Fascism, war, and the Germans. There we found more hope, more cheerfulness, than in France. There is something about the very soil of Italy, permeated with history and art, that has always appealed to us. The affinity of the Italian people for art, which had always impressed us, again came to the fore on many occasions. We visited several villages that had been destroyed by war and rehabilitated—modestly, with the minimum of means, but how beautifully in every architectural detail! At the national exhibit of reconstruction, there was so much taste and skill in displaying the "before" and "after" that I asked Professor Vinzentini, head of the department, Ministry of Public Works, how they had achieved it. He half-smiled and answered, "We are a poor country, but when there is need for artists, we have no problem. Each artist was given a room and the material, each handled the matter in his own way."

We had long discussions about the program to revive the south of Italy, where agrarian reform was overdue; conferred with the central manufacturers' association and trade-union people, had several meetings with Corrado Gini, an old acquaintance of Wolik's, and other academicians; discussed financial problems with the director of the Bank of Italy and the plans for reconstruction, with the staff of the Ministry of Reconstruction. Involuntarily, comparisons with Italy after World War I came to our minds. In 1950, life was not yet fully organized, but we saw no evidence of the chaos so characteristic of the years 1918-19. There were many problems, many difficulties, but also blueprints for reconstruction, the desire to work, to move ahead.

The really depressing country to see in 1950 was Germany—physical destruction, suspicion, the knowledge that Germany was hated everywhere and by everyone, the feeling that someone had cheated the country of its dreams of grandeur. A country can take a military defeat with dignity, but here was deep moral defeat, and it dogged every German, faced him wherever he turned. In The Netherlands, Swiss visitors wore a little Swiss flag in their lapel so as not be confused with Germans and to get replies when they spoke in German. In Oslo, the murals in the new City Hall, which display the historical events in the life of Norway, represented the German occupants with almost inhuman faces. In every country, there were inscriptions on buildings where occupying forces had executed a worker, a soldier . . . In the churches, names of persons killed, hanged, or taken to Germany were engraved in marble. Everything passes, but not so quickly. We ourselves could not forget the millions put to death in gas chambers. The stay began to get on our nerves, and we left Germany earlier than we had planned.

The Scandinavian countries were basically healthy—most important, healthy in spirit. Of course, Norway had suffered much, and it was pitiful to see empty shelves in the once abundantly supplied stores in Oslo. But the people had preserved their dignity and their self-respect, and we heard many tales of heroic actions during the German occupation. Our contacts with people, specialists in various fields and Government officials, were pleasant, enlightening, and without the slightest tension.

In Oslo, Wolik called up Professor Johan Vogt, the outstanding Norwegian demographer, and said, "This is Woytinsky." Vogt asked, "Are you the son of Professor Woytinsky?" Surprised that Vogt could have known his father, Wolik said yes. Vogt invited us to his home and told us what train to take, saying that he would meet us at the station. When we came out and recognized each other, Professor Vogt said, "I expected to meet your son. I believed that the man who published that great work *The World in Figures* must be some hundred years old by now." We visited Professor Vogt again when several influential people from the Government were at his home. The world is small, particularly for people who move on the same wave length: Two years ago, at a gathering in Storrs, Connecticut, I met a professor from Oslo. Now, when he heard my name, he said, "Don't you remember that we spent an evening together at Vogt's house?" and told the guests about Professor Vogt's miscalculation of Wolik's age.

The Foreign Service, told by our Embassy in Oslo that we wanted to see as many Government economists and researchers as possible, scheduled meetings for us from nine in the morning till five in the evening, every hour on the hour, including lunchtime. We were accompanied everywhere by Norwegian officials, who frequently took turns. Not knowing "the way of life" in a northern country, we followed this crowded timetable for three days, though by the end of the day we felt exhausted. On the fourth morning, we asked to make a short stop at the Embassy to pick up our mail and while there, mentioned our schedule. The reaction was one of disbelief and compassion and also admiration for our stamina. Anyhow, recess for lunch was promised beginning with the next morning. That very noon, however, as we were talking with the president of the Central Bank in his office, a large tray with sandwiches and coffee was brought in. He had had an appeal from the Embassy to feed the starving visitors.

This was the time of the Marshall Plan in Europe. We saw its operations in many places and, of course, in each of the ten countries we visited, we discussed the economic situation, plans, and prospects with the American officials. The Marshall Plan was then the central focus of European life, and even in Sweden, which had received very little assistance, the benefits of the Plan were evident. The director of a large Swedish bank explained it in these meaningful terms: "By saving Europe, you saved us."

We were impressed in Sweden to hear the heads of industrial organizations talk about the trade-union people. While they opposed the latter both politically and across the bargaining table, they never questioned their personal integrity. Nor did they deprecate the labor leaders as human beings; we were told that on occasion they went on hunting or fishing trips with them and enjoyed their company.

We sent tons of material to Washington, directing it to our home, to a family of friends who had a large basement, and to the Washington office of the Twentieth Century Fund. On returning home, it was quite a job to collect all those endless packages, and sort and arrange the contents. Also, many agencies put us on their mailing lists for certain types of material, so that new documentation from Europe continued to flow in. In addition, we found mountains of material at home—from the United Nations, many agencies in the United States, associations, and so on.

Back at our desks, we plunged into our work anew, and after about a year the manuscript of the first volume was ready for delivery. We had received wonderful cooperation from the many experts in individual fields in reviewing the manuscript. Whether or not we had a personal contact with them, all graciously read it, and the comments were most helpful. I have no doubt that we could not have obtained such kind, well-wishing support in any other country. Printing took a long time, perhaps partly because of changes we made in the galleys. These changes, made in the interest of the quality of the books, required much time and energy on our part, and also, on the part of the publisher. We therefore refrained from making changes in the page proofs to update the material.

These two volumes on world economics became our calling cards abroad, though they were a little too heavy a card case—about ten pounds together. On later trips, we found them in almost every university library; several times, professors and even students brought their personal copies and asked us to autograph them. At Wolik's lectures in foreign universities, the two volumes were always present on the table (either the university dean or the U.S. cultural attaché had put them there), and seeing them, the students addressed Wolik most respectfully. The press was very generous, and many admiring letters came from readers in this country and foreign countries. The intellectual dividend was grand, and greatest of all was the satisfaction and joy at working together, at being united in work of which we had dreamed for many years.

Shortly after the release of the first volume in June, 1953, we delivered the manuscript of the second volume to the Twentieth Century Fund for publication, and felt as if a mountain had slid from our shoulders.

There was still a great deal of work to be done on the second volume, but we needed a break in the heavy work schedule we had begun in November, 1947. Our destination was the West, supplemented by Hawaii.

We stayed at Lake Tahoe, hiked in the Sierras and Yosemite National Park, made many side trips, and then left the car in the garage of friends in Los Angeles and flew to Hawaii. There, everything appealed to us— the magnificent scenery of the islands, the glowing sunsets, each more exciting than the last (every night we decided not to take more pictures of the sunsets, and every night we succumbed to their fascination); the dramatic sky, the boisterous play of the waves, the beautiful flowers, the multiracial population, colorful clothing, hula dances. Everything charmed us. We hiked in all directions, rented a car and drove about, flew from island to island, explored the national park on the island of Hawaii. It seemed that the people living amid all that beauty had a carefree, gay, hopeful spirit. Where else in the United States could one find signs on municipal beaches telling people, "This is a muncipal beach. Have fun"?

On the way home we stayed several days with our friends in Los Angeles, revisited the Grand Canyon, then stopped at the Arches National Monument, Utah. Unfortunately, Wolik overexerted himself there by taking pictures under the burning sun without protecting his head. By evening he felt tired, weak, and dizzy. From then on, he could not stand heat, and we would drive from five in the morning until noon, with several stops in between so that he could lie down and rest on the grass in a park for a little while. Then we would take an air-conditioned cabin, where he rested until early the next morning.

I was afraid to turn to a strange doctor in strange cities, because of a bad experience we had had on leaving Los Angeles, when I got an infected tooth. We had stopped in San Bernardino, and we went to a dentist recommended by a large drug store. He examined the tooth, wanted to hospitalize me, "put to sleep," and would not say how long I would have to stay in the hospital. We refused and drove back to Los Angeles, to our friends' dentist. In fifteen minutes, my tooth was out. I rested for a few minutes and suggested that I drive through Los Angeles, because Wolik could interpret a city map better than I. This we did, without any ill effects. So I wanted to bring Wolik home as rapidly as possible, and would have made the trip faster if he could have stood more hours of driving.

At one filling station, we picked up an air-conditioner, very primitive but still helpful. Every time we passed a park or a forest, I knew that Wolik longed to get out of the car, and I was torn between the desire to satisfy his wish and an awareness that we'd better speed toward Washington. In one park, where Wolik had stretched out on the grass, with a pillow under his head, a man looked at him and said, "He is passing away," or something of the sort. Clearly he thought Wolik beyond hope. I gave him a look that sent him away in a hurry, but fear gripped me. That midnight, I suggested that if Wolik could stand it, we would start right away and try to reach home late in the afternoon. We drove that night under a pouring rain, the windshield wiper was out of commission, there was not a car on the highway. It was a nightmare! But we were back in Washington around four in the afternoon, and the doctor came an hour later. Next morning, Wolik felt better, and two days later we took a walk around our block. A few more days, and he was himself again!

THE "GREAT DEBATE"

In the last part of November, 1953, Colin Clark published two articles on the U.S. economic situation in the *Manchester Guardian*. In them, he predicted that the United States would have a depression of great magnitude unless the Government took drastic measures: No less than $25 billion of additional purchasing power must be pumped into the national economy to produce significant changes and lift the American economy out of the morass into which it was sliding. These sensational articles stirred up great excitement in the United States. Colin Clark probably was better known in this country than any other foreign economist, and had an excellent reputation. Every American newspaper, every weekly, every business magazine commented on those predictions.

Suddenly, the National Industrial Conference Board was on the telephone. They had decided to invite Colin Clark to present his views before the business community of the United States; would Wolik agree to debate with him? Wolik said, Yes, it would be an interesting opportunity to meet the best representative of the Keynesian school face to face on this very important subject. Colin Clark also accepted the invitation and expressed his pleasure at having Wolik as his opponent.

The board sent invitations to its members throughout the country. A few days later, they let Wolik know their pleasure at having received some 300 telegraphic acceptances to attend the meeting; after a few more days, another letter: more than 500 acceptances; then more than 750 acceptances. It was clear that the U.S. business community was worried, the economists were interested, and the press would be fully represented.

Wolik worked on this report with great care, going over every economic series related to the subject, checking and rechecking every figure. He knew that it was to be not just a newspaper article or a paper to be discussed within the small group of professionals, but a debate in a national forum, a debate on a question of greatest import to every businessman, to every person in the country. He also knew that he was going to oppose an economist and statistician of international distinction, whose skill, knowledge, and imagination he respected and with whom he felt congenial in various ways. He knew that every newspaper and weekly of standing would report this debate. He had accepted the invitation because he was convinced that there was not going to be a depression, especially not one of the magnitude predicted by Colin Clark. As Wolik said in his address, ". . . depression? No! . . . A recession? Yes. If we call a recession any downward or leveling-off movement even on a very, very high level, then we have a recession. But this is a recession of a special type, a type which has never been described in our textbooks. Because a baby must have a name, I suggest we give a name to this type of recession—it is a *recession de luxe.*"

I had no doubt of Wolik's success, though I would have preferred to have him talk after Colin Clark, as would have been natural. But he was scheduled to open the debate, in accordance with Clark's wishes. I told Wolik jokingly, "You don't have to worry a bit! Who likes a Cassandra foretelling troubles, especially if she arrives from the other side of the Atlantic? They will grab your smiling projection with both hands!"

Finally, the big day arrived. Two ball rooms (North and East) in the Waldorf-Astoria Hotel were filled to capacity, with many people standing along the walls. In attendance were the heads of most American corporations, business economists, teachers of economics, reporters of important periodicals, students. When it was over, a few reporters following the Keynesian line declared the debate a draw, but the general consensus was that Wolik had won. Much more important, of course, was the fact that the development of the American economy took the direction predicted by Wolik and not that forecast by Clark.

After the meeting, the chairman of the board congratulated me on Wolik's success. I thanked him, and so as not to show how pleased I was, I said, "Of course, I realize my husband's English is no match for the consummate English of Professor Clark." He reassured me: "Never mind the English! We on the board knew that Professor Clark's English is better than your husband's, but this was not a competition in English. The vote in the board in selecting your husband to speak for the American economy was unanimous."

CHAPLAIN ALFRED OLIVER

During the war, our vacations were short, and the gasoline ration limited our range. We decided to spend our two-week holiday in a small boardinghouse in the Virginia mountains. After unpacking, we were sitting on a bench awaiting dinner when a couple came in—he, tall, erect, looking like a military man but in civilian clothing, with a steel collar; she, rather small, smiling, unaffected. They joined us, and while Wolik and the man sat together and talked, I chatted with the wife. She told me that her husband was a military chaplain, that she had been with him in Manila, in the Philippines, before the war until all the women were sent home. She and her daughter had then bought a car in California and traveled slowly across the country "since time was the thing to spend." Her husband, an Army chaplain with the rank of colonel, became a war prisoner and participated in the death march.

The Japanese mistreated him, breaking his neck, and he could not turn or bend his head. Now they were back home again in Washington.

This is how Wolik described his first conversation with Chaplain Oliver:

> I asked him about the campaign in the Philippines, the death march, the prison camp. He talked about his missionary work in China, the death march, and people who were with him, some two thousand men in prison camp, but said very little about himself. Then I asked him about his steel collar. He answered slowly, choosing the words: "You see, I was the senior officer in the group. They wished to humiliate me in order to break the morale of my men. They tried to humiliate me by beatings." I remarked: "All jailers think they can humiliate a prisoner by mistreatment. They do not know that it is much worse for a man to see mistreatment of those who depend on him and not to be able to intervene." The chaplain asked gently, "Where did you learn that? You were not there." "I have been in other prisons," I answered.*

At dinner time, we sat at different tables. Next morning when we came for breakfast, the Olivers were leaving. The chaplain came to say good-bye, gave us his card, and said he hoped to see us in Washington. Though we were impressed by them, we were too busy to get in touch with them. Then, one Sunday afternoon, when we were upstairs dressing to go somewhere, the doorbell rang. I ran down in a robe, expecting a telegram or a special-delivery letter, and saw the Olivers at the door. It was an awkward situation. I could not leave them in the living room and make myself presentable, Wolik was shaving, we could not ask them to wait because we were already late. We all tried to make the best of the situation, and they asked us to come for dinner a week or two later. We went, and found ourselves in the company of several generals, who were probably as uncomfortable with us as we were with them. The only thing about that evening that interested us was that when one of the generals wanted the chaplain to tell about the experiences of which he had talked to Wolik at their first meeting, the chaplain refused, saying that he did not like to talk of them.

As Wolik wrote in his memoirs, *Stormy Passage:*

> A strange closeness developed between the gallant soldier-priest and me, a closeness that lasted to his death. Very different roads brought us to captivity, but our experience in an important section of our lives had been the same, and in captivity each of us had learned the same things."

Outwardly, it might seem that we had nothing in common—not work nor friends nor interests—but Wolik and the chaplain reached

* *Stormy Passage*, p. 192.

each other in the first hour and a friendship developed between the Olivers and ourselves. Even the fact that our attitude toward religion was totally different from his did not lessen the chaplain's warm feelings toward us. He simply said, "Both of you have God in your hearts. This is all that matters," and we never touched on that subject again. Of course, he always said grace at meals in his home, and we asked him to say it at ours so as to make him and Mrs. Oliver comfortable.

The chaplain told us many stories from his prison-camp years. He had been the only minister there, and so he had established an inter-denominational service for all prisoners—Christians, Jews, and others. One of his prison-camp experiences stood out most clearly in his memory:

The prisoners were starving; a handful of rice was their daily ration. They had eaten the bark of the trees, insects, practically everything they could lay their hands on. They were emaciated; there were no drugs or other medical resources. Mortality was high, nearly every day somebody died. Our chaplain suffered morally as well because religious funerals were not permitted, and dead bodies were simply thrown into a large pit. The only contact with the outside world (except for a secretly built radio kept hidden from the guards) was the civilian war prisoner whose task it was to deliver barrels of rice to the camp. Several times the chaplain thought of asking the man if he could obtain and smuggle in drugs, but he always refrained from doing this because of the deadly danger to which that would expose the civilian. Yet when mortality in the camp became ghastly, he finally approached the man. The latter told him that he had practiced dentistry in Manila before he was taken prisoner and had contacts with some pharmacies because of his profession. He promised to explore the situation and do the best he could.

After that, there was always something extra in the barrel with the rice—a little package of aspirin, or quinine, or some other drug. This went on for some time. Then the Japanese, sensing their approaching defeat, made a few small concessions, including permission to hold a funeral service on the ground where many prisoners had been dumped into pits. The service took place very early in the morning. The chaplain feelingly described how pitiful the prisoners looked, with their sunken eyes, their worn clothing, their tattered shirts through which one could see their ribs; some could hardly stand on their feet. The funeral service, so far from their own country, in such complete isolation, was very sad. Many had tears running down their faces. Unexpectedly, the civilian, whose name was Aaron, came forward and sang the mournful prayer that the Jews sing on the Day of Atonement, the Kol Nidre. The chaplain told us that he had never heard anything more moving. Perhaps it was their loneliness and despair that gave that prayer so forceful an effect on him and the other soldiers, who sobbed openly. Soon afterward, the dentist was caught smuggling drugs into the camp and was arrested and sent to the mainland for sentencing. The ship carrying him there was hit by American bombs and sank with its crew and him. When

Chaplain Oliver returned home after the end of the war, he got a post-
humous medal for Aaron and tried for a long time to have a film made
of that story and of life in their camp, but was unsuccessful.

We once visited the Olivers in their summer home in Ocean City,
New Jersey. I cannot recall how it happened that I was alone with the
chaplain—perhaps Wolik was talking with Mrs. Oliver in another
room, or was writing while she was busy with household work. I commented on the beautiful floor in the living room, where we were sitting,
and the chaplain answered meditatively, "I myself laid out the floor. You
may not know it, but I have a special affinity with wood. In my youth,
when I worked in the lumber business, I used to judge the quality of
wood as to its grain, how it would look in a polished state, and other
features, just by glancing at the logs arriving from South America. We
got shiploads of very expensive wood from there, and my boss relied on
my judgment. For example, he let me select the wood for the walls in
the study of Mr. Vanderbilt."

Intrigued by this unexpected revelation, I said, "Chaplain, you raised
a question in my mind. May I ask you something, and if you find my
question out of place, please say so." He replied that he would try to
answer it, and I asked, "You have just told me that you were a businessman, a lumberman in your youth. How did it happen that you became
a minister?"

He was silent, then looked at me and said, "I have never talked about
this, but I will answer your question. One Sunday I went to church with
Carole, then my fiancée. During the whole sermon, I was thinking of
the next day's business and making calculations in my mind. Suddenly
I heard the Lord's voice saying, 'I want you to serve me as a priest.' It
came like lightning, and I replied inwardly, 'Lord, I am not good for
this. I am not prepared to be a preacher. Perhaps I have not given
enough support to the church; I promise to give it more money.' But
the Lord insisted, 'I do not want your money, I want *you!*' I begged
the Lord to release me, argued that I had no abilities for that work,
but the Lord would not yield. I saw there was no way out for me and I
gave in, begging the Lord that if after a year of service my work did not
please Him, He would then permit me to return to private life. The
Lord consented. As we left the church, I said to Carole that I was going
to give up my job next morning to become a preacher. She could not
understand what had happened to me and objected strongly, but when
we returned home, I locked the door to the living room and gave my
first sermon before her. She never again objected to my decision."

If I had not had complete faith in the chaplain's integrity, complete
trust in his words, I might have hesitated to believe that story, but his
sincerity and truthfulness were beyond question for me. I thanked him
for his confidence and accepted his story, though I am still baffled as to
how to explain his conversation with the Lord.

The chaplain showed great fondness for Wolik, respected his judgment, leaned on his arm when climbing steps—help that he rejected

from other people. He showed much attention to me, and was so tolerant that he did not object to my smoking at his home and had an
ashtray ready for me. Sensing that the Olivers must have disliked
smoking, I tried to restrict myself to three cigarettes during the evening,
which was not easy. Too bad that I gave up smoking too late for him to
know it.

Every time the chaplain was ill, Mrs. Oliver asked us to visit him at
Walter Reed Hospital, saying that it would please him. I recall our last
visit there, not long before his death. He lay prostrate in bed, uncovered. I noticed that he did not pull up the blanket when we entered
—he who so meticulously observed the social graces. It pained me as a
sign that he was not of our world any longer. His thoughts were already
somewhere beyond. As we took leave of him, I felt that he realized that
we would never meet again.

8. *At Home*

YEARS PASSED. Two short words can best epitomize our twenty-five years in the United States—we were *at home,* in the full sense of the word "home." The drama of our life was in the past, yet for all its quiet and peace, our life here was full—of work we loved, writing, reading, traveling, political interests, friends, hobbies, gardening, photography.

In the personal life that belonged only to us two and that we carefully kept to ourselves, lyricism reached its culmination. More than ever before, we were one in thought, feelings, attitude toward life and people —in everything. There were only a few days—I could probably count them on my fingers—when we were not together.

We felt a relaxation from the tensions we had lived through, felt solid ground under our feet. We had found home. This strengthened the life-asserting spirit in both of us, and—crucial to me—especially in Wolik; this set all the bells ringing in and around us. Wolik liked to repeat, "Life is fun which just begun," from Gilbert and Sullivan. Indeed, the innate cheerfulness in Wolik's nature, earlier muffled by outside pressures on his life, came to the fore. The pressures, the political complications and battles, the stubborn struggle to maintain dignity and preserve life itself, could now be pushed aside.

YEARS OF FUN

All these years stand out in my memory as unending fun and joy in life with Wolik. He was brimming over with puns, wit, jokes, some of which only I could understand because they related to some personal experience. He was an inimitable mystifier and, with the most innocent expression on his face, liked to pull someone's leg. How many times I had to hasten to explain that Wolik was joking so as not to let others repeat his jokes as facts! If we were invited out, he would come down, all dressed except for his pants, and say, in a business-like manner, "Are you ready? I am waiting for you." Or he would say with a twinkle in his eyes, "Why does it take the women so long to change?" If I laughed, he would recite Tolstoy's poem about an official who went to an important celebration

without pants. Sometimes we were so absorbed in our work that dinner
was late. He would come down from his study and say, as if checking on
himself: "Isn't it funny? I can't remember whether or not we have had
dinner tonight." Occasionally, he found me at my desk: I had everything
ready on the table, but in order not to press him and yet not to lose time,
had gone back to my desk to finish a paragraph or a computation. Wolik
would enter our kitchen (the "family room," as he called it), show surprise as he looked around, and then say with satisfaction: "Am I not right
in saying that angels prepared this meal? How is it that Francis of Assisi
could catch them by surprise, and I always fail?"

Wolik liked to make statistical jokes about the medical profession. One
such joke was: "Statistics have shown that more people die in the hospital
than in the theater. So when you are sick, go to the theater and not to a
hospital." Another was: "Statistics show that more sick people go to the
doctors than healthy ones. So if you don't want to be among the sick,
don't go to the doctors." Everyone laughed at such jokes, but alas, for
himself Wolik was pathetically right: He got no more help from the doctors and the hospital than his jokes would imply.

When a friend complained that she still had difficulties with arithmetic,
particularly multiplication, Wolik showed her an ingenious way of using
the fingers to multiply. She was fascinated and told others about it.
As a result, friends, both adults and youngsters, wanted to be shown his
"multiplication table." If we left a shop with two packages, Wolik must
carry both to "maintain the balance." If he chose to do something
around the house or to repair a necklace or bracelet for me, he pretended that he was in deadly earnest about it, that it was "a job for a
man."

It had been our great fortune that we loved the same things, and that
we could not only work together harmoniously, but could also enjoy
outdoor life together, even strenuous mountaineering. Nothing was too
fatiguing for us, and we adjusted ourselves to every condition in travel,
from the most primitive to the most elaborate. Wolik's sense of humor
and sweet temper made everything seem charming, unusual. Sometimes
friends showed surprise when they saw Wolik interestedly making toys on
a dull winter Sunday or tinkering in the workshop, or absorbed with
me in doing a jigsaw puzzle. I recall our taking some friends to Char-
lottesville; when we were walking to the restaurant at lunchtime, Wolik
stopped in front of a window displaying some new toys. One of the
friends, of the same age as Wolik, said to me with astonishment in his
voice, "I look at your husband and envy him that life still holds so many
wonders for him. To me, this is past long forgotten."

Wolik disliked what he called "mousy" colors. He never wanted me
to wear a gray dress or suit, and enjoyed seeing me in bright clothing.
One antipathy of his that persisted through his life was born in his
prison years: Because prisoner's garb was striped, he objected to wearing pajamas or shirts made of striped fabrics.

My office (the Economic Warfare Board) once sent me to New

York for two days for a meeting on nonferrous metals. A letter from Wolik began:

> My housekeeping is first class. Breakfast—eggs, grapefruit, cheese. Lunch in the cafeteria. Dinner late, at about 10 P.M. The menu: chicken, green peas, cheese, fruit. [I had left everything prepared.] I have come to the conclusion that one can have all one's meals without spending too much money. My total expense—$1.30. Of course, one has to know *how* to avoid unnecessary expenses. Yes, I did spend some money on nuts, but I am not considering this an expense: the nuts are untouched.
>
> Everything all right, but I forgot the key to the front door. Had to crawl into the house through the window . . . Traffic on the way home exceptionally light. Would you believe it, I met only two cars and one truck, while three cars and a five-year-old boy on a tricycle passed me. Otherwise not a soul in the streets. Nevertheless, I drove most carefully, stopped in front of each house. Got so worn out that on arriving home went to bed at once.

From the next day's letter:

> Again drove through empty streets. Not a soul! As in the story about Lady Godiva. Have not forgotten the key, but forgot my wallet. So went to the bank, got some money. Am sure you had a more profitable day. If your book is ready, be on your guard with the publishers. They are all brigands. If they offer a lump sum, don't accept less than $10,000.
>
> I began to feel lonely without my dearest Emmotik, but I realize that this is just the beginning. Soon will appear the publishers, reporters, photographers, receptions, banquets. There is nothing to do about it, this is fate . . . Well, I will have to accept this.

On my return to Washington, I found the following telegram, on a sheet of Western Union paper, on my desk:

> Still Emmotik is best of all, and I love her very much. As to Wolik, he is, of course, no great shakes, but there are worse than he. W.W.

There was never anything commonplace about Wolik. He wrapped the smallest happenings of everyday's life in a mantle of fun, and there was no end to his gay inventions. His thoughts always moved on a high plateau above the small irritations of life. We had many names for each other, sweet, tender names that we never used in the presence of others; many expressions, funny or serious, that meant a lot to us but that nobody else understood because they seemed unrelated to the topic of conversation. Thus we continued our dialogue: one private word, one glance, and we were alone in the crowd.

Like Voltaire, Wolik believed that what one needed was the unnecessary, that only the superfluous was really necessary. We had one short period in Paris, after leaving Hitler's Germany, when we just barely got by. Yet, for my birthday, Wolik brought a luxurious silver manicure set to make me feel that we were not hard-pressed after all. An old friend, a Swiss physician, who was staying with us at the time glanced at it and said, shaking his head, "Just what your household was lacking! And you tell me that Wolik has no sense for practical things."

Once I said to Wolik, "Have you noticed the difference beween us? You are impractical but economical, particularly so far as your own desires are concerned. I am practical but not economical." Wolik's satisfied conclusion was: "Together we are both impractical and uneconomical."

One winter, Mr. Rat worked his way into our house. After many unsuccessful attempts to get rid of him, he finally died in the garage, in which we had cemented all the holes to block his entry into the house and thus also his escape. Wolik's version was that the rat had died of a broken heart, shaken by the inhumanity of people who lived in a large house and denied him a tiny place in it to protect him from the winter cold.

Wolik pretended to be lazy and liked to compare himself with the crocodile, slow in motion, slow in understanding. Occasionally he asked me, "Really, isn't there a great deal of similarity between me and the crocodile? No, don't laugh! Please, try to be serious, this is not a laughing matter." When some friend mentioned that Wolik was always so poised, or wondered how he could maintain his good humor, Wolik teased me afterward: "Can you beat that? Who will believe your constant complaints about my bad temper when I am so sweet?" And he would assume a fierce expression that made him look as if he were ready to tear the place apart, and then would laugh contentedly.

Yet Wolik could be sharp as a razor when he disapproved of an attitude or act. When the United States entered the last war, a young colleague came to consult Wolik about his intention to avoid the draft. Wolik listened patiently to the young man's argument that his work would contribute more to the country than his serving in the Army could possibly do, then said, "You have asked for my opinion. Here it is: You are a coward. You want to live in a free country and enjoy all its advantages, but you would leave the privilege of defending it in time of danger to others." The young man enlisted that same day.

In Mexico City, a man came up to Wolik after his lecture on the U.S. economy and said, "Why does the United States keep armed forces in Mexico in pursuit of its imperialistic policy? Do you want to subjugate us?" Wolik looked at the interrogator, saw that he was not an illiterate worker but a man of education, and answered, "You are lying and you know that you are lying. I am not going to talk to you." "You have not answered my question," insisted the man. "Yes, I have," Wolik replied, and turned away.

It has always been my observation that people who work intensively have more time within the same twenty-four-hour day than those who do nothing. Just as stretchable nylon hose expand to larger sizes, so busy hours expand to take in many extra things. Anyway, this was true for us.

Few among our friends—and all of them have been people with substantial jobs and many additional commitments—have worked as steadily and with such absorption as we did, day in and day out. Yet we were always available to our friends and had time for ourselves. It was the natural way for us to live, the natural way to treat our friends—to read what they wrote or published, to hear about their plans and comment on them if asked to, to invite them to our home and accept invitations to theirs. The stretchable time for ourselves included a variety of pastimes.

Does reading belong to leisure? It definitely did for us. Of course, we read almost the whole day when we were not writing, but this was work. Leisure reading was time taken from work, from other types of recreation, occasionally from sleep. Sometimes we read different things and told each other about them, but when some book was really exciting or important, we both read it. Still, Wolik read more than I and retained more, though—or perhaps because—he read more slowly than I. In the last four or five years of his life, he may have reread the entire Greek literature, the Roman classics, all the important books of the Middle Ages. In the last week in the hospital, when both of us hoped and believed, because of the doctors' assurances, that he would soon return home, he asked me to buy the Koran, saying that he wanted to refresh his memory of its content. Often, before turning the lights off, I read poetry aloud. Though Wolik knew much of it by heart, he liked to listen to my reading. Of course, we received a large number of professional and general magazines, in both English and other languages. We read the outstanding nonfiction books, and occasionally we read the latest fiction, though often disregarding the best sellers.

Traveling came next, though it was usually combined with reading. We seldom left home without several books, some new, others to reread. I have described some of our travels in the western United States, Canada, and the Caribbean. We also explored the eastern states—New England, New York, Pennsylvania—and some southern states, including much of Florida. Even in Washington, we took long or short hikes, according to time and weather, and thoroughly explored every path in Rock Creek Park, the tow path and the Great Falls area, the Skyline region. We walked over many sections of the Appalachian Trail, climbed various mountains in the Adirondacks, hiked around many lakes. We were immune to inconveniences and occasional misadventures, such as when, on top of McIntyre Mountain in the Adirondacks, we got caught in a heavy downpour with no shelter near by. We decided that rather than be drenched there, we would dash down and find a shelter in the valley. We found it in a tavern, where we were given the billiard room and two sheets. Our clothing and shoes were dried at the kitchen stove while we had tea and soup to warm ourselves.

We crossed Florida several times in all directions and stayed at nearly all its most interesting spots, but preferred a small village on its west coast, without a movie house but with a splendid beach stretching for miles. Every day we would walk at least three miles along the beach to our favorite swimming place, for the sake of walking, and then return the same way. We collected many interesting shells during those walks, and at night, when the weather was uninviting and kept us inside, we made them into all kinds of funny animals. We collected driftwood and on our return to Washington, Wolik made wonders of it—intriguing pieces that he hung on the porches and in the garden. All that was needed to find odd creatures in the twisted roots and tree limbs was to have eyes curious and keen enough to recognize the inner hidden grain and the possibility of shaping the wood in one way or another. Some of Wolik's creations have been conversation pieces for years.

In traveling with Wolik, the fun began long before we started a trip. Though he might be under the heaviest work load, Wolik always found time to examine maps, trace our trip on the globe in his study, read guidebooks and books on the history and arts of the countries to be visited. He drew me into every detail, and we saw in our minds' eyes the places and the monuments in those distant countries.

Abroad, especially in the Far Eastern and Latin countries, Wolik, who ordinarily disliked shopping and for whom I therefore bought everything that did not require exact measurement, enjoyed strolling in the native markets and acquiring, on whim, products of native craftsmanship. His pockets were full of trinkets, toys, odds and ends. If he noticed something that he could not buy at once, he tried to return and get it. Some curios were really a nuisance in air travel, such as the very brittle masks from Bolivia or the big tin rooster from Guadalajara that Wolik assessed as *the* pieces without which we could not possibly leave Bolivia or Mexico. They were difficult to pack, but they gave him so much enjoyment that it was a pleasure to satisfy his wish. So we carried each of them in a separate basket by hand on scores of flights, though we were already loaded down with cameras, brief cases, coats, overnight bags.

On our return, it was Wolik's job and pleasure to find a place for the new treasures, to build additional shelves, make new frames. There is nothing precious or valuable among our mementos, but each reminded us of a particular area or a special occasion. One friend told me, "There is nothing to show off in your home but so much to see," and another said, "How do you achieve the impression of unity? I bring home a few articles from a trip, and they never seem to fit together when I display them, but in your home the products of fifty countries seem to like one another." Who knows? Perhaps they felt Wolik's loving care and interest.

We acquired a circle of friends in Washington and gathered them at our home from time to time. To prevent the habitual division of the sexes after dinner, in accordance with Anglo-Saxon tradition, we suggested that we all discuss a particular question—perhaps election prospects or returns, the international situation or a national event of importance, or the economic outlook in the United States. When the group was comfortably assembled, Wolik would introduce the topic and draw everyone into the discussion by a kind of roll call. Of course, there was complete informality; serious and humorous questions were raised; jokes and laughter interrupted the talk. Yet nearly everybody, or so we thought, felt that the evening had been more interesting and stimulating than it usually was when conversation drifted into small talk.

Our friends were almost exclusively Government or academic people, as is true of many gatherings in Washington homes. In our case, the informal atmosphere was due to the complete unpretentiousness and to the congeniality of the crowd. Above all, I believe, it was Wolik who gave the tone of friendly humor and cordiality; somehow everyone felt free and easy with him, and it warmed my heart to see how beloved and happy he was among friends.

Once a year we held a large garden party for some seventy-five or eighty people. The guests included casual acquaintances, who were invited for the regular hours, from four to seven or so. But close friends, some thirty or more, stayed on for an informal dinner and conversation; they rarely left before midnight. In the fall, we often persuaded those who had vacationed abroad to tell of their summer adventures or showed our latest slides or movies.

PHOTOGRAPHY

Photography is a subject in itself. As I have mentioned, Wolik made slides and I took movies. Many of Wolik's transparencies were highly artistic and imaginative, and had dramatic composition. In the beginning, scenery attracted him most, but later he began to take close-ups of flowers, of people, and when possible, of animals. He needed time to take pictures and disliked being hurried, and he was almost always successful. When we returned home, he arranged his slides in trays and gave travel talks to our friends after each trip.

Though movies were my hobby, Wolik actively participated in them. He built a title-maker for me, and we spent many an evening preparing titles that moved on the screen. It required a great deal of patience to push a letter half an inch again and again while I took single shots which, in combination of sixteen, produced the impression of moving on the screen.

The movie camera permits one to do many tricks, and Wolik and I took advantage of this. For example, Wolik would go into our garden and pick roses, and I would film the scene with the camera upside down and after the film was developed, would reverse it. On the screen, one would see Wolik arrive in the garden with arms full of roses and proceed to put each flower on a bush. Once, I wanted to say "Thank you" at the end of a film and so our friends, after a movie on Mexico, saw flame appear on the screen and a burning scroll with charred corners unrolling itself to become a flat, large sheet on which clearly appeared the words "Thank you." To make this, Wolik and I went to our basement, stretched a wire from one corner to the other, and attached to it a large sheet of paper bearing the desired words. Then he set its corners on fire, and I filmed the scene with the camera upside down.

During our trips, we invented all kinds of amusing movies. One was about a very large Chinese shell that we bought in Florida. Wolik swam some distance away from me while I was shooting at eight frames per second instead of sixteen; then he disappeared under the water, came up with something covered with seaweed, and swam back to me with one upraised arm holding that precious thing, which turned out to be the enormous shell, most unusual for that area. On the screen, the pace was doubled, so that the waves looked agitated and Wolik's efforts to hold on to his find seemed nothing short of heroic. Another time, I shot a film showing our summer trip by the movements of our hands and feet only; the rest of us never appeared on the screen.

To enable us to make the titles while we were motoring across the country, Wolik framed a pane of glass and bored a hole at the bottom of the frame for the tripod. We bought a set of large letters with glue on the reverse side. Then I would set the appropriate word on the pane and film through it—WATERFALL, SUNSET, or whatever. On our return to Washington, I spliced and respliced my films until we were completely satisfied, then sent them for comment and criticism to *Home Movies Magazine* in Hollywood. One film was returned with an award of two stars and another with three stars.

Our trips abroad were not so well suited to picture-taking as the domestic ones. There we did not have the car to carry the heavy equipment, and more important, the purpose of the trip was research, lecturing, meeting people. We could not possibly go to offices with cameras, looking like tourists. Also, the weather did not always cooperate; sometimes it was sunny on weekdays and rainy on Sundays. Despite these and other difficulties, we usually managed to bring home a good many pictures. Some friends used to say they had seen "the world in pictures" at our home.

GARDENING

Gardening was another cherished pastime. Except in bad weather, we worked in the garden an hour or a little more every day. Our garden is not too large but it is rather difficult to tend because it is both terraced on a slight slope and crowded with plants of all kinds. Walking between the rows of flowers calls for truly acrobatic exercises. Wolik loved gardening and always selected the heaviest jobs, but he also enjoyed reading and writing under the large shady trees at the back. I soon discovered that I had a farmer's soul, always wishing and needing more land than I had.

We lived in three houses in Washington—first, a bungalow with a small back yard, then a large house with apple trees, a grape trellis, and flowers in the back yard, and finally in the present house, which we bought in 1946. From the beginning, the neighbors assumed that I had a green thumb, not because of any gardening skill on my part but because of my love of this occupation. Now I am considered almost an authority on gardening, though I fail no less frequently than others.

Thanks to that reputation, I acquired—unexpectedly and touchingly —the night-blooming cereus of the bungalow's neighbors. This elderly middle-class couple welcomed us when we moved in and occasionally offered us, over the fence, a bowl of cherries from their tree or a part of an apple pie; I reciprocated with home-grown apples or something else. One night they called us over to watch the blooming of that beautiful and mysterious flower. We admired it very much, and saw it open every year thereafter. Then we moved several blocks away and did not see those neighbors for years. One day the old lady telephoned me to say that her end was approaching but she wanted the night-blooming cereus, her great joy for many years, to live on. She had a daughter in Washington, but she would not entrust the plant to her; would I take it? I did, and since then the plant has bloomed not only for us but for many friends and neighbors to whom we gave its young "babies."

Our garden differs somewhat from most gardens in Washington; it spreads over a tiny elevation and is terraced. The first, highest terrace is near the house, and three succeeding terraces negotiate the downward slope to the lawn below ("the foot of the mountain," as Wolik jokingly called it). Beyond the lawn is a miniature creek crossed by two tiny stone bridges, and a second flagstone terrace. The garden is small, but crowded with every kind of plant. Because of the excellent soil, flowers and weeds grow in profusion, and at times the garden looks like a jungle. Because of its abundance, most of our friends have plants from our "nursery" in their back yards; some plants have traveled as far as Long Island, Syracuse, and even Indiana. But no matter how many we gave away, our garden has always remained overpopulated.

Wolik followed lovingly the changes caused by each season. In the spring he delighted in observing the young, tender, pink-coated leaves on the trees, but he also loved the brilliant colors of the foliage in the fall. I still find leaves in books, where he had put them to dry. He enjoyed the flowers in our garden and everywhere else, and he loved to have plants in his study during the winter. His eyes caught beauty in everything—in the timid snowdrops venturing in the cold air, in the sharp, black designs of the naked trees in the winter, the icicles hanging like tears on frozen tree limbs, the triumphant entry of spring and its very scent in the air. He admired beauty wherever it exists—in the human face, in painting, in architecture, in literature, especially in poetry, in every facet of life—and his admiration was both intense and active.

WINEMAKING

Our gardening included an adventure in winemaking. In the house we rented on Massachusetts Avenue, we had two long vines of Concord grapes. The first year we did nothing with them except to invite the neighbors to share them with us; many dropped to the ground, making the garden very messy, and the birds feasted on them. The second summer I called up the grape expert at the Government's Beltsville Farm and asked for advice. Assuming that we had only a few bunches of grapes, he suggested that we keep them wrapped until they ripened. When he learned that we might have some 300 pounds of grapes, he threw up his hands, or so it seemed from the way his voice sounded over the phone. I took his advice, the more readily as wrapping material was pouring into our house: Wolik had participated in the discussions on the 1940 Census, and neat brown envelopes with preliminary reports on individual counties and cities filled our mailbox every day. Soon our garden looked like a part of the Census Bureau, with each bunch of grapes tucked into a separate envelope.

Still, the basic problem of what to do with that abundance had not been solved. Then a friend suggested that we make wine out of the grapes and offered to supply the equipment. We thought that this would be fun and set a date. A week later the mail brought a letter from the Alcohol Revenue Unit. David had informed it of our venture. The letter gave us permission to produce up to 200 gallons of wine and added that the inspector would visit the "premises for winemaking" on that date. Everything being official, we sent out handbills inviting "job-seekers" to appear at nine in the morning of the scheduled date on our premises, in work clothes; food would be provided, children admitted. David brought large and small barrels, an iron press, and other equipment.

We posted the letter from the Alcohol Unit on the front door that morning. More than thirty "workers" arrived. Immediately requests started: "Where is the ladder?"; "I need clippers"; "We need a pail"; and so on. Wolik and I rushed to oblige the eager grape pickers, who competed with each other, but there were not enough baskets, bowls, pots. Finally, every available receptacle was filled, including the sink. In the meantime, I was filming various scenes.

The next step was to clip away the twigs. This operation lasted until it was time for lunch, which was served picnic-style in the garden. Then we rolled out the large barrels, filled them with grapes and turned the hose on them to wash them thoroughly. After that began the most responsible job: grape-pressing, with everybody taking a turn. In between came supper. The air was filled with jokes and laughter, and I filmed until dark.

At about ten that night, the grape juice was poured into large barrels. David asked for sugar and for cheesecloth to cover the barrels with. Not forewarned, I had neither in the house. Consultation followed, trips here and there were taken, and an hour later the job was finished. Exhausted workers stretched themselves on the floor in our exceptionally large living room; others slumped in the armchairs. By midnight, we celebrated the occasion with a soft punch.

Next morning we left the keys to the house with David and another friend. They watched the fermentation in the barrels every night and in due time transferred the liquid into the small barrels. These had a small hole; into this, they pushed a tiny pipe, its other end placed in a glass half-filled with water. This is what we found in the basement on our return home. Two months or so later, the bubbling in the glasses stopped, and our wine, good light wine, was ready—some 40 gallons. We gave half of it to David, the initiator and the "capitalist," since he owned all the means of production. The rest we served at home, and when invited to dinner took a bottle or two with us, with special labels prepared by Wolik, such as "Extra Dry Statistics" and indications of the year of production, the row in the wine cellar, and other usually required data.

The film has been shown many times. Almost everybody liked it because almost everybody was in it.

OTHER PASTIMES

As I have said, the day is long if time is not wasted. Thus Wolik found time for carpentry, home repairs, frame- and shelf-making. One day we were walking along our street to the hardware store for a pane of glass for the frame that Wolik was holding and had just finished. A man stopped us to ask where he had got the frame. On learning that Wolik had made it himself, the stranger became excited and showed us a sketchbook he was carrying. He was a painter, he said, and he was spending a fortune on frames, paying exorbitant prices for them. Would Wolik make frames for him? Amused, Wolik told him that frame-making was just a sideline and that he had another occupation that took all his time. We shook hands and parted.

And Christmas cards! We discussed the subject, and Wolik drew them. Some friends have kept the whole series, because there was such fun in them and also the story of progress in our work and life. For the children, Wolik cut out paper dolls—boys and girls to stand in a circle holding hands as in a square dance, butterflies, all sorts of animals, and "magic" faces.

Only recently, friends in Connecticut wrote me that the children still preserved as a precious thing a "magic" drawing that Wolik made years ago. It showed a man with a friendly smile, but when the drawing was turned upside down, there was the same man now angry, almost irate. I still remember the excitement of little Charles, some five years old, when Wolik gave him that drawing. There was a large crowd in the living room, and Charles went from one guest to another, saying again and again, "Just look! This way he smiles, and that way he is angry. The same man! It's magic!"

For a time, we played tennis, but when it became complicated to arrange hours at the neighboring tennis court, we shifted to Ping-pong. We installed a standard table in the basement, and every now and then ran down for a quick set of three or five games. We never were good tennis players, but we did rather well at Ping-pong. Wolik liked it and excelled in it. Once he tried his skill against a national champion of France and came out with flying colors. In Paris, we had learned to play billiards when we had a table in our apartment. Later we bought a small type of billiard table and played for relaxation. In the garden, we played badminton and other games.

Nearly any game that called for physical exercise appealed to us, but hiking remained our favorite. Hiking was not only a certain relaxation from work but also a source of ever-renewed contact with nature. Nothing escaped Wolik's eye during a hiking trip; he noticed every change in the air, in the trees, in the leaves, and he loved the physical fatigue after a long hike or climb.

Wolik never criticized any of my shortcomings. If I drove too fast for his taste, he called me *"Skakunchik"* (a lovely, untranslatable Russian word meaning a dashing, carefree runner); he never objected to my smoking but called me *Moya kurilochka* (again untranslatable, something endearing like "my darling smoker").

Usually we worked at least a half-day on Sunday, then read the newspapers. Occasionally I took up the crossword puzzle in *The New York Times* or the *Saturday Review,* and turned to Wolik for the difficult words from mythology, Roman classics, military science, sports, and science in general. He liked this collaboration and often asked, "Any difficult words?"

I could continue but am afraid to—it may begin to look as if we were pretending to work while spending all our time on amusements. Fortunately, our reputation was so firmly established that Wolik said jokingly, "If we stop doing everything, our friends will still insist that we must have a respite not to collapse from exhaustion." In general, Wolik's theory was that laziness was the mother of all human progress: People invented labor-saving devices and machinery in order to work less, not more. Observations and the ability to draw conclusions from observations also contributed to progress. How did people discover that roasted meat was tastier than raw? According to Wolik, by repeating what they saw happen accidentally. Once a structure burned with a bull inside. People ate the meat and found it was more palatable than the raw meat they ordinarily ate. Next time they built a structure, put a bull inside it, and set fire to the building. Gradually, they eliminated the roof, then one wall after another, and finally discovered that the meat of a bull burned in the open air was no less tasty than that of one burned with a building. Simple, isn't it?

One of Wolik's characteristics that worried me and kept me on the alert all the time was that he had no sense of self-preservation, or a very weak one. Thence came not only his exceptional courage but also his lack of concern for the hazards to which one is exposed now whether at home or abroad. Wolik told me that his attachment to life was feeble before we met. On his trip to Arshan before our marriage, he once found himself in danger on a hanging cliff and was reluctant to exert himself to reach a safer place. He was almost ready to close his eyes and let himself go. In this respect, we were different. I was ready to live forever, with Wolik, of course, and never thought of death, except in the hospital in Rome. Wolik accepted death as a natural end of life. He would say occasionally, "I will be satisfied if I live five more years." To make him merry or amuse him, I would reply, "Not before I am a hundred, shall I even consider my age." Both of us were of one mind however—to live meant not to vegetate, but to live happily, usefully, enjoying every facet of life and work to our complete satisfaction.

TEMA

One day during the war I received a letter with a strangely familiar handwriting on the envelope. I looked at it, but could not identify the writer. On opening it, I recognized Tema's handwriting before I saw the signature. She had been my friend from the time I was thirteen years old, but life had separated us for some twenty-five years, after 1917. And now there was her letter telling me that she and her husband, Yasha, were in New York for the winter—she studying journalism at Columbia University, he working as a mechanic on a destroyer. They had two daughters—Isabelle, who had graduated from Vassar College and was married to a professor of psychology at the University of Connecticut, and Carrie, who was a student at Oberlin College. Tema had tried unsuccessfully to locate me before that winter, when they came to New York and she got my address very easily.

My friendship with Tema lasted about half a century—from 1906 until 1955, when she died of a heart attack in our home in Washington. The beginning of our friendship was rather unusual. Tema lived in Dvinsk (now Daugavpols), some 150 miles from our town. Her classmate and close friend, Yadviga, was transferred to my high school when her parents moved to Polotsk. Soon we became friends, and Yadviga told me about Tema and wrote to Tema about me. We exchanged greetings for some time and then began to correspond. Tema loved to write letters all her life and did it especially well. I cannot remember what I wrote about, but most probably my letters were very dull in comparison with hers. This did not impede our friendship, however, and Tema wanted to meet me and invited me to her home in Dvinsk.

I now understand my mother's lack of enthusiasm for the visit. Neither of us had ever met Tema or anyone in her family, and I had never traveled by train before. Mother did not want me to go, but I decided to go nevertheless. Most probably I would not have gone against Father's will, but he was in Siberia, building army barracks. It made the situation even worse that on the day of my departure, Father's niece came to visit us. I had just enough money; it has been given to me by some relatives on my birthday.

I stayed with Tema for a week, affirmed our friendship, and returned happy, hoping to find Mother in a forgiving mood. But she hardly talked to me. She had written Father about my behavior, and he had ceased to mention me in his letters. I was upset and tried to explain the importance of the new friendship, but Mother was hurt. It was the first and, as far as I can remember, our family's only challenge to her authority.

Some months later, Father fell gravely ill. His life was in danger, but Mother could not leave eight children and embark on a ten-day trip. We were terribly depressed and lived from telegram to telegram. When Father recovered, there was a celebration in the family. Mother made peace with me, and so did Father, explaining that he had made several promises during his illness, and one of them was to forgive me.

Tema was not pretty. She was big, with big hands, big feet, and a rather plain face. But her voice was soft and warm, and there was something forceful in her bearing. Her dramatic sense, her sincerity, and her fine humor attracted people to her. She had a big heart and a sparkling temperament. Before she graduated from high school, a young officer, Victor, son of a general, fell passionately in love with her. Even more surprising, his sister, Nina, became Tema's lifelong friend, and his mother wanted Tema for her daughter-in-law. This was surprising, because the general's family came from the cream of society while Tema was a poor Jewish girl. Tema was fiercely proud of her family and unconcerned about her poverty. At a ball to announce the engagement, one of the guests, not knowing that Tema was Jewish, said something offensive about the Jews in general. Tema saw at once that in the society she was about to enter, she would be exposed to such attitudes frequently. Then and there, she told Victor that she would never marry him. No amount of persuasion could change her mind. Nevertheless, her friendship with the general's family remained as solid as before.

We graduated from high school the same year but I, with a gold medal, was accepted at Bestugev Women's College (a college having about the same relationship to St. Petersburg Imperial University as Radcliffe has to Harvard: the same teachers, the same finals, state examinations at the University, the same rights), while Tema, with lower marks, could enter only a private college, which did not give her the right to live in the capital. In Tsarist Russia, only certain categories of the Jewish population could live beyond the pale—merchants of the first guild, graduates and students at Imperial universities, doctors of medicine, dentists, midwives, and certain categories of skilled workers, such as seamstresses. There were several fine private colleges in St. Petersburg, and some Jewish girls first obtained a certificate as midwife or seamstress by passing the required examinations and then registered at those colleges. Much depended then on the police of the precinct. If an officer was not satisfied with the bribe he had received, he might, for example, wake the student during the night to send her to a woman in labor. Tema did not want any such arrangement. She was given the passport of a gentile girl friend and entered college under that girl's name.

This complicated our life. We roomed together, and every time there was a ring, we picked up the phone or ran to open the door in fear that the landlady would discover that Valentina was, in reality, Tema. This went on for a couple of months, and as we were young, the situation provided many amusing incidents. Then Tema went to see the dean of my college, a well-known professor of law. He was horrified when she told him of her "clever" scheme. He explained the danger to which she had exposed herself and ordered her to return home at once and never to be so "clever" again!

Tema went back to Dvinsk. Strangely, the months we lived together rather strained our friendship; we were too different in so many respects. Later, when the pattern of our lives was firmly established, neither of us minded this difference, but college age required a greater congeniality than our temperaments and interests permitted.

Tema began to teach in Dvinsk, while I spent the following years in St. Petersburg during the winter and at Irkutsk during the summer vacation. We nearly lost each other. In 1917, Tema came to Petrograd, as it was then called, and we were friends again. After that, until I received her letter from New York, I did not know what had happened to her.

It was wonderful to receive a greeting from my childhood, so remote, nearly forgotten. Yet when some meetings took Wolik and me to New York and we planned to see Tema and Yasha, I became apprehensive. Would we be friends or strangers? And would Wolik like this association?

Tema and Yasha had one room in a typical New York apartment in which nearly every room was rented, with a common kitchen and bathroom. Very soon I saw signs of Tema's civilizing influence, even under those conditions. To give her a chance to talk with Wolik, I went to the kitchen for a glass of water. There, a roomer greeted me and said, "Since your friend came here, our place has become so peaceful. Before we were always quarreling for space in the icebox, a burner on the range. She suggested that we assign everyone a shelf and schedule hours for using the kitchen. She is so friendly." In the bathroom, I found on the wall an appeal in Tema's handwriting to keep the place neat and clean. I could not help laughing. Tema had not changed.

On the day of our arrival, however, Tema and Yasha were upset. They had just received a letter reporting that a snow slide had destroyed the dining-room pavilion in their tourist camp in the Adirondacks, their basic source of income for twenty years or more. The letter was from a state policeman, a member of the troop situated opposite Tema's camp, which was on the highway leading to Canada and therefore carefully controlled. The letter said:

> Dear Mama and Papa Yoffe:
>
> We have sad news for you. Last Sunday a terrible storm raged at Raybrook and brought loads of snow down on our road. Much was destroyed, and your dining room is gone, broken to pieces. But don't worry too much and don't come here. We all went to work and saved what we could. We put everything worth saving in the garage, and by the time you return, the wood will be dry and usable. Also, Bill said that he has $2,000 in the bank and will be glad to lend it to you so that you can build another pavilion.

When I got back to Washington, I found a letter from Tema telling me how happy she was to find me and (not knowing our circumstances) offering to share with us everything they had. Next summer we motored through New England and stopped at Tema's camp for a few days. It was lunchtime, and I heard her say to the waitress, "I have company and do not wish to be bothered. Please take care of the customers." About half an hour later, the girl came back: "There are three people, they want borsch." Tema said impatiently, "Tell them we have none." The girl reappeared: "The guests want to know *when* you will have borsch." One of the policemen dropped in, was introduced to us and said, "Mama Yoffe, I'm dead tired. How about a cup of coffee?" While Tema was pouring the coffee, her younger daughter, Carrie, came in. The policeman gave her a brotherly hug and said to me, "This is my gal, a sweet kid."

In the afternoon, two old ladies came from Lake Placid to visit Tema and to meet us. One of them, widow of a millionaire, took me aside and said, "Your friend is an exceptional person, so upright and so warm. You must be very proud to have her for a friend." Yet she knew that to make ends meet and to give their two daughters an education, Tema had worked in the restaurant and Yasha as a janitor in the school for several winters.

Despite their very limited means, Tema maintained dignity in her and her family's life—by hard work, respect for knowledge and high purpose in life, inborn pride, and the capacity to appreciate and bring out the best in people. A large and not very harmonious family had a camp near by in which every member possessed separate cabins and accommodations. When Tema's daughters were established in life, she and Yasha spent their winters at Bradenton Beach, in Florida, a very modest little place on the Gulf where they managed to live on their summer earnings from their tourist camp. For Christmas, Tema always sent citrus fruit to her neighbors across the road, and once one of them said, "You are always so nice to us. I wish we knew something we could do for you." "Oh," replied Tema, "you can do a great deal. When we come back in April to open our place, the water pipes are frozen, and it takes hours before we get water and can warm ourselves up. If you would have a cup of tea for us, it would be wonderful." The next spring, tea was served when Tema and Yasha arrived, and they heard there had been competition among the women for the privilege of preparing it. A year later, a hot meal awaited their arrival. These are small incidents, but they illustrate Tema's ability to live on good terms with people on all levels and civilize them. I could tell many more such stories of her.

In the fall and spring, on the way to and from Florida, Tema and Yasha stopped in Washington to see us and we went to Bradenton Beach every year for ten or twelve days for a restful visit with them. Though Tema and I were very different, we felt like sisters. Fortunately, Wolik liked her very much and was always amused at her vivid storytelling. She was high-tempered and exploded easily, but had a fine sense of humor. She had a very special admiration for Wolik, and often wanted me to reassure her that he truly liked her.

Tema died unexpectedly. She and Yasha stopped by late one afternoon in April, 1955, on the way to their camp. She was tired but soon relaxed and made plans for the next morning. At dinner time, we had a friend in, a writer, and we talked about various books and authors. Wolik and I urged her again to write the story of her camp, something like a book recently published, *Japanese Inn.* She became animated, told of people who had stayed at the camp the previous summer. Our trip to Japan, scheduled for the fall, worried her. She foresaw all kinds of dangers—catastrophe in the air, the outbreak of war, and others— and tried to persuade me to give up the trip. I laughed and reassured her. Before she went upstairs, she embraced me, and in an outburst of sudden tenderness, said, "You are so frail, so delicate compared to me, but I want to lean on you, get some strength and some cheer from you. You and Wolik will always be our dearest friends, won't you?"

Next morning, she did not feel well. I went to her room, took her a glass of orange juice, and suggested that she rest awhile. She stretched out, saying, "Please raise the shade, let the sun come in." I went downstairs. A few minutes later I heard Yasha cry out. Tema had closed her eyes and passed away.

9. *Our Travels*

WORK CONTINUED on our second volume on world economics, *World Commerce and Governments*—galleys, page proofs, index, corrections, answers to queries. Unexpectedly, we received a letter from Takeo Naoi in Tokyo from which we learned that he and several others were translating our first volume, *World Population and Production,* into Japanese for publication by Mr. Yamada. Naoi asked us to clarify several sentences. In this manner, the question of a trip to Japan was raised. At about the same time, Wolik received an invitation to present a paper to the international meeting of the Congress for Cultural Freedom in Milan in September, 1955. We decided to try to wind up our work on the second volume, leave Washington, and let the book come out in our absence.

As we planned the trip, the program grew from day to day. From Japan came an invitation to Wolik to give ten lectures, mainly to business groups such as the Association of Manufacturers, the Chamber of Commerce, a group of bankers, and so on. The Department of State asked Wolik to lecture before university students. This meant that our stay in Japan would be longer and more interesting. Some friends let the Indian Ambassador know about our trip, and Wolik had a talk with the Indian cultural attaché about lecturing at Indian universities and consultations with the Central Planning Board.

REVISITING EUROPE

We began our trip of nearly nine months with a visit to Spain and Portugal, the only two countries of Western Europe, except Ireland, where we had never been. There is no need to describe the excitement of visiting the Prado Museum in Madrid, the glory of Spain. We spent four days there and hated to leave, but we wanted to see Andalusia, too. We went there by bus for the first time on a guided tour, which made it impossible to make side trips and stops for photography. Occasionally, the bus stopped for an unexpected reason. Once, we all waited somewhere for more than an hour, without knowing why until the guide explained that one of the passengers (an American, by the way) had asked him to halt while he made his confession to the priest in the monastery there. When the passenger returned, purified and ready to go out into the world with a sinless conscience, the bus resumed the trip. It was almost unbearably hot, and when somebody complained, our guide offered a little paper fan, explaining that this was air conditioning *à la Espagnol*.

Seville and Granada charmed us, and our greatest regret was that we were tied up by the tour and so could not spend at least a few more days in each. We promised ourselves to return to these cities some other time for a longer stay. In Córdoba, we looked sadly at the Christian church installed within the grandiose mosque. To us, this was the same type of religious desecration, only in reverse, as we had seen in Constantinople, where the Moslems had built a mosque within St. Sophie.

Somehow the fact that the famous Giralda was originally built by the Moors for their religious services but was now a part of the Christian cathedral did not have the same effect on us. Fortunately, Córdoba's mosque's initial splendor and majesty had defeated the efforts to transform it into a church. Wandering among the countless columns in the spacious halls, we almost ignored the superimposed structures, until unbelievably we noticed workers breaking up some Moorish carvings on the wall of a corner chapel. It seemed incredible that such things could happen in our time. Even if one could forgive acts of intolerance in the heat of fierce struggle in the fifteenth century, nothing could excuse such action today.

Though Spain was better off economically in 1955 than just after World War II, when her people had been near starvation, we saw much poverty, along with evidence of some incredibly large fortunes. We drove for miles beside vineyards and olive groves belonging to individual landlords and also saw miserable patches of peasant land and the wretched huts of landless farm workers.

The people were friendly, sometimes touchingly so. We asked a stranger for directions in Córdoba. He started to explain, then suggested we take the trolley that he was going to take. He paid our fares and refused to let us pay him back. Then he showed us where to get out, and stood up and lifted his hat as he said goodbye.

We spent a week in Portugal—most of it in Lisbon, but also in Coimbra, Setubal, and other places. We enjoyed many beautiful days in both Iberian countries—beautiful scenery and beautiful man-made sights, and many simple pleasures such as a lobster lunch in a fishing village among talkative, animated workers, or listening to the fandango songs, a kind of Portuguese "blues," in a little cabaret in Lisbon. Both countries offered much more than we had time to see, but we had to be in Milan for the Congress for Cultural Freedom.

As usual at such gatherings, we met many people—some we had known, others for the first time. We were particularly glad to see M. A. Aldanov, the noted Russian writer, and had several meals with him. He did not look well and could hardly make the few steps to the nearest restaurant, but conversation with him was a delight. A man of broad historical and literary knowledge, a fine example of the old Russian intelligentsia in manners and way of thinking, he possessed both background and perspective in discussing political events. Every allusion, every reference to a writer, a political personality, a historical occurrence was understood without explanations. We grieved when he died several years later.

Wolik presented his paper, "The Road of Freedom," and participated actively in the debates. He made several radio talks, for French and Italian radio stations, and had invitations to conferences in other countries, which he declined so as not to shorten our trip to Greece. One point in Wolik's paper that attracted particular attention was his observation that while totalitarian countries pose as people's democracies and erect a façade of parliamentary institutions and elections, no democratic country has ever attempted to gain popular support by pretending to be a dictatorship.

We took the airline limousine to the airport for our flight to Athens. The only other passenger sat with his back to us, and we did not exchange a word during the long drive. We had to wait half an hour or longer for our plane, and set down for a cup of coffee in the restaurant. From its window, we saw the lonely figure of our fellow limousine passenger walking back and forth. On the spur of the moment, we invited him to have coffee with us. He was very pleased. A professor of astronomy at the University of Athens, he had been attending an international congress of astronomers in London and was returning home. He spoke only Greek and French, and so had felt lonely during his entire trip. In the plane, he took the seat next to Wolik, and they talked animatedly during the flight.

We arrived in Athens at midnight, where our professor was met by two young instructors. He said something to them in Greek, and they got our luggage and took us to our hotel, some 25 miles from the airport. We had not expected such a friendly reception and were delighted to meet members of Greece's intellectual fraternity from the moment of arrival, and even before. At the hotel, our new friends awoke the sleeping janitor and waited until he found our reservation and took us to our room. We invited the astronomer to a meal in a restaurant a few days later, and all of us were pleased that a cup of coffee had brought us together.

We had two unforgettable weeks in Greece—five days in Athens, five days on a cruise to some Aegean islands, then a drive across the country in a rented car with a Greek chauffeur, Angelico, who could speak some English. Legendary heroes of the Greek myths became alive, legends became historical facts—all because of continuous explorations of Greek, French, Swedish, American, and British archaeologists in many parts of Greece. Wolik, much more familiar with the early Greek period and archaeological discoveries in Greece than I, was a wonderful guide.

Ghosts from Minoan and Mycenaean times walked with us as he talked during our travels from Knossos in Crete to Mycenae, the city of Agamemnon. Shadowy names, long forgotten or buried in teen-age memory, came to life when Wolik recalled Greek myths or descriptions in the works of Homer. In Epidaurus, we sat in the amphitheater and imagined performances in the center. In the brightness of the southern sun and under the spell of Greek architecture and sculpture, my college studies suddenly came back, and we talked about the age of Pericles, about the magnificent blossoming of art, literature, philosophy in that tiny area, the cradle of our civilization. It was particularly inspiring, even elevating, to remind ourselves of the enormous contribution to humanity made by that territory so insignificant in terms of space and physical power.

We were especially lucky in Mycenae, though it did not seem so when we arrived late in the afternoon. The only hotel was primitive, our room was small and provided with pitcher and bowl instead of bathroom or even washstand. Dinner was dull, just acceptable. There were five other people in the dining room, and they were talking in Greek, very animatedly. Then several workers arrived, stretched a map on the neighboring table, and entered on a long discussion. We got up very early next morning, and when I came to the dining room after packing our bags, I found Wolik in a lively conversation with a member of the evening's group, whom he introduced as Professor Papadopulo, head of the Greek archaeological mission in Mycenae. I was no less excited than Wolik at this unexpected opportunity. The ruins were about a mile away, and the entire group got into our car. We spent the day with them, and Professor Papadopulo took the time to re-create everyday life in the palace with his vivid description, indicating every important detail. His young assistant showed us the subterranean way to the water source and the burial place of Agamemnon and Clytemnestra.

As we walked in Olympia, Delphi, and other places, we could see archaeologists scattered all over the area. They usually paid no attention to tourists. Once Wolik spoke to a young man working in a trench, but without lifting his head, he made a sign that he did not understand English. Wolik then mentioned that Professor Papadopulo had told him of the work going on there and had advised him to see some of it. At this point, the young archaeologist jumped up out of the trench and stood before us. A pupil of our professor, he suddenly displayed a good command of English and a great willingness to show us everything, particularly when he heard that his teacher had given us so much of his time.

Our impressions of Greece were particularly strong because we felt sympathy with the Greeks of today. We liked the open, honest look of the children, the courage and unbroken pride of the adults, the friendliness without a desire to ingratiate oneself. Even our chauffeur showed us this attitude. He recommended that we buy melons at a village he said was famous for them. Of course, we did not need any, but we suggested that he select one for us and some for himself and his family, at our expense. He thanked us and took two for himself. An hour later, at another village, he asked permission to stop, then went off and returned with two huge bunches of grapes for us. We thanked him and accepted the grapes; the equality between us was restored.

IN EGYPT

A greater contrast could not have been found than that between Greece and our next stop, Egypt. There, too, great art and great skills once flourished. The temples and monuments in Luxor, Karnak, Memphis, Giza, in the valleys of the kings and the queens, were overwhelmingly impressive. The murals in the tombs of the pharaohs, painted some 5,000 years ago, seemed as fresh and bright as at the time of their creation. It is hard to understand how the huge, massive statues and obelisks could have been produced and handled, without tools, by the most primitive means and endless human patience.

Ancient patience, that is what we saw in Egypt in 1955. We were in a boat on the brown, muddy waters of the Nile, moving along its shore, overgrown with reeds, behind which were villages hidden from our eyes. We saw two peasants drawing water from the river in a bucket and emptying the bucket on their land for irrigation. They were singing something monotonous and cheerless. I asked the guide to translate. He shrugged and said there was only one word: patience! It seemed as if the peasants had been standing there for thousands of years, singing cheerlessly—patience! We could read this song in the faces of the Arabs as they sat on the dirty ground and conversed, as they walked about in long robes that swept the dirt along, as we met begging adults and bothersome, insolent children at every step.

Why such degeneration in one people, and such pride and courage in another? Was it because Greece had created the civilization of free people, free independent cities, free thought, because its arts glorified humans, while Egyptian art had been the servant of the rulers, stiff in design, rigid in thought? In Egyptian representations, nobody was permitted to match the pharaoh in size, not even his wife, who was depicted as reaching only to his knees.

We admired the unsurpassed craftsmanship of the ancient gold- and silver-smiths of Egypt, the brilliant and expressive murals, the sculptures and monuments. Yet we could never have that warm feeling of closeness that took hold of us in contemplating Greek art, so natural, so uninhibited. Nor did we feel anything approaching the sympathy we had for the Greek people. We were told afterward by several people of different nationalities that animosity to foreigners was a fact of life in Egypt. They were surprised that we had ventured into the native section of Cairo without an Arab guide, and warned us not to do it again. Well, we survived and Wolik considered their worry groundless, but I must confess that I felt uncomfortable under the cold, suspicious looks of the people around us and was relieved when we found a taxi to take us back to the hotel.

Yet there were days of real thrill in Egypt. In the Valley of the Kings we were fascinated by the grandiose though somber scenery and the fabulous murals in the tombs. The guide suggested that we drive to the Valley of the Queens, but we let him go ahead with the car and, instead, walked up the mountain separating the two valleys. From its top, the panorama was superb, almost unreal in its immensity and calm. We were alone in that gigantic amphitheater, with a few human beings and the guide's car appearing as insignificant spots a great distance from us. We remained there for a while, and then slowly descended to visit other tombs and study their paintings. The guide was surprised at our eccentricity; it was the first time he had met people who preferred a strenuous mountain climb to a comfortable drive. Of all the tomb paintings we saw that day, one stands out in memory as really touching and humane—that of the pharaoh accompanying his dead son to the kingdom of death and presenting his boy, obviously scared and insecure, to Osiris.

There were some human surprises. An Egyptian student approached us in the streets of Cairo saying that he had heard us speaking English and asking permission to join us so that he could obtain practice in that language. As we walked along with him and inquired about the way to reach Giza, he offered to take us there and to other pyramids if we wished. He seemed pleasant, and we agreed. He proved to be knowledgeable, and we asked him to come along again. He once mentioned that his uncle had a curio shop; we went there with him, bought a beautiful tray and other souvenirs for ourselves and our friends, paid for them, and asked to have them shipped to Washington. When they had not arrived several months later, as Washington friends reported to us, I wrote to the storekeeper about it. I promptly received a reply framed with typical Oriental courtesy. First, he inquired about my husband's and my health, then he prayed to Allah that everything should be well with us, and finally he expressed the hope that the purchases, shipped long ago, had reached us by now. I decided to write off the whole affair as a lesson teaching that one should not entrust his money to a stranger met on the street in Cairo or to his relatives. My suspicions were unfounded. The articles had indeed been shipped without delay but had remained on the shelf in the Central Post Office in Washington, awaiting our arrival and inquiry.

In Luxor, we talked to a salesman in a shop and learned that he was from the Sudan. Somehow our questions about his country reached him, and he told us of its beauty, its proud and strong people, his family in Khartoum. If only we could go there, we would love it! He would get in touch with his family and make us their guests, they would take us around. He did not want us to leave the store and asked to see us next evening at our hotel. He was so warm and persuasive that we began to feel sorry that the trip was not possible. If we had had a week to spare and transportation to the Sudan had been less complicated, we might have succumbed to the temptation.

We spent our last night in Cairo with a member of Nasser's Cabinet. Mutual friends had written him about us, and he invited us to his home. We met his wife and children; all spoke English. It was a relaxed atmosphere in the home of educated people, and the conversation was interesting. The host made one remark that we let pass unchallenged despite our amazement: he declared that Egyptian medical science was on a very high level; perhaps he even said that it was second to none. Apparently, he was impressed by Wolik, because he suggested arranging a meeting with Mr. Nasser, who would be interested in talking with him. Our flight for Hong Kong was scheduled for four the next morning and our luggage was already checked, so Wolik thanked him but declined the offer.

IN THE FAR EAST

Hong Kong was a marvel. We were dazzled by the fantastic combination of a teeming Oriental world and magnificent scenery. Wolik could not tear himself away from the superb harbor, where every type of craft of every flag and size from every part of the world competed for space: warships, massive freighters, oilers, liners, junks, Chinese sampans with tall, colorful sails. The streets, too, are exceptionally picturesque, with huge calligraphic signs on every little shop and wares on the sidewalks. We explored the narrow, almost vertical side streets several times and had the impression of moving in an anthill.

We observed with appreciation the efficiency with which the British ran the city against heavy odds—Red China at its side, the enormous pressure of the refugees, the shortage of housing, and the problems of health and sanitation and of merely maintaining order in so over-crowded an area. The ferry between the mainland and the island func-tioned like a precision instrument, carrying masses of humanity in both directions every five minutes.

Yet, order is one thing, and poverty is another. It was depressing to see so much poverty concentrated within so small an area, to see a whole village of boats where each family lived in a shaky sampan, sleeping and eating in dampness and filth, using the polluted water. Wherever we looked, there was overcrowding, and the lack of sanitation was appalling.

Nevertheless, industry was expanding, new factories and shops were opening, and there was no feeling of immediate danger from Red China. We drove out to the last village before the Chinese border and walked al-most along it. Seeing a woman on a balcony, we asked her for directions. She came down and walked with us for a while. What was she doing there? She and her husband headed a Protestant mission from the United States; next to them was a Catholic mission. Wolik remarked half-questioningly that living among strangers, they must be on friendly terms with their American neighbors. "Oh no! We lived next to each other for two years without speaking. Recently we have started to exchange greetings on the street, just 'How do you do?' or so." Proselytic missions competing with each other amidst a people with their own religion.

IN JAPAN

Finally, we took off for Tokyo on October 17. Because of change in the schedule we arrived late at night. By about one in the morning we had completed customs and the other formalities of arrival. Loaded down with cameras, brief cases, overcoats, field glasses, we walked up the staircase and came upon a large group of Japanese, some with cameras aimed at us. I looked back to see whom they were meeting, but there was nobody else; we were the last to leave. There were our publisher, Mr. Yamada, the translator, Mr. Naoi, and reporters from Tokyo newspapers waiting to meet us!

Despite the late hour, four or five persons accompanied us to the hotel to discuss the announcement of the next day's lecture in the morning newspapers. They showed some disappointment at hearing the topics of the three lectures Wolik had prepared—the modern economic system and Marxian theory, the outlook for the world economy, and the economic system of the United States. They indicated politely but insistently that they wanted something else. Indeed, they had prepared a large notice that the lecturer would discuss the economic perspectives in America, the subject of greatest interest to the Japanese public. Wolik was tired and not too eager to change the topic of his first lecture, but he smiled and asked what they thought of the title "How Long Will Prosperity Last in the United States?" This was just what they had hoped for. The meeting ended on a very happy note, and the newspapermen rushed off to their offices. That lecture became the most popular. Even the universities often preferred it to other subjects.

Again and again during our three months in Japan, we were surprised to find that Wolik and his writings were well known. In every university, we met professors who had used one or more of his books. *The World in Figures* was almost universally available, and many university libraries also had various books published by Wolik in the United States. The embassy received requests from universities and various public organizations for lectures by Wolik. As a result, we crisscrossed Japan in all directions.

The interpreter engaged by the Embassy before our arrival gave up in the middle of the first lecture, because he was not familiar with the technical terms used by Wolik. Fortunately, we had Mr. Naoi with us. He had translated most of our *World Population and Production* into Japanese and so could take over the translation at a moment's notice. In Japan perhaps more than anywhere else, it is essential to have a translator who knows the subject matter as well as both languages. The Japanese language is not yet fully equipped to deal with modern technology. In an economic publication, for example, among the intricate Japanese symbols, one may find such words as "flexibility" and "integration" printed in English because the Japanese language has no equivalent terms. The interpreter must be able to follow the specific terminology used in the lecture and explain it in a roundabout way. Naoi-san, as we soon started calling him à la Japanese, accompanied us to all meetings and conferences and traveled with us wherever we went. This helped us very much. Wolik and Naoi-san formed a very congenial team, and we established a warm friendship with him.

Japanese scenery is enchanting, in both natural beauty and beauty created by man—the exquisite gardens, tastefully placed monuments, lovingly cultivated parks, tidy rice fields, magnificent temples and palaces, lovely lakes and ponds. Japan is heavily populated and its islands are crowded, but it looks neat and Sunday-dressed, everything on a small scale. Land is utilized with greatest care; the rice fields begin only a foot or so from the highway. When we looked down at the streets from the television tower in Nagoya, we saw that every patch of land, even if no bigger than a handkerchief, was cultivated and green.

Nowhere in the world have we seen anything like the untiring devotion of the Japanese farmers to their fields. Machinery was rare on those tiny patches of land, and there were no draft animals, only people working from dawn till dark, diligently, stubbornly, carefully. One evening our train stopped beside a field. From the window, I watched a farmer breaking the soil with a spade, lifting a chunk and placing it aside, next to the others. If he had had a surveyor's instruments, he could not have worked with more precision. Every chunk was exactly like the others, as if it had been measured on all sides.

We admired the artistic abilities of the Japanese, their love of art, which they express in so many ways. We visited artistic workshops, art exhibits that occupied one and sometimes two whole floors in a department store, the Institute of Industrial Arts. Tokyo's department stores were like museums; everything was a pleasure to see, from the gorgeous kimonos to lacquered trays, china thin as paper, beautiful silks, elaborate dolls, exciting wood block prints, and scrolls.

Along with neatness in everything goes frugality. The people know that their land cannot yield surpluses. In a cafeteria of a department store, we sat down for a cup of coffee next to a Japanese woman with a little boy of three or four. I watched the boy clean up his bowl of rice—not a grain was wasted—and thought of American children picking at full plates and leaving much of it to be thrown into the garbage can.

To us, Japan was in a class by itself. It was neither European nor Asian, though there were some features of each in its life and organization. In Japan, the old and new seemed to live in the same person without apparent conflict. In his home, the Japanese lives as he has for centuries—sleeping on a quilt laid on the floor, sitting cross-legged at the single low table in a room, dressed in a kimono and with slippers on his feet, eating traditional food. A little later, he changes to European clothing, goes to his Western-style office, where there are chairs to sit on, uses modern inventions like the telephone, typewriter, calculator, perhaps an IBM machine, until evening, when, returning home, he plunges back into the fifteenth or sixteenth century.

We wanted to stay in the Japanese inns, and so experienced both their charms and discomforts. The charm was in the lovely rooms, very attractive in their simplicity, with beautifully polished wooden walls and screens opening to the garden, which was landscaped with the taste and ingenuity needed to make its usually small space look bigger than it really was. The discomfort? We exchanged our shoes for slippers at the entrance and next morning, when we wanted to visit the garden before breakfast, had to wait for the shoes to be brought from the garden side. On arrival, as soon as we reached our room, we were asked what we wanted for dinner and for breakfast next morning, and when we wanted to take our baths. Used to Western hotels, where one unpacks and rests in privacy, we could not understand the curiosity of the servants and wanted to get rid of them. But they insisted on getting answers to their questions, and gradually I realized that, not having central heating and occasionally having only charcoal stoves, they had to know in advance what to prepare.

The bath produced special complications. Because hot water had to be carried in buckets, it was impossible to provide separate baths for each member of the family, and so it had become customary to wash oneself before entering the bath, which then was used by all family members in turn. The Western hotels in Japan provide individual bathrooms, of course, but in the traditional Japanese inns, it was hard to know whether each of us had a fresh bath. Privacy is less prevalent in Japan than in the West. A man stuck his head into the bathroom when I was in the tub, and a maid opened our door without knocking when Wolik was undressing. The Westerner in Japan need not suffer such small inconveniences unless he asks for them by staying in a traditional inn. Moreover, they loom smaller or bigger depending on one's attitude toward travel and novel experiences. To us, the charm outweighed the absence of habitual comfort.

Generally speaking, the Japanese house, beautiful as it is, seems to me to be adapted only to such hardened, unspoiled people as the Japanese. I inquired if it permitted the occupant to take a casual rest during the day; the answer was no. There are no couches or armchairs, and the bed mattresses are brought out only at night. During the day, there is no place to make oneself comfortable. At least, few Westerners would find it restful to lie on a mat-covered floor.

We traveled in Japan by plane, train, boat, and car. Wolik lectured at the Universities of Tokyo, Kyoto, Fukuoka, Osaka, Kobe, Nagoya, Sapporo, Oturo, Sendai, and many other cities. It was winter and rather chilly. The university buildings were not heated. The students often wore their coats, and it was suggested that we should, too. Occasionally, a little iron stove was provided for the benefit of the lecturer, and Wolik would warm his fingers over it before drawing a chart on the board. In Hokkaido, the northern island, such palliatives would not work. It was bitingly cold when we arrived there, and we were delighted to find that the houses were heated.

In order not to repeat himself, Wolik expanded and varied the content of his lectures by introducing topics raised in preceding discussions. It took some effort to start a discussion after the lecture or even to elicit questions from the students. They were rather self-conscious and avoided asking questions for fear of appearing immature to the guest lecturer or their own professors. The customary faculty meeting after each lecture was more animated. The topic selected for discussion, often differing from that of the lecture, ranged from techniques of economic forecasting to a planned economy within a capitalist society. The faculty members showed a surprising familiarity with the American and English economic literature and seemed to know everything Wolik had published, even an article in the *Review of Economics and Statistics* that he himself momentarily could not remember.

Our schedule was rather full, and at times it was very heavy. In Fukuoka, for example, Wolik had four lectures and a press conference in a single day, and at night there was a dinner party with many Japanese, which meant another discussion of many economic problems on their minds. Yet the USIS representatives in that city told us that interest in economics, and particularly in what Wolik had to say, was so great that they could work up a schedule like that for him for the next two weeks if he agreed.

Very often we were invited to a luncheon after the lecture. We would be seated across the table from the dean or the president of the university. This was always a solemn affair, partly because, more often than not, every sentence had to be translated, and partly because there was a much stronger sense of hierarchy in Japan than in this country, so that the conversation was mostly restricted to the center of the table, between the head of the university and ourselves. All attempts to initiate a conversation with our neighbors failed.

I was nearly always the only woman at the Japanese gatherings. At the embassy reception for us, about forty academic and Government people and their wives were invited, but only two wives came. One of them was German, and the other sat the entire evening without saying a word. Once, when the president of the Central Bank, the late Mr. Araki, invited us to a luncheon in the bank with several of its directors, one was accompanied by his very attractive wife. She spoke English fluently and told Wolik that this was the first time that she had been invited to such an occasion. Evidently she was invited because of my presence. At one luncheon, after Wolik's talk to a business association, the host asked me to say a few words to the group, in particular about my impressions of Japanese women. I said that I would be glad to report my impressions if the Japanese men would give me a chance to meet their wives.

Actually, I did meet many Japanese women by lecturing to them. There were professional women among them, some of whom participated in municipal affairs or welfare organizations. I could sense a desire among the women, particularly the young generation, to break out of the traditional role assigned to them. But it was not easy to do so. Sometimes a woman in the group would say, "Mrs. So-and-so wanted to come, but she could not leave the house." After I heard that explanation several times, I inquired into it and learned that the Japanese house was never left alone. Someone was always there to guard it against accidental fire or larceny. When I said that we had left our house locked up for nine months with no one living in it, the astonished reaction was, "Aren't there any thieves in the United States?"

The contrast between two concepts of failure came to the fore at a lecture in which I spoke about the social structure of the United States and touched upon the mobility of labor and the frequent labor turnover in our factories. One woman said, "In our country if a man loses his job he may never get another one. He is considered a failure, because otherwise his boss would not have parted with him. How is it in your country?" I replied, "Just the opposite. If a young man takes a job after he graduates from high school or college and holds it throughout his life, he is regarded as a complete failure, a person without any initiative, any drive. As a matter of fact, I never heard of such a case." The entire group laughed.

We tried to see as much of Japan as possible. During the national festivals, we spent the day among the crowds, which sometimes exceeded a million persons. The day of the Meiji celebration, we went to the beautiful park very early, before the crowds began to overflow all the lanes and trails. At the main gate, we met Mr. Araki, and I noticed that Wolik, while discussing economic problems with him, kept looking again and again at the stands at the park's entrance, where novelties and sweets were displayed. As soon as we were alone, Wolik hastened there and selected a bright toy representing a sort of twig with seven traditional gods of happiness. Nearly every visitor to the park carried a camera, and Wolik was photographed many times, so amusing and unexpected to the solemn, ceremonious Japanese was the sight of that smiling, gray-haired stranger with a bright toy in his hands. The day was sunny and warm, and the huge park easily absorbed the enormous crowd. Theatrical and sports performances were presented in various sections of the park; we watched jujitsu performers displaying their art with great skill and formal dignity.

While visiting a museum one day, we noticed that something unusual was taking place in one corner of the park in which it was located. We saw colorful screens partitioning off a section of the park from the spectators. In front of and behind the screens moved Japanese women in gorgeous kimonos. We found a spot from which we could photograph the group, then hesitated, since the screens clearly indicated a desire for privacy. One lady observed our dilemma and invited us to watch the proceedings—a performance of the traditional tea ritual. Some twenty young women in beautiful kimonos were seated on a rug spread over the lawn, creating a brilliantly colored spectacle of grace and femininity, and harmonic blending of bright colors. Wolik took pictures, and I, as a woman, was invited to take part and enjoy the special tea and delicacies. We could only smile at each other, for lack of a common language.

Wolik addressed the annual meeting of business associations on Kyushu island at a luncheon for men only, but both of us were invited to dinner at a fancy restaurant. When we arrived, we saw about forty Japanese businessmen, a burning hibachi in front of each of them, sitting on the floor along the three walls of a large room. On the fourth side was a stage. Midway along the wall facing the stage were two seats for us, also on the floor, of course. To my surprise, six geishas were serving the guests; I had been told that women are not invited to entertainment provided by geishas, but here they were. One of them, quite old, was famous in Japan as a collector of traditional songs. The geishas were especially attentive to me, and one of them said, "We are so glad that you are here." To my natural question "Why?," she replied, "If you were a Japanese lady, you would be jealous and treat us badly. That would spoil the evening."

After dinner, the geishas sang and danced to the accompaniment of the samisen. After an intermission, a man dressed like a samurai, with the sword at his side, appeared on the stage, and sang and danced while the geishas played their instruments. It was a superb performance, and we applauded wildly. He reappeared as a hobo and his humorous performance again delighted the audience. He made his final bow in his ordinary clothes, and turned out to be the executive secretary of the association, to everyone's complete surprise. The audience roared.

Our publisher, Mr. Yamada, showed us exquisite courtesy. Wolik, who had had dozens of books printed by both commercial publishers and institutions in many countries, including the United States, was taken by surprise. Mr. Yamada had met us at the airport with his entire staff. Three days later, he came to the Imperial Hotel bringing us the Japanese edition of our *World Population and Production* wrapped in a *furoshiki,* a silk handkerchief. We were touched by such exceptional attention but would have been speechless if he had told us that our book was not to appear until January and that the copy he gave us, on October 22, had been bound especially for us. He invited us to spend several days with him and his son and daughter in Hakone, one of the finest resorts in Japan; because he did not speak English, he invited Naoi and his daughter, too.

We were lodged in the finest hotel. Mr. Yamada arranged several mountain drives to show us Mt. Fuji from all sides, and a cruise on Lake Hakone. The hotel had a pavilion, once the property of the Imperial family, for special occasions, and Mr. Yamada invited all of us to dine there on tempura and other Japanese dishes. We were overwhelmed by this friendliness and courtesy, but he felt that this was not enough attention to pay the authors of a book he valued very highly. He treated us to the kabuki theater and dinner in a fine restaurant afterward. There he presented us with a full collection of Hiroshigo prints and other beautiful publications. We were embarrassed by such generosity and did not know how to reciprocate. Since Mr. Yamada was interested in art, we wrote to friends in Washington asking them to send him several of the best art books on American paintings and design. But these, of course, fell far short of his lavish presents to us.

The Japanese theater was an exciting experience. The intense dramatic atmosphere on the kabuki stage, the solemnity of the speeches, the ancient, elaborate costumes, the grim-faced actors, held us spellbound for hours—literally hours, because the kabuki shows last almost the whole day. Fortunately, there are intermissions, during which one can get a snack or a full meal in the restaurants within the theater. To the right of the stage was a platform for the samisen players and the narrator, all in ancient costumes. We could not understand a single word of the narrator's chant but the poignancy of his voice was moving; at one point, tears ran down his face in streams. All the kabuki actors are men trained, during a long apprenticeship, to impersonate women. We also saw an all-woman performance, including the impersonation of male roles, in Takarazuka. In both cases, the illusion was complete.

In Osaka, the bunraku puppet show captivated us. Although there were up to sixteen black-robed men on the stage, the spectators are supposed to understand that they cannot see these manipulators of the puppets' arms and legs. Indeed, when the heroine took her life by plunging a sword into her breast, we saw only her, oblivious of the black shadows.

We were invited to spend Christmas Day with an American friend and his Japanese wife. She was very sweet and attractive, but they lived in loneliness, having lost contact with both the Americans and the Japanese. Somehow they felt that we were different and so invited us. She, in particular, thought that we would understand what she did not expect others to understand. Her main concern was the future of her baby, a boy with a distinctly Japanese face. In a Japanese school, the children would consider him neither American nor Japanese. She was afraid that the same attitude might prevail in an American school. Consequently, Michiko and her husband were thinking of moving to Honolulu, and she wanted me to tell her everything I knew of Hawaii. In doing so, I tried to encourage her, but her anxiety was so deep-seated that it could not be easily dissipated.

We spent the New Year's holiday in Tokyo. There, it lasts almost a whole week, and the Government offices are closed for at least three days, and sometimes five. This is the biggest celebration in Japan. Much alcohol is consumed, and during these days, inebriated Japanese behave not too graciously on the streets.

On New Year's Day, a Japanese professor with whom we had become good friends came to take us to the traditional book fair in the university district. While we were in our hotel room talking, I saw from the window policemen and the assistant manager of the International House in the garden. Our friend went out on the balcony to find out what had happened, and reported back, "Nothing of importance. Last night two men broke into the basement and were caught. Burglaries often occur on New Year's Eve. Traditionally, all debts must be paid by the New Year." He was puzzled when we laughed.

After the New Year's holiday, we went to Nagoya, one of the most highly industrialized cities of Japan, where Wolik was scheduled to talk to both business people and students. There, our meeting with the mayor turned out to be especially interesting. Evidently, he had been importuned by foreign visitors many times and was tired of describing, over and over, his city's destruction under heavy bombing in the last months of the war and the work of reconstruction in progress. So he met us rather boorishly, clearly indicating he was busy. But when Wolik inquired rather closely into the city's plans and remarked that they reminded him of Rotterdam's reconstruction program, the mayor suddenly became interested and animated. He ordered all the city's reconstruction plans to be brought out, called a conference of other members involved in that work, and had plenty of time for us. He kept us for lunch, and presented Wolik with a beautiful statue of Buddha when we left him.

Both of us were asked to talk in Hiroshima. Though we were eager to see that city, we went there with great apprehension and discomfiture. When we arrived, I was told that the group of women that I was supposed to address were waiting for me. I went straight there, and was so intent on watching my listeners that I cannot remember what I talked about. I could not discover any stamp of Hiroshima on them and did not know whether they were survivors of the tragedy or newcomers.

We spent the evening with the USIS representative and his wife. Their only child, a girl of ten or eleven, was enrolled in a Japanese school and spoke the language quite well. Our impression of the family was that we had the right people at the most sensitive post in Japan. As we walked with them next morning, several Japanese stopped them to exchange remarks, and many others greeted them in the friendliest manner. Their daughter was with the Japanese children, and the group was cheerful and talked animatedly.

However, when we entered the museum of atomic horrors, we stopped talking. We felt such pain, such sadness, that we could hardly move from one photograph to another. It was a heartbreaking experience, but we felt we had to expose ourselves to those horrors. Yet we did not notice any animosity in the Japanese crowd around us. Perhaps they felt like the radio operator on our ship in the Inland Sea who said to Wolik, "War is bad, not the bomb. If we had had it, we, too, would have used it." Several people told us that while the destruction from the atomic bomb had been horrible and spectacular, routine bombing had inflicted greater damage on Japan. One conventional bomb could send whole districts of matchbox houses up in flames, with many people suffocated or burned to death.

Japan's leading economic magazine, the *Oriental Economist,* had published many of Wolik's articles after World War II. During our stay in Japan, it printed most of his lectures and an interview with him after our arrival in Tokyo. Before our departure, the editors of the magazine invited us to a final conference. As a token of appreciation and respect, the editors presented us with a beautiful Japanese doll. They could not have done better to charm Wolik. In Washington, he built a special shelf, glassed it in, and enjoyed showing it to friends as a symbol of gracious refinement in human relations and of most unexpected refinement in the relations of editors to contributors.

We were driving through the streets of Kyoto one day when Wolik noticed, on a theater building, a poster showing a man in a knight's jacket, wide-brimmed hat, broad lace collar and cuffs. He stopped the car and got out to inspect the poster, which announced the presentation of Friedrich Schiller's play *The Robbers* on the occasion of the sesquicentennial of Schiller's death. Nowhere else, except perhaps in Germany, would this date have been commemorated or even remembered. Wolik was thrilled by this interest and knowledge of a European drama in the Florence of Japan and admired the poster so much that he was promised that a copy of it would be sent to him in Tokyo. The Japanese economists who were showing us their city were touched by Wolik's unaffected appreciation and love of art and the theater. I saw them exchange grateful looks, and one of them said to Wolik, "You have the eye of an eagle. Who but you . . . ?"

The U. S. Embassy in Tokyo cabled the Department of State in Washington this report on Wolik's tour:

> Woytinsky widely known and respected among economists and intellectuals and [his] stay here enabled Embassy make wider contacts [with] these groups than any other specialist.

In contrast to many other countries we visited, there is dignity in the personnel with whom the traveler in Japan comes in contact. The guest is not importuned; nobody stretches out his hand for a tip, or "backshish." The hotel adds 10 per cent to the bill for service, and no further tips are expected. But we had stayed in Japan's International House for longer and shorter periods during three months, and I wanted to show our appreciation to both the office and dining-room staff. On the day of our departure, I bought two large trays of delicacies— tarts and candies—and presented them at both places. That night a group of Japanese friends gave us a farewell dinner—held, at our suggestion, at International House. During the dinner, an envelope was handed to me. It contained a letter from the staff saying how pleased they were to have had us and thanking us for the treat. Everyone had signed it—some in English, others in Japanese. It was dignified, and underscored the fact that all of us were people. I cannot think of another country where the reaction in such a case would have been as dignified.

Just as our arrival and stay in Japan had been warm and touching, so was our departure. Nearly everyone we met left a little present for us, as a token of friendship and appreciation for Wolik—a book, a piece of china, a silk scarf, a handkerchief. Michiko made a summer kimono for me. Every university had given Wolik a present—a painting, a book, a cloisonné vase, or a doll—some item that was a regional craft specialty. We were unaccustomed to this practice and we loved the presents as mementoes to take home and show our friends. There was nothing of great monetary value, of course, but we appreciated these tokens the more, knowing that they were expressions of warmth, not efforts to ingratiate.

IN THAILAND

Scenically, Thailand is a fairy-tale country. Nature created it enchanting, with the innocent look of a carefree child; man enriched nature's handiwork by building resplendent palaces with colored tile roofs, fantastic temples with golden spires and superb ornamentation. Add to this the azure sky, lush vegetation, and mild climate, and one feels like a visitor in a dream world. With its innumerable canals, large and small watercourses, Bangkok reminded us of Venice. The people, smiling, lighthearted, moving swiftly, were a gay contrast to the sedate, ceremonious Japanese.

Unlike Japan, Thailand is not haunted by the fear of overpopulation. Given twice as many Thais as today, the people could produce rice, fish, and other foodstuffs for themselves and still have surpluses for export. The soil is fertile, and there is water everywhere. There is also enough feed for the large herds of buffalo we frequently saw at work in the fields.

In Thailand we were guests of the Central Bank; Mr. Charabatara, head of its research department, met us at the airport with the program for Wolik's meetings and lectures at the university, before the country's Economic Association, and before the bankers' group. Being on our own, without any Government commitments, we felt freer in the use of our time. Moreover, the Central Bank had generously provided us with a car and a chauffeur for our fortnight in Bangkok and assigned two young economists to accompany us on trips to the most important points in the country, including Ayudhya, the ancient capital of Thailand.

Thanks to the Bank's courtesy in offering us its motor launch, we saw the famous "floating market" of Bangkok. The chauffeur came shortly after 4 A.M. one Sunday and took us to the launch. What a picture! Children and grown-ups were swimming in the brownish water along both banks of the Me Nam River and canal. Monks in their orange robes walked on the rickety sidewalks, and women came out of every door to drop rice or other food into the monks' bowls. The canal was crowded with barges carrying all kinds of produce and goods. Brisk business was going on between the people living in the houses on stilts along the canal and the merchants on the boats. Most of the barges carried only vendors, some of whom were also buyers. The people seemed to be carefree; laughter was heard on all sides.

The Bank had obtained permission for us to visit the inner part of the King's palace. We were told to dress in black because an official ninety-day mourning period was in effect on account of the death of the King's mother. The Bank economist who accompanied us wore a black band on his sleeve. On our way to the palace, he stopped the car, dashed into a store, and returned with a black band, which he put around Wolik's sleeve. In the palace, we were greeted by the majordomo, who took us to the chapel where the King's mother was lying in state. Next to the coffin, on the floor, several mourning women were sobbing and lamenting loudly. The majordomo told us to bow three times. This ritual accomplished, he offered us seats and ordered Coca-Cola to be served, nearly in front of the dead lady. This struck us as incongruous, but we maintained our solemnity.

Evidently, one funeral was not enough, for we soon walked into another one. We were visiting the compound of a large temple, containing many towers and chapels, when a procession of schoolchildren with two teachers came by. To film it, we followed the children into a huge tent and, thinking there might be a school performance, we entered —and were trapped. Instead of the children, we saw, in a kind of a hall, many people. We were led to a table, given a feather pen, and told to sign. Then somebody took us inside the tent, where there were many people, some seated, others standing. We were seated. We looked around but could not figure out what we had stumbled into. A half-hour passed, and large trays of food were brought to us. We declined with thanks, explaining that we had just had a heavy breakfast. After a few more minutes we decided to try to get out. We rose from our seats, whereupon a solemn man came up to us and led us, of all things, to a coffin in which his dead mother was exposed. The people around it were relatives or friends; the children had come from a school that she had supported during her lifetime. We bowed, paid our respects to the dead, and her son took us to the exit. Beside it was a table from which he took two large new handkerchiefs from a pile and handed them to us. Their purpose? To be used when crying at the sight of his dead mother. It was clear that we had entered through the wrong door.

As in Japan, I was always the only woman among assemblages of men at lectures and interviews. Even when on our last night in Thailand, Mr. Charabatara (or Mr. Chamra: we called him by his first name on his suggestion) invited us to his home for a farewell dinner—a real Thai dinner, excellently prepared and delectable—neither his wife nor his children were present. Obviously, the social separation of the sexes was complete.

IN BURMA

While Thailand seemed smiling, despite the political insecurity within and without its borders and despite the evident poverty, Burma was devastated by war and civil war, and the Government's power extended over only a small area beyond the capital city. Outside this, trains were stopped and the passengers molested or robbed, electric installations were wrecked, roads barricaded, people assaulted. But as long as we stayed in Rangoon, life seemed normal—the stores and the schools were open, newspapers appeared, the streets were full of people.

Wolik gave a lecture at the university, and a few days later the dean of the economic faculty asked him to lecture again. Wolik explained that, to his regret, he could not; we had an appointment with the Secretary of Agriculture that morning and an invitation to tea with the Chief Justice; the next morning we were to leave Burma. The dean shifted Wolik's appointment with the Secretary to a later hour. Not having any material with him, Wolik took the latest *U. S. Statistical Abstract* from the university library and, turning its pages, interpreted some of the important statistics—population and its growth, the labor force, unemployment, agricultural and industrial output, national income, taxation, social security, and so on. After he finished, the dean said meditatively: "All these are facts which we did not know. Obviously, we have to revise our thinking about the United States."

There is a funny footnote to that meeting with the dean. Several years later in Washington, at the home of a friend, we met a member of the International Monetary Fund from Burma who reminded us of Wolik's lectures at the University of Rangoon and remarked how effective they had been. Neither of us could remember having met him, and only hours later did we realize that the impeccably Western-dressed economist was the dean of the faculty in Rangoon, who had worn there his native dress—a bright silk *pasoe* reaching to his ankles, actually a long strip of silk wrapped around his body in long, soft folds. He had looked like a different person then.

We visited Burma at a time when its Government was not receiving American aid, having rejected it because it had been conditioned on Burma's taking sides in the Cold War. However, many officials disapproved of the Government's decision. The Chief Justice told us that, in his opinion, Burma had cut off its nose in order to save its face. At tea in his house, I saw his wife pass the open door of the living room, but she did not come in.

Perhaps we were too sensitive, but we felt almost guilty when, on a Sunday outing with Burmese friends, food was spread out picnic-fashion for us but nothing was offered to our chauffeur. We could not say anything but neither could we meet his eyes.

The intellectuals in both Thailand and Burma told us of their countries' problems and difficulties, of their plans and hopes. There seemed to be no barrier between them and Wolik. They did not weigh their words; they seemed to feel, by some mysterious chemistry, that there was an understanding friend willing to use his knowledge and experience in advising them and having *their* good in mind. In the streets and parks, Wolik felt at ease with the crowd. I could see that he attracted them by his sincere, unaffected interest in everything around him and by his warm smile. Even the monks came up to tell him about their way of life and walked beside us for some distance. When we sat in a park or on the steps of a temple, children often came to ask Wolik to let them use his binoculars or to photograph them.

IN INDIA

In Wolik's discussions with Japanese economists on how to raise the productivity of labor and the standard of living, education was never among the problems raised. Japan had about the same literacy rate as the United States. It was a country of readers, and the number of books published in proportion to its population was greater than that of this country. As soon as we left Japan, we began to be impressed by the importance of education to economic development. In India, Wolik stressed the significance of education not only as something socially desirable but as a fundamental factor in the modern economy.

We went to India as tourists. We knew no one in that huge country; none of our friends had any contacts there. In addition, we had been told several times that we would be subjected there to hostile questioning. A trip to India seemed to promise little pleasure. Nevertheless, we went and were richly rewarded.

Our first stop was Calcutta, where we arrived late in the evening. Early next morning an Indian journalist, K. K. Sinha, called. He had been informed of our arrival by the Congress of Cultural Freedom, and he offered to show us his city. Intelligent, well-educated, Western-oriented, and open-minded, he was most helpful in introducing us to India. We spent several days with him and saw much, even the railroad station where the refugees from East Pakistan squatted on the floor in family groups, holding their only earthly possession, a brass pitcher. Some Indian students objected violently to Wolik's taking a picture of the station with the refugees. One of them shouted that the Americans always stressed India's poverty in their pictures and that Nehru would have expelled us had he seen *what* Wolik was photographing. Mr. Sinha said something to them in Bengali and advised us not to argue with them. This was the only act of unfriendliness toward us personally during our three-month stay in India.

Next morning, the Ramakrishna Mission called to invite Wolik to give a talk. We had never heard of Ramakrishna or his Mission, but after the Mission priest came to explain its purpose and attitude of genuine tolerance, Wolik agreed. It was our first contact with an Indian audience, and therefore particularly interesting. To enable Wolik to get the feel of the audience, the Mission invited us to attend a talk scheduled the day before Wolik's lecture. The audience was mixed; along with people in Western clothing were some in Indian garb, including ladies in elegant saris and bare-chested men with long hair, probably members of some religious groups. The speaker was a beautiful, middle-aged woman (Srimati Rukmini Devi, as we were told later) who discussed the role of art in civilization and the dance as the spiritual epitome of art and culture. Her talk was like a poem, presented in excellent English, and we were charmed by it.

At Wolik's lecture the next day, the audience included a professor of economics, home for a short time from his work in Egypt for the United Nations. He was accompanied by his wife, daughter, and son-in-law, and he explained to us that he had brought the young couple, both economists, so that they could get inspiration from an older team working as one. The audience was as mixed as the day before, but the discussion following Wolik's lecture on the outlook of the world economy showed that the listeners understood the subject. It also showed us that in India any correlation between education and external appearance, particularly clothing, was purely coincidental.

On reaching New Delhi, we went to the embassy and found a letter from India's cultural attaché in Washington, which had followed us from Japan to Thailand, Burma, and finally India, bringing invitations from sixteen Indian universities to lecture and be their guests. I was surprised and touched that the invitations to lecture were addressed to me also and that they offered us the hospitality of the university guest houses. Since our embassy did not express any desire to be connected with these lectures, we followed the suggestion in the letter and got in touch with the Undersecretary of India's Ministry of Education. To be guests of the universities and to lecture under the auspices of the country's Ministry of Education was, for us, an incomparably more favorable prospect than to be sponsored by our embassy.

As we traveled along both coasts during our lecture trips and made contacts with academic and Government people, with students and people in the streets and on the highways, we began to feel closer to India and to appreciate the great challenge and the enormous difficulties it was facing. We began to understand the sense of urgency, the nervousness in the Government's efforts to achieve at least some small, telling improvements in the situation. Sharp, contrasting impressions, provoking bewilderment, compassion, admiration, closed in upon us sometimes within a single day, even a few hours.

In Benares, we went to the university one morning, unannounced and without any introduction, and found ourselves within half an hour engaged in a lively conversation with two professors who had noticed us on the campus and inquired if they could be helpful. From there we went to a dealer in brocades and embroidered stoles of exquisite craftsmanship. He took us to his workshop, where several poorly dressed youngsters were working with golden threads at the looms. An hour later, in a boat on the Ganges River, we were thrown back several centuries as we watched teeming pilgrims, naked or half naked, bathing in water in which we had just seen a dead cow being sunk to the bottom. Along the bank of the river, we saw a man cremating his dead father's body, then another man breaking the skull of his dead relative to release his spirit. The other bank of the river was bare, without people, without buildings; people were convinced that anyone who went there would die.

Shaken and depressed, we left the boat and on the way to the hotel, stopped to join a crowd assembled around a young man, probably a priest. We could not understand a word of what he was saying except for the name of Buddha, which came up again and again. His gestures were expressive, his voice soft and melodic, his smile warm. Wolik, familiar with the language of gestures, began to interpret the priest's narration to me. His voice, his dancing body, took us back to the Ramakrishna Mission and to the eloquent woman's talk on the spiritual value of art. Here as there was the universal language, just as close to the Indians as to us—the language of beauty, art, and humanity. The grim pictures on the Ganges faded from our memory, while we stood in the crowd and listened to the story of Buddha's life.

Back at the hotel, I noticed Wolik looking out the window from time to time. When I asked why, he told me that he had sent the man who had served us as a kind of guide to the dealer we had visited early that morning to buy a stole that he had liked very much and wanted me to have. We did not know the name of the man and we were scheduled to leave the city next morning; I was sure that we would see neither him nor the stole again. But if Wolik's action appeared impractical, the motive was loving, and so I said nothing to discourage him. I noticed, though, that he became a little uncomfortable when, by eight in the evening, his messenger had not shown up. Shortly thereafter the man came, however, bringing a beautiful, gold-embroidered stole. He explained that with two generous tips—from Wolik and the dealer—he had bought a football for his boy and had stopped at home to surprise him with it. Wolik was triumphant; his trust in humanity had been vindicated and he had gotten the stole for me! All this in one day, and the gorgeous stole, too!

When we asked if it was routine to throw dead animals into the Ganges, the answer was that all dead animals were "buried" in the Ganges, as were holy men and very small children. When I tried timidly to check the statement, a ranking official casually remarked, "I guess there are plenty of crocodiles at the bottom to quickly dispose of the dead bodies." This cut me off short. Yet we did have a common language with him in talking about many other things. Occasionally a gulf like that appeared in discussion and made us feel that we were living in different worlds.

In Bombay, we stayed at the Taj Mahal Hotel. It was an excellent hotel, but when Wolik put his hand out to pick up a glass of water at the dinner table, our guest, a well-known Indian economist, warned, "You should drink only bottled water in India. I may drink this, but you are not immunized from childhood, as I am." Right he was! We were shocked to read in the next morning's newspapers that a corpse had been discovered in the city's water reservoir, and the municipal authorities urged the people to boil water before drinking. Countless thousands in the city did not have the facilities for doing this. Yet Bombay prided itself on its modern plant for pasteurizing milk.

There were many charming impressions, too. At Kutb Minar tower, we saw a colorful group of young girls on a meadow. They noticed that we were photographing them and jumped up to join us. In a minute, we found ourselves in the center of the teen-agers. They laughed, bombarded us with questions, and several offered us sections of peeled oranges they held in their hands. Another time, when I gave a talk in a girls' college, they threw leis around my neck and then arranged themselves in a big circle on the floor. It was an unusual experience to talk standing to listeners seated on the floor, but there was no chair on which I could sit.

Human life is cheap in India. We spent a day in the school for social work in Baroda and read afterward, in an article written by its dean, that in their field work, the students faced such facts of life as the parents' refusal to give blood for a transfusion to a sick child because they could have another child, or the husband's refusal to be treated for venereal disease because if he infected his wife and she died in childbirth, he could marry again.

Life in India is full of surprises for a Westerner who is not attuned to them. A day in the caves of Ajanta and Ellora left us speechless at the sheer power of imagination, the ability to conceive and produce such a monument and superb work of art and faith by using the solid rock of forbidding mountains as both the raw material and the setting. Words are too small when one faces such forceful, gigantic creation— mountains transformed into temples, with endless columns of Buddha and colorful murals inside the caves.

In a mountain resort in the Nandi Hills, the superintendent gave us two rooms that Gandhi had once occupied after an operation. In chatting with him, I expressed some interest in the many big monkeys running around, and he remarked in a matter-of-fact tone, "They do not bother us, and we do not molest them. You know, our god Hanuman was a monkey." That ended that conversation! One of Hanuman's descendants later paid us a visit. Entering the dining room, I saw a big monkey sitting comfortably at the table and holding the melon that the swami from the neighboring room had given to us. At my exclamation, the monkey dropped the melon and ran out, while I called myself a fool; if I had had more sense, I would have quietly picked up my movie camera and gotten a priceless picture.

Yet, right there, amidst the monkeys of divine origin, we spent the evening with a professor of biochemistry, a man of broad knowledge and understanding, and a swami who inspired respect at first glance. This is India, and each part of it is genuine. The Indians look with justification and pride at the mute witnesses of their country's past grandeur— the towers covered with imaginative bas-reliefs such as the Kutb Minar tower, the Taj Mahal mausoleum in Agra, the magnificent gardens of the Mogul rulers, the imposing palaces, the endless sculptures testifying to the Greek and Persian influences, the Red Fort and Big Mosque in New Delhi, and other monuments of unsurpassed splendor, commanding beauty, and artistic inspiration. The more disheartening is much of the reality of today!

In Calcutta, we got our first shock at the incredible poverty of the Indian masses, and this shock has never worn off. Poverty cried to us everywhere, from emaciated faces, skinny legs, children thin as rakes, from the sight of families huddled under rugs for a night's sleep on the sidewalk next to our hotel. In the city's outskirts it talked to us from the lines of "tents"—four or even two poles set in the ground and covered here by a rusted sheet of tin, there by wornout burlap; from the caravans of primitive carts pulled by buffalo on the way to market. Beggary, the concomitant of poverty, pursued us as soon as we stepped out of the hotel's protection into the street. It stretched its arms toward us even when our cab stopped at an intersection for a red light.

We realized in India that the concept of poverty was very stretchable; that while poverty should not necessarily exclude life in dignity, there were gradations, and a state of poverty could be reached at which millions of human beings existed much below the elementary attributes of human dignity.

Yet when I mentioned to an Indian friend, a member of the Parliament, that I had seen in a village hut nothing but a few rags in a corner, his casual reply was, "Poverty is no disgrace in India." When I answered, "Poverty is no disgrace anywhere, but people usually try to do something about it. It really degrades those who do not seek to overcome it," he merely shrugged his shoulders. Only six years later did I happen to find that my reply had been given much more impressively by Pericles some 2,500 years earlier: ". . . poverty we think is no disgrace to acknowledge but a real degradation to make no effort to overcome." I felt as surprised and proud when I stumbled on this sentence of Pericles as the *bourgeois gentilhomme* of Molière when he discovered that he had been talking prose all his life without realizing it.

The sight of women making pancakes of cow dung and then throwing them against the walls of their huts to dry in the sun, and of the walls decorated with them was at once disgusting and disheartening. India's exhausted soil badly needed those fertilizing substances, which were burned as fuel in cooking meals and thus literally went up in smoke. Handling cow dung was apparently woman's work. We saw women walking to the markets bearing on their heads baskets filled with dung cakes. Little girls with beautiful, sad eyes collected animal dung along the highways, wearing silver bracelets on their arms and silver rings on their ankles. Our Western outlook could not bring those two features into a common focus.

Later we learned that Indian villagers hoarded silver and gold, mostly in the form of women's jewelry. Bracelets, necklaces, rings welded on their ankles and even toes constituted a dowry carried on the body for both prestige and safety. The hoard of gold and silver in the villages is estimated to be worth several billion dollars. An Indian economist told us that gold markets operate in almost every city and offered to take us to one if time permitted. These markets are patronized not only by the rich but by people who live in misery but have preserved some crumbs of their inheritance.

The cohabitation of cities by people and cattle was dismal. We had known that the country held almost as many cattle as people. I myself had written about this in the section on agriculture in our *World Population and Production*. But it is different to know something from books and to see it with one's own eyes. The books tell of poor-quality cattle, nearly always hungry, of their drain on the limited supply of foodstuffs, their moderate usefulness, and so on. Our eyes saw cows, their ribs barely covered by hide, walking on the sidewalk, lying in the middle of the street while people walked carefully around them and cars drove to one side to avoid hitting them. Our eyes saw cows grabbing edibles from the market stands and merchants afraid to repulse them. The books did not tell of the demonstrators who gathered in front of the Taj Mahal Hotel in Bombay, where we were staying, and raised their fists against the Westerners inside and cursed us, the meat-eaters, for killing their mother, the cow.

In the streets, we saw the moving beauty of India's women and children. In the markets and railway stations, Wolik could not turn his eyes away from some young mother clad in the poorest garb yet worthy of being painted by Raphael, from a child who looked like a little angel. This beauty amid poverty was much more captivating than that exhibited amid luxury; it was genuine, effortless, and unforgettable. Delighted, Wolik repeatedly sought the best possible angle to capture it with his camera.

A parliamentarian from Mysore showed us the housing development built by the transport company for its employees in Bangalore, the state's capital—a group of small cottages, very modest but neat and, considering everything, adequate. Before one of them I noticed a young couple with a baby in the mother's arms. I introduced myself and asked if they would mind showing me the inside of the cottage. They were friendly and asked me in. There was a narrow hall with a room on each side and a closed toilet with space for a tub, I was told. The exit led to a kerchief-size back yard, and beyond was no man's land, with a dump near by and cottages scattered at its borders. Not a blade of grass showed, and the soil was parched and hard as stone. I asked how long they had lived there. "About two years." Aroused by the apathy, I said, "What different attitudes people have in different countries! Would you believe me that if an American worker moved into this cottage, he would probably use his first free day to clean up the dump and try to raise something, at least to have green grass around, or a few flowers?" Later I regretted my words, because there was also not enough water (I saw the queue at a public faucet in the development) and not enough money for seed. In any event, I could see how difficult it was to take each step upward, to achieve even the smallest improvement.

And so it was wherever we looked—everything had two sides. If one saw only one side, the impression was incomplete and the judgment often wrong. In the same city, we visited a little school, or rather a combination of school and nursery, for the children of local social workers—not a typical school but one for privileged children. Our friend's very attractive granddaughter and an adopted charming little boy went to that school. The girls, with twinkling bells on their ankles, danced for us, while our friend held the boy in his lap. Later he told us that his wife, a social worker, had bought that boy for five rupees (about a dollar) from a woman in a railway station. Though selling children was not unusual in his country, it had outraged his wife that a baby would be offered to passers-by in a station. Again, both unspeakable misery and human compassion and indignation were in style!

What impressed us in India more than in any other country was the complexity in every feature of life—the complexity of its long history with continuous warfare and numerous dynasties that had split the subcontinent into hundreds of petty princedoms; the complexity of its people, created by the merging of many racial types; the complexity of religious beliefs, of castes and tribes; the complexity of languages, without any one truly national language. After my lecture at the Maharani College in Jaipur, Rajasthan, I discussed education in India with two teachers. One was from East Punjab and the other from West Punjab, and they could communicate only in English. No author in India can write for everybody; to scores of millions, his language will be totally unknown.

At times, the impact of such complexities faded from our consciousness, particularly when we were with intellectuals. Thus we found ourselves at immediate ease with Professor R. K. Mookerji, who at once conceived a great fondness for Wolik. On our first visit to his home, he began to call Wolik "Baby," indicating that trivial matters cannot and must not occupy his superior mind. More than two years after Wolik's death, he wrote to me that he could not reconcile himself to the fact that our "Baby" had left us. At that first meeting, he surprised us by saying, "American women are slaves. How can you accept spending time on household chores? A woman who can write a book must be freed of such menial tasks. There are enough people who can do nothing else." I laughed and told him that I would not want to have servants around me and that I had time for everything. He shook his head and said gently, "Yours is the slave's satisfaction. Write books and let other people work for you!" Later, whenever he wanted to suggest something practical to us or to advise us where to go, whom to meet, and so on, he would ask for me, not wishing to bother the "Baby" with such trifles.

The university students were under the spell of Western ideas, eager to learn and seemingly eager to reconstruct India and, in addition, the world. They filled the auditoriums, listened quietly to Wolik, and then respectfully asked loaded questions. For Wolik, an experienced speaker and a scholar, it was easy to answer every question on its merit and to broaden its meaning and implications, without showing that he under-

stood the student's intention to be critical or even sarcastic. This dis-
armed the youngsters, and many times they cheered Wolik's good-
natured and humorous replies. They crowded around him after the
lecture, evidently glad to have a chance to exchange their thoughts with
him. This happened particularly often in the provincial universities,
which could offer only modest accommodations and therefore were
seldom visited by American lecturers. Indeed, the accommodations were
sometimes very primitive, though they were the best the university could
offer. To us, the only thing that counted was that the students and faculty
members were genuinely interested in the lectures.

Knowing that we were born in Russia, the teachers and students occasionally compared their country with Russia in their talks with us or
in the question period after the lecture. In this, they showed the
same ignorance of Russia's past and present that we had come to take for
granted. It surprised them to hear that even at the beginning of this
century, Russia had a per-capita real income several times as high as
India had in 1956; that even half a century ago, Russia had an aggressive,
enterprising managerial and industrial class and intelligent, qualified
workers; that literacy had been expanding, that the country was on the
eve of introducing compulsory elementary education, and that university
teaching was on a level with that of the other European universities; that
Russia's literature, music, theatrical art, ballet, painting, and architecture
were recognized the world over for their high accomplishments. Naïvely
the Indians had thought of Russia as a half-barbarous country that the
Communists had raised to a great power.

To bring the comparison closer to home, I once put it this way: "You
know of your Community Development program, one of the most promising features in your Government's development program. It sends
officials to the villages to encourage the people to dig wells, improve
their huts by adding windows and chimneys, and make other improvements. Well, the Russian peasants did not need such encouragement
from the Government. They dug the wells and built their houses,
larger or smaller depending on their means, with stoves and windows,
and supplied them with hand-made furniture.

"Here's another example. On our honeymoon, we bought a rowboat
and traveled down a large river in Siberia, in the wilderness, for more
than three weeks. Every night we stayed at a peasant's house, invariably
finding a clean bed and wholesome food, enough to eat that night and to
take with us for the next day, since the villages were thirty or forty miles
apart. Can you imagine any young couple spending such a honeymoon
in your country, going to the first village house they came to and always finding acceptable accommodations and good food? You must
honestly answer no! Yet this was possible in Russia forty years ago. This
should show you the difference in standard of living between Russia
before World War I and your country of today. The Russian peasants
have given their country great poets, writers, actors, musicians, leaders
of industry and science, professors, and generals—all this not with the

help of the Government but despite the obstacles erected by the Tsarist Government. Inertia and fatalism have not been characteristic of Russian life."

These remarks provoked more questions from the students, eager to learn about that mysterious land the U.S.S.R.

Wolik was less known in India than in Japan, though most universities had his books, especially our two volumes on international economics. In general, American authors were poorly represented in the libraries of Indian universities, as compared with British authors. We were sorry to see that our foreign-aid program had neglected to supply the universities with books. To us, books seemed a more powerful weapon than guns.

Occasionally, however, we met professors who were familiar with Wolik's writings in their particular field. For example, Professor Gupta in Jaipur had awaited Wolik's arrival to confer with him about a sampling of the working population in that area that he had just completed and was starting to analyze. I happened to come in during one of their discussions and asked to see some of the cards of his sample. The first I pulled at random asked: "Your occupation?" and was answered, "Begging"; the next question was, "How long have you practiced your occupation?" and the answer, "Twenty years."

To our mind, the crucial test for India was whether its Government could break the centuries-old inertia of the people and their passive acceptance of poverty and ignorance, and kindle in them a desire to act and a determination to improve their lot. The most modern steel mills and airplane factories built by the Government with foreign aid would not make India a better country to live in, but the arousal of the people from their apathy could and would. It seemed to us that with the best of intentions, Indian planners were setting out to build a new house for their country by starting with the roof, and not even considering that the foundation might not be strong enough to support it. We could not see how a modern economy could operate with illiterate people at its base. Yet most Indian intellectuals were fascinated by the vision of industrialization and showed little enthusiasm for the basic, though slower ways of creating a healthy modern economy. Preaching the necessity, not just the desirability, of broad elementary education was unavailing. "Sometime later, yes, but not now, when we need steel mills, chemical plants, and so on!" Some of the planners had never even been to a village and seen those pathetic village schools. Often they had only three walls, with the fourth side open, and the children, of different ages, had no seats but crouched on the floor. In some "schools," there was not even a blackboard; often a single textbook had to serve all. Usually there were only a few girls. The absent ones were needed to help the mothers take care of the younger children.

We discussed these problems with Indian friends at the university meetings and privately, and the discussion went round and round in the same vicious circle: India could not afford to spend her meager means on more education, yet she could not modernize her economy without managerial skills and without workers with at least an elementary education.

We were surprised that the Community Development program, concerned with the well-being of most of India's population, created little interest among academic people. We spent many a day in the villages, talking to their leaders and officials, the doctors in the modest maternity homes, the schoolteachers. It was refreshing to see energetic young people proud of improvements already achieved and full of plans for more. They were eager to show us every new feature in the village that promised to improve the life of its people. Patiently, Wolik would get out of the jeep to see the reservoir for holding rain water or a tiny "people's house," or a recently dug well, and always he found some words of encouragement. It was quite a strain to drive in a jeep on bumpy, dusty roads under the burning sun, but Wolik was too interested in what he saw to be aware of any discomfort. Yet to many high-brow intellectuals, these achievements were peanuts, not worth consideration. An Indian pilot who recognized Wolik from a newspaper picture and stopped to talk to him on his way to the cockpit, later wrote to him after he had read Wolik's article on Community Development: "I am a layman and my job is flying airplanes . . . but being an Indian and knowing what little I do about India, all I can say is that . . . your article on Community Projects told me more about the resurgence of rural India than all the Indian newspapers put together." In Madras, we induced a young professor to accompany us on a trip to some villages and got him to see and appreciate the work being accomplished, with no recognition from the press, in villages that he had never before visited.

It was amusing to observe the Indian intellectuals' different attitudes toward Great Britain and the United States. The British had left India "most graciously," we were told many times. Now the term "imperialist" had shifted from the British to the Americans. Many of the Government and academic people had graduated from Oxford or Cambridge or some other British university and retained numerous youthful memories in common with the British. Once the occupation of India ended, those memories were revived. There were no such ties with the Americans; instead, the attitude toward them was determined by the Indian's position taken in the Cold War, by his ideological reaction to the bad word "capitalism" and the good word "socialism."

This attitude would have been irritating if it had not been amusing. Fortunately Wolik, because he was being consulted with great respect by top economists and Government people, could, in his usual warm and modest way, express his opinions with complete frankness, whether he agreed or disagreed with the prevailing concepts. The Indians were quite unprepared to hear from him, and have him document it, that the public sector in "capitalist" United States was considerably larger than that in "socialist" or "socialist-oriented" India.

The Sikhs have a reputation for being ferocious warriors, but in everyday life they give a different impression. The first Sikh whom Wolik met, with traditional turban and long beard, was working in the offices of the International Labor Organization in Geneva. Wolik went to talk to him about labor problems in India and was surprised, to put it mildly, when that member of the international staff began to talk with great pride about his people's way of killing their enemies mercilessly. Incredulous, Wolik listened for a while, then he laughed and said to the Sikh: "Listen, you may mystify other people, but you are not fooling me. I'll bet you have never had any weapon in your hands but a fountain pen. With all your decorative headgear, you are still an intellectual, a peaceful employee of the ILO. So let's not talk about killings any more. I have several questions to discuss with you." The Indian looked disappointed at his failure to impress Wolik with his belligerent talk, then smiled and said: "I should have known better. You are a hard nut to crack."

I saw the Sikhs in India for the first time. Indeed, they looked dangerous, but on various occasions in New Delhi we found them friendly and helpful. In the official travel bureau, a Sikh employee was very patient and kind to us in arranging for a room when we arrived a day ahead of our reservation. The taxi driver we most frequently engaged was a Sikh, and we liked to talk with him. He spoke softly except when the Moslems were mentioned. Then, by the expression on his face, one could imagine the satisfaction with which he might stab a Moslem, his hereditary enemy.

Our most restful days in India were in Srinagar, Kashmir, a town in the foothills of the Himalayas. The flight there, between towering glacial ridges, was unforgettable. We stayed in a hotel with beautiful grounds and an unequaled view of the mountains. The building had once been one of the Maharaja's palaces, and its enormous rooms seemed too formal and cold, but the surroundings defied description. It was heavenly to stretch out in a gondola moving on Lake Dale and savor the beautiful sky, the wonderful air, the dazzling peaks of glaciers, and the gorgeous flowers and blossoming trees. We went up to Gulmark, first in a car and then on horses. It was wonderful to walk in deep snow on the trails through the sparkling forest and again, as years before, see a panorama of glacial peaks, even more majestic than those in Switzerland and the Tirol.

Because we were going to spend the whole day on the heights, we asked the hotel management for two box lunches and were told that they had been put into the car. It was a surprise to find that the hotel had provided a complete service with table, tablecloth, silver, and all the other appurtenances—evidently a custom established under the British. Unexpectedly, we met two young students in the shelter on top. Seeing nobody else around, they told us that most of the people in that area were Moslems and would prefer to join Pakistan. We were, of course, noncommittal. But this was not the first time that we had heard such a statement. The coachman, boatman, and storekeeper all had found a way to squeeze into their talk a reference to the Moslems, who constituted nearly 95 per cent of the population. One priest even had the fantastic idea that to pacify the sentiments of the people, the United States should take Kashmir under its wing.

IN CEYLON

We made a side trip to Ceylon and spent two enjoyable weeks in the "Pearl of the Orient," without any official commitments. We rented a car with a chauffeur and drew up an itinerary that included many historical and otherwise interesting points. The weather was excellent, the vegetation lush and beautiful, and the time was all ours! If there was a sour note, it was provided by the chauffeur, a fanatical Catholic. Whenever we visited an old Buddhist shrine or temple, he could not restrain himself: "This is a godless place. It should be destroyed. What is there to see?" Wolik's reaction was categorical: "I have never approved of cannibalism, but I begin to understand why some missionaries were devoured."

We once stopped at a rubber plantation and penetrated into the forest to watch the workers swiftly emptying the latex from small cups tied to the trees into buckets. Deep in the forest, we noticed a shack, in front of which sat a woman with a baby in her lap; a little girl of six or so stood nearby. Though there was little light, we wanted to take a picture, and pointing to our cameras, asked the woman for permission. She nodded yes, but then motioned us to wait and went into the shack with the children. When they reappeared, the little girl wore a pink dress. The mother's pride in the child, her desire to show her in the best outfit in those poorest of conditions, were both touching and pathetic. We were deeply moved; here again was the universal language of humanity.

Another day we visited a tea plantation, with hills covered by tea plants and hundreds of workers picking the leaves. In the hallways of the company building we were astonished to see the workers and office employees walking about in their shoes over the leaves piled on the floor. We hesitated to do the same, but the head of the company stepped onto the leaves and waited for us to follow him. We closed our minds and did as the others did.

We arrived at Ceylon during the election campaign. It was a very spirited affair. We saw posters everywhere—on buildings, on trees, on special boards, in the windows, on trucks and cars. Because most of the people are illiterate, the political parties identified themselves, both during the campaign and on the ballot, with symbols—an elephant, a handshake, a workingman, and so on. We could not read the text on the posters, but during our cross-country trip we saw clearly that the opposition party was represented better in the country than it was in the Parliament. In some towns and villages, we saw its posters and flags only. Yet before our departure, when we paid a courtesy call on the ambassador, the latter answered Wolik's question about what results he expected from the elections, by saying, "Oh, I have no doubts. Sir John [the head of the Government] will win, perhaps with a somewhat smaller majority." The young man who handled press relations in the embassy felt otherwise: "Workers on the tea and rubber plantations will ask their boss for whom they ought to vote and then vote for the opposite ticket." A week later, the election returns left the unbeatable Sir John with only eight seats in the Parliament and brought the opposing party to power. Thus, as tourists driving through that lovely country, we actually gauged the people's temper more accurately than our permanent diplomat!

In ancient, long-forgotten times, Ceylon had a very intricate irrigation system, a vast network of reservoirs stretching over thousands of acres, built with great engineering skill and in subtle harmony with the surroundings. They provided plentiful water for the paddy fields in Ceylon's "dry zone" in the north and east. In the face of continual invasions from southern India, the people migrated to the southwest part of the island. Deserted and neglected, the reservoirs became the prey of the jungle, filled with sediment, and lay unused for centuries. Some restoration work was started under the British. Point Four helped to clear some, and several important restoration projects were under way when we were there. What so far had been cleared of wild vegetation and heavy layers of dirt was impressive evidence of the remarkable skill of the engineers of antiquity. Surrounded by lavish tropical plant life, the huge reservoirs, with excellently laid foundations and well-protected banks looked majestic and blended so well with the scenery that they seemed to be nature's rather than man's creation.

Ceylon offered much to see—the ancient cities of Anuradhapura and Polonnaruwa with their dagobas (Buddhist temples), statues of Buddha, and miles of palace ruins, swimming pools, royal baths, and temples; Kandy, the beautiful botanical gardens near it, and the famous Temple of the Tooth; the fantastic Sigiriya rock, rising up to 600 feet with the palace and fort on its top, and the superb frescoes portraying mysterious women on the way up—a difficult climb, but we made it. At another place, Wolik was fascinated by the statue of the Sinhalese king reading from the book of law.

IN PAKISTAN

Our final stop in the Far East was West Pakistan. We had been ready to return home when a cable from the Department of State reached us in New Delhi, asking if Wolik would lecture in Pakistan. Though we had been counting the days until our departure for Washington, we did not want to refuse, and cabled that we would go to Pakistan for as long as a fortnight, if that was acceptable. It was, and so we went to Karachi. Unknowingly, we arrived at a most awkward time, during the Ramadan fast. Lectures could not be given at night, when people, starved during the day, comforted themselves with food and drink and relaxed. And so Wolik's lectures and our meetings with officials and academic people were scheduled for the early hours of the day.

The contrast between New Delhi, the capital of India, and Karachi, the capital of Pakistan, was obvious. In New Delhi, India had inherited the magnificent palace for the President and the office buildings for Government agencies. In Karachi, a provincial town suddenly raised to the status of national capital, Pakistan had no large buildings at all and had to achieve that transformation overnight. Moreover, Pakistan not only lacked Governmental buildings but, what was much more important, had no experienced Government employees. Almost all the natives employed by the British Civil Service had been Hindus; Pakistan lacked even low-echelon people.

An even greater handicap was that the new country was divided into two parts, which were separated by thousands of miles. Considering the enormous difficulties that Pakistan faced from the day of its birth and the tragic events in the wake of the division of the subcontinent into two independent countries—the flight of the Moslems from India and that of the Hindus from Pakistan, the massacres on both sides, the millions of refugees crowding the roads—Pakistan was entitled to feel a certain satisfaction for what it had achieved in less than a decade. Improvements were badly needed at every level, and we heard many complaints, but the most important fact was undeniable: Pakistan existed and intended to continue to exist!

We stayed a few days in Karachi, then flew to Lahore for a series of lectures. In that old university city, among the eggheads, we were more in our element, and had long discussions on a variety of subjects. The U.S. consul was most helpful, inviting us to a round-table discussion with the Government people one night, and the opposition leaders the next.

To facilitate Wolik's lectures in Peshawar and Rawalpindi, the present capital of Pakistan, the consul provided us with a car and chauffeur, enabling us to see much of the country. The chauffeur was not fasting; traveling people, he told us, did not have to fast if they fulfilled their obligations afterward. I doubt that he did so, but that was not our concern. He was pleasant, an excellent driver, and knew the country. Somehow he got the idea of attaching himself to us and going with us to the United States. Every once in a while, he dropped a remark directed at Wolik: "If you take me with you to America, I would drive you anywhere you wanted to go. Wouldn't that be convenient?" Or, "You must not carry such a heavy brief case. Let me carry it. I will always do that for you in Washington." Though we tried to discourage his expectations, he did not give up easily and kept finding new reasons to persuade Wolik of the convenience of having him around.

In one Pakistani college, we had our first glimpse of co-education, Moslem style. Wolik, from the dais, saw students of both sexes in the auditorium, but they were separated by a screen, reaching from ceiling to floor, which prevented them from seeing each other. Indeed, they entered through opposite doors.

Though we were eager to return home, we tried to see as much of Pakistan as possible and enjoyed our stay very much. The scenery at times was grandiose, particularly on the trip to the Khyber Pass. It was also rich in reminders of history, of which both of us were always very conscious. I particularly loved them because Wolik excelled in reconstructing ancient times and their atmosphere. We saw relics from the time of Alexander the Great and the invading armies of Persians, Mongols, and others.

Maintenance was an equally serious problem in India and in Pakistan. Several times in New Delhi we rode in an almost new cab that was rattling, its ashtray gone, its upholstery spotted. The drivers were unimpressed by our comments that it was a pity for a new car to be in such a condition. In Karachi, we saw a camel walking with difficulty on sore legs and were told that the animals were used, without care, until they could not move any more. On the way from Lahore to Peshawar, we were shown development work in some villages. In one, drainage ditches had been dug recently at several places to let foul water escape, and now were so clogged with refuse that the water could only trickle through.

In one Pakistani village, we stopped at the cobbler's to see him work and to buy native slippers. We asked him how many children he had. He lifted two fingers. Surprised, I said, "You must be an exception. Everyone else we talked with has a large family." His wife raised three fingers, and our interpreter explained that there were two boys and three girls in the family.

In Karachi, we entered a large store in search of native products. There were beautiful rugs, splendid wood carvings, and many other attractions, all too heavy for airplane travel. The storekeeper then showed us a white silk scarf with gold embroidery, and explained that the design had been made in wax and then sprayed over with gold dust. While he was talking, an old man entered the store, and the merchant introduced him to us as the last remaining craftsman in that line. The old man was pleased and offered to show us how he worked. I bought several silk kerchiefs and a plain white silk scarf and asked him to embroider them. He did this in our presence. On paying, I noticed that the storekeeper turned over the money for the gold embroidery to the old man, who thanked him and left. I asked, "Does this craftsman work for you? You gave him the full sum paid for the decoration." He replied, "The man is old. He has his work table here and earns a little from time to time. I don't need his money," and pointing to the store, loaded with expensive things, he added modestly, "Allah has given me enough." This was our last day in Pakistan, and we were glad to leave that country on so kindly a note.

10. *Home, Sweet Home*

It was the first time we had been away from home for so long, more than eight months, and we were eager to return to Washington. Moreover, it was becoming increasingly hot in Pakistan. The temperature fluctuated between 106° F. and 116° F. Our only means of relief was to keep the shades down and the ceiling fan gyrating day and night. There was no cold water to drink, and in the bathroom one had to use sun-heated water from the open tanks on the roof. Around noon, faucet water was almost boiling. No wonder we counted the days until our departure. Wolik dreamed of ice-cold milk and I of ice cubes for water.

Wolik delivered his last lecture in Karachi in the afternoon, and an hour later we drove to the airport for the fifty-hour flight to Washington. We did not stop anywhere in Europe, and were excited and happy at seeing the New York skyline and unlocking the door to our house, a few hours later.

During the flight, we talked hopefully about having a good rest on our return. Now that our two volumes on international economics had been published, we envisaged no immediate obligations and wanted time to digest our impressions of the trip.

No sooner had we arrived, however, than requests began to come in— for lectures, reports on our trip, articles, talks here and there. The Department of State asked us to prepare a pamphlet on the questions about the United States that had been put to us most often abroad and the answers we had given. The *Encyclopaedia Britannica* asked for an article on world trade by Wolik, and one on world food supplies by me. Mountains of mail required sorting and answering. Moreover, despite all his desire for relaxation after the rigors of lecturing and traveling in the Far East, Wolik felt "crammed like a bomb" and was eager to get back to his desk.

We plunged into work and "normalcy," spending no fewer than ten hours a day, and often more, at our desks. With his impressions of India fresh in his mind, Wolik wrote four articles on it for the *New Leader*. Shortly thereafter, Harper & Brothers sent him a flattering letter and offered to publish them in expanded form as a book. Still, the pressure, though heavy, was not so continuous as in previous years. Instead of one seven-year study, we had individual commitments, each taking several months.

Both of us were in a happy mood. The trip had been successful, we had not lost a day either abroad or on our return because of sickness, our contacts with intellectuals and scholars now nearly spanned the world, we had seen many beautiful sights and gotten much inspiration. We renewed the impressions and sensations we had experienced in the Far East by reading books on its art and history. Though we had some regrets at not having seen more, we realized that, with the lecture load, we could not possibly have attempted more sightseeing. But the lectures had been the most important factor in familiarizing ourselves with the life and spirit of those countries. The questions and reactions of the students and the discussions with faculty members had given us many insights into their thinking and feeling that we could not have obtained otherwise.

To share with our friends what we had seen and learned during the trip, we gave after-dinner travel talks with slides and film and had discussions on the problems in the Far East and U.S. foreign policy. We also tried to devote at least one hour daily to the garden, which looked like a jungle when we arrived home, weeds dominating the scene. Occasionally we hiked along the tow path or in Rock Creek Park, but we did not venture beyond.

Betweentimes, Wolik built a shelf with many sections calculated to house the souvenirs from Japan, India, and the other countries. One special project was to build a glass case for the beautiful doll presented to us by the *Oriental Economist*.

As the months flew and one commitment after another was completed —the articles for the *Encyclopaedia Britannica* sent, the book *India, the Awakening Giant* in the hands of Harper & Brothers, the pamphlet for the Department of State delivered, and so on—we began to think of another trip. Before our lecture tour in the Far East, Wolik had never wanted to accept invitations to speak, whether at meetings or social affairs, but to his surprise, he had found our first lecture trip a source of great satisfaction and great fun. I, too, had never been particularly eager to complicate our travels with commitments, but our experience in the Far East had inspired me with the desire for more trips of that kind. Thus, to the teasing question of our friends, "What new worlds are you planning to conquer?," we had a ready answer: "Latin America."

We began to talk about Latin America during the hikes along the canal or in the woods, and to read about its scenic and historical attractions. First we thought of visiting three or four Latin countries, but that list gradually expanded to include more than fifteen. We decided to offer a lecture tour of Latin America to the Educational Exchange Service of the Department of State, which regarded our Far Eastern trip as a most successful venture, and to undertake it independently if the Department was not interested. Its reaction was positive and almost immediate. This time the Department wanted us to work as a team. We began to prepare our lectures—Wolik wrote five and I, three. I started to study Spanish in order to be able to communicate freely with the people in Latin America, and to translate Wolik's lectures into Spanish and deliver my own in that language.

In the midst of all this came a request from the House Subcommittee on Foreign Trade Policy for Wolik to do an article on U.S. foreign-trade policy. So we had to squeeze this too into our jammed schedule.

Studying Spanish was fun. The language seemed easy, and I decided to read in the original at least one major novel for each country we expected to visit. I did not achieve that goal, partly because of lack of time and partly because of difficulty in obtaining the books I wanted. I took private lessons from an excellent teacher, a Spanish refugee, intelligent and educated, so that we could talk about almost everything—literature, art, music, politics, and so on. But she was busy and could give me only two hours a week the first month, then four hours a week, and during the last month before our departure, she agreed to two additional hours a week on Sunday. After the first month, I translated for each lesson articles from *Harper's, Saturday Review,* or the *New Leader*—with the help of a dictionary, of course. Because I was versed in several languages and always interested in writing, I could produce poor but not hopeless translations. During the third month, I translated our eight lectures and, with the teacher, edited them. The Department of State processed them and sent twenty or more copies of each lecture in both English and Spanish to the embassy in each of the countries we were going to visit.

Despite the ease with which I could read Spanish novels and even translate literary or political articles into Spanish, I felt very insecure and feared the approaching real test when I would have to appear before Spanish-speaking audiences and interpret Wolik's lectures and the questions in the discussion period. I confided my worries to Wolik, but with his usual optimism he declared his confidence in me: "You will surprise the world. There is nothing at all to be concerned about except that your success will turn your head!" This did not reassure me at all, and I searched for opportunities to listen to Spanish or to converse in it. The best I could do was to listen to the BBC news report in Spanish, but it was measured reading, fully articulated, not the rapid, temperamental talk I expected to have to cope with in Latin countries.

In the meantime, our close friends from Syracuse begged us to visit them before leaving on so extensive a trip. Not wanting to interrupt my Spanish lessons, I wrote that we could come only if Sylvia could arrange conversation hours with a Spanish teacher. She replied that her colleague in the University's Romance Department had agreed to give me two hours daily.

When he came the first time, he asked me, in Spanish, questions that, to say the least, surprised me. Why was the Department of State sending me to Latin America? Was I going to negotiate treaties in any of those countries? And so on. All this was sheer nonsense, and I tried to explain to him the purpose of the Department's educational exchange program, telling him that our trip was one of many arranged every year. At the end of the lesson, he said to me, "I must confess that I regretted having consented to teach you, and this morning I simply hated to come. I understood from your friend that some lady, after a month or two of Spanish lessons, was considered so competent by the Department of State that it was sending you to represent it and lecture at Latin universities. In my resentment, I wondered what your Government must think of Latin countries if it considered a person with so little knowledge qualified for any responsible work there. I began to think that there might be other than educational purposes, I mean political purposes, in which you might be more versed than in Spanish. All my apologies, *señora,* and it will be a pleasure to see you tomorrow." I teased Sylvia about the misunderstanding she had created.

Wolik's triumph came after my fourth and last lesson. Thanking the professor for his help and patience, I asked him what he thought of my Spanish, particularly whether he thought I would be able to understand the questions after the lectures. He reassured me: "Oh yes. Perhaps not every word, but you will grasp the meaning, I am sure." Though encouraged, I said, "I shall have six or perhaps eight hours more of Spanish lessons in Washington and hope to do a little better than now." He smiled and with mock seriousness remarked, "With those extra lessons, you should be able to teach Spanish." I protested. "Please don't laugh at my efforts. Wouldn't you agree that with every month spent in Latin countries my Spanish will gradually improve? You know, we shall be there more than eight months." Sweeping his hat in a broad arc like a Spanish grandee, he said, "When you return, *señora,* you could give Spanish lessons to me." Later that day, Wolik invented all kinds of waggish situations to permit him to say again and again, "What did I tell you?" He turned to Sylvia with a twinkle in his eye: "Just watch that *señora,* she is out to conquer Latin America," he said.

As our departure from Washington approached, our home, our garden, began to look ever dearer and more attractive. Why were we starting this new adventure? Wouldn't it be better to remain home and work here? But Wolik was all set for the trip, intrigued by the prospect of seeing another world, thinking of all the places he had wanted to visit since his boyhood—the ruins of the Inca kingdom, the jungles of Brazil, the Amazon, the Galápagos Islands.

Finally, the day of our departure arrived. An hour before we left the house, our neighbor across the street, an Air Force colonel, came by to give us a note to his classmate, now cultural attaché in Buenos Aires. I mentioned that despite all my efforts to empty the refrigerator, there remained bits of this and that. What should I do with them? "No problem at all! Do you have a carton in the basement?" He ran down, returned with a box, and began packing the leftovers, meanwhile giving a running account of what would be done with them. "We'll have a fiesta, invite Sam and Ruth and drink to your health!" We were charmed by his gay camaraderie. What other colonel in the world, of even the smallest air force, would do this? None! Eight months later, when we came home one Sunday morning around four o'clock, we found our refrigerator freshly stocked with bread, butter, bacon, eggs, milk, and so on. "Only in America!"

11. *Latin America*

OUR LECTURE TOUR was to include all the countries in South America, six countries in the Caribbean and Central America, and Puerto Rico. It would take some eight months, with stays of a month to six weeks in the larger countries and from about ten to fourteen days in the smaller ones.

Preparations for this trip were much better than those for the Far East tour. The Department of State sent out to all the embassies advance copies of our lectures with biographies and many pictures of us at work, at home, in the garden, and also sets of our two volumes on international economics to serve as a calling card. Now we were better informed about the work and arrangements of the Educational Exchange Service. At our first trip we had known so little about its usual arrangements that Wolik never raised the question of remuneration, and had been completely satisfied at having his traveling expenses paid. It never occurred to us to ask for any part of my travel expenses, though I worked throughout the trip. It had therefore come as a genuine surprise when, on reporting to the Department on our return to Washington, Wolik was handed a check for his services abroad, with the words, "According to the reports from our posts, you did a superb job. It would be unfair not to pay you a salary when everybody else gets one. All our thanks." Not having expected anything of the sort, Wolik could only say: "Anything can happen in America!" Though I did not get any check, I was completely satisfied with the acknowledgement of my work by the Department in its letter to Wolik: "We cannot thank enough you and Mrs. Woytinsky for the splendid job you are doing in winning respect and understanding for our country abroad."

LECTURING IN LATIN AMERICA

From the day we arrived in Bogotá, Colombia, at the end of July, 1957, until the day we left Guatemala City, in April, 1958, we were in a mill-race: lectures, radio talks, press conferences, round-table discussions, receptions, meetings with embassy people and with Government, academic, business, and labor people in each country; visits to housing developments, Point Four projects, schools, factories, estates and plantations, fairs and markets. At night, in the hotel, we read memorandums and publications given to us at universities and government offices during the day, so as to be able to discuss further the questions raised during the interviews and in private conversations. We traveled continually from one city to another, back to the capital, then somewhere else, and made nearly sixty flights in all kinds of aircraft, frequently starting at four or five in the morning.

Packing clothing was at times a complicated problem, because temperature differences in many Latin American countries depend not on the time of the year but on the altitude. In Peru, flying from Lima (512 feet) to Cuzco (over 11,000 feet), or in Ecuador, flying from Guayaquil (a seaport) to Quito (over 9,300 feet) meant a change from summer warmth to winter cold within a few hours. In La Paz, Bolivia, the cultural attaché met us with an oxygen tank which he placed in our hotel room for the duration of our stay. We did not touch it but appreciated the embassy's thoughtfulness.

We received excellent publicity. The newspapers reported our meetings every day and often printed page-long texts of Wolik's lectures. In each country, we had at least two press conferences—one on arriving, in which we stressed the dual purpose of our visit, to lecture on problems of economic development and the United States economy, and to learn more about the host country, and another on the eve of our departure, when we were bombarded with questions about our impressions of the country. Special articles were written about us and our teamwork. The newspapers stressed my *perfecto castellano,* referred to me as "Doña Emma" or "Doctora Emma" and to us as *pareja* Woytinsky or *matrimonio* Woytinsky. We were photographed hundreds of times. Wolik, much more photogenic than I, was recognized by waiters in restaurants and drivers and passengers on buses.

All in all, Wolik lectured at thirty-five universities and I gave talks at about twenty. Requests for Wolik's lectures kept coming, but our schedule was so heavy that at times it was impossible to accept. At other times, it was impossible to refuse. After Wolik had talked at four universities in Bogotá, we were preparing to leave Colombia when the president of the fifth university insisted that Wolik must lecture at his institution, too. Having learned that we were to leave in two days, he scheduled the lecture for the next day, Sunday.

It was easy and at the same time difficult to translate Wolik's lectures into Spanish—easy because I was thoroughly familiar with the subject and because he remained within the framework of the prepared text, and difficult because I had to be on my toes all the time, ready for any unexpected comparison that might pop into his mind or for a new and imaginative conclusion. More difficult, particularly in the beginning, was the discussion period with its sometimes inarticulate questions. When

Wolik did not feel like going into the subject, he suggested that I answer the question, giving additional material to expand on some of his statements.

During the first few weeks, I felt unsure of my Spanish and therefore somewhat tense. By the end of the day, I was fatigued from the strain of discussing in Spanish many different topics—from the methodology of statistical surveys and problems of economic development to taxation, financial and foreign-trade problems, agricultural reform, the status of education—and in between, indulging in plain social conversation. Gradually, without my noticing when and how, my tenseness evaporated, and sensing the people's appreciation that I was talking their language, I was at ease.

The first language problem arose in Brazil, where Portuguese is the national tongue. Though nearly all educated Brazilians understand Spanish, it would have offended national pride if Wolik's lectures had been translated into Spanish. The embassy provided us with a translator, a senior student majoring in economics who spoke English reasonably well and had spent six months in the United States. Ramon was a likable young man, but unfortunately, a very poor translator. He could not find the proper words, and worst of all, he had no memory. To help him, Wolik paused after each sentence, which was in itself a strain, but became exasperated when Ramon said, "Sir, do you mind repeating the sentence?" Sometimes a professor would take over. Other times, I translated into Spanish and a professor gave the Portuguese version. In Haiti, we both lectured in French, the national language. In personal meetings and social conversations, Wolik often communicated directly when English, French, or German could be used.

Wolik was at home everywhere—in Haiti, poor and illiterate, as much as in Argentina or Chile; in Bolivia, a country caught up in revolutionary turmoil, as much as in Mexico, the most stable and advanced country of Latin America. Without attempting to do so, he captivated both the press and the universities. As had happened also in the United States, the reporters occasionally used provocative headlines in accounts of press conferences—in Rio de Janeiro, for example, "The American Economist Says We Spend Too Much" and "The Trouble with the Latin Americans Is That They Spend More Than They Have." Naturally, Wolik had said nothing of the sort but in answering the question on the origin of inflation, he had referred to the policy of printing money as one cause of inflation in many countries without naming any of them. We felt uncomfortable when we saw those headlines but were reassured when, in the funicular taking us to the Sugar Loaf Mountain, several people recognized Wolik and came to shake hands with him, saying good-naturedly: "You said that we are spending too much. Right you are!"

Generally, the reporters showed great respect for "the grand old man," at the same time enjoying his humor, his gay repartee, his friendly and unpretentious manners. He was blessed with that wonderful gift of communicating with people from all stations of life. Whether he talked to workers or industrialists, professors or students, before a simple or sophisticated audience, he was always himself but instinctively found the right approach to others. As a result, we did not leave a single country without being urged to stay longer and to return. After Wolik's talk at the University of Buenos Aires, for example, the dean asked if he could give five more lectures.

The introductions given Wolik before he spoke were often a source of amusement. The dean or chancellor who chaired the meeting would ask me to provide him with biographical data. I knew from experience that the less I said, the more chance there was that a reasonably accurate statement would ensue, and so I would give a few essentials and suggest some short, simple sentences. What we heard a few minutes later usually bore no resemblance at all to what I had said. Wolik and I would look at each other and suppress our smiles. But once out of sight, we would laugh about it together, and Wolik would playfully insist that I must have inspired those exaggerations and the occasional nonsense.

After Wolik had given several lectures in the San Marco's National University and I had lectured in the Peruvian-American Institute in Lima, we flew, in accordance with the Embassy's schedule, to Arequipa, a beautifully located city, the second most important in Peru. Wolik had an especially successful evening. The largest auditorium was packed and the audience was most responsive; almost every answer Wolik gave to questions was met with applause. After the lecture, Jesuit Padre Corvy came to congratulate us, then said to me: "I shall attend the lecture tomorrow and bring you a present." Surprised, I tried to dissuade him, but he insisted I must have a souvenir from that area! Alas, we never saw Padre Corvy again or his present! Anticipating that his would not be the last such promise, we decided to set aside a special shelf to be called "the shelf of Padre Corvy." Every time someone promised to bring a memento to our hotel, we thanked him and solemnly said, "We shall put it on the shelf of Padre Corvy. That's where we keep the souvenirs from our trip to Latin America."

Once Wolik was interviewed on TV in Rio de Janeiro, right after the Brazilian ambassador to Buckingham Palace and before Miss Brazil. At the end of the program, the interviewing reporter shook Wolik's hand, thanked him for his appearance, and suddenly said, "You know, we produce excellent cotton and now we make fine fabric. I shall present you with a shirt of Brazilian cotton so that you can show it in your country." Taken aback, Wolik replied, "I had not expected this, but thank you just the same." Sitting in the studio, I had time to consider how he should have answered the interviewer, and when Wolik returned, I said to him, "For the first time, we had a real chance to get a present, and you muffed it. You should have turned to the camera and said, 'All you Brazilians, you are witnesses to the fact that I have been promised a shirt. Don't let him forget it!' " Of course, that cotton shirt from Brazil earned a place on the shelf of Padre Corvy!

Wherever we went, the students were alert and listened intently. At the National University in Bogotá, the editor of the college magazine, wanted to interview Wolik, who suggested he come to the hotel next day. He arrived with written questions, brought a copy of the magazine, *Pensamiento Economico (Economic Thought)*, and showed us his last article, "Reflexiones de Una Generación." We answered his questions, and then he told us about his plans and his family. His mother had died, his father was a worker earning twenty-eight pesos ($5) a week; he had two brothers and three sisters. He had worked since he had been in elementary school, lost several years after high school, then enrolled in the university. He studied during the day and worked in the evening, collecting rents for a real estate company. "What about your brothers and sisters? Do they go to school?" "Not all of them. Father and I can carry only two." Wolik asked why he had chosen economics, and the boy tried to explain: "When a poor boy is lucky enough to enter the university, he studies medicine or law. These professions promise good fees, good living, a car. But nobody cares about helping people like us. We must learn why we are poor, how to get better conditions. I decided that economics would teach me this." He was not alone in coming from a working-class family, but earning one's education was not easy: "When you go to class without breakfast, it's hard to concentrate on what the teacher is saying."

My first lecture was on the social structure of the United States. Among the students was a tall, well-built Negro. To my surprise, he got up after I finished, and with highly complimentary words, suggested that the university obtain the text of the lecture for distribution among the students. It was the next student, a white lad, who raised the question of racial discrimination in the United States. We had faced this question many times, I more often than Wolik, because one of my topics—the social structure of this country—lent itself more readily to a discussion of it. Our response was to acknowledge the fact of discrimination stemming from Civil War days, acknowledge its ugly features, describe how it had developed, but also tell of the progress in race relations made during the decades we had lived in the United States and of the attitude of the Government and the enlightened sector of the population. As we became better acquainted with race relations in Latin countries, with the treatment of the Indians and the obstacles in the way of their education and social acceptance, I began to conclude my answer by declaring that in all the countries we had visited, there was discrimination against some part of the population, and though discrimination against a minority marred the image of the United States, in many countries discrimination was directed against the majority of the population. Though I did not mention any country, the question was dropped.

When we visited Brazil's Villa Redonda, the largest steel plant in

Latin America, and saw the white and black children of the workers and employees splashing together in the company's swimming pool, its director, who was taking us around, said pointedly, "Here we have no Little Rock!" What could we say? Just, "Good for you!"

Often Wolik had to reply to complaints that the Latin countries were paid low prices for their raw materials and produce by the United States, but had to pay high prices for U.S. manufactured goods. Usually his explanations met with approval, though it was hard for the students to accept his statement that they had an exaggerated faith in the ability and obligation of the United States to solve all problems, and that only a real cooperative effort between their peoples and the Americans could bring lasting results. Of course, some Latin Americans understood this. Once we met a Jesuit padre, the spiritual adviser of Colombia's trade unions, who had spent several months in the United States. In answer to our question about what had impressed him most during the visit, he said, "In your country, people believe in God but they try to ease His task by taking care of themselves, and only occasionally beg for help. In my country, people are such fanatical believers that they expect the Lord to do *everything* for them, without their lifting a finger." At times, it seemed that some Latin Americans had the same faith in the United States.

Generally speaking, our policy was to frankly acknowledge wrong where it existed historically and to discuss each question without evasive answers—essentially the same attitude which we had adopted in the Far East. No matter how loaded their questions, the students showed great respect for Wolik and great courtesy toward me as a woman.

ON THE WESTERN COAST

Though each country in South America has its own characteristics and personality, the countries on the western coast have more in common with one another than with the countries on the other side—in geographic conditions, ethnical composition and so on. We started our tour with Colombia and went on to countries on the western coast—Peru, Ecuador, Bolivia, and Chile. They had been less accessible to European immigration than the countries on the Atlantic side, and in each of them, with the exception of Chile, the majority of the population is of Indian blood. The undersized, undernourished Indians, often bent under heavy loads and avoiding the eyes of the white people, are pathetic to see. We asked ourselves whether the Incas had always been so small. It seemed incredible that the forefathers of these puny people had conquered the Andes, laid roads still usable, built temples that have survived centuries of neglect. Now they were regarded as an inferior race. One businessman said to us, "The Indian with money is a Mestizo, and the Mestizo without money is an Indian." A city dweller was annoyed: "There is no room in the cities for the Indians; they should be forbidden to settle here." A Peruvian economist characterized their role in the country's life by saying, "They are not a part of the economy; they consume what they produce."

The greatest defender of the Indians whom we met was Haya de la Torre, who apologized that he did not have much time but would be glad to answer our questions. Wolik asked:

"What are Peru's main problems?"

"The Indian question, agriculture, education—three aspects of the same problem."

When Wolik said that he was glad to hear this, Haya looked at him penetratingly and at once grasped that here was a real understanding of his country's problems. Now he had all the time in the world. He talked to the two of us as if we were a large audience, waving his arms as a condor moves his wings in flying, in Wolik's description. He said:

"Do you know our people, the Incas, the only people in the world who have been able to work the soil above the clouds, in the Andes? Exploited for centuries, never given a break! Some say the Indians don't care about education. Nonsense! I have seen Indian boys walk five miles over the mountains to the school. Oh yes, they are eager to have their children learn to read and write. The white men have told them that they lost their land when their forefathers pressed their thumbs to papers that settled that question once and for all. The Indians want, desperately want, to have their boys learn to read those papers, to find out the truth. We, the white people, are responsible for their misery. We have cheated them, abused them! They are lethargic, suspicious. Who is responsible for this? Theirs is not lethargy but hopelessness. How can they trust the white people? Oppressed, taken advantage of at every opportunity, they have withdrawn into themselves."

We listened spellbound. There was no chance to interrupt or ask another question. The door to our room half opened, and somebody looked inside so as to remind Haya that people were waiting for him. But unconcerned, he continued:

"The Indian problem is the problem of national unity, of our existence as a nation. The agricultural problem merges with it as does the problem of education. We need rural cooperatives, better roads, we need drainage of jungle land, irrigation. Our greatest need of all is for schools, education for every child! Only with education will the Indians become full citizens, recover their dignity, gain the respect denied them by my countrymen!"

He developed his ideas more and more. The door was furtively opened again and again, but nobody dared to interrupt Haya. Venomous looks thrown at us told better than words of the irritation of the people waiting for him. Timidly, first Wolik, then I tried to remind Haya of the people who were waiting for him, but he was too deep in thought to hear us.

Finally, the door opened and closed again, and I summoned the courage to say that we would be more than happy to come again when he had time to see us but that we must not keep his visitors waiting any longer. Wolik supported me, and Haya got up: "Sorry, we must break off. I wish we could continue."

Peru and Haya de la Torre became inseparable in our minds. Many times during our trip we were asked whether we had met Haya, and the fact that we had and had been impressed by him created a bond between us and progressives in many Latin countries. He is the most outstanding political leader in Latin America, yet the most controversial in Peru, his own country—too radical for the reactionaries, not liberal enough for the leftists.

In a private home in Bogotá, Colombia, we met Colorado, one of the trade-union leaders. He had just returned from a trip to North Africa and told us, "When I saw the miserable conditions in those countries, I said to myself, 'Well, they have just come out of colonial domination. But what about us, an independent nation for more than a hundred years? What have we achieved to be proud of?" He asked Wolik to talk before the trade unions. Our Ambassador, Mr. John Cabot, expressed a desire to attend the lecture. Thereafter, Colombia's Minister of Labor announced he would attend; he could not be absent when, for the first time, an American ambassador was to be present. The trade-union leaders were delighted. The workers' protest demonstration against the rising cost of living had been set for shortly after the lecture, and the trade unions had tried vainly to get the Minister of Labor to receive them. Now they would have him as a captive audience.

Wolik talked about technical and human factors in economic development and, as usual, I translated. Then Colorado commented on the lecture enthusiastically, and said that Wolik was a great world scholar concerned with human and labor problems, and praised my knowledge of Spanish, acquired specifically for talking to and with them and the other people in all Latin America. Several questions were later directed to the Minister of Labor, who refused to answer until the Ambassador and we had left, saying that internal problems would not interest us. Colorado and two other unionists quickly invited Mr. Cabot and ourselves to have a drink in another room while the Minister was left in the lion's den.

As in the Far East, we tried to combine each lecture trip to a new area with a study of its problems and special features and sightseeing. Peru was especially rich in historical and scenic attractions. So we very willingly accepted the invitation from Cuzco University, though we had been warned that the head of the exchange program, an influential member of the faculty, was a Communist.

The flight was in an unpressurized plane, and as soon as we were above 17,000 feet, the stewardess, without much ado, pushed a tube connected with an oxygen tank into every passenger's mouth.

Scenery, history and the works of man combined to make Cuzco one of the most fascinating places in all Latin America. Established among forbidding mountains by the first Incas in the eleventh century and captured some 400 years later by the Spaniards, it still had many massive stone walls and buildings from Inca times. Only a few miles from Cuzco stands the proud and defiant fortress Sachsaihuaman, a reminder of the incredible skills of the Incas. It consists of cyclopic boulders, each many times as high as a man, so tightly sharpened and so keyed to the neighboring stones by re-entrant angles (the polygonal system) that even now it seems a needle could not penetrate between them. How they could have been moved and shaped to form the wall cannot be imagined. Truly, a miracle of human superiority and a victory over all natural obstacles. While we were looking at the fortress and down at Cuzco, with its narrow, cobbled streets, a shepherd appeared with llamas. We had been looking for llamas everywhere and had almost lost hope of seeing and photographing them—and here they came, against the most suitable and beautiful background, at a brilliantly sunny hour! We were in heaven, and most appropriately two Indian children in native clothing—a boy and a girl—ran down from the neighboring hill. The boy was playing a primitive flute and the girl was dancing to his tune. The scene was so charming that we did not even mind that it had been staged by their practical mother. We could see, in the distance, the hut from which she could watch for tourists at the fortress, then dress the children and send them out to gather tips.

A few years before our arrival, Cuzco had experienced an earthquake. There had been many casualties, and many historical buildings had been destroyed. Some were still lying in ruins, others had been restored, and the cathedral was being reconstructed. One of Cuzco's influential citizens told us that his city was a kind of "forgotten man" and that the catastrophe had been truly a blessing in disguise, forcing the Government to do something for Cuzco.

Who could leave Cuzco without seeing Machu Pichu, that marvelous Indian city perched atop lofty mountains, that mysterious treasure of the Indians, kept secret from the Spanish conquerors for some 400 years? Certainly not Wolik and I, even if we had to climb it on foot! Fortunately, a small, rickety train took us up there. At the top, we were overwhelmed by the sheer grandeur of the scenery, the breath-taking boldness of conceiving a city literally hanging in the clouds, the prowess of making this dream come true. What a people the Incas were!

Outside the capitals, we lectured in provincial universities and binational institutes, which gave us much insight into the life of each country. In Peru, the embassy wanted us to lecture not only in Lima, Arequipa, and Cuzco, but also in two small towns, Trujillo and Piura. At Trujillo, we visited several near-by projects of Servicios (cooperative organizations of Point Four and the host country) and the incredibly rich museum, with products of Indian tribes found in the pre-Incan ruins of Chan-Chan, and Chan-Chan itself. The museum shelves were crammed with pottery, hand-woven fabrics beautiful in pattern and surprisingly rich in color, articles made of obsidian, crystal, and other minerals—all of marvelous skill, many delicately chiseled. Other articles not yet sorted and registered were heaped on the floor. Many sites remain unexcavated, and friends, including embassy people, told us that they were still finding in the ground various objects of pre-Inca and Inca times, each of them keeping to himself "his" area of chance discovery.

An exciting surprise awaited us in Piura, a sleepy, dull town with nothing to see, nothing to do. Even the market was uninteresting. We walked aimlessly along the streets, and seeing a church, entered it—and were electrified. It was full of light; its walls were of beautiful bluish marble. Above the altar ran the words of a prayer carved in the marble, with musical notations. The church had not been completed, and workers were setting mosaic pieces on the floor and tools were lying here and there. A priest came up and asked gently, "Do you wish to visit my church? I shall be glad to take you around." Of course, we wanted to and we talked in three languages, mixing French, Spanish, and Italian. As we walked with him, we felt that he had come out of the Renaissance. "Everything inside has been brought from Italy, my native country— marble, mosaic, paintings, sculptures. There will be no dust in my church, no wood carvings to accumulate it. The walls will be water-hosed and clean. People come to the church to get relief, inspiration, to feel happy in the presence of God, not to be depressed."

We asked about the words and musical notations on the walls. "I play the organ and sing with the congregation. I could no more live without music than without bread."

In the crypt, he said, "See how much light there is even here, and there is also air conditioning. People should find consolation in their sorrow." To my question: "Padre, when will your church be completed?" he folded his arms piously and answered, with his eyes gazing up, "Only Providence knows." He told us that he had been born in a small town near Rome. When his father had taken him to Rome occasionally, he had been chiefly interested in architecture, even at the age of five. This had become his profession; his two brothers were medical doctors. When the Piura church was to be reconstructed under the auspices of Brothers Redeemers, they had turned to their office in Rome, and our padre, himself a Redeemer, had been chosen for that work. Somehow neither he nor we wanted to part, and he invited us to see his house and the patio. There he talked of each plant separately, and with touching pride he said, "Each has come from Florence. When I am taking care of them, I feel I am in Florence, and it warms my heart."

In Valdivia, Chile, both of us gave talks at the new university, and the following Sunday, the university arranged a trip for us to see the countryside. At the suggestion of the driver, we made a small detour to see a rodeo in the neighboring village. We could not have asked for more—a village festival without any other tourists, the Chileans attractively dressed for the occasion, the horsemen—one built better than the next, all courteous and poised—the excellent Chilean thoroughbreds, the festive tables of food, the beautiful weather, and the friendly Chileans, pleased to have admiring, happy guests.

The rodeo itself was much more attractive than the Western rodeo in the United States. The bulls were forced to run along the walls by the pressure of the horsemen riding alongside. The trick was to perform this maneuver gracefully, without forcing the bulls to their knees or harming them in any way. A hacienda owner, sitting proudly on his beautiful horse and reminding one of a feudal lord in an old painting, was the chief performer of the day. Among the horsemen, many were workers on his land, but one could not distinguish them that day from gentlemen, so freely and gracefully did they move around. We photographed many scenes of the rodeo, while the horsemen explained to us the essentials in the performance and told of Chile's famous rodeo performers. It was fun to be with the boisterous, friendly crowd!

On the way back, the conversation with the driver turned to lottery tickets, which are sold at every street corner in all Latin countries. Yes, he had been buying lottery tickets for many years. Did he ever win? No, never! Then he had been throwing his money away; he could have acquired something valuable for all the money he had spent on lottery tickets. His reasoning was different, and probably it is valid for all the little people who buy such tickets. "What my wife and I want above all is our own little place to live in. We know we shall never be able to save to buy one, and our only wild chance is to win in the lottery. The money we spend on the tickets wouldn't be saved anyhow—there are always too many things we need. And the lottery ticket— this is our way to dream, to hope. No, we would not give up our chance to hope." We were touched, and against our better judgment, bought two tickets for him, with the wish that he might see his dream come true.

On many occasions, we noticed how unwilling or unprepared the Latin middle-class people, the intellectuals and, of course, the higher strata of the population were to have anything to do with manual work. This attitude is instilled from childhood. In the streets, one would occasionally observe a husky boy on his way to high school accompanied by a little Indian girl, who carried his books. In the lounge of a hotel, several little girls came up to ask us about the United States. I wanted to know their names, and each gave hers until it was the turn of the youngest girl, about six or seven years old, who held a dog in her arms. One of the bigger girls said to me with a possessive air that this was her servant (*mi muchacha*) and so she did not consider it necessary to give her name. During our lecture at the university in Barranquilla, Colombia, the USIS representative who accompanied us, a tall, jovial Texan, caused a sensation when, in the discussion, he mentioned that in his student years he had worked in a butcher shop, cut and trimmed meat for the customers. The amazement on all faces was a sight to observe!

Yet, there were signs of changes. The car in which our Point Four representative was driving us, got a flat tire. To our surprise, the local agent of Point Four said to him, "Let me change your tire. You have on your best suit." This was almost a revolution in the way of thinking and acting, a true "Yankee" victory over tradition!

POINT FOUR

As we looked around, met people and traveled, the profile of life in Latin countries became more and more evident: poverty, illiteracy, inertia, unhygienic living conditions, on one hand, and carefree living, wealth, contempt for manual labor, on the other. We concluded that the source of poverty and degradation lay not so much in the lack of capital for investment and economic development (though this was a factor, too) as in the backwardness of agriculture, which employed the majority of the population but was incapable of providing enough food for the country even at its low nutritional standards. This backwardness was conditioned by obsolete forms of landownership and tenure, and by the illiteracy and poor health of the masses.

In many villages, the standard of living was no higher than in India, or even worse because of the severe, inclement climate. Some of the worst conditions we saw were in Tunja region, in northern Colombia. It was market day in Tunja; everybody, man or woman, was dressed in black. After the colorful, bright native markets in the Caribbean, black was particularly depressing. We were told that families were large and death was common, so black clothing was most economical.

The Point Four representative wanted to show us an "improved" farm. We drove several miles in search of that place and finally discovered it amidst rubble and filth. We entered the one-room house—no trace of furniture, no table, no chairs. In the right-hand corner was the "bed," a hole in the ground covered by dirty rags. The dirt floor was untidy, and the only sign of "improvement" was the oven, which had replaced the hearth of three stones in the middle of the room. The children, scantily clad, had sores on their legs and arms; the 4-S girl (4-S is the equivalent of 4-H in the United States) did not look a bit cleaner. Again, here was not only poverty but dull inertia. Winters in that region are cold, yet the family had had neither the energy nor the initiative to carry in at least the pieces of wood we saw lying about outside so as to have something to sit on instead of crouching on the icy floor.

We were encouraged to find much better conditions in central Colombia. There, the Point Four agent brought us to a farm shared by three generations: an old man, owner of the farm, and his wife; their two sons and three daughters, all married, and their children. This was obviously a substantial family. The rooms were furnished with chairs and tables, the windows had curtains, the floor was clean, and there were photographs and prints on the walls. While we were talking with the old couple, their grandson, a boy of fourteen, disappeared, and then returned in snow-white trousers and white shirt. He was slim, a little shy,

and as nice as only a boy of his age can be. A member of the 4-S club, he
had a project of his own: Point Four had given each boy a little pig on
condition that he raise it according to instructions. The pig remained
the property of the agency until it was repaid in kind from the first litter,
whereupon each boy then became full owner of the first pig and the
rest of the litter. Prizes were given for the best-tended pigs, and our
host's grandson had won a prize, which he showed us. The old farmer
was proud that the boy's pig was bigger and healthier-looking than his
"unscientific" pigs had ever been. Wolik took the boy's picture, and I
said to his grandmother, "I will call this picture the 'hope of Colombia.' "
She thanked me with tears in her eyes.

This was, of course, one of the best farms in the area but as we drove
along we saw a few other farms of about the same type—several windows in front, a wing at one side, a covered porch.

Many saw little promise in the work undertaken by Point Four in
cooperation with the local governments, its projects, the 4-S clubs, and
the like. Where they did operate, however, they were laying foundations
of lasting effect for future farmers, who, once they became of age, would
use their knowledge for more productive work and better living. Moreover, as we saw so clearly in Colombia, Peru, Ecuador, and Bolivia, the
youngsters were slowly influencing their parents to try new ways. We
spent a day in Bolivia with an American extension agent and 4-S boys
and girls who eagerly watched his every move in preparing the seed
beds and planting, and then followed his example, each on his or her
assigned plot. Another time a Peruvian extension agent took us to see
the work of the 4-S club near Trujillo, with seventy members—fifty of
them boys and the rest girls. They had plots provided by a hacienda
owner, for whom they worked all day for five sols (about 25 cents);
then, working in the evenings and at dawn at their own plots, they
earned five times as much. Some plots looked mediocre, others were excellent; the barn for raising chickens and rabbits had been built by
eighteen boys, each of whom had his own section.

Wolik calculated, with the agent, the cost of the project. The club
members had paid for everything we saw from their first harvest—tools,
seed, fertilizer; they had dug the ditches, built the road between the
plots. The cost to the extension service came to about $10 per boy for
three years' training. Each thereafter would probably produce four times
as much as he could have produced without training. In both above
cases, we were told, the parents of the young 4-S members were coming to
watch their work and were impressed by the results of new methods
applied by the youngsters.

As far as we could judge, the American extension agents and other
agricultural experts were accepted wholeheartedly in Latin American
villages. In one Brazilian village, we met a native agronomist and asked
him, "How do our agriculturists compare with the experts sent by the
FAO [Food and Agriculture Organization of the United Nations]?"
The reply of the Brazilian was: "The FAO people come to study us and

write reports about us. Your people come to live with us and show us how to produce more and better food."

Point Four had worked rather well in Peru largely because it had been a cooperative effort from its inception. The U.S. financial contribution was often only a fraction of the local funds; most valuable and most valued by the Peruvians was the technical help in planning the projects, supervising them, and training local people to take them over. We saw the name of this joint organization, Servicio, throughout Peru and visited many of its projects.

Servicio's Health Center in Peru was located in Rimac on the outskirts of Lima, the capital. Just as Lima, with its magnificent plazas, impressive churches, and monumental Government buildings, is not Peru, so Rimac, the hearth of misery and slums for its 150,000 inhabitants, is not Lima. The Health Center, a nucleus of a considerable organization for preventive medicine, had a small group of dedicated doctors, nurses, social workers, and sanitation experts. We talked with many of them—a surprisingly large proportion had studied in the United States, while others had visited here. Practical idealists, they were crusading for sanitation and cleanliness, saying that the enemy they were fighting was not only ignorance but also lethargy and suspicion, born of misery and helplessness.

We spent a day in Chosica's Normal School of Servicio, a small but beautiful teachers' college. The director impressed us by his emphasis on the quality of future teachers. He required the same educational standards for a teacher in a primary rural school as for one in a high school or vocational school. The rural teacher had the greatest responsibility of all, because his task was to lay the foundation for the whole educational system and because, for most of his pupils, education would be limited to what they learned in the rural school. Dedicated and competent teachers were therefore needed for primary schools, and they were entitled to equal pay and prestige with other teachers.

One day we visited the Servicio's School for Tropical Agriculture, located about twenty miles from the capital. Of the two directors, one was American, the other Peruvian. Among the teachers, we found to our surprise, were two women—a young Brazilian, pretty and vivacious, who was an expert in poultry; and the other older and more reserved; I do not remember her special field. There were about forty students; we saw them working in the field, cultivating the soil, digging a ditch. This was an impressive sight in a Latin country, where manual work is usually spurned! Yet the American director told us that his most difficult task was something else—to bring the students to trust one another. Distrust toward everybody else was so deep-seated that though they lived in an isolated school, they kept their meager belongings under lock and key.

Distrust was a rather common feature. A university professor told us that in sending an article to a magazine, he had to take all kinds of precautions to keep it from appearing under somebody else's name. In

Lima, during the lunch hour, the stores on the main avenue covered their doors and windows with padlocked shutters. I asked a merchant, "Is this an old custom, or do you really consider it a necessary protection?" "It is absolutely necessary" was his answer, and he was not impressed by my remark that window-shopping should be included among tourist pleasures.

October was approaching, and we were told that we would see women wearing a purple robe with a white cord around the waist and the picture of a saint on the breast, and that men would be wearing purple ties. Those who were dressed this way would be praying for forgiveness of a sin or asking for some Divine favor. On the second of October, we had invited a young Peruvian couple to dinner; he was a journalist, had spent several months in the United States on some kind of fellowship, and spoke English very well. He and his attractive wife had taken us for a drive one Sunday to show us the country and then to a restaurant for a meal with her father, who had just been discharged from an important Government position. A man of substantial means, he was planning to go into private business but, according to his daughter, was taking the loss of his socially eminent position rather hard. When the young couple appeared at the door, the first thing I noticed was that she was wearing a purple robe, and the first thing she said to me was, "Isn't it wonderful? I put this robe on only yesterday, and guess what happened today?" I looked blank, and she finished triumphantly, "Today my father was reinstated in his previous position. Isn't that marvelous?"

We grasped every opportunity to visit the rural schools. Often the school was a shack, a dilapidated house. On the way to Cuzco, we saw a school consisting of two classrooms divided by a flimsy screen. Some thirty children in each class sat shoulder to shoulder on narrow benches. The teachers invited us to see the work done by their pupils. We looked into several copy books and could not believe our eyes. The handwriting was neat and clear; there were drawings made with colored crayons. In the next grade, too, careful work. A pitiful school in terms of space, light, equipment, and sanitary condition, the children barefoot, some in rags, some perhaps unwashed since birth. But their eyes were bright, and the young teachers knew their job.

Several times we stopped to visit schools on the haciendas or estates. Some were adequate, others very bad. The worst one we saw in Ecuador had one classroom, more than 100 pupils, and not enough benches and desks. About thirty children were perched on the stairway leading to the attic. We were told that an additional school was to be built shortly, and we saw some building material in the yard.

After a visit to a pathetic school like that, the monumental and ostentatious luxury of some of the new Government buildings were particularly irritating. Friends asked us to tea at the Army Club in Bogotá. Observing the lavishness of the Club, Wolik said wonderingly, "I have always thought that our Army was bigger than that of Colombia, but we have nothing to match this splendor!"

Educational supplies and books were badly needed almost everywhere. The paucity of textbooks was unbelievable. Suffice it to say that
the professor of economic geography at the National University in
Santiago, Chile, wanting to consult Wolik on his subject, had brought
the *only* book on economic geography available, which had been received from CARE and which he, as the teacher, had kept. To him, that
book was a precious possession, and when we said that books of that type
and on that subject were counted by the dozen in the United States,
his eyes lit up. We thought that a little initiative might enable the
universities to obtain books and other publications from the United
States in exchange for university magazines and monographic studies.
Unfortunately, our aid agencies and Congress have not valued the importance of books as highly as that of some military equipment. We
appreciated this fact on our first day in Latin America. The USIS library occupied the first floor of the embassy's building in Bogotá. Before taking the elevator upstairs, we decided to take a look at the library. We introduced ourselves to the librarian, who said, "You have
come just in time to get the last glimpse of our library. We are closing
tomorrow." "Why?" "No appropriations." "Do you have regular readers?" "Yes, more than three hundred." We were speechless.

Wolik and I discussed our impressions of what we had seen and
heard, and again and again came to the conclusion that the plans for
economic development in Latin American countries exaggerated the importance of steel mills, chemical plants, and machinery-producing works
and neglected the problem of human resources. Wolik's favorite lecture
was on technical and human factors in economic development. "The
main task is to destroy the poverty of the poor," he would say. "The
difference between your country and the United States is not in how
the rich people live in our countries, but in how the masses of the people
live. Investment in the people, in their well-being, education, and health,
is the most profitable investment any nation can make!"

Some professors, including several university presidents, congratulated Wolik for his courage in expressing unpopular convictions, which
could break the spell of the prevailing theories of economic revival
through accelerated investment of domestic and foreign capital. But
more often than not, the economic planners were skeptical. One able
economist ridiculed Wolik's argument about the effect of mass illiteracy
on economic progress: "Education has no economic value in the village.
A big hacienda owner told me that he had never seen a literate worker
cut sugar cane with a machete better than an illiterate." Wolik replied,
"If you are satisfied with ancient methods of production, then indeed,
education is of no value. But you were telling me that you are planning
a modern economic system for your country. Such a system cannot be
built on illiteracy and machetes." In Brazil, a professor of economics
and an important figure in the country's planning for economic development said during the discussion that knowledge would reach the village
by "contamination" from peons who had worked a year or two in the

cities and returned home. The students, too, often argued for quick industrialization, minimizing the importance of elementary education.
But at the invitation for questions in Bela Horizonte, Brazil, a student
got up and said thoughtfully, "I have no questions. All I want to say is
that until tonight I had never heard that people are important in
economic development. Strange, I never thought of this, and I want to
thank the lecturer for the new vista he has opened up to me."

In Rio de Janeiro, we had an appointment with a ranking official in
the Ministry of Education described to us as an outstanding educator.
When we entered his office, he came out from an adjoining room, where a
conference apparently was going on, and asked the purpose of our visit.
Then he sent a clerk to get the printed materials on the educational
system in Brazil, and showed little disposition to spend more time with
us. Disappointed, we might have left him had he not said impatiently,
"What is the use of talking about education? Nobody is really interested in it. Education is not considered important in my country!"
Hearing this from an educator was startling, and Wolik replied that to
us, this was the crux of Brazil's future. Suddenly our host, who had continued to stand to indicate that he was busy, called to his assistant to
take his place at the conference, asked us into his office, and unbur-
dened himself: "You can't interest anybody in education, especially
elementary education. The middle class? Yes, they began to appreciate
it, but only for their youngsters. They support outlays for colleges, but
not for public schools. The labor unions? They ought to understand
that only education can open the way up for them. If they had sense,
they would fight for elementary education, but all I meet with is indifference!"

At times, it seemed as if he were talking to himself. He showed us
charts and tables illustrating conditions in every area of education in
Brazil, and told how he had failed again and again in his efforts to
arouse interest in what to him was a vital matter. Pleased to find kindred souls with understanding of his work, he embraced Wolik, shook
hands with me, and taking us to the elevator, said warmly, "God bless
you! I feel better after talking with you."

When the advantages of spending limited precious resources on
education were questioned during the discussion after one of my lectures
in Quito, Ecuador, I used the following argument: "I am told that a
thousand German and Austrian refugees settled in your city. They arrived without any property or money, without a knowledge of Spanish.
Within a decade, they not only have established themselves and are
making a decent living, but also are providing work for thousands of
Ecuadorians. Yesterday I visited the artistic workshop of one of these
refugees and saw sixty women working on looms and producing fine native textiles for export. What the refugees brought with them were
knowledge and skills, and these were more valuable than money. If they
had come with money, not skills, they would have become public charges
long ago. Now, suppose a thousand of your compatriots were forced, for

one reason or another, to move to a European country. What would become of them within a decade? You can figure this out yourselves."

Our Latin American friends repeatedly put this question to us: "Who needs your military equipment? If you arm us in the hope that we will play any role of importance in case your country is attacked, you flatter us and deceive yourselves. Our combined strength is no greater than that of a mouse in case of a new world conflict. All you achieve by sending us military equipment is to arm our Governments, often dictatorial, and to strengthen our military. Also, you encourage rivalry among our countries. When Chile gets some special equipment, a warship or new planes, Peru considers herself obliged to get them, too, and vice versa." We had no answer for this.

MEETING COMMUNIST OPPOSITION

Two hours before Wolik's lecture in Cuzco, the head of the university's exchange program, a known Communist, let us know that because of construction work, the lecture had been canceled. We had been warned in Lima that this had happened to an outstanding Spanish refugee and might happen to us. We were luckier than he. Shortly thereafter we had a visitor, a professor of law, who came to pay his respects to Wolik. On learning of the trick played by his Communist colleague, he expressed his indignation and asked Wolik if he would be willing to lecture before his class at eight the next morning. Wolik, pleased, said he would. In the morning, Professor T. came to take us to the university, where several posters announced the lecture and invited all students to attend it. Wolik gave his talk, the newspapers reported it, and several professors expressed their pleasure that the Communists had been outwitted.

In Bolivia, we encountered a Communist dean of the economic faculty. Actually we had wanted a chance to go to Sucre, the old capital, but instead the embassy had arranged our lectures in two Communist strongholds, Oruro and Cochabamba. We concealed our disappointment, but luck was with us. First, motoring across the Altiplano, the 12,000-foot plateau along the Andes, offered us not only beautiful mountain scenery but also glimpses into the hardships of life on stony, sterile soil in an ever-cold, windy region. The Bolivian economist who accompanied us pointed out, here and there, buildings or chapels where people had been killed in the bitter political strife. At several points, we met armed villagers. Then, unexpectedly, as we entered a mountain village, a scene from the pre-Spanish time unrolled before us. The entire population, dressed in fantastic, colorful costumes, with floating white feathers no less than some forty or fifty inches tall on their heads, were dancing, singing, shouting. Musicians were playing enormous instruments. We jumped out of the car and madly took pictures. Never did we see anything approaching this scene of unconcerned gaiety and picturesque, almost absurd costumes, amidst the world's highest mountains!

Wolik established immediate contact even here. He found a woman who seemed especially representative of that wild scene and indicated his desire to take her picture. In no time, her husband joined her, patted Wolik on the shoulder, and stood smiling with pride at being selected, with his wife, as the best performers at the festival!

Soon we reached Lake Titicaca and glided in a boat over its glittering water under the blue sky and bright sun. What more could one wish? From high-school years, the name "Titicaca" had been to both of us the symbol of something inaccessible, of something that one could not even dream of ever seeing, of something mysterious beyond description. We laughed like children, wanted to stay there a day, a week, a month.

Of course, we had to leave to reach Oruro the same evening. There, Wolik did not encounter the opposition we had anticipated. In fact, two students who had visited the United States confirmed his characterization of the American economy. Later, the college president and several teachers asked us to go to a near-by restaurant for a friendly conversation.

Next morning we visited the famous tin mines, nationalized by the revolution and almost idle, and saw the living conditions of the miners in the valley, the familiar, cheerless picture. Then we flew to Cochabamba. Our talks were scheduled as a part of "Economic Week," opening the academic year. As usual, we paid a courtesy call on the dean of the faculty, Dr. Anaya, and presented our two volumes on international economics to the university library.

The hall was packed with some four or five hundred students and professors. The dean introduced us in such flattering terms that we wondered where the Communist opposition was coming from. After the lecture, however, he cut the discussion short and said to Wolik, "That was a very interesting talk, but I disagree completely." Intrigued, I asked, "About what, Dr. Anaya?" "About everything. The United States is ruled by General Motors, Standard Oil, and Du Pont. The democratic apparatus is nothing but a veneer." He gave us the full Communist line on conditions in this country. The students gathered around us and listened. We argued at first, but seeing his thickheadedness, I said, "When you visit the United States, you will see how wrong you are." "I will go if you get me a visa," he replied.

Back at the hotel, we discussed the situation. Having been told that the dean was a Party member, we thought that he might cancel my talk next night; or the students might be indoctrinated and might not come. On the other hand, we did not want to close an avenue for reaching young minds or make it impossible for other lecturers to obtain an invitation. With all this in mind, we decided how we would handle the situation. On arriving at the university the next evening, we saw the notice of my lecture at the entrance. The faculty room was crowded, and the dean was sitting morosely in a corner. Wolik asked him for permission to say a few words to the audience before the lecture. Suspicious, the dean asked, "About what?" Wolik explained that he wanted to thank him for being tolerant and for letting him develop ideas with which he disagreed. The dean seemed pleased.

The hall was as full as the night before. Wolik got up and said that he wished to thank Dr. Anaya for giving him the opportunity to talk to them the preceding night despite the disagreement in their points of view. To us, he said, the difference between the free world and the totalitarian countries was, first of all, in freedom of thought and speech. Their dean had shown respect for academic freedom and, because of this, he said, turning to the dean, "The day may come when you will change your point of view and join our side." The audience applauded. After my lecture the dean thanked us for our contribution to Economic Week and invited the audience to join him in wishing us success in our lecture tour in Latin America, good health, and a safe return home.

ON THE ATLANTIC COAST

As we continued our trip—from Chile to Argentina, Uruguay, and Brazil—we became more and more aware of the distinct difference in the composition of the population and native ways of life. The Atlantic coast had been more readily open to immigrants from Europe than the Pacific side of the South American continent, while the impassable mountains made penetration overland nearly impossible. There are fewer Indians in the east-coast Latin American countries, and the original Spanish (and in Brazil, Portuguese) population had been diluted considerably by the influx of Germans, Italians, and other Europeans. In Argentina, particularly in its cities, English influence was of long standing. Except for several specific regions, such as northeastern Brazil or southern Argentina, the standard of living was substantially higher, and we did not see the appalling poverty of the west-coast Indian villages.

Nobody could call Argentina an underdeveloped country. Before Perón, it was the richest country in Latin America. Literacy was rather high, the middle class was considerable, the professionals constituted an important layer of the population, land was fertile and agriculture would have had every chance to be prosperous if the country had had a stable, strong, and democratic government. City businessmen concurred in this view. In Mendoza, for example, the president of the business association, in reply to Wolik's question as to what Argentina needed for economic development, said, "Freedom and a sound government."

The country was beautiful—we loved its spaciousness, its green fields stretching to the horizon, its magnificent mountain scenery, its fine cities. But when a member of the Municipal Council and his wife drove us to the edge of Buenos Aires, we saw along the railroad tracks the worst slums we had ever seen; slums plus bordels plus saloons of the most repulsive kind. We were told that the city was powerless against the politicians who protected their owners. From there, we drove to the imposing apartment buildings erected by Perón for his followers. The picture was not totally depressing; we spent the next day at a housing development built by cooperatives, where decent apartments were accessible to lower-middle-income groups.

One of our first lectures in Buenos Aires was at the National Academy of Science. Its president impressed us by his venerable appearance and his measured, quiet manner of speaking. He showed us the splendid library and conference rooms and said, "I have spent many years here in loneliness. Perón wanted to become a member of the Academy, but I opposed him on the ground that according to our statutes, only eminent scientists could become members. He did not consider it practicable to dissolve or close the Academy, so he forced some scholars to withdraw and canceled the membership of some others. I have been here all by myself." Several days later, Wolik gave a talk on the world population to a distinguished audience there.

We both lectured at the Argentinian-American Institute. Then Wolik caused quite a stir by expressing a desire to talk to the trade unions. The USIS had no contacts with the labor groups, and no other lecturer had ever asked for a meeting of that sort. This surprised us the more, because before our arrival, the USIS had printed two of Wolik's lectures in an edition of 25,000 copies and then, to satisfy the demand from the trade unions, had had to print another 25,000. Anyway, a contact was established after some search; Señor Gregorio, head of the textile union, one of the thirty-two so-called free unions that were opposed to the Peronista unions, came to see us at our hotel and we agreed on a day for the lecture.

On arriving at the union headquarters at 6 P.M., we were led to a small conference room where several union leaders were awaiting us. When the conversation stretched on for about two hours, we began to think that this was all Señor Gregorio had been able to arrange and, rather disappointed, were ready to leave. Just then someone came to announce that the meeting was ready. We were taken to a hall filled to capacity with no fewer than 500 people, and were told that a microphone had been installed in the large yard outside for those who could not be accommodated inside. People stood along all the walls throughout the meeting.

The chairman who introduced Wolik said that he had heard Wolik's name for the first time from President Aramburu, and so was particularly impressed by Wolik's desire to spend an evening with the workers. This was one of our finest meetings in Argentina. Wolik talked on Marxian theory and the modern economic system, and gave many suitable examples from the workers' life. He held the attention of his listeners to the end; the discussion lasted more than an hour, with questions coming even from the yard. Some questions were directed to me, and Wolik shifted others to me, which obviously pleased the audience, surprised to see such intimate collaboration. By 11 P.M., the meeting was over, and refreshments were served in another room, where fifty or more labor leaders assembled to continue the discussion and consult Wolik on various problems. When we left, I was presented with an enormous bouquet of red roses, and Wolik was thanked again and again for his interest in the trade unions.

Wolik was no less successful before the Forum of Free Enterprise, where the listeners, important landowners and businessmen, were interested to hear about the economic system of the United States and had many questions about the public sector of our economy, the role of the Government, the monetary policy, taxation, and so on.

We lectured also in Mendoza, Córdoba, and Rosario, thus gaining an insight into the life of the country. People in the provincial cities were usually very pleased to have visiting lecturers, so that before our arrival our calendar was filled with luncheons and dinners given by the university people, newspaper associations, municipal officials, and business groups; also, arrangements were made for visiting museums, monuments, and parks, and usually for outings, too. We were invited to a cherry harvest on a large farm, where we saw hundreds of cases packed with choice cherries for export to Brazil and later found a case of cherries in our car; to a bodega (wine cellar) in grape-raising and winemaking Mendoza; to schools, efficient modern plants. Nevertheless, we were able to steal an hour or two for ourselves here and there just to walk through the streets without an escort, take pictures, and occasionally talk to strangers.

We failed in only one matter in Argentina. We wanted to see some large haciendas and had received several invitations that, for one reason or another, ended up on Padre Corvy's shelf. However, we did spend a full day on an extensive, well-managed hacienda in Uruguay. The souvenir its owners insisted on sending to our hotel also found its place on the famous shelf.

We were very much interested in the political life of Argentina— under Perón and during our stay, on almost the eve of the first free elections in a decade. We were impressed by President Aramburu, who had promised free elections and was trying to educate the people to their importance. Unfortunately, the democratic forces were not united, and the main party—the Radical Party—was split by personal ambitions. To get elected, Frondizi split his party and, with the aid of Peronistas and Communists, obtained the necessary majority, thus destroying his country's chance for a stable democratic government. Many professors expressed their concern about the results of pending elections. The newly elected dean of the economics faculty in one large city frankly told us that if the new Government wanted to have someone else in his position, the change would be made; university positions were in the hands of the Government.

Professors in Latin countries were seldom devoted exclusively to teaching except for the so-called "contract" professorships. Lawyers and medical doctors usually took on teaching for prestige or for political reasons for two or three hours a week, often disappearing as soon as the bell rang for dismissal and having no contact whatsoever with the students.

Businessmen, agriculturists, and city people told us about the fear under which they had lived under Perón, when servants could not be trusted and not even their own children, who had been taught to report on what they had heard or seen at home. To us, this was a familiar story!

The Latin American countries that possessed oil fields, whether or not developed, greatly resented U.S. policy in this area. Rightly or wrongly, they accused this country of not wanting to help them unless they let the large American corporations participate. Many times we saw a defiant poster in various Latin capitals: "El Petroleo es Nuestro" (The oil is ours). There was a deep-seated distrust of the American oil companies for having interfered with internal policy and having pursued their own interests to the disadvantage of host countries. Strangely enough, that resentment was never extended to their own governments for having permitted such conditions to develop. For some political groups or leaders, this problem has overshadowed everything that the United States has done for their country, including Point Four aid, technical assistance, shipments of free food, and loans.

It was difficult to understand what really was the interest of the United States in opposing governmental oil operations in Latin countries and why it insisted that they develop their oil resources with the help of U.S. oil companies. The explanation given to us was that those governments were incapable of doing that job efficiently. Granted this, it still was questionable whether it was necessary to build up so much suspicion and nearly hysterical resentment about insignificant oil fields and feed the already passionate nationalism in those countries.

At the first round-table discussion at Brazil's Central Bank, Wolik expressed interest in the controversy raging around Brasília, the new capital in process of construction. We were immediately offered an opportunity to visit it. The Government's plane for four (the pilot, a Brazilian economist, and ourselves) took us to the interior of the country, where a new city was being created in a jungle. The model of the future city showed many original, even exciting, architectural features; some of the buildings promised to be exceptionally striking. The layout of the capital, with its government offices, diplomatic residences, university and schools and large boulevards was highly imaginative, and the idea of opening the interior and providing it with better roads was unquestionably sensible. Whether this was the most practical way to integrate the neglected interior into the country's economy and whether this grandiose undertaking was well-timed were, of course, other questions.

Our first impression of Brasília was "organized chaos," in which were participating some 20,000 workers imported from the crowded areas along the Atlantic coast. Barracks to house them, shops in shacks, banks and airline offices in hastily erected makeshift buildings, temporary residences for visiting officials, were scattered within an enormous acreage crisscrossed by unpaved, muddy roads.

We discussed with each other the wisdom of this undertaking from the economic point of view, but we were fascinated, nevertheless, by the scope of the plan, by the flight across the unexplored country and everything we saw in Brasília. Because of the unfavorable weather, the pilot suggested postponing the return to Rio de Janeiro until next morning. The family of the Finance Minister, who happened to be in Brasília, invited us to stay with them in the temporary building. Sitting in a candlelit room and hearing the raindrops beat against the roof and the windows, I saw myself back in my father's brickyard works in Siberia. Our host's little boys found their way to Wolik's heart and soon started calling him the "Grandpa of Brazil."

Some magic about Wolik attracted children to him everywhere. I cannot say what it was—his soft smile, twinkling eyes, the friendliness with which he watched them move around, his way of talking to them, his animated interest in their games and pranks. All I know is that they unerringly selected him among all the adults. At Copacabana Beach, several boys noticed Wolik in the water; one came up to him, asked some questions, and in no time he was surrounded. Swimming around him, they continued the conversation, laughing and obviously enjoying his company. Another time, in Santos, the coffee port of Brazil, we asked directions of two youngsters; they attached themselves to us, showed us the city, treated us to sugar-cane juice squeezed in a most primitive way at a stand (there was no way to refuse that unfamiliar liquid) and generally were eager to hear about the United States, Russia, the world. Interestingly enough, one of the youngsters said to us, "Brazil is the most democratic country in the world. There is no discrimination of any kind here."

Speaking of Copacabana Beach, it was some excitement to take a dip on the last day of December and then at night merge with the huge crowd and watch the voodoo rituals, with endless candles illuminating the water, hear the mysterious songs, see thousands of people kneeling before the Queen of Water. There was much laughter, noise, gaiety in the air, and a beautiful sky full of brilliant, glittering stars over our heads.

In the morning of that same day we were in the business section of Rio de Janeiro and unexpectedly saw how the office secretaries and clerks celebrated the last day of the year. All the windows in the office buildings were open, and out of them flew the outgoing year's calendars. The air was full of little sheets of paper, and the pavement was blanketed with them.

In nearly all Latin American countries, we met Spanish refugees from Franco, German and Austrian refugees from Hitler, and Russian refugees from Stalin. The latter, the oldest, were almost all naturalized citizens. Our name in the newspapers told them, of course, that we were from Russia, and one or more would attend our lectures or call on us at the hotel.

Our most colorful caller was in Salvador (or Bahia), Brazil. Returning to the hotel after a lecture, we found a note in the letter box: "Having learned of your arrival in our city, I consider it my duty and privilege to welcome the famous Russian economist. Would you please make me happy by calling me up in the British Club." Signed: Ataman of Kuban Cossacks, General So-and-so (I do not remember the name). The combination of the title Ataman of Cossacks and the British Club in a provincial city of Brazil was, to say the least, bizarre. Amused, we called up the General and asked him to come for a drink. He came loaded with a bulging brief case. Rather short, with military bearing, he ceremoniously kissed the hand of "the Russian woman" and greeted Wolik with emphatic respect.

No encouragement was needed to get the General's unusual life story. As soon as we sat down, he pulled out of the brief case notebooks with pictures, newspaper clippings, letters from VIPs, and so on. In short, he had been the commander of a large Cossack unit in the White Army organized in Russia against the Communist *coup d'état;* had been heavily wounded; raised to the status of a general and, together with the remnants of the defeated White Army, sought refuge in Yugoslavia. Young, enterprising, with no hope of returning to Russia, he wanted broader horizons. In search of them, he wrote to the presidents of all the Latin American countries, offering to establish an efficient agricultural colony of 200 Cossacks if their transport, land for settlement, and working equipment were provided, partly or fully, on a loan basis. A favorable answer came from Peru. He assembled 200 strong-bodied, healthy, energetic Cossacks, chartered a boat, and arrived, with man and horse.

Telling of the impression made by the appearance of his cavalcade in Lima, on the Plaza de Armas, he became eloquent, almost poetical. Well he might be! We could visualize the crowds of short Indians excited and almost terrified at the sight of slender, tall, well-built Cossacks, splendidly dressed with two rows of cartridges adorning their breasts. Some marched solemnly, others rode on beautiful horses. The President of Peru came out to welcome them. The crowd went wild when some Cossacks, skillful horsemen, jumped and, standing erect on their horses, rode around the Plaza. Probably the Peruvians had not seen anything of the kind since the appearance of Spanish conquerors. Mass was said in the cathedral, and his men charmed the Peruvians by their powerful trained voices.

There can be no doubt that the Cossacks, excellent agriculturists, could have organized a model settlement of high productivity that would have benefited not only them but the host country. Unfortunately, the propitious beginning had a poor ending. After the festivities in the capital, the Cossacks took up the area assigned to them and waited for the equipment to work the land. But they were asked first to build roads to connect their area with the neighboring city. Though unfamiliar with road construction and eager to settle down, they complied, built roads and housing accommodations. Then they began to ask more vigorously for the promised equipment. Apparently, there were some irregularities in the handling of appropriations. Accusations and counteraccusations forced the General to go to Lima to appeal to higher authorities. His romance with the daughter of a Cabinet member further complicated matters. Finally after negotiations and troubles, he and his men became frustrated by the red tape and the difficulties of the unfamiliar language and ways of life. He then suggested that those who felt dissatisfied should return to Yugoslavia, while he would organize a chorus from those who remained.

If I remember correctly, fewer than 100 stayed on. Then a new epoch began, in which his chorus toured all the Latin American countries. Again pictures, clippings, letters of praise and congratulation, appeared on the table. They traveled throughout Latin America and were acclaimed everywhere for their singing, dancing, fancy riding. His group continued to shrink. Some Cossacks married Latin American girls and left, others found new professions, some died. After several decades, his chorus was dissolved, and now the General was living on a small pension or salary from the Government of Brazil, functioning as the Ataman of some 2,000 Cossacks scattered throughout that country. He knew them all, supplied information and certificates at Government request, and so on. Our last question: "What was his connection with the British Club? "Very simple. The chef was one of his Cossacks."

The General talked for an hour or longer with great animation, but when he finished, he suddenly looked like a punctured balloon. There was nothing more to talk about. He was happy to tell his life story and relive it once more. Amused, we were good listeners, but we were worlds apart. All he could do was to leave. He collected his precious possessions, bowed, thanked us for the pleasure of meeting us, and left.

Wolik gave a talk on the U.S. Social Security system before the Brazilian trade unions. In command of every detail of that system, he presented a well-rounded picture of its operations. We could hardly believe our ears when one listener after another got up to attack it: "You want your people to work until they are sixty-five years old before they get benefits? How can you be so cruel? Who wants to, who can, work to such an old age? We want to stop working at fifty-five or fifty and have some years of leisure and rest." When Wolik said that in the United States many people did not want to retire at sixty-five and preferred to work till seventy or longer, the chairman, somewhat embarrassed, tried to explain the difference in attitudes. "You have to understand that in our tropical, damp climate, people age sooner, are exhausted earlier, than in the temperate zone. Also, you cannot compare the working conditions in your country's airy, well-lighted, comfortable plants with those in our stuffy, unclean, crowded factories, insufficiently lighted, with poor seating facilities, and so on. Housing conditions are also very different. We want to retire earlier because life in our country is shorter than life in the United States. Each one of us hopes to have at least a couple of years of leisure before he dies."

The more we traveled, the more we were impressed by the quality of the newspapers in Latin America. In Montevideo, the capital of tiny Uruguay, the local papers could match practically any U.S. paper except *The New York Times*. Latin American dailies were on a higher cultural level than ours; like most important European newspapers and pre-Soviet Russian newspapers, the Latin American dailies published not only serious economic and political articles but also extensive essays on literature and art, both local and international, and historical and other scientific articles. To us, this was an indication of the importance of the intellectuals and the growing middle class in Latin countries; without them, such papers simply could not exist. The papers carried fewer pages of advertising, but found space to reproduce some of Wolik's lectures verbatim. Much space was always devoted to happenings in the United States, in contrast to our papers, which print information on Latin American countries chiefly when there is a revolution, an earthquake, or a visit by the American President.

Of course, the United States is a single country, in contrast to some twenty countries south of the Rio Grande. Nevertheless, they resent being neglected and taken for granted. One professor said to us, "Every schoolchild in our country knows of George Washington. Who in your country knows of Bolívar?"

Really, why couldn't our large newspapers devote a page or two weekly or biweekly to life in Latin America—not only political events but also cultural and educational matters, their literary best-sellers, paintings, and architecture—and occasionally publish articles by outstanding Latin writers, historians, political journalists, and economists? We sensed a great reservoir of good will for the United States, and were told again and again that while the eyes of their educated classes had always been turned toward France, Italy, and other European countries, the psychological orientation has been shifting toward the United States, particularly since the war. On various occasions professors, businessmen, students, and even workers, farmers, and soldiers told us that they would like to live in the United States or to visit it. Curiosity about this country was noticeable everywhere. This does not mean that we did not meet with criticisms of the United States. Of course, we did! But what about the statements in this country of Latin America? Are they always complimentary, and how much real knowledge do they show?

Indeed, we did not always find real interest and knowledge about Latin American countries among our representatives there. Several times we were surprised to learn that our cultural attachés had little contact with the university people. In two very important Latin American countries, we introduced our cultural attachés, who had been there for some time, to the president of the university in the capital. In one of the largest Latin American countries, our officials had not known any economist on the university faculty. In other instances, in contrast, we met local intellectuals who were on the best terms with our officials, and we saw how effectively the two sides cooperated.

Some features of American life were especially appreciated and had inspired economic thinking and planning. First of all was the Tennessee Valley Authority. We saw its influence in the project for integrated regional development in Chillan, in Chile; in the Cauca Valley Project, in Colombia (referred to by local people as the Lilienthal Plan, because David Lilienthal had greatly contributed to its formulation); in the Papalcapan, in Mexico; and in various development plans in Brazil. Collaboration between the American and local staffs was at its best, and at none of those projects did we hear anything but praise for the U.S. approach to regional problems.

Our itinerary listed Venezuela as the last country in South America (we did not plan to stop in Paraguay). But a day before our departure from Brazil, the embassy received a telegram from Caracas about the troubled political situation there and the expected fall of the dictatorial government of Jiménez. Clearly, the time was not favorable for our lectures. So instead of Venezuela, we left for Puerto Rico, where we spent ten enjoyable days, lecturing, meeting Government and academic people, visiting schools, housing developments, plants. After six months in South America, it was a wonderful relief to be under the umbrella of the U.S. Public Health Service with fresh water and unpolluted milk!

IN MEXICO AND THE CARIBBEAN

We were familiar with Mexico and several Caribbean countries, particularly Guatemala, each of which we had visited several times and crisscrossed in different directions. But those had been tourist trips for the sheer pleasure of hiking and relaxation, without commitments and programs, away from everything and everybody. This time every day had been arranged well in advance, without prior consultation with us. Though the schedule was frequently crammed, we never objected, even when Saturdays and Sundays were chock-full of meetings. Still, naïvely believing that we could dispose of Sunday at least, we decided to postpone our flight from Port-au-Prince, Haiti, to Kingston, Jamaica, until Monday morning so as to enjoy at least the "rehearsal" of Mardi Gras in Haiti, and we rearranged our airline reservation accordingly. Told of this, our cultural attaché in Port-au-Prince invited a large group—both Americans and Haitians—to his home for Sunday afternoon to meet us. Since almost no one had a home telephone, the invitations went from the embassy by mail. The telephone system, we had been told, was still operating as it had been installed and left by the U.S. Marines in 1915.

A tragicomedy followed. Returning on Saturday night to the hotel, we found a letter from another embassy official about an urgent request from Jamaica that we come on Sunday as scheduled; he would call early in the morning to discuss the matter. Our first move was to try to reach him or the cultural attaché by telephone. Not finding their numbers in the directory, we called the embassy, and the marine stationed there told us that no one but the Ambassador had a telephone at home. In the meantime, a long telegram from Jamaica arrived: our broadcast had been arranged for 2 P.M. on Sunday; there was to be a cocktail party for us with university people, a dinner at the Finance Minister's home. At the end came an irritated question, "Jamaica wants to know why Woytinskys cannot come on Sunday?" Unwilling to get the ambassador out of bed for such a triviality and unable to get in touch with anybody else in the embassy, we capitulated and decided to give up the festival and the rest of the plan.

But would we be able to obtain flight tickets? At eight in the morning, I went to the airline office, while Wolik stayed at the hotel to await the visit of the embassy official. The airline clerk told me that the plane was fully booked; I insisted, and he began to look for another flight, with a stop at the other end of the island. Just as I was preparing to accept this, the manager arrived, looked up the list of passengers for the first flight, and declared that we were on the list: Our cancellation had been overlooked. That is how things work in Haiti!

After that, we never suggested the slightest change in the prearranged schedule.

In the fifteen years since we had last seen Mexico, it had changed greatly. One no longer saw barefooted Indian women in the streets of Mexico City or babies hung on their mothers' backs as before. The markets, once crowded and filthy with rotten refuse, were clean, with drinking water fountains scattered here and there. The butchers wore white aprons and hats; fruit and vegetables were neatly arranged. The place around the Guadalupe Shrine, once a nightmare of stench and filth, had been cleared of market stands; the access to the cathedral was paved. Standing there, we watched dozens of people, mostly women, traverse the great length of that plaza on their knees while over at one side colorfully dressed Mexican actors were performing an old play about the arrival of Spaniards in Mexico.

Wherever we looked, we discovered signs of change. But as we traveled from the capital to provincial cities and then to villages, such signs were fewer and fewer. Still, progress was noticeable everywhere—progress inspired by the country's long-drawn-out revolution and by the impact of the United States example.

In the beautiful city of Guadalajara, next in importance to Mexico City, we met people active in state and local government. One of them, Señor F. M. Ascensio, the state treasurer, devoted a day to showing us what they were doing and trying to achieve. After taking us to some of the best housing developments and a charming kindergarten within one of them, he drove us to the slums, from which they could only slowly move people to better living facilities.

I shall never forget our pathetic walk through a dark corridor to the interior court of a compound crisscrossed by narrow alleys, with low, windowless barracks on each side. The ground was littered with trash, in which naked children with bulging bellies crawled and rummaged.

Then we passed a long row with public latrines on one side and laundry tubs on the other. At each tub was a woman. As we walked, Señor Ascensio ahead of us, he closed the door to each latrine. That it never occurred to any of the women to close the doors to the stinking latrines was the worst mark of human degradation one could imagine. I was glad Señor Ascensio did not have to face us, for I felt his embarrassment perhaps as strongly as he did. All he said when we were out of that compound was, "How can you expect people to be civilized and be good citizens when they have never lived in decent conditions?"

Yet there was also much cheer and fun in Mexican life. In a small town one evening after dinner, we stepped out of the hotel to get some fresh air before going to bed. In the streets, we noticed people moving in one direction; we followed them and came to a little church where, we were told, the saint of the day was to be celebrated. In half darkness, two men brought some contraption of wood and straw and erected it in the center of the churchyard, surrounded by an iron fence. What followed was one of the most brilliant, imaginative fireworks we had ever seen. First, a silver rain started to drop around the contraption, and children began to dance under the rain. Then the figure of the saint with the halo around his head, began to climb slowly up and up a flaming ladder. When he reached the top, he stretched out his arms as if to bless the crowd, which broke out in some religious song. The naïveté and yet the artistic skill of these fireworks, put together with the most meager of means and by the cooperative efforts of nearly everybody, and the spontaneous participation of the crowd in the festivities, made this a charming spectacle. How much better than the expensive official fireworks in Washington on the Fourth of July!

As in Brazil, where the Government arranged our trips to Brasília and Volta Redonda, so in Mexico, the Ministry of Public Utilities arranged a two-day trip for us to see Mexico's Tennessee Valley project, then to the newly constructed electric installations, already in operation. These trips not only provided us with economic and technical impressions and information, but also gave us some insight into the election campaign then in full swing in Mexico. On entering each village, we saw from afar huge posters with the portrait of the presidential candidate, covering the entire wall of the first house. As we drove on, party signs, posters with single sentences from the candidate's speeches, promises, resolutions of the labor unions to support him, succeeded one another. We asked the economist who accompanied us whether such an intensive campaign was really necessary. He shrugged his shoulders: "Evidently, yes!" On another occasion, a journalist rather skeptical of the Government policy said, "In your country, people may not be free during the whole year, as some here pretend, but they are entirely free on election day, when nobody knows in advance what the results will be. In my country, the situation is the reverse: we are free the whole year, but on election day we all vote the same ticket."

In the poorest of all the Caribbean countries, Haiti, we were moved when the dean, after Wolik's lecture at the university, said to the students: "We envy the United States for having such an ambassador of good will, who has found for even our poor little country, words of friendship and encouragement, words that we have seldom heard before." We visited the newly built church, with murals painted by local artists. The scene of the Last Supper was indicative of the people's feelings. Christ and the disciples were depicted as black men except for Judas, who had a white face!

The attitude toward Wolik in Latin America had a special quality. To the intellectuals there, he was more than an American. He was a world citizen, born in Russia, thoroughly familiar, from personal experience, with nearly every European country (thus with the countries of their origin), *and* an American whose ideological equipment embraced the whole world. To the labor leaders in Latin America, he was *their* man, who had been all his life in close contact with the labor movement—in Russia, Germany, France, and other European countries, and in the United States, who had written many studies on the workingmen's problems, with whom they felt at home. They especially appreciated the fact that despite his world-wide reputation as a scholar, he wanted to meet them and talk with them. This combination created an atmosphere of intimacy that is difficult to express in words but that all felt keenly. Among the intellectuals, some could converse with him in English, older people often talked to him in French or German; he began to understand Spanish and even Portuguese, and occasionally could answer a question during the discussion, without awaiting my translation. Wolik was well acquainted with the political history of the Latin American countries and knew the realities of their economic conditions. All this made for easy communication, for an unrestrained, warm exchange of ideas and knowledge. His unaffected, eager interest in every feature of life, the glint in his eyes as soon as something new came to his attention, drew people to him. Of the many articles written about us in the Latin American press, I will quote only one:

> The distinguished economists are a couple that, in addition to their great contribution to the understanding of many basic problems of our time, offer the fascinating attraction of their literary knowledge, of the dangers that they courageously faced together and of their intimate collaboration in service of science, that is, of truth. Hence the halo of human sympathy which surrounds them, strengthening in many ways the well-deserved respect for their high scientific qualities.

Of course, the author had Wolik in mind, first of all if not exclusively.

We did not notice such striking changes in Guatemala as in Mexico. The capital city seemed to have a little more business than before, more traffic. Tourism had grown; old hotels in favorite tourists spots, such as at Lake Atitlan, had expanded and new hotels had opened. In Quetzaltenango, the city second in importance to Guatemala City, there was even less change, except for the new university buildings, including the new library, called Lincoln Library.

Our schedule in Guatemala followed the familiar pattern—we talked in the universities and binational Institutes, met official and academic people. University life was affected by internal conflicts, often politically colored. Some professors tried to ingratiate themselves with the students, sought their support. The students dominated the streets. One day they would demonstrate against the university administration; the next day they would march to ridicule church processions. They were an unruly group.

There was still, under the ashes, a smoldering resentment against the U.S. intervention in Guatemala's affairs. Whether the accusations were true or false no longer mattered; sides were taken and changed, and some kind of dissatisfaction colored all the discussions. We did not seek political discussions, even tried to avoid them as fruitless, particularly since we were not informed on the many details used in the arguments and counterarguments. Yet, politics crawled into almost every conversation.

Between meetings and lectures, we went to the picturesque native markets, a never-weakening attraction in that small country. This time we could talk directly with the people, inquire about their life, their children, their way of making a living, their crafts. What a difference it made to dispense with the interpreter!

While in Quetzaltenango, we decided one day to drive up to a mountain village that, we were told, still lived its own secluded life, unaffected by civilization. We left the car at some distance from the village and hiked in one direction, then in another. In the village, we saw African-type tents on both sides of a dirt road. From one tent, two men wearing pink coats with embroidered sleeves emerged. We wanted to talk with them, but they were reticent and answered monosyllabically. Just when we were ready to believe what we had heard of this remote village, shrill sounds broke the air—somebody had turned on the radio in one of the tents.

A little incident showed us that an intelligent worker could still be superior to a mechanized attitude in production.

While I was filming the beautiful rain forest in Puerto Rico, I heard a strange click inside my camera and realized with a sinking heart that something inside had broken. It was late Saturday, and early the next morning we flew to Cuba, then to Haiti, and finally, Jamaica. In none of these countries could I get my camera repaired. Only passionate amateurs can understand how I felt—especially in Haiti, a paradise for photographers—with a broken camera in my hands. It was maddening! My last hope was Mexico City. Immediately on arrival, I went to the largest photographic store, which had a big repair department. Yes, they could fix the camera; a broken spring needed replacement. The camera would be ready next afternoon. Alas, next day I was told that that spring was not available; it was ordered from the United States by telegraph.

After three weeks of disappointment, we left Mexico with the camera unrepaired. In Guatemala City, there was a little camera shop across from our hotel. Discouraged by my fruitless efforts, I did not even want to try again, but Wolik insisted and so I went. The store owner sent me to his repairman around the corner. He took the camera into the darkroom, and on reappearing, said that while he could not replace the broken spring, he would shorten it, and since only the very tip of it had come off, I would hardly notice the difference. Next morning I had my camera, and I never replaced the spring.

In El Salvador, the interest of the economists was concentrated on the possibility of organizing a common market of the five small Caribbean countries—El Salvador, Costa Rica, Honduras, Guatemala, and Nicaragua. Wolik was consulted on its prospects. He supported the plan for its various features, one of which was the possible encouragement for developing the industrial plant for the regional instead of the much too limited domestic market of each individual country. Asked to give his judgment on the recession in the United States, he said that he was confident of an early pick-up in business, basing his opinion on the first small but telling changes in the economic indicators.

Friends from the embassy took us to a tiny mountain village where the entire population, adults and children alike, were engaged in preparing the tiniest curios—Easter eggs, toys, even a tiny farmhouse with a poultry yard, people occupied in various jobs, animals, a cat on the roof of the house or barn—all this on a board perhaps 5" x 7" or 6" x 8". Some of these articles were so minute as to be hardly discernible without a magnifying glass, yet each was painted in different colors and made true to form. We had bought some articles of this sort years ago in a curio shop, on our first trip to El Salvador. Now we wanted to see that village with its people and workshops.

Jamaica does not belong to Latin America, but we included it as a Caribbean country. The contrast between Jamaica and the neighboring Haiti was overwhelming. One had just become independent; the other had been independent for more than 100 years. Yet in everyday life, literacy, and the caliber of public officials, university people, and journalists, standards were so much higher in Jamaica than in Haiti that to compare them would almost be like comparing day and night.

Jamaica had inherited the British Civil Service, and we were impressed by the intelligence and broad knowledge of various members of the Cabinet. The Prime Minister, Mr. Manley, charmed us with his quick understanding of every question raised, his excellent formulations, his wit, his broad outlook. The University of Jamaica was of a rather restricted British type for the top layer of the society, but apparently it was planning to open its doors wider. We gave talks there and radio interviews, taped three more broadcasts, and gave a page-long interview to Peter Abrahams' weekly, *Public Opinion*. Thanks to the intimate relationship between our cultural representative and local intellectuals —writers, painters, newspapermen, teachers—we met many more people in Kingston in eight days than in some other countries in a fortnight.

Jamaica's scenery is superb, the vegetation is rich beyond description, and the local crafts are very attractive. No wonder we would have preferred to remain there longer, but our rigid schedule permitted no such indulgence.

We completed the tour of Latin America convinced that here, as in the Far East, there was a stirring for a change, some change, any change. We sensed everywhere a great restiveness among the intellectuals, and hence a vague dissatisfaction and instability in thinking. The masses, too, were affected by this attitude—more in some countries, less in others —but all seemed drawn toward something that held promise of better times. There was no stagnation, even though progress often seemed very slow indeed.

The main question was how to direct life into new, fresh channels. We stressed the necessity of making greater efforts in education, which creates new demands, raises the quality of work, stimulates initiative and independent thinking, and is the foundation of the economy in our technological age. We were not at all sure, however, that we had made any headway in getting those ideas across, though we had found strong support here and there. In India, we had been told that there were a million college graduates without jobs who spent their time in fruitless discussions—what use would it be to have more of them? We wondered why those graduates did not go to the villages and small towns to spread knowledge, as Russian youth had gone in Tsarist times. In Latin America, too, every country was seeking the golden fleece of fast industrialization. If we had talked about building more factories and increasing the investment in industrial plant as the most urgent need of those countries, we would have been much more to the liking of many local economists.

We never heard mention of the practicability of using several shifts for fuller utilization of existing industrial capacity or of attempts to increase the productivity of labor and thus equalize, at least approximately, prices of domestically produced goods and those imported from abroad. If efforts in these and similar directions had been undertaken, perhaps some resources for educational needs would have become available.

Finally we were on the plane to Washington. We were in good spirits. According to the opinion of our embassies and the statements of university people and press and Government officials in Latin America, the lecture tour had been a success. Personally, we had learned a great deal in those eight months about the individual countries, their political history, their long-range and immediate needs and problems, the attitudes of the various socio-economic groups. A name like Concepción, or Guayaquil, or Manaus, which we might not have known at all or of which we might have had only a vague recollection from high-school geography, now brought to mind a picture full of life and of people we had met, a distinct place with its own problems and attractions.

There were many wonderful things to remember—the invariable

friendliness with which we were received everywhere, the generous attention of the press, the genuine interest of the students in our, particularly in Wolik's, lectures, the many fruitful and pleasant contacts with
the intellectuals, the chivalrous attitude toward me as a woman and a
member of the team, the gorgeous scenery, the easily approached people
in the markets, in the villages and city streets. We left Latin America
charmed and grateful, like warm friends who loved much in it and also
deplored much in it, and wished and hoped for changes to better ways
and higher standards of living.

12. *Our Last Years*

BACK HOME! Again that wonderful feeling of privacy, which one never has in a hotel! We were sick and tired of changing countries, cities, hotels, beds, of constantly being with people, often not of our choice, of seldom being alone! Just to stay home—in the house or in our lovely garden—seemed like heaven!

The Department of State arranged a meeting for us with the analysts of the Latin American countries. We reported our impressions and answered questions about individual countries. Since we had found that good will toward the United States prevailed in spite of various grievances and criticisms, our over-all appraisal was that there was an encouraging climate for cooperative efforts in the interests of the United States and Latin America.

This meeting occurred on the eve of Vice-President Nixon's visit to Latin America, where so explosive a reaction awaited him. Though we did not expect the violence he faced, we had no doubt that a friendly reception for him was out of the question. Nobody who had branded the New Deal period as "twenty years of treason" or with similar epithets could then, or can now, expect to be received as a friend south of the Rio Grande. It was enough to enter any of the Latin American countries to see that they venerated Franklin D. Roosevelt. From most airports, we drove along F.D.R. boulevards, past F.D.R. hospitals, libraries, high schools, youth organizations. Even among the conservative groups in Latin America, there was recognition and appreciation of F.D.R.'s Good Neighbor policy. Nobody known to have attacked him could then, or can now, be welcomed by the university students in any Latin American country. Only sheer complacency and ignorance of the political attitudes of the students could have led one to expect that students would listen and argue with so bitter an opponent of F.D.R. as Mr. Nixon.

We were very sorry to see that much of the good work done by Point Four and the USIS in Latin America was destroyed unnecessarily and clumsily by that incident. The reaction of the American press and policymakers was more than awkward; to us, it was pathetic in its lack of understanding of the prevailing attitudes in the Latin American countries, particularly among the students. The assumption seemed to be that we needed only to supply more money to reverse the students' attitudes.

Wolik used his own weapon to bring Latin America closer to the thinking public in our country—the written word. He wrote a series of articles on Latin America for the *New Leader,* and other articles for Spanish and Portuguese magazines, which were printed and commented on in the Latin American press. He also wrote a pamphlet, *The U.S. and Latin America's Economy.* After our trip to the Far East, the Department of State had asked us to prepare a pamphlet on questions about the United States and our answers to them, and this had been published for the benefit of other American lecturers. Now we offered to prepare a similar pamphlet on Latin America (in both cases, without remuneration, of course), but there was no special interest and the reply was negative.

We then turned to our personal problems, the most urgent of which was Wolik's eyesight.

CATARACT OPERATION

Several months before we had left for Latin America, cataracts had begun to form on both of Wolik's eyes. The ophthalmologist found the condition not ready for surgery, and Wolik continued to work as usual, from early morning till night. Occasionally he complained of a deterioration in his vision, and at night, the street lights bothered him. Though he loved driving, he gave it up, being unsure of his vision.

During our tour of Latin America, his vision became more and more affected. He no longer could read at a glance the notes and statistical data that he carried with him for his lectures. On our return to Washington, the doctor examined Wolik's eyes and could not understand how Wolik had managed to read, write, and even take pictures with only a fraction of normal vision. He did not know Wolik's unyielding attitude toward physical impairment, his energy and persistence. Nobody but me had noticed what strenuous efforts were required for him to work with his gradually deteriorating eyesight, and I could not help him because he did not want to concede physical defeat.

Now the doctor recommended surgery on one eye in a fortnight. Though we were assured that removal of a cataract was routinely successful, one could never be wholly certain. I searched the library for articles on cataract and its removal. We continued to work but we were worried, though we managed to appear cheerful. Shortly before the operation, Wolik said, "I will be satisfied if I can work at least two hours a day." This remark hit me like a bullet, but I said reassuringly, "After the operation you will work more than you do now, and that is what bothers me—you may forget our plans to go to the Fiji Islands and Tahiti."

Wolik worked until the last minute before going to the hospital; I took him there straight from the examination of a Ph.D. applicant at George Washington University, in which he participated as a member of the board. Wolik disliked taking drugs, regarded medicine as a nuisance, and found himself a hospital patient for the first time in his life, unless one counts his faked stay in a prison hospital in an attempt to escape.

At the last moment, the hospital was not able to provide the promised private nurse. It was imperative to keep the patient from touching the operated eye. I was afraid that Wolik, when sleeping, might press the eye or try to remove the patch, and insisted on staying with him at least the first three nights. With that permission and even a cot, I sat through those nights, reading to him and watching him. Of course, I also stayed with him during the day. With both eyes bandaged, he was as helpless as a child, and I fed him and read to him until he became drowsy. Uncomfortable as he was in bed, he dictated to me the articles about our impressions of Latin America for the *New Leader*. I copied them a few days later when I could return home for a night's sleep.

The doctor was positive that the operation had been successful. We were hopeful of recovery, but Wolik was very impatient, and we counted the days until the unoperated eye could be uncovered, until he could leave the hospital, until the patch could be taken off the operated eye, until the new glasses were ready. All this took about two months. At home, too, I fed and nursed Wolik, read to him, took his dictation on articles, aware of his constant yearning to become independent and able to move around freely. At times he became discouraged at the slow pace of recovery, and so I stressed every tiny improvement. Finally, the big day arrived—Wolik came out of the doctor's room with perfectly adjusted eyeglasses and clear, sharp vision. He was overjoyed, never having truly believed it was possible, and so was I.

As soon as we reached home, Wolik wanted to inspect my eyes and was glad that I had his favorite gray eyes that day. We celebrated the beginning of a new era by a long hike. For the first time in more than a year, he could enjoy the brightness of a sunny day and all the shadings of forest life. We had a glorious time!

OUR LAST JOINT WORK

In the meantime, we had accepted two commitments—to prepare the article on the United States for the new edition of the German *Handwörterbuch der Sozialwissenschaften (Encyclopedia of Social Sciences)*, and soon thereafter to make an analysis of the state of the American economy for the Public Affairs Institute in Washington. Both offers— *korabliki*, "little boats" in our terminology—had reached our shores on their own initiative, at a time when we were not ready to launch our own *korabliki*. Had the American *korablik* arrived ahead of the German, we would not have accepted the latter, because both projects involved rather speedy delivery. Yet the American project was too challenging to refuse. We had already started work on the article for the German encyclopedia, and so decided to complete it before taking up the study of the American economy.

Thus we resumed our "normal" schedule, Wolik working with a

vengeance to make up for the lost months. Probably few can understand the satisfaction we felt at being again at our desks and working independently, yet together—few, because I know of no other couple who could or did work as one, without any other thought than to give the best one had and to assist the other to bring out his or her best. This was particularly important to me; even when I could do my part by myself, I felt the security of Wolik's support, and this doubled my strength. Of course, Wolik did not need my support as I needed his, but he loved our joint work and stressed on many occasions, seriously or jokingly, how wonderful it was to have so complete a unity as ours. In his article "Scholar and Man of Action" in *So Much Alive,* our late friend Paul Studenski compared us with the well-known British economists Sidney and Beatrice Webb, who also worked together. We heard this comparison rather often, and it was always meant as a compliment. Though the Webbs produced many worth-while works and left an undeniable imprint on England's literary and cultural life, I do not find this a happy comparison. I can think of nothing more prosaic than Beatrice's description of her marriage with Sidney Webb as a "partnership," and her description of their engagement in her diary, July 7, 1891:

> We are both of us second-rate minds; but we are curiously combined. I am the investigator and he the executant; between us we have a wide and varied experience of men and affairs. We have also an unearned salary. These are unique circumstances. A considerable work should be the result if we use our combined talents with a deliberate and persistent purpose.*

As to the attitude of Sidney Webb, she characterized it in these words:

> The plain truth is that his emotional life—all his capacity for personal intimacy, and for over-appreciation of another's gifts—has been centered in his wife and partner, and his wife just because she is also his partner.†

I may be wrong, but I would like to believe that, with all his acerbity, Bernard Shaw would not have said of me as he said of Beatrice Webb after her death, "There was as much poetry in Beatrice as in a steam engine."

Anyhow, we were again "plowing Shakespeare," in the colorful expression of Edmund Kean. We enjoyed writing about the United States for that important German publication, giving our image of this country and our interpretation of its basic characteristics—geographic, demographic, political, social, and economic. We worked intensively at home and in various libraries and had the manuscript ready shortly before Christmas.

Without taking a respite, we then turned to the survey of the Ameri-

* Beatrice Webb, *My Apprenticeship* (London and Toronto: Longmans, Green and Co., 1926), p. 398.
† From her Introduction to Beatrice and Sidney Webb, *Our Partnership.*

can economy. This was much more controversial than an over-all description of the United States. We planned to analyze the experience of the three postwar recessions and extract from them the lessons for future economic policy. Wolik plunged into this work with all his energy, and it was difficult to get him down from his second-floor study for a walk or a visit with friends. At night, however, before going to bed, he liked to pace back and forth in the living room and the adjoining sun parlor, sharing with me the thoughts and conclusions that had come to his mind during the day, and to show me the charts he had been working on. In this particular study of the American economy, our work was more interwoven than in that on international economics. In the earlier work, each of us had about a thousand printed pages or more to write independently. In the current project, we were preparing a booklet of a hundred pages and wrote all the text jointly. For example, Wolik would write some statements on the cost of recessions, unemployment, or industrial production, and turn them over to me to comment or add some thoughts, fill in figures, or draw up tables for longer periods to guide our thinking. Or I would prepare a few pages on agricultural problems and foreign trade, provide them with tables, and Wolik would expand the text or suggest changes in it. Wolik prepared all the charts, and I, most of the tables. We read and reread the material until we both felt it was ready.

The main lesson we drew from the three preceding recessions was that while the economy of the United States was strong and resilient enough to withstand "the hurricanelike deflationary spiral," the cumulative impact of the successive economic dislocations was grave. In Wolik's words, the vulnerability of the American economy was "like that of people in modern society who need not fear an epidemic of plague or cholera but have little or no defense against the common cold." The periodicity of "common colds" afflicting our economy in postwar periods was undermining its strength and retarding its growth. Our over-all conclusion was that it was necessary to prevent or at least iron out recessions by a set of measures, the most important of which was to expand the public sector of the economy when the private sector began to contract.

A quarter of a century earlier, Wolik had fought for an active economic policy in Germany, then to conquer the raging economic crisis. This time, he called for an active economic policy, amidst the recovery of 1958-59, to prevent the impending economic setback. With the same uncanny insight and commanding knowledge of economic realities with which, in 1947, he had predicted all the successive recessions, he warned in 1959 that another periodic economic dislocation was just a year or so ahead.

When our *Lessons of the Recessions* appeared, the Public Affairs Institute arranged a meeting with well-known economists to hear Wolik's appraisal of the situation. I remember that one of them said: "When I go home from a meeting at which one fresh idea has been expressed, I consider the evening well spent. What then to say of tonight's meeting, of these fireworks of ideas, brilliant analysis, bold policy suggestions?"

Yet this survey appeared not only in a time of recovery and therefore of psychological relaxation, but also when the nation's attention was focused on the approaching national elections, with their own preoccupations and careful maneuvering. Whatever the reason, the survey did not receive much attention; at least, we were not entirely satisfied.

OUR LAST TRIP ABROAD

Between the delivery of that manuscript and its appearance in print, several months went by in which we were occupied with galley proofs, various articles and talks on the same subject—and plans for a new trip. This time we decided to travel for rest and pleasure, to proceed leisurely, without obligations, to rent a car in Paris and drive across France and Spain, possibly Italy, then fly to Israel and Turkey. Preparations were much simpler than for our earlier journeys. There were no lectures to write, no special language to learn, and the trip was to last three months instead of eight or nine. Actually, Wolik was willing to stay away longer, but I was not so eager to wander as before. Whether this was a premonition or weariness, I cannot say, but though I did not dampen Wolik's enthusiasm, I showed less fervor for travel than he.

Instead of flying, we took a boat and found the crossing rather boring. In Paris, we met Russian and Spanish friends and otherwise spent our time in walking in the streets and along the Seine in a kind of nostalgia, visiting our favorite spots and museums or sitting in cafés and watching people go by. Then we rented a little Dauphine and set out in the direction of the Loire Valley.

The country never looked to us as beautiful as that fall; people seemed at ease and friendly, the roads were good and so was the food. If I were to complain of anything, it would be that there were too many châteaux, or rather too many winding, steep flights of stairs. I worried that this climbing was too much of a strain for Wolik. It was impossible to hold him back. His eyesight was perfect, and he wanted to explore every corner, and found special pleasure in taking numerous pictures. Not sparing himself, he climbed steps, hills, and fences, and trudged back and forth until he was satisfied with a chosen angle and composition. I had a new camera, considered the finest of its kind, but I did not handle it as well as my old one.

We saw many signs reminiscent of the last war and the German occupation—on the houses, in the churches, on the tombstones in cemeteries: "Shot for resistance," "Exported to Germany for work and never returned," "At this corner the occupants hanged two men," with their names, ages, and the dates. Inside the churches, there were little silver or marble plates with prayers for a son or husband who had fallen at the front or had been executed by the invaders. We also noticed other, happier inscriptions with thanks for recovery or the birth of a child, or naïve thanks of students who had passed their examinations: *"A la Reine des Sciences"* (To the Queen of Sciences).

In a church belonging to a château where, we were told, town people had been admitted on special occasions, I inquired if any distinction had been made among the various groups of the population. *"Mais oui, madame, il en avait des paroisses des souliers et des paroisses de sabots"* (But, of course, madam, there were parishes of leather shoes and parishes of wooden shoes). In another castle, which looked like a forbidding fortress, a corpulent woman took us around and called our attention to an old painting of Christ: *"Regardez les muscles, les épaules larges de ce personnage"* (Look at the muscles and the powerful shoulders of that fellow).

We reached the climax of excitement at the Lascaux Caves, with their wall paintings, about 30,000 years old, perhaps the most grandiose, the most incredible, the most overwhelming human monument in the world. We stood in rapturous admiration of the creations of the naked, "savage" cavemen who had produced those overpowering murals in half-darkness, with only two natural paints at their disposal and probably boulders used to reach the ceiling of the huge cave. We became ecstatic looking at the painting of the deer crossing the lake. Perhaps what stirred us most was the irrefutable evidence of the craving in the human beings, even at an almost animal-like stage of civilization, for beauty and self-expression in creative art. We felt as though we were in the Sistine Chapel of the Glacier Age. How miserable, how shallow, how expressionless, are the paintings of today, as compared to those in the Lascaux Caves!

Driving on highways, lined for miles and miles with tall, old trees, was like moving in an endless park. Then we crossed the wine country, where people were harvesting the grapes. Wherever we stopped to watch their work and take pictures, we were given more grapes than we could consume. We revisited St. Jean de Luz and Biarritz, where we had vacationed one summer long ago, and then entered Spain.

The change was immediate. Now we were in a country where getting gasoline and, even more, its quality, were ever-present problems, where the villages looked pathetically poor, where we could not force ourselves to stop at a village store—dark, unclean, exhibiting spoiled produce in the window. Nevertheless, the scenery was often beautiful and the weather favorable, and we decided to spend a week in the little village of Potes, high in the Cantabrian Mountains. The drive to it on narrow, winding roads amidst the somber, naked mountains stirred our imaginations. We found accommodations in a small boardinghouse and were included in the family circle the very first night. We dealt mostly with the landlady, a sturdy, simple, but intelligent and pleasant woman and her two daughters—the older, married, more sedate, and satisfied with her lot, and the younger, clearly in search or expectation of a husband and naïvely trying to raise her own value by stressing her modest knowledge of French. She felt this set her apart from other girls in the village. Her mother, amused by this childish attitude, winked mockingly at her.

That isolated mountain village had not been spared by the Civil War —houses had been burned, family ties torn and friendships broken, killings had been a routine matter. We heard heart-breaking stories about individual families, were shown where executions occurred. There, as later in all of Spain, anyone who talked to us of the war meant the Civil War. Spain knew no other wars in our time.

We hiked from village to village, climbed mountains, occasionally drove in one direction or another. Few villagers had seen a woman at the wheel of a car, and someone was always looking at me with undisguised surprise. Sometimes we heard approving remarks about French women, made in the belief that I was French, a next-door neighbor, so to speak. When we were leaving Potes, the proprietress of the pension begged us to return and then admonished Wolik to take care of me. Directing her gaze at me, she said to him, *"Vale mucho"* (She is worth much) and gestured how I operated the wheel. Several times thereafter I found under my napkin at the dining table a little card with *"Vale mucho"* written by Wolik.

From the mountains we drove to Madrid, where we got in touch with the economists at the embassy. They called up one of the best Spanish economists and told him of our arrival. He asked us to dinner the next night, at nine o'clock, Spanish style. He drove us through various old sections of the city, showed its most interesting buildings and plazas, and then took us to one of the famous restaurants to treat us to its specialty, roasted suckling pig.

The conversation lasted well into the early morning. With a sure knowledge of political and economic conditions in the world, our host scintillated with sharp formulations that depicted the situation in his country without exaggerations. He was frank with us and showed full trust in our discretion by not asking to keep to ourselves what he said. "In the bones of every Spaniard is the deadly dread of civil war. None of us would ever want to see it again." About Franco: "Nobody will lift a finger to oust Franco, but nobody will lift a finger to protect or save him."

The next night, at a dinner given by an American economist, we found our Spanish friend present in the large group. Looking straight at us, he put his finger to his lips, indicating that he would not want to share his views with the other people in the room. The same confidence in us was shown by several other Spanish intellectuals. Some visited us in our hotel; others asked us to their homes.

Of our time in Spain, we particularly enjoyed the week in Palma, on Majorca, and the drive along the Costa Brava. Unfortunately, the rented car developed some trouble and, at the border of France, of all places, it refused to move. Even the Spanish road patrol was unable to help us, and they suggested that Wolik cross the frontier on foot in search of a mechanic while I stayed with the car. Traffic in both directions was heavy, and everybody looked at me, sitting in the car off the road, apparently under the surveillance of the border police. Finally Wolik returned in a truck with a French mechanic who diagnosed the trouble: The clutch had to be replaced. He would need twenty-four hours to do it. There was nothing we could do but stay overnight in the French frontier village of one street. In any event, its accommodations were more acceptable than we would find on the other side of the border.

Fortunately, there was a tiny hotel, and even a room with a bath. Next morning, we went reconnoitering and discovered that Le Grand Maréchal Vauban, the military genius and outstanding statesman during the reign of Louis XIV, had built a fortress on the mountain towering above that region. Even I knew of General Vauban from my work on French agricultural statistics (he had made the first estimate of France's agricultural output and also had prepared the world's first schedule in which the census of land and livestock was combined with the census of the population, houses, and enterprises). Wolik was thoroughly familiar with Vauban's writings on military and financial problems and so was thrilled at the unexpected chance to see the fortifications he had erected. Thus the dull wait for the car repair turned into an adventurous hike. We climbed to the fortress and, though it was closed to visitors, walked round and round to see all its special features and take pictures. Late in the evening the car was ready and, not wishing to spend another night in the village, we drove on to Perpignan.

From there we motored through the region full of Roman monuments —aqueducts, arenas, bridges, theaters—and of memories of papal power, then along the Mediterranean coast with Cannes, Nice, and other cities that we had planned to see sometime but never had.

In Nice, we returned the car to the renting company and flew to Rome, then Naples, and went by train to Paestum. That ancient town was high on our must list of places to visit, and it fully justified our yearning. The day in Paestum was like the last caress from Italy, her loving goodbye to Wolik. Nature and history combined there to make that visit unforgettable—the scenery, serene and full of charm, the wonderfully preserved Greek temples, the endless opportunities for photographing, the Italian children who surrounded Wolik and followed him. From Paestum, we continued by bus to Amalfi, Sorrento, Salerno, then by train back to Rome and by air to Tel Aviv, Israel.

IN ISRAEL

We arrived in Tel Aviv on Wolik's birthday. We were not prepared for what that little country offered us—the economic, political, and cultural achievements in one decade punctuated by two wars, the confident spirit of its people, the austerity of life, the historical reminiscences at every step, the attitude of concern for children and education, the lovely scenery, and all this in a climate of optimism and intense work. We stayed a little less than a fortnight in Israel, but we saw much in that short time. Unexpectedly, we found friends in the Embassy, the Government, and the Histadrut (Central Federation of Trade Unions). We were offered facilities to see everything we wanted—we visited the Negev Desert, Sodom and the Dead Sea, Beersheba, Jerusalem, Haifa, several kibbutzim, and spent a night in the kibbutz on the shore of Lake Galilee. We visited German, Moroccan, Arab, South African, French, and Spanish settlements, and talked in many languages with people in that multilingual country.

We were so impressed that we decided to write a book on Israel, collected materials and statistical documentation, talked with specialists in many fields, bought books and illustrations. When we were alone for a short time, we discussed the plan of the book and decided that Wolik would write preferably on theoretical economic problems, national income, balance of payments, foreign trade and labor problems, while I would take industrial production, agriculture, natural resources, population and immigration, social and cultural problems.

Everybody with whom we talked had a personal story to tell—one's family had been killed in the gas chamber, another had escaped from Poland or Russia, still others had been expelled from Egypt or Yemen. All had lost almost all their earthly possessions. Those who had come from the European countries had a profession and were, with a few exceptions, well educated, while the immigrants from the Arab countries more often than not had been illiterate, although some were skilled craftsmen.

Attachment to their new country, which gave people from many lands a sense of unity and security, was strong. The elevator boy in our hotel had come from Egypt, and when I asked him if he had adjusted himself to the new ways of life, he looked at me without understanding. "What do you mean? *This* is my country." The taxi driver who took us to the cemetery on Herzl's Hill in Jerusalem had fought in both wars and said, "If we have to fight again, younger people will be called up, but if necessary I am ready." The woman who made our beds in the Dan Hotel in Tel Aviv was from Romania; she cried as she told me that she and her husband had been permitted to leave Romania and had gone on the insistence of their only son, who believed that it would be easier to get out if he was alone. But the Romanians ceased to give visas. "Our life has lost any meaning without him, and we need more people to defend the country."

Pride in national and local achievements was great, sometimes childishly naïve, as when a lady in charge of public relations said while taking us around a new, well-built modern hospital, "Only we in Israel can build something so beautiful!" On the other hand, it was inspiring to hear a cab driver say, "You haven't seen the Weizman Institute? You must see it before leaving. A great thing." As in all newly independent countries, nationalistic feelings were strong, but we did not meet with expression of hatred, not even toward the Arab neighbors. All we heard was, "If they would leave us in peace!," or "Peace is all we need to grow and develop."

The strongest impact came from seeing revival of the land, dead for centuries and now vibrant with life. Buoyant settlements, groves of citrus fruit, green fields along the frontiers of Lebanon and Jordan on Israel's side; tents covered with hides, camels pulling wooden plows that lifted the barren, arid soil, on the Arab side. How to explain the apathy, the inertia, of the primitive man, unmoved by the spectacular sight of revolutionary changes before his very eyes? How to comprehend that lack of curiosity, the absence of any desire to try to achieve something better than their neighbors, even if only out of pride or a sense of competition? Was this the so-called "Oriental fatalism"? Was this spite? We watched this human puzzle with concern and had no answer.

As for the people of Israel, who had been forcibly kept off the land for centuries in most countries of the world and described as a people without any attachment to the soil, they now excel as soil conservationists and arouse the sincere admiration of American and European specialists in this field. A colonel who headed the political education of the Israeli Army talked of the land in poetical terms: "Our land had been unproductive, unloved, neglected, exposed to sun and wind. It lay in sterility, waiting for people to come, to water it, to bring it back to useful life. Haven't you seen how contentedly it breathes now, how generously it repays our loving care?"

No less stunning was the revival of Hebrew. We asked several intellectuals if it was possible to express new ideas in that obsolete language, and the answer was yes. There were many bookstores, and in their windows publications in Hebrew represented a substantial part of display.

Another outstanding feature was the appearance and behavior of the children. In that warm climate, they swarmed on the beaches and in the parks. Healthy, cheerful, well built, they moved freely around but were not noisy. Among them were many with fair complexions and blond hair. Wolik picked out two little girls in a school crowd—one smoke-black and the other with blue eyes and blond hair—for his picture.

The heads of the kibbutzim (communal agricultural settlements) showed great concern about the future of their communities. The old members who started these collectives half a century ago or even earlier, are gradually dying out; many of the younger members leave, preferring city life, which has become much more exciting and offers many more opportunities than ever before. To recruit new members from the newcomers is not easy. Those who have come from Soviet Russia or the satellite countries are alarmed at hearing of communal life in the kibbutzim. This reminds them of the kholkhozy, and nothing can induce them to join a kibbutz. The German newcomers often hesitate because they do not want to turn over their assets or their titles to reparation payments to the new community. However, there have been German refugees who joined the kibbutz, became its great patriots, and increased the communal funds by their assets.

We visited several new moshavim—villages based on private land ownership, but working, buying, and selling as cooperatives. Here, we were told, the life and kind of work depend on where the members came from. No problems have arisen with newcomers from the Western countries but much preliminary educational work has been required to introduce those from primitive Arab countries, like the cave dwellers of the North Atlas Mountains in North Africa, to such fundamentals as sleeping in a bed instead of rolling up in a blanket on the floor or on the ground, sitting on chairs rather than floors, using forks and knives rather than fingers. At the same time, they have been taught Hebrew.

We wanted to see an Arab village, and arrived in Baka at the time of a council session. Some twenty or so sedate Arabs in Oriental garb were sitting solemnly when we entered. They bowed to us, we bowed to them. Cigarettes and coffee were brought in. Wolik, who had never smoked, sensed that he must not refuse and unhappily held his cigarette. The chief greeted us, and Wolik responded with a few words. Then we were taken around, saw the new school, maternity ward, and just across the small stream, the villagers in Jordan. There was something ominous in that inescapable proximity, though one asked oneself, "Why can't there be a good-neighbor policy instead of animosity?"

We paid a courtesy call on an Arab member of the parliament (Knesset). Again, cigarettes, coffee, refreshments. Perhaps this meeting would have been as strained as the preceding one, except for the help of a little girl of three or four. She wanted to stay with her adoptive father, the congressman, and the guests, but a servant came and carried her away in his arms. She cried loudly and as soon as she was set on her feet, she ran back to us and pressed herself to her father. The servant did not dare to snatch her out of his master's embrace. Unruffled, the child looked at us with her eyes, big as cherries, and smiled happily. This charming episode broke the tension, and we all became people, simple human beings. We asked the congressman for permission to photograph him with the child, and though he was a little embarrassed, he went out into the garden where there was more light.

The days were hot, the sun was high. Wolik who rarely covered his head, proudly wore a Basque beret acquired in Spain. It was very becoming to him, and the Foreign Service employee who accompanied us on one trip, exclaimed, "You look like Rodin!" Later when he took off the beret, the girl remarked, "And now you look exactly like Einstein." Wolik laughed and said: "You don't know—I am a first-rate magician. With the beret, I am Rodin; without it, I am Einstein. Sheer magic! Have you ever seen anything like it?"

We spent one night in a kibbutz at Tiberias. The people, the atmosphere in the large dining hall, the night walk in a community where every structure had a story to tell, a story of hardships and sacrifice, of work and disappointments—all this was new and exciting and became particularly so when the lights in the Syrian military camp on the other side of Lake Galilee suddenly blazed.

We were always amused in the streets of Tel Aviv or Jerusalem when, asking in English for directions, we got our answers in German, Russian, or Spanish. Many Government leaders had come originally from Russia, which had supplied a considerable number of the idealists who had organized the original kibbutzim and struggled heroically against all odds to make real their dream of a better society on that historical ground. At lunch in Technion, Haifa, our host on the right, the Vice-President, spoke Russian with me, as did our host on the left, the chief librarian. Many knew Wolik, some even from Russia, by name or from his writings, others from Germany or Europe, still others from work and books published in the United States. We were urged to stay longer, to return next spring or fall, and we said we would.

Both of us were moved and saddened by the Military Cemetery in Jerusalem. Located on the Herzl's Hill, it offers an unobstructed view of the city. All the tombs were made like symbolic resting places: beds with pillows at one end. When a group of fighters died together, their graves were arranged accordingly. We saw graves aligned like the planes of a squadron in air formation. For sailors serving with the British Navy who lost their lives when the ship was hit by a torpedo, the tombs were put under water, with the captain's tower erect and the tombs clearly seen. We could not read the Hebrew inscriptions, but we saw with great emotion the pathetic figures indicating the age of the deceased: seventeen, eighteen, nineteen. As always, the best, the most valorous, the most idealistic, who registered as volunteers, were the first to be mowed down, those poorly equipped and little-trained youngsters with few adequate weapons in their hands but armed with a valor that defies danger and death.

After having seen money spent on a grand scale in many under-developed countries, we found Israel's policy of austerity particularly impressive. In Beersheba, a member of the Knesset raised the question, whether Israel could afford to introduce television. He felt that it was premature and unwise to burden their young economy with the expenses for such luxuries. This was in November, 1959. I do not know how the situation is now. His wife was almost delirious with joy in talking of their new apartment. Curious, I asked to see it. She was proud to show it, and we found it to be three average-size rooms, with a tiny bathroom and a kitchen. This was the great good fortune so enthusiastically described by the wife of a member of Parliament! We imagined how other people must live in Beersheba, a city growing by leaps and bounds.

Alas, there was one cloud on the horizon, no matter how much I tried not to notice it. Even when we were in Amalfi, I had begun to notice a sharp pain in my left side. When I sat quietly or lay down, it would ease up and then vanish. In Israel, the pain returned every day, occasionally several times a day, sometimes even at night. It was worst when the pain hit me while I was talking. Not wishing to show my discomfort, I would continue to talk, but I was forced to slow down or sometimes to stop. I recall our visit to a plant that was making pipes for channeling the water of the Jordan River to the Negev Desert. It was a very hot day, the sun was merciless. We walked about with the engineers, stopped here and there to observe something, climbed narrow steps to watch work done inside, then walked again. A cutting pain struck me suddenly, but I had to move on with the rest of the group and even to answer questions. It was probably foolish, but when the pain felt strong enough to knock me down, I merely pressed my hand against my breast under my coat to get some relief.

Why did I not go to a doctor in a country where there were many excellent physicians? I hated to envisage what probably would follow: I in a hospital, Wolik's enjoyment ended, inevitable inconveniences that loomed terrifically big. So I said to myself, If I am *that* sick, we must go home immediately, as we now can in a single day, and not burden friends in Israel with my and our trouble. If I am not seriously sick, then I know I can stand the pain and not ruin our trip. As a matter of fact, as soon as the pain disappeared, I was my own self and enjoyed everything no less than Wolik, expelling worry like an unpleasant invader.

After our journey to Sodom and the Dead Sea, I told Wolik of the recurring sharp pain, and he insisted on canceling our trip to Turkey and flying to Washington immediately, as we then did.

Now I often think that if I had gotten medical help in Israel, perhaps things would have worked for the best, perhaps I would have been more helpful to Wolik during his illness. These are cruel thoughts, and it is pointless to talk of them.

OUR HEART ATTACKS

Back in Washington, we got in touch with our doctor and made an appointment for the next day. He examined us and gave both of us a clean bill of health. The following day, during luncheon at a friend's house, Wolik's face suddenly became bright red, then white, and again unusually red. We all got up from the table, and after Wolik had rested a little while in a chair in the living room, he suggested that we drive home. A young doctor, the son-in-law of our hosts, who happened to be there, took Wolik's pulse and advised us to take him to the nearby hospital, which we did. Wolik later told me that he had believed he was going to die and had reconciled himself to it. His cardiogram showed a light heart attack. I stayed with him till night and refused to spend the night at friends' or have them come to stay with me. Saying, "I am made of steel. Please don't worry about me," I took our car and drove home.

Late in the evening, my familiar pain returned. Certain that it would soon vanish, I started to read, but it persisted all night. At about six in the morning, I got up, arranged this and that, had breakfast, made a few necessary calls, packed various things for Wolik and, in another bag, for myself. Then I called up the doctor and asked him to arrange for a bed for me in the same hospital, and asked our neighbor to drive me there. First, I went to see Wolik to reassure him that I was trying to get into the hospital to be near him, then I went for an examination. My cardiogram also indicated a heart attack. To my great disappointment, I was put into a separate room in another ward.

Two days later, just when I had complained to the doctor that there was no reason for me to be in the hospital since I could get the same medical care at home, I had a severe heart attack. Two doctors, assistants, and nurses stayed with me from seven in the evening till midnight, stuffing me with drugs and injecting various solutions. When I asked one of the doctors if this was a thrombosis, he answered, "It is debatable." Later he told me, "We thought we might lose you that night." After midnight, the intern came to see me. Noticing his Spanish name, I asked him from what country he had come, and when he said Nicaragua, I shifted to Spanish. We chatted until he reminded me not to talk too much and left, admonishing the nurse in my presence that she take good care of me, "a very exceptional person."

Now of the two of us, I was the serious case. Soon Wolik was wheeled into my room for a short visit, and he told me that he was working in bed on the proofs of our article for the German *Encyclopedia of Social Sciences.* He had been begging the doctors for permission to get out of the hospital and wanted to go home, but there was no home without me. So I called up our closest friend, who was teaching at Syracuse University, to find out if she could possibly come to be with Wolik; she thought she could arrange to do so after a week or so. In the meantime, Frances, our household help who had been with us for nine years, would move in, the doctor would visit Wolik twice a day, and I arranged that friends and neighbors would see him at short intervals.

For the first time in our lives we were physically handicapped, and we were deeply moved by the reaction of our friends. We were showered with flowers, books, magazines, letters, telephone calls, and visits.

We worried about each other, but Wolik sounded confident, and the doctor thought that he was doing well. I, too, began to feel stronger, could get up, take a few steps, sit at the window and watch construction workers across the way, read and eat in a chair. Then suddenly I had a relapse, more serious than the earlier attack. The room swam before my eyes. Again doctors, drugs, injections, oxygen; I was to be fed and not to move my arms.

The important thing to me then was not to alarm Wolik, who himself was not out of danger. In this I failed, because the telephone was put beyond my reach. It rang, and certain that Wolik was calling, I tried frantically to get the nurse and have her tell him that I was out of the room. It worked that time, but he called again half an hour later and, not receiving an answer, he got the head nurse and then the doctor on the phone. Both told him about my relapse, and shortly thereafter he appeared, white as a sheet, trembling: "I cannot live without you." I made light of my situation—just a slight dizziness, the doctor evidently wanted to relieve himself of any responsibility, nothing to worry about, and I would be back home very soon. Though I did not succeed completely, Wolik who had thought to find me dying, went home more hopeful than he had come.

When the doctor arrived, I was cross with him. Why did he have to frighten Wolik? Didn't he know that Wolik had not yet recovered and might get another heart attack? We quarreled, and I thought he would leave me in the care of some other doctor and not come again. But he called at night and ordered sleeping pills. Afraid I might die in my sleep, I refused to take them and did not close my eyes during the night. Next morning he scolded me for this, but I said, "Never mind me, take care of my husband, and we both will be all right."

Sylvia arrived, and I knew that Wolik had the best of loving care. This helped me, too. Sylvia brought him to see me every day; we talked frequently on the telephone, wrote little notes to each other. Christmas was approaching, when the hospital tries to send home as many patients as the doctors will release. I was on the list and was taken home on a stretcher. Wolik met me with eyes full of tears, but I was cheerful. It was wonderful to be home and be together again!

Again the thought of leaving Wolik alone haunted me. I could not visualize him alone, managing the small things of life. I reproached myself for having accustomed him to be free from trivial, everyday matters which could become a heavy burden just when he would be at his lowest emotionally. This was my fault, I told myself. Wolik was not *that* helpless when we met, but I had always considered his time more precious than mine and so relieved him of everything that I could. The price for this, however, was that Wolik lived in a world in which all practical things arranged themselves, so to speak. As long as I lived, this was fine, but knowing that my life might end any hour, I worried about Wolik. As soon as I was alone with Sylvia, I asked her to promise me that she would help Wolik to weather the worst time without me.

Our dining room was transformed into a bedroom, and the neighbors had keys to the house. Sylvia stayed for a week or so, until her sons were to come home from college. Despite small occasional troubles, we were recovering, slowly but surely. Wolik began to work longer hours. Since he could not go upstairs to his study, he worked in the living room, sitting in a big armchair and using a lap board instead of a desk. He called that place his "den." I wanted him to rest more and stay in bed longer, but was not always persuasive enough, the more so as I was drowsy a part of the day and the doctor was noncommittal. Sylvia left, but life was organized in terms of doctor's visits, household help, shopping, and so on. The neighbors on both sides of the house were most helpful.

As soon as I could get up, we would sit on the porch for a while and feel the spring in the air. Finally, we could take a walk around the block, and soon thereafter, use our bedroom upstairs. Everything pointed to a definite turn for the better.

Then complications started, which now, in retrospect, appear to have been avoidable. Wolik had pains in his leg—phlebitis. Again ambulance, hospital, injections. He spent five days there, and on my urging the doctor permitted him to go home. I nursed Wolik, made the injections, administered the drugs, helped as best I could and knew how. Just when he began to feel better and to get out of bed, severe itching set in, probably caused by some antibiotic. But Wolik had taken so many drugs that it was not easy to find the culprit right away. Then he had coughing attacks that shook his body and weakened him. Nevertheless, he continued to work and wrote a pamphlet that appeared later, *The Prosperity Issue in the 1960 Election*.

Finally, Wolik was up again, and we were both so much better that we could walk for half an hour or so without being unduly fatigued. We were counting the days until our full recovery. Wolik was revising his memoirs; I read the proofs of our article on the United States for the German publication, typed and retyped parts of the memoirs and the new pamphlet, handled the correspondence, nursed Wolik, kept the household, and so on. We were not too strong, but we were busy and did not worry.

A telephone call from the National Industrial Conference Board in New York came, asking Wolik if he would be willing to present a paper on the U.S. share in world trade as the opening speech at the conference on "American Enterprise: The Next Ten Years." Wolik reported his convalescence and, with a reservation concerning an unexpected setback, accepted the invitation. We began to prepare the documentation, and as usual, Wolik outlined orally the major points of the paper. We were glad of this opportunity to break away from the cheerless, monotonous days concerned with illness and all that illness implied. It was like a turning point, a return to normalcy.

Then, about a week later, Wolik did not feel well one night. I immediately called the doctor, getting him out of a professional meeting. Wolik had another heart attack—again not too serious. We moved back to the first floor, arranging it as a hospital—this time in the living room, on Wolik's wish. I stayed with him twenty-four hours a day, snatching bits of sleep when he slept, reading to him when he could not sleep. There were nights when Wolik was very uncomfortable, and in desperation I tried one thing and another, cooling his forehead with towels drenched in cold water, making tea, giving him drugs, and so on. Impatiently we waited for the morning and the doctor's visit, and though he really brought no help, there was always a slight hope that he would. Friends came, mail arrived, the telephone rang—all this helped to fight the pain for a moment.

Despite sickness, Wolik continued to work; he wrote a series of articles on problems of the American economy for the *New Leader,* and pursued the revision of his memoirs. In between, he read much. Staying in bed affected his health; he ate less, lost some weight. Still, it never occurred to me that Wolik would not recover. He was "so much alive," so full of fun, he joked and laughed so youthfully.

In the meantime, we received the printed program of the conference in New York, at which Wolik was scheduled to give the first speech. He had to let them know that he could not come—the first time in his life that he could not attend a conference on account of sickness.

Pain began to harass him more and more. At times in agony, he would hold my hand and say through his gritted teeth, "Only for your sake, only for your sake!" He meant by this that otherwise he would not care to stand that much pain. I could have beat my head against the wall to quiet the pain inside, and now, at times I feel that we should then have done with life together. Neither of us would have had to suffer any more. But I was so confident, so blind, so sure that we would again be strong and healthy, that even the memory of that awful time would disappear like a nightmare.

It seems to me that there were moments when Wolik lost confidence. Once he said to me, "You will write the book on Israel." I held back my tears and replied, "We will write it together as we always have." Another time he wanted to say something about our separation, but I interrupted him, "Wolik, my dearest love, don't torture yourself and don't torture me. We will live through all this awful suffering and pain. Believe me, we will!" I talked of our future trips to sunny countries, to unknown places on our must list. Little by little, his dark thoughts would disappear and he would become animated and relaxed, and would smile again.

Once, about two o'clock in the morning, I went to the kitchen to make tea for him and saw, in the window across the street, a couple dancing on the balcony. There was no sound, no one was visible except the couple moving gracefully in half-darkness. I stood fascinated by this unexpected spectacle and, when the tea was ready, told Wolik of what I had seen. He said calmly, "I saw it, too." "Where? How?" "In the window here." He sounded so positive that for a moment I believed him. Then, realizing that he was pulling my leg, I laughed and said, "You deserve a prize. For the first time, you have succeeded in fooling me." Wolik was pleased no end, and this eased the sadness that night.

I do not know what my own health condition was at that time. I was still on a heavy diet of drugs, but swallowed those pills mechanically and gave no thought to myself. It irritated me that when friends called, they expressed worry about my health, but Wolik was within hearing of the telephone, and I did not want to say that his condition was more serious. They all insisted that if I continued to take care of Wolik, I would certainly collapse and, to persuade me not to disregard my condition, they told me again and again that I must spare myself for Wolik's sake. I knew that Wolik did not want anyone but me to care for him, and my natural wish, too, was not to have strangers around.

Yet, during these last years I have not been able to help thinking that if I had been less absorbed, every hour of the day and night, in doing the immediate, the urgent thing, perhaps I could have done more for Wolik by realizing earlier how dangerous his condition was, by turning to other doctors. It is heartbreaking to feel that this and that could have been done differently, perhaps with better results. I feel great bitterness toward the medical profession and medical help, though there have been four medical doctors in my own family. All I wish now is to die in my sleep, so as not to depend for my life on any of them. As long as I live, I will feel that Wolik could have been saved, that he could have lived longer if I had not been as sick as I was then.

Wolik began to have such terrible pains that I could not stand it any more than he, and once I suggested that perhaps if he were in the hospital they would help to relieve his suffering better than I could. He did not reply to this, but later when I suggested a consultation, he said pitifully, "They will take me away." Under some pretext, I rushed out and cried as never before.

Soon the doctors decided to perform a prostate operation. I went with Wolik in the ambulance and said firmly to him, "This is the fourth time that I am taking you to the hospital. I give you my word that I will bring you back as I have the three previous times. Oh, my love, I hope so much that we will have better times after this." I saw in Wolik's eyes that he was trying to remember these three times—the cataract operation, the heart attack, and the phlebitis.

An X ray was made before the operation, and the surgeon came to tell me, "All the doctors are surprised that your husband's bones look like those of a young man; not a trace of aging. What is his secret? Has he drunk much milk?"

There is no sense in re-creating those sorrowful days in the hospital. Wolik never complained, but on the last day of his life, when he could not keep from moaning, he suddenly said, "I know that I am a failure" —for not being able to keep quiet. At this, I broke down for the first time in his presence, and with limitless tenderness in his voice, he said, "My Emmochka is worn out!" Through my tears, I tried to explain to him that I was crying because of my helplessness, my inability to ease his suffering. It was not I who was worn out, but he, and this was why I cried. How could he have such thoughts about himself? Didn't he know that he was the most wonderful, the most heroic being in the world? When we were home again, I told him, we will analyze Wolik, to show him how little he knew and understood the real, the true Wolik.

To divert his sad thoughts, I wheeled him through the hall to the visitors' room. A doctor passing by stopped to say, "If I did not know that Einstein had died, I would think he was in that chair."

I brought Wolik the latest issue of *Survey of Current Business*. He looked carefully at the tables, read the text, and then said to me, "Compare what the figures say with the text—such a contradiction!"

The last morning it seemed that Wolik for the first time had withdrawn into himself, or perhaps he was not fully conscious. I called a consultation of our doctors. What a mockery! Nothing to worry about, they said, and the wound from the operation was "clean as a whistle." A few hours later I began to realize that Wolik did not react to my voice, even when I begged him to show me with his eyes that he heard me. Again two doctors, and a last prescription which I could not get at once because the hospital pharmacy was locked for the night.

Wolik was in an oxygen tent. I laid my head next to him for the last time.

The full circle is closed: My life began when I met Wolik, and it ended when he left me. As before when I had been alone, existing but not living a full life, I move around, work, meet people, and seemingly am alive. But without the flowering of our love, the vibrant joy, the sunny laugh, the triumphant feeling of oneness with Wolik, there is no real life.

Epilogue

No ONE I have known or heard of or read about, nobody in the whole world, could match Wolik's wonderful combination of strength and gentleness, of greatness and innate modesty, of brilliance of mind, grace of humor, incredible courage in action and thought, and poetic perception of life.

Wolik was a born writer. To express himself, he grasped a pencil and was writing as the thoughts formed in his mind. His writing was on so objective a level of scholarship that on occasion he simultaneously published the same article in periodicals holding diametrically opposite positions—for example, in Wall Street's *Barron's* and the liberal *New Leader*.

Wolik was a born speaker. I heard him speak before enormous crowds, friendly and antagonistic; speak, not read a prepared piece, to university students and scholars, to workers and soldiers, industrialists and officers, highly sophisticated people and the illiterate. He felt instinctively what to say and how to say it, usually captivating the audience with his sincerity, integrity of thought, and humor.

Wolik was a born scholar. When he was not writing, he was reading. At fifteen, his father, an outstanding professor of mathematics, told him that he could learn nothing more in that field in a university. At his father's summer preparatory courses for the entrance examination to Russia's highest technical institutes, the youngster, not yet out of high school, taught physics and geometry. Before he entered St. Petersburg University at nineteen, he had written a book on economic theory, *Market and Prices*, which the eminent professor of economics, M. I. Tugan-Baranovsky, took for the work of a young professor.

Wolik was a born leader of men. As a university student, he organized singlehandedly a desperate and unruly crowd of thousands of unemployed in Russia's capital, St. Petersburg, into an orderly, disciplined movement. Elected to the presidency of the Council of the Unemployed, he managed to force the reactionary Municipal Council of the capital to open feeding stations serving 40,000 meals a day, to provide rent money and interest on pawnshop loans, and even to initiate public works for thousands of them—something unheard of anywhere at the beginning of this century—and this in Tsarist Russia! Without trying and against his desire, he became the gospel for thousands of men and their families. His gospel was against violence, against drunkenness on the job, for maintaining regular work and discipline among men who were embittered against the society, against their former employers, against the Government, men who knew that they had been defeated and could be easily incited to any act of desperation and madness.

In the entire progressive movement in Russia, nobody matched the feat of this youngster, who was without practical experience, without ability for or interest in political maneuvering. No other leader in that revolutionary era could truthfully say that he was loved and trusted by the thousands who depended on him as was Wolik. He knew only one aim—to help "his" unemployed, to whom he was the only hope and the embodiment of compassion and understanding.

In the ten years of prison and exile to which his revolutionary activities led, he was as great as ever. Thrown from a sophisticated, well-to-do environment into one of the worst prisons of Tsarist Russia, exposed to hunger, humiliations, and mistreatment, he did not surrender to self-pity or apathy. With every means at his command—his pen, his knowledge of law, and the keen ability to appraise every situation—he fought to break the regime of terror and protect his fellow inmates, political prisoners and common criminals alike, against sadistic tyrants. By his revelations, smuggled out of prison and published simultaneously in the Russian and European press, he forced the Government to initiate an investigation and liquidate at least the worst abuses.

Wolik set himself exceptionally high moral standards. Because of the recognition of his talents, because of the efforts of his parents, several opportunities were offered to him to escape the murderous conditions in the ill-starred penitentiary of the Castle of Ekaterinoslav—opportunities acceptable even to the rigid honor requirements of Russian revolutionaries. Wolik would have considered some of them appropriate for others and would not have blamed anyone for taking advantage of them. But he rejected them for himself because he felt that he must share these horrors, that he could not live with himself if he left his companions after what they had lived through in common in prison.

Even there, without access to a library, he continued his scholarly work and wrote a book on the theory of wages. He could so concentrate on writing, as one of the other inmates told me later, that he did not lift his head when bullets whizzed through his cell. In the forty-four years of our marriage, he did not say one word of complaint about his youth in prison and exile. On the contrary, I could see that he considered those years a part of his growing into better understanding of people and appreciation of nature.

In the second Russian Revolution of 1917, Wolik again fought for the democratic future of Russia, risked his life repeatedly, not out of lust for power or to satisfy personal ambitions, but for the freedom of his native land. "He gravitated almost intentionally toward the most dangerous tasks," one Russian historian said of his activities during that period—in the ominous July days of the Bolshevist uprising, during the mutiny of General Kornilov, and most of all, during the Bolshevist *coup d'état* against the Provisional Government, when "It was a miracle that he was not lynched."

He showed again his dauntless spirit by remaining in Germany until the last day on which the opposition to Hitler in the trade unions was alive. At the decisive meeting when the request for their participation in the Nazis' May Day parade was on the agenda, Wolik urged the Executive Board of the General Federation of the Free Trade Unions not to capitulate to Hitler's demand. He was no less aware than the other members of the Board of the danger incurred by such an attitude, but he argued that the honor of the labor movement was at stake at that critical moment. He cast the only vote against the unanimous decision to accede to the Nazis' request, and then resigned.

Wolik had not only physical courage but exceptional intellectual courage. When he believed in an idea, as in the fight against the economic depression in Germany in the 1930's or during the "battle of projections" on the postwar American economy in the 1940's, he knew no hesitation and never prepared intellectual alibis in the event that his projections would turn out wrong. On the contrary, he went out on a limb without fear and purposely sharpened his conclusions so as to leave no room for doubt or for later excuses.

Wolik was a wonderful teacher—three universities could not have taught me a part of what I learned from working with him. The range and breadth of his knowledge and interests were incredible, and he had the unusual ability to teach without trying to, just by drawing one into the stream of his thoughts and mental associations. Even more important, Wolik possessed and instilled in me, too, self-discipline in work and the priceless capacity to work efficiently and to concentrate on work, regardless of any disturbance within or without. He could work for ten or twelve hours a day and more, if necessary, without becoming fatigued. Yet he found time to read books on philosophy, history, literature, to take beautiful photographs, to work in the garden and the workshop.

In the truest sense of the word, Wolik was an encyclopedist. His range of knowledge embraced economics, mathematics, sociology, demography, statistics, the political history of many countries of the world, philosophy, physics, history of literature, arts and religions, poetry. He had a good knowledge of geology and meteorology, and was familiar with the literary output of many countries. His frame of reference was immense, and his speech sparkled with historical and literary associations, illuminating comparisons from the heritage of all ages. To be associated with him meant to learn and grow all the time.

Perhaps especially because of his years behind bars, Wolik's love of nature was powerful and deep. I have never met anyone who so rapturously enjoyed scenery—the mountains, the sea, the forests, the fields. To be outdoors with him was sheer delight. His rapport with nature was complete. He had a sure sense of orientation, always found the best point for a lookout. Whenever we became thirsty on a mountain hike, he would pause to listen and then go unerringly where the sound of dripping water led him—to a little spring or a tiny waterfall running down the slope. In the Siberian wilderness, when we saw an approaching rain, he would cut some large branches from the trees, stick them into the ground, and bring their tops together, making a tent of sorts. We would slip in and get enough protection to be amused and enjoy the fun.

As a human being, Wolik was wonderful; as a husband, he was perfect. I would never attempt to describe the supreme happiness of our intimacy. One may wonder how such an exceptional being could have lived among us and how he could have fallen in love with me and have loved me until his last breath. That *is* a miracle, and nobody can make me believe that miracles do not happen. They do!

Index

Index